Shalom/Salaam:
A Story of a Mystical Fraternity

# Shalom/Salaam:
# A Story of
# A Mystical Fraternity

by
Thomas Block

FONS VITAE

First published in 2010 by
Fons Vitae
49 Mockingbird Valley Drive
Louisville, KY 40207
http://www.fonsvitae.com
Email: fonsvitaeky@aol.com

Copyright Fons Vitae 2010

Library of Congress Control Number: 2010932255
ISBN 9781891785481

Printed in Canada

# Contents

I dedicate this book to those who make my life complete: Debbie, Dalya and Mollie. With much love —Thank you!

# Introduction

More than a decade ago, as I explored the thought of spiritual masters from many faiths, I came across a brief allusion to the influence of Sufism on a few medieval Jewish thinkers. Although this at first appeared to represent little more than an unsubstantiated claim, the possibility of such a relationship struck me as not only fascinating, but also deeply important. This supposed mystical fraternity ran contrary to the contemporary narrative between the children of Isaac and Ishmael; it was a subject that I, as a Jew interested in my own spiritual roots, felt compelled to explore.

Jews and Muslims, as I understood it then, were longtime enemies. How could it be that a spiritual link existed between the two, which might have influenced medieval Judaism? At that time, I thought that the association between Muslims and Jews involved nearly 1400 years of enmity, and a present-day battle over a piece of land in the Middle East, which both People claim.

Although not a lettered academician, I followed an inner impulse so strong that it ended up taking nearly a dozen years of my life, and countless hours in the Library of Congress, to satisfy. After initially searching in vain for confirmation of this Muslim-Jewish fraternity, I finally discovered an author who had undertaken substantial research in this area: Professor Paul Fenton of the Sorbonne. I spent hour upon hour pouring over obscure academic texts, following leads described in Fenton's notes and bibliography, exploring other valuable sources, which then led to further, even lesser known sources for my research. Eventually, a hitherto unrecognized story emerged that I believe needs urgently to be fully explored.

Far from coming across evidence of but one or two discrete medieval interactions, I discovered more and more articles, buried in little known journals stretching back more than a century, concerning Jewish mystics and thinkers who studied with, and took on the ideas of, Islamic mystics and thinkers. By the time I closed my last, faded folio and looked at my notes, I was able to trace an unbroken line of Islamic mystical influence on the development of Jewish thought and practice from the inception of Islam, into today's Jewish liturgy and contemplative practice.

Scholarly investigation on this subject dates back more than one hundred years, starting in the late 19th century in Germany, then moving to the seminal work of Shlomo D. Goitein (Institute of Advanced Study, Princeton) in the middle of the last century, who devoted his life to translating the medieval documents discovered in the Cairo Geniza (a repository for religious and other texts in the synagogue where Moses Maimonides prayed). This went on to include Alexander Altmann (Founder of the Institute of Jewish

Studies, University College, London), Israel Efros (Rabbi and Rector of Tel Aviv University) and more recently the work of such scholars as Moshe Idel (Hebrew University), Paul Fenton (Sorbonne) and Diana Lobel (Boston University), as well as a smattering of independent-minded professors who have provided invaluable insight into this story. Utilizing their research, I was able to piece together the various aspects of this centuries-long tale.

In virtually every case, the research of these scholars has been sequestered in obscure journals or academic tomes. This information has never reached the general public. Books on medieval Jewish mysticism are being written *today* that do not include a single reference to Islam or Sufism. There has not been a scholar willing to make the claim that Sufism was a central influence in helping shape Jewish spirituality, refashioning the religion as it is currently practiced.

It must also be noted that Sufism was certainly not the only influence on medieval Jewish thinkers. They enjoyed a varied intellectual milieu the likes of which they had never before known. In addition to a wealth of Jewish and Muslim thinkers, the educated medieval thinker had access to works by Plato, Aristotle, Galen, as well as Neo-platonic works, Hindu stories, Persian musical treatises, scientific collections from various backgrounds, ancient mathematical treatises, medical essays and a host of other sources on philosophical and theological subjects. Additionally, many of the ideas taken on from Sufism came to the Islamic mystics via other, earlier influences. It was a spiritual blend – but one which often came to the medieval Jewish thinker via Sufi and Islamic intermediaries.

The Jewish-Sufi spiritual fraternity hardly developed in a vacuum. The relationship between Jews and Muslims had strong positive resonance almost from the time of the Prophet Muhammad's revelation. For instance, a preeminent historical figure in the body of the Koran is Moses — his name being cited more than 100 times.[1] According to Professor Shlomo Goitein, the Koran contains so many accounts and theological ideas found in Talmudic literature (c. $2^{nd}$-$5^{th}$ centuries) that a reading of the Muslim Holy Book offers a fairly comprehensive view of the fundamental beliefs held by the Jews.[2]

These initial positive interactions affected the relationship between the two People. When Muslim armies swept across the Straight of Gibraltar in 711 and began their conquest of Visigoth Spain, the invaders trusted the thankful Jews for their help as garrison forces to secure and guard conquered cities, as the Muslim armies pushed north.[3] For Jews, these "marauding" warriors represented an army of liberation!

As part of the Islamic quest for knowledge, Muslim leaders encouraged Jewish scholars to play a major role in the life of Islam. Professor Norman Roth notes in *Jews, Visigoths and Muslims in Medieval Spain*: "Jews were prominent among the scientists, mathematicians and physicians encountered in (Islamic) biographical and literary encyclopedias. In addition, Jewish scholars drew heavily upon their contemporary Muslim colleagues for their knowledge in such fields as astronomy, mathematics, physics and medicine. The greatest Muslim scientists and philosophers had Jewish students."[4]

Perhaps the most surprising aspect of the relationship, however, is that the often positive and respectful social interaction led to a direct connection between theologians and mystical thinkers of both religions, linking these two together in ways that few today would suspect. Mysticism lies at the heart of all religions, representing a manner in which an individual can develop proximity with God. That Jews and Muslims would come together at such a central focus of their faith – where humans most clearly endeavor to encounter the Divine – struck me as not only fascinating, but also vital to understanding the Jewish-Muslim relationship, especially in our era, when the appreciation of this historic affinity is clouded by political exigencies.

The story of the "Jewish-Sufi" begins with famous and intellectually powerful Jews such as Abraham Maimonides (d. 1237, Egypt) and Solomon ibn Gabirol (d. 1058, Spain) – both of whom continue to be influential within Judaism today, though their Sufi tendencies have remained shrouded. Abraham Maimonides, son of the pre-eminent Jewish thinker Moses Maimonides (d. 1204, Egypt), wrote one of the most important works on the interior life of medieval times, "A Comprehensive Guide for the Servants of God," which was almost entirely influenced by Sufism. Although submerged in the sands of history, for nearly half a millennium it was a vital source for Jewish mystics yearning to better understand their own religion.

Abraham Maimonides founded a dynasty of Jewish-Sufis, descendents of his who, while decidedly and profoundly Jewish, believed that Sufism offered the pre-eminent spiritual model for the ancient religion of Israel. Five generations of Maimonidean descendants not only served as pre-eminent Jewish leaders, but also quoted Sufi sages, wrote Sufi treatises and included Sufi modes of worship in the medieval Egyptian synagogue. The reverberations of these contacts influence Judaism to this day.

Solomon ibn Gabirol, who predated Abraham Maimonides by nearly two centuries, was well known as a Jewish poet, philosopher and writer of liturgical hymns, many of which are still performed in synagogues around the world. He penned one of the basic songs of the Jewish *Sabbath* (day of rest) rite, *Adon Olam* (Lord of the World). What is often overlooked in the popular biographies about Ibn Gabirol, however, is that his pre-eminent spiritual mentor was a Sufi, Muhammad ibn Masarra (d. 931, Spain), and much of his thought and work are based on Ibn Masarra's teachings.

It is important to recall how different were those times from today, for both Jews and Muslims. At the height of Islamic power, from the 8th-12th centuries, ninety percent of all Jews lived under Muslim rule.[5] While Jewish citizens certainly did not enjoy the same rights as the Muslim majority, it was for the Jews a Golden Age, an unprecedented period of legal acceptance and religious and scientific advancement.

By the time the Kabbalah, the most important Jewish spiritual system since Biblical times, was being formulated in the 13th century, Sufism was so important to Jewish thinkers that Islamic ideas permeated this spiritual practice. Sufi manners of worship, Sufi terminology, even stories first told of the Prophet Muhammad all found their way into Kabbalistic writings. Later, 15th and 16th century Kabbalists were drawn to fundamental aspects of the Kabbalah that stemmed from Sufism. They also continued to have direct contacts with Islamic thinkers in the Holy Land. At the time that the Baal Shem Tov (d. 1760) was developing Hasidic worship in Eastern Europe, Sufi antecedents were so prevalent in medieval Judaism and so compelling to the European Jewish leader that Islam, again, played a central role in the creation of a novel Jewish mystical response. I trace this lineage in the pages that follow.

Let me note that I have used the term "Jewish-Sufi" throughout the text to denote specific Jewish thinkers who were deeply influenced by their Islamic spiritual cousins. This is not to say they viewed themselves as "Jewish-Sufis;" they did not. Virtually all of the Jewish personages discussed herein considered themselves wholly Jewish, and their Islamic mystical innovations in keeping with historic Judaism. However, I use this term in order to pay homage to the deep influence of Sufism on Jewish mystics, and Jewish religious practice in general. It is my conclusion that the development of medieval Judaism and even contemporary Jewish practice cannot be fully understood without acknowledging and comprehending the influence of the one (Islamic mysticism) upon the other (Jewish mysticism). The term "Jewish-Sufi" honors this fraternity.

It is vital also to set this book within its proper social context: although is deeply sourced and academic, this effort is ultimately a Track II (citizen-diplomat) peacemaking document written by an independent writer and historical researcher, and fueled by a passion for both Truth and peace. This work is a proposal based on historical affinities, as well as specific interactions between Jewish thinkers and Sufi mystics and their ideas. On some points, academics might disagree with my thesis; in fact, I document many instances where my narrative runs contrary to some of the most recognized Jewish scholars over the past century, such as Gershom Scholem (first Professor of Jewish Mysticism at the Hebrew University of Jerusalem), Paul Fenton (Sorbonne) and even Moshe Idel (Hebrew University). In other places, the conclusions are based on the scholarship of a single thinker, such as the work of Professor David Blumenthal (Emory University), and his work concerning the Sufi influence on the thought of Moses Maimonides.

What I offer is a mosaic of influences which, in my mind and I hope that of my readers, resolves itself into an image of a deep and lasting influence between Jewish mystics and Sufi thought. This is not a book based in wishful thinking. What I present has been deeply considered: a Sufi thread is shown to run through Jewish thought from the 9th century, into the 19th century and even today. However, for some academics, my thesis, or some parts of it, will appear to be outside what is generally accepted within the scholarly world. But I must share my findings.

A quote from Professor Harvey J. Hames of Ben Gurion University (Israel) offers wonderful insight into the difficult and delicate work it takes to attribute ideas to individual sources, especially when one group (medieval Jewish thinkers) often went out of their way to hide their foreign sources:

> A lack of citation of chapter and verse [in most work written by medieval Jewish-Sufis] raises the issue of what constitutes proof or evidence of cross-cultural influences or borrowing. This is not an easily resolvable question, and standards of what constitutes proof differ among scholars within their own disciplines and among disciplines themselves. Sociologists and cultural anthropologists often talk about acculturation or the diffusion of cultural traits – concepts, which, while not necessarily conclusive, are more than suggestive. Historians of religion discuss criteria such as accommodation, cultural symbiosis and religious commonality. To these, it is possible to add geographical proximity and … a long and well-documented history of cultural interaction among members of the three monotheistic faiths in the Iberian Peninsula. Since, in a discussion with important theological implications, direct quotation from a Muslim source by a Jew could be counterproductive, one would expect to find indirect evidence – the use of similar motifs in similar contexts – and this is precisely what one does find [so often in medieval Jewish spirituality].[6]

I hope that readers will consider my book as a whole, and understand that the thrust behind these years of research has been to point to a nourishing place of spiritual affinity between these two great faith traditions.

This book in no way claims to offer the final word on this story. *Shalom/Salaam: A Story of a Mystical Fraternity* simply hopes to help begin a conversation. My primary motivation in undertaking this study is to initiate a dialogue within popular culture concerning this story of spiritual comity. This tale of mystical fraternity is important not only for its historical significance, but also for the relevance it has to the contemporary situation between Jews and Muslims. Looking at today's news, it is easy to believe that Judaism and Islam *never* enjoyed a period of mutual enrichment, a time of peace and reciprocal respect. Hatred runs so deep and the relationship is so combustible, it is hard to imagine that these pervasive attitudes cannot be traced back to the founding of Islam (c. 630). In this climate, positive truths such as those outlined in this book are overlooked and even denied.

This book is offered as part of the dialogue of peace. *Shalom/Salaam* represents a reality of shared roots that we can no longer afford to ignore. Despite the tremendously challenging political and social situation between Palestinians and Israelis, Muslims and Jews, bridges of the living spirit can be built between the two communities. *Shalom/Salaam: A Story of a Mystical Fraternity* is one attempt to highlight and encourage such a profound and brotherly connection.

## Endnotes

1. Goitein, S. D. *Jews and Arabs*. New York: Schocken Books, 1964, p. 55.
2. Ibid. p. 50.
3. Roth, Norman. *Jews, Visigoths and Muslims in Medieval Spain*. New York: E.J. Brill, 1994, p. 73.
4. Ibid. p. 170.
5. Ben-Sasson, Menachem. "Varieties of Inter-Communal Relations in the Geonic Period." *The Jews of Medieval Islam: Community, Society and Identity* (Daniel Frank, ed.). (Leiden: E. J. Brill 1995: 17-32), p. 17.
6. Hames, Harvey J. "A Seal within a Seal: The imprint of Sufism in Abraham Abulafia's Teachings." (*Medieval Encounters 12.2*, 2006), p. 171.

Shalom/Salaam:
A Story of a Mystical Fraternity

# Chapter 1
# The Muslim-Jewish Cultural Affinity

Once upon a time, a widely circulated Jewish document described Islam as "an act of God's mercy."[1]

The contemporary Muslim-Jewish relationship is a lightning rod for geopolitical tensions worldwide. The area of Israel/Palestine represents for many people the embodiment of an intractable enmity. The two People appear to share an aversion so intense for one another that partisans the world over feel compelled to take sides and pass judgment.

While a great deal of this friction clearly grows out of the current political situation, tradition also plays a role in the contemporary justification for the acts of war. Legends and historically based memories have grown up on both sides of the conflict, fanning the flames of hostility. This "habit" of hatred has saturated the education, media and culture on both sides of the border between Israel and the Palestinian Territories.

### Abraham, Isaac and Ishmael

The seeds for today's climate can be traced into the deepest past of the human narrative, which goes back more than five millennia. The story of Abraham, and his sons Isaac and Ishmael (Genesis 16-21, from the *Torah*, or Jewish Bible; Koran 37:100-113), sets up what appears to be an unbridgeable chasm between the two heritors of Abraham's covenant with God.

This tale upon which the traditional parameters of Muslim-Jewish relations were founded appears different in each faith. For Jews, Genesis 16-21 tells the story of Abraham's God-sanctioned relationship with two women. Sarah, Abraham's wife, was unable to conceive, so God enjoined Abraham to take Sarah's maidservant, Hagar, to bear him a son. Hagar bore Ishmael, who was designated Abraham's heir. Thirteen years later, God informed Sarah that in her 90th year she would deliver a son, who would become the rightful inheritor of the Abrahamic covenant with God. After the birth of Isaac, Hagar and her son Ishmael were sent into the wilderness, though God assured Hagar that from her son would issue a "great tribe."[2]

While there is no direct assertion in the Biblical narrative that Ishmael became father of the Arabs and, henceforth, the Muslims, the term "Ishmaeli" did come to signify, even in later Biblical stories, a wandering desert tribe that engaged itself in trading. Further along, during the time of the Second Temple (520 B.C.E – 70 C.E.), Jews had much contact with the Arab people, and the name "Ishmaeli" was accorded to them throughout the Talmudic period (c. 200-500).[3] The history of familial relations between the two People can be found in various other ancient Jewish sources as well. For example, Arabs are referred to as *dodanim*, or "cousins," in Isaiah 21:13.

A different version of the story was revealed to the Prophet Muhammad (d. 632; Medina). One vital change in the narrative was that the Koran (3:66) states: "Abraham was not a Jew or a Christian, but he was an upright man, one who submitted to the will of God" (which is the definition of a Muslim). With Islamic revelation assuring that Abraham embodied the central tenet of Islam, submission to God's will, and with the Jewish revelation having come long before the Islamic religion and making no mention of Islam at all, a fertile seed of potential discord was sown. One cannot question a revelation – be it Jewish or Islamic – and when two are as variable as are these stories of the Abrahamic lineage, it is not difficult to see how conflict among literalist followers of both faiths might arise.

This is not the only disparity between the two versions. The Koran also implies that it is Ishmael whom Abraham is asked to sacrifice (and not Isaac, as per the Jewish narrative) to prove his fealty to God and who, therefore, receives God's blessing for submitting to God's will in this manner. The Koran (37:102-113) relates:

> When he grew enough to work with him, he said, "My son, I see in a dream that I am sacrificing you. What do you think?" He said, "O my father, do what you are commanded to do. You will find me, God willing, patient."
>
> They both submitted, and he put his forehead down. We called him: "O Abraham. You have believed the dream." We thus reward the righteous.
>
> That was an exacting test indeed. We ransomed him by substituting an animal sacrifice. And We preserved his history for subsequent generations. Peace be upon Abraham. We thus reward the righteous. He is one of our believing servants.
>
> Then We gave him the good news about the birth of Isaac, to be one of the righteous prophets. We blessed him and Isaac.

In the Islamic version, Isaac clearly is born after the incident of God's demand to sacrifice Abraham's son.

### Jewish-Islamic Cultural Entanglement

Despite this ingrained, oppositional aspect of the revealed histories of Jews and Muslims, relations between the two People were positive almost from the outset. They speak languages so closely related that medieval Jews created a mystical understanding of Hebrew through their study of the Arabic tongue. The basic, democratic social organization of the two groups was as alike as it was unusual for medieval times, with their respect for the individual within the greater community essentially unheard of in other parts of the ancient world – a political facet that has remained with both of them for the duration of their histories.

As the pre-eminent 20th-century Jewish Islamicist, Professor S. D. Goitein (Institute of Advanced Study, Princeton) notes in *Jews and Arabs*:

> Israel and the Arabs present the type of a society which is characterized by the absence of privileged castes and classes, by the absence of enforced obedience to a strong authority, by undefined but nonetheless very strong agencies for the formation and expression of public opinion, by freedom of speech and for a high respect for human life, dignity and freedom ... Israel and Arabs alone preserved their primitive democracies, and the moral attitude implied by it, at the decisive hour in their history: when both people became the bearers of religions that were destined to mold the development of a great part of the human race.[4]

Sifting through Jewish-Islamic history, we find more that positively links the two People. Although there is an ongoing debate among Islamic scholars, most practicing Muslims believe that on the authority of a verse in the Koran (5:5), they can eat meat that has been ritually slaughtered not only by Muslim butchers, but also by Kosher Jewish ones. Jews and Muslims today may have a hard time merely sitting at the same negotiating table together, but when they retreat to their respective homes, they might each be eating a joint cut from the same religiously sanctioned roast.

Regardless of these similarities great and small, "familial relations" can cut two ways. The rapport between Muslims and Jews has become as complicated as it is intertwined, a tale of respect, hatred, love, disgust, murder and shared mystical inspiration. The early, dubious impetus provided by the story of Isaac and Ishmael has recently solidified due to political events, and become accepted as a supposed "tradition" of mistrust and outright loathing, refashioning a relationship that was often positive for more than one thousand years.

## Muhammad, the Koran and the Jews

No religious leader or movement comes into being in a vacuum, and Islam was no different. Surrounded by people of various faiths, including Jews – a religion and culture that Muhammad respected – Islam emerged into an atmosphere suffused with the ancient monotheistic creed. S. D. Goitein maintains: "Islam is from the very flesh and bone of Judaism. It is, so to say, a recast, an enlargement of the latter."[5]

The Koran clearly states that its message did not depart from the communications of past prophets, but that this was the final prophetic revelation, which reiterated and clarified the message of the earlier Jewish and Christian scriptures. "Believe in the *Torah*, the *Zabur* (Book of Psalms) and the *Evangel* (New Testament)," Muhammad stated.[6] As the *Encyclopaedia Judaica* relates, the Koran, representing an extension of Jewish and Christian revelations, reaffirms points of essential doctrine, prophets and even holidays. Earlier religious symbols appear throughout the Koran, showing how Islam flows naturally with previous monotheistic practices.[7]

### Jewish Influence on Early Islam

The status of the Islamic revelation as a reiteration of the "message of Abraham" can be seen in many of the Koranic stories about the Jewish prophets.[8] For instance, as mentioned in the introduction to this book, a preeminent historical figure in the body of the Koran is Moses (*Musa* in Arabic) – his name being cited more than one hundred times. Stories about Moses, some recognizable to Jewish readers and others seemingly more obscure, pervade the Muslim Holy Book.[9] As the Koran relates (46:12): "Before this book there was Moses' book ... and this book (the Koran) confirms it in the Arabic language." According to Michael Sells in his *Early Islamic Mysticism*, the Koranic Moses offers a prototype of one who has directly encountered God.[10]

Even more important than the specific Jewish law and lore that is emphasized by the Islamic revelation, the Koran verifies fundamental aspects of the Jewish belief system. Basic Islamic concepts such as the belief in one God as the creator of the world and the designer of human destiny, and the insistence that this God represents justice and mercy, before Whom everyone high and low bears personal responsibility (a very important point, given the strictly stratified culture of seventh century Arabia), reaffirm ideas from the earlier Jewish prophets.[11]

### *Isra'iliyat*

Early Muslim commentators used *Isra'iliyat* (Tales of the People of Israel) to explain obscure or unelaborated portions of the Koran, as well as expound on pre-Islamic history.[12] Professor Steven Wasserstrom asserts in his book *Between Muslim and Jew* that Koranic commentary is filled with Talmudic (c. 2nd-5th centuries), *halakhic* (Jewish law), *aggadic* (non-legalistic oral teachings), *midrashic* (commentaries) and other Judaic material.[13] The themes of these *Isra'iliyat* covered the prophets and their warnings, the Jewish people's sufferings and rewards, individual Jews' indiscretions and punishment, sayings of wise men, premonitions of the appearance of Muhammad claimed to be found in the *Torah*, stories of Moses and even descriptions of the Muslim community and specific Caliphs,[14] retroactively applied to Jewish history and the Bible.

Initially, these mostly Jewish additions to Muslim interpretation were respected and utilized within normative Islam. Ismail ibn Kathir (d. 1373; Damascus, one of the most important exegetes of the Koran) relates a *hadith* (saying of the Prophet Muhammad) that states: "Convey from me, even if it be an *aya* [verse of the Koran], and narrate from the Children of Israel, and there is no sin in that."[15] According to Sheikh Ahmad Shakir, an Egyptian *qadi*, or judge (d.1958), Abdullah ibn Amr ibn al-As (a Companion of the Prophet Muhammad) "reported that the Prophet permitted the study of *Isra'iliyat*."[16] M. J. Kister notes in *Israel Oriental Studies II* that another *hadith* reported by Amr ibn al-As states that the Prophet interpreted a dream of his, in which he had honey on one of his fingers and butter on the other, by stating: "You will read the two books, the *Torah* and the Koran."[17]

Although the acceptance of these stories is verified in the *hadith* and by the actions of the Prophet's Companions, the subsequent history of *Isra'iliyat* is a bit more problematic. The ebb and flow of acceptance of *Isra'iliyat* within Islam parallels the wax and wane of the political fortunes of Jewish-Muslim relations. Recently, for instance, events in the Middle East have "launched an Islamic reconsideration of *Isra'iliyat* within Islam, [which] are now seen by many Muslim scholars as metaphors for the infiltration of contemporary Islamic life by Western and Israeli distortions."[18] Regardless of the specific attitude of Muslim interpreters toward *Isra'iliyat*, the deeper connections to which their existence within Islam points are impossible to ignore.

Within one hundred years of Muhammad's revelation, there arose in early Islam a class of professional raconteurs, whose subject was mainly the "Prophets," i.e. the Jewish, as well as previously unknown, heroes of the Koran. Those experts wove their responses to Muslim questions from various sources, and in particular from the vast literature of the *Midrash*, the popular (Jewish) exposition of the Bible. When none of these sources could fill in the gaps, they added bits and pieces from other tales and sources, and even from their own inspiration. According to S. D. Goitein, some of these *Isra'iliyat* even found their way back into later Jewish *Midrash*, which from that time on contained some Koranic material.[19]

### Jewish Influence on Early Sufism

Other aspects of the Koranic revelation confirmed Jewish antecedents. The Koran reiterated the highly dedicated religious life of Jewish forerunners, tying Islam and Judaism together at their mystical cores (which, as we will see, allowed medieval Jews to "reclaim" ancient Jewish spirituality through their study of Islam). Malik ibn Dinar (d. 748; Babylonia), a disciple of Hasan al-Basri (d. 728; Babylonia, considered the "patriarch of Muslim mysticism" by the pre-eminent Islamic scholar Annemarie Schimmel[20]), quotes copiously from Jewish sources, specifically the early Jewish Pietists (c. 2nd – 5th centuries).[21] Living half a millennium before Muhammad, and known through their representation in Talmudic literature, these gentle Jewish practitioners came to represent for Ibn Dinar the height of Islamic piety.[22] As David Ariel, President of the Cleveland College of Jewish Studies, notes in *Approaches to Judaism in Medieval Times*:

Perhaps an answer as to why Malik [relied on] *Isra'iliyat* [as opposed]

to *hadith* ... lies within the tendencies of second and third generation
Islam. The opposition of the Caliph Umar I [d. 644, second Caliph in
Islam after Abu Bakr] to recording *sunnah* [traditions of the Prophet]
reflected a general reluctance to expand the corpus of the *hadith* at a
time when the Koran was being established ... The strictures against
reliance upon *hadith* led the early Pietists, including Hasan al-Basri and
Malik ibn Dinar, to turn to other sources of legitimacy. The sense of
veneration for the Hebrew prophets, the presence of Jewish converts
in and around Baghdad and the desire to encourage further conversion
led to an unusual openness to Jewish sources. The receptivity to Biblical and rabbinic legends of exemplary spirituality, conceived under the
broad heading of *Torah*, as in the case of Malik, made it possible for
early Muslims to turn to Jewish models of piety without posing a chal-
lenge to the authority of the Koran.[23]

Islamic mystics appeared at times to be extensions of the earlier Jewish
Hasidim. In even the most detailed aspects of their worship, these Jewish
practitioners prefigured Sufi practice. The Talmudic mystics eschewed all
extravagance; they stayed away from government and even Jewish authorities; in dress and behavior, the Hasidim appeared as mourners; they formulated their teachings in short, aphoristic sayings of a mystical flavor and
cared not at all what other people thought of them. In all of these details,
they foreshadowed the Sufis, as each detail mentioned here with regard to
the Hasidim of the Talmudic era applied also to the Islamic mystics.[24]

Professor S. D. Goitein addresses the question of why later 10th-15th-
century Jews were drawn to the Sufis for mystical inspiration, instead of
to the earlier model of Jewish piety. This point is of great consequence
to this study, as many scholars and lay-people today insist that the Sufi
ideas that so captivated Jews were actually Jewish ideas first. While this
is in some (though certainly not all) cases true, the fact remains that the
immediate inspiration for the medieval Jewish thinkers was usually their
contemporary Islamic mystics. It was the Sufi interpretation of past ideas
that influenced medieval Judaism.

> Where the Jewish Gnostics of the fifth and sixth centuries stammered,
> the Muslim mystics of the ninth and tenth centuries were able to speak
> out eloquently. Thus, despite the largely common background, Muslim
> pietism became a far more complete and impressive system of thought
> and morals than early Hasidism, and was able, in its turn, to exercise
> a tremendous influence on Jewish minds, which were well-prepared to
> accept it.[25]

It is vital to consider this mutual influence, from the Talmudic Hasidim to
the Islamic mystics, then to medieval Jews, as many Sufi-oriented Jews

declared that they followed the ways of the Sufis because they (the "Jew-ish-Sufis") were in fact reclaiming an ancient Jewish mystical practice that had been lost to the Jews, and taken up by the Sufis. They felt certain that they were bypassing nearly a millennium of calcified Jewish worship to reach back toward the earlier Talmudic mystics and Biblical prophets, via the intermediary Sufis.

## A Surprising History of Mutual Respect

From the early 7th century, when Islam emerged on the Arabian Peninsula, until the dissolution of the powerful Arab Caliphate at the end of the 15th century, Jews often lived freely and prospered under the umbrella of Muslim control. And it was fortunate that they did, since at the height of Islamic rule, nearly 90% of the world's Jewry lived within this rich culture.[26]

From the inception of Islam, Jews viewed Islamic rule in a positive light. According to Professor Yom Tov Assis (Hebrew University), in his article "The Judeo-Arabic Tradition in Christian Spain," Jewish citizens took great comfort in the downfall of their Christian oppressors, who had treated Jewish subjects with a humiliating apartheid. In addition to being freed from the yoke of those cruel leaders, many Jews viewed the victory of Islam over its adversaries as the precursor of their own messianic age,[27] a belief that became important as Jewish mysticism flowered under Islamic rule.

### Jewish-Muslim Religious Symbiosis

The Jewish-Muslim connection involved more than just the esoteric practitioners of both paths. The similarities between the normative aspects of the two religions are striking, providing much impetus for the often-positive interrelationship between early Muslim practitioners and their contemporary Jews. Professor S. D. Goitein outlines a series of likenesses between Judaism and Islam:

1) Islam, like Judaism, is a religion of *halakha* (Hebrew), in Arabic *shari'a*, that is, a God-given law that regulates minutely all aspects of life.

2) This religious law is based on the Oral Tradition called in Arabic *hadith* and in Hebrew *Torah she-be'al peh* (Oral Torah), which supplements the written law.

3) The Oral Tradition falls into two parts, one legal and the other moral. In Muslim and Jewish texts they assume the same form of maxims and anecdotes.

4) A free and unorganized republic of scholars developed Muslim *shari'a*, echoing Jewish *halakha*. Islam (like Judaism) never had a hierarchy of religious dignitaries.

5) The logical reasoning applied to the development of the reli-

gious law is largely identical in Islam and Judaism.

6) The study even of purely legal matters is regarded in both religions as worship. The holy men of Islam and Judaism are students of the divinely revealed law.[28]

There grew out of the concurrences between the revealed traditions, as well as the early Jewish influence on the growth of Islam, impetus for an ongoing dialogue between the two faiths and cultures. "The process operating in the highest spheres of the spiritual relations between Islam and Judaism is echoed in the absorption of considerable sections of the ancient Jewish popular literature into its Arab counterpart, which, in turn, made the former [the Jews] ready to accept the influence of the latter [Muslims]."[29]

### Islamic Influence on Jewish Religious Practice

Jews under Muslim rule were strongly influenced by the regenerative force of their host religion. Jews of medieval Islam went so far as to re-create the Muslim *hajj*, or prescription that at least once in a lifetime an observant Muslim must make a pilgrimage to the holy city of Mecca. Islam's Jews instituted a Jewish *hajj*, with the need to "Behold Jerusalem" at least once in a lifetime becoming almost a religious duty for them.[30] As the vast majority of Jews lived under Islamic rule, there was a constant journeying of observant Jews, plying the waters of the Mediterranean, fulfilling this Muslim-inspired religious duty.

Jews were not reticent about relying on the Koran to help clarify spiritual issues. Moses ibn Ezra (d. 1138; Spain) notes that he took no issue with citing the Koran in his exposition of Jewish law: "I paid no attention to the hatred of some of the hypocrites of the sages of our community," he avowed, who were upset that he based his exegesis on the Islamic holy book, since earlier (Jewish) scholars like Saadia Gaon (d. 942; Babylonia, a preeminent Jewish philosopher and head of the Talmudic academy in Sura) and others had used the Koran to clarify obscure prophecies in the Bible. Ibn Ezra also quotes another Talmudic phrase that would be oft repeated by Sufi-leaning Jews: "Everyone who says a wise thing, even among the nations of the world, is called wise [*Megillah* 16a, from the *Mishna*, or codification of the Oral Law]."[31]

Jewish practitioners could go too far, however, even in this open-minded Golden Age. For instance, during this period a *responsum* (religious edict) was issued to the effect that "a leader of liturgy in a synagogue who dared to sing prayers to popular Muslim tunes must be silenced (indicating, perhaps, that the practice of doing so was not uncommon.)."[32] In fact, the *Jewish Encyclopedia* notes that we do have record of a specific medieval Muslim "tune" that is still sung in Sephardic synagogues, attached to one of the most important Sabbath songs, *Lekha Dodi* (Come My Beloved).[33]

Jewish Scholarly Expansion Under Muslim Influence

As Islam moved out of Arabia and conquered ever-vaster lands to the north, east and west, it did not view its new subjects as the Romans had theirs; these latter had crushed their vanquished. For the Muslim peoples, the rich scholarly and wisdom traditions of the Syrian, Persian, Hindu and Jewish cultures were no sooner conquered, than they were translated into Arabic and acculturated into the daily life of the nascent society. The Jewish population, in the process of changing its own daily language from Aramaic to Arabic, profited greatly from this scholarly influx. This heretofore inward-looking people suddenly had access to a vast compendium of fresh world-views and ideas.

Another factor for the constructive interaction between Jews and Muslims was the open-minded rule of the early Muslim Caliphs. The Abbasids (750-1258) allowed non-Islamic groups an amount of autonomy. During this era, Jews were held in such high esteem that the head of the Jewish community also enjoyed an official position within the Muslim Caliphate. Recognized as the spokesman for all of the Jews in the realm, he was given the title of "Exilarch,"[34] which signified the leader of the "exiled" peoples of Israel. Said to be descended from the House of David (1037 - 967 B.C.E., the second leader of the Kingdom of Israel), the Babylonian Exilarch attained a position of splendor.[35] Part of the reason for the respect paid by the Muslim leaders to the Exilarch was that they, like the Jews, regarded David as one of the great Prophets, and with their respect for lineage, ranked very highly the scions of such an ancient and noble line.[36] Muslims refer to him as *Sayidina Daud*, "our lord David."

To get a sense of the inter-confessional atmosphere in the capital city, one need only read the words of a 9th-century Islamic theologian visiting Baghdad for the first time:

> One of the Spanish theologians – Abu Omar Ahmad ibn Muhammad ibn Sa'di – visited Baghdad … Upon his return he met the famous scholar Abu Muhammad ibn Abi Za'yd, who asked him whether he had an opportunity of attending, during his stay in Baghdad, one of the theological assemblies. "Yes," he answered. "I attended twice but refused to go there a third time." "Why?" "For this simple reason, which you will appreciate: At the first meeting there were present not only people of various [Islamic] sects but also Magians, materialists, atheists, Jews and Christians, in short unbelievers of all kinds … One of the unbelievers rose and said to the assembly: 'We are meeting here for a discussion. Its conditions are known to all. You, Muslims, are not allowed to argue from your books and prophetic traditions since we deny both. Everybody, therefore, has to limit himself to rational arguments.' The whole assembly applauded these words."[37]

Jews participated in even the most vital Muslim activities. The Jews Masha'allah ibn Athan (745-815), Shu'aib (late eighth, early ninth century), Sahl ibn Bishr (first quarter of the ninth century) and Anul-Tayyib Sind ibn Ali all worked as Muslim court astrologers in Baghdad, delving into such important intricacies as the occult sciences and the making of talismans.[38] In addition, the Jewish liturgical poet Yosef ibn Abitur (d. 1024; Spain) interpreted the Talmud for the Muslim Caliph al-Hakim (d. 1021; Egypt).[39]

Friends from Childhood

This positive interaction was hardly accidental – it was woven into the upbringing of Jew and Muslim alike. Young Jewish boys were trained from their youth to appreciate and excel in the Muslim world. In addition to studying Hebrew, the *Torah* and the Talmud, Jewish children attended *madrassas* (Muslim schools), studying everything from the Arabic language and grammar to the Koran and Muslim law.[40] By attending these schools, Jewish children operated on an equal social and scholarly plane with the Muslim boys, and the seeds of later collaboration were planted in both societies.

This relationship was hardly a one-way street, as Muslims sometimes even found their way into a Jewish house of prayer. A well-known edict issued by the Jewish leader of the Talmudic academy in Babylonia (Iraq), Hai Gaon (d. 1038) states: "It is permitted to teach Arabic calligraphy and arithmetic in the synagogue together with the sacred law. Non-Jewish children may also study in the synagogue for the sake of good relations with the neighbors."[41]

It was not just an elite sliver of the Jewish population that profited from the new cultural influences and social opportunities. A sizable minority of Jews read the new literature and studied the sciences in Arabic. As Professor Abraham S. Halkin of the Jewish Theological Seminary notes in *The Great Fusion*:

> The vocabulary of the Islamic faith finds its way into Jewish books; the Koran becomes a proof-text. The Arabs' practice of citing poetry in their works is taken over by the Jews. Jewish writings teem with sentences from the works of scientists, philosophers and theologians. Indeed, Arabic literature, native and imported, becomes the general background of all that the Jews write.[42]

Jewish society, so long walled off from the cultures within which it existed, opened and flowered. The time between the 8th and 11th centuries is known as a Jewish Golden Age, when Jews reached social and religious heights that they hadn't known in almost a thousand years – and wouldn't know again for another eight hundred years, until the arrival of the great waves of Jewish immigrants on the shores of America.

### Intermingling in Daily Life

The average Jew hardly lived a life segregated from his Muslim hosts. Medieval Jews inhabited homes that were exactly like those of their Arab neighbors, shared their interests in gardens, fountains and other architectural adornments, and enjoyed the accoutrements of the middle class Muslim lifestyle. Many Muslims and Jews shared houses together, living as tenants in a home owned by a member of the other religion.

They cooked and ate the same foods, allowing for the differences in Jewish and Muslim dietary restrictions. In clothing, as well, there was very little difference between Jews and the majority.[43] Jewish citizens even extended invitations to their Muslim neighbors to attend drinking parties, which caused problems for both, as wine was forbidden within Islam and sacramental for the Jews. S.D. Goitein relates:

> Muslims occasionally joined Jewish drinking parties, which caused some difficulty, because wine, due to its sacramental character, should according to law be handled only by those within the fold. When such newcomers would enter, sophisticated keepers of the law would drop honey into the wine. The use of honey was forbidden within the Temple service (Leviticus 2:11); consequently its admixture converted the taboo beverage into a regular soft drink. Moses Maimonides ruled that the Egyptian *nabidh*, which was [wine] diluted with honey, was not to be regarded as wine; the benediction pronounced for it was that pronounced over water. Thus, the Muslim visitors could freely partake of the beverage, as could the Jews.[44]

Jews were deeply involved in the everyday life of the state. They frequently attained positions of influence disproportionate to their numbers within the greater community. A medieval Egyptian Muslim poet laments the secular success of the Jewish population in this short refrain:

> The Jews of our time have attained the goal of their aspirations:
> The honors are theirs and so are the riches.
> Counselors and kings are taken from their midst.
> Egyptians! I advise you, become Jews, for Heaven itself has turned
>   Jewish.[45]

Jews enlisted in Muslim armies and participated as members of the Muslim police force, giving them sway over Muslim malefactors.[46]

The Jews of Islam not only echoed their hosts in numerous domestic and professional manners, but the interrelationship was so fertile that they became Muslims' business partners. Oftentimes, Jews would act as agents (*wakil*) for Muslims, and vice versa. The best-known form of shared enterprise was called a *commenda*, in which one party would provide the capital and the other would execute the work. While one might guess that the Jews were most likely providing the work, due to their inferior status as a minority, in fact, a *commenda* functioned both ways, with sometimes the Jews and sometimes the Muslims supplying the capital. Many such connections were formed between members of the two religions.[47]

Business relations between the two People were so common, that Moses Maimonides was asked to rule on the specifics of commercial relations between Muslim and Jew. In response to a question concerning joint ownership in a store, Maimonides writes that in places where Muslims and Jews shared commerce, the profits should be divided equally. He adds: "They may agree that the profits of sales on Friday [the Islamic holy day] go only to the Jew and that those of Saturday [the Jewish *Sabbath*] go only to the Muslim."[48]

The convivial relations between the two religions were such that during the entire five hundred year long Abbasid period, there were no documented cases of forced conversions by Jews to Islam.[49] This bespoke an unusual respect by a majority religion of that era – one that allowed the minority Jews to practice their birth religion in peace.

### Jewish Jurisprudence

Jewish jurisprudence, which before and after the Golden Age was strictly rooted in a rabbinical interpretation of the Bible, grew porous during this period, allowing for a lively interchange with Islam. While the stated position of both Jewish and Muslim authorities was that each community was to be ruled by its own system of courts and judges, chosen from within the community itself, the reality was different.[50] For instance, although strictly prohibited, Jews with legal complaints sometimes turned to Muslim courts. This behavior became so widespread that it was codified by various religious edicts, from both Muslim and Jewish authorities. Norman Roth notes in *Jews, Visigoths and Muslims in Medieval Spain*:

> A tenth century Muslim juridical decision stated that if one [Jewish] party appealed to a Muslim justice and the other to a Jewish [justice], the case must be decided by the Jewish judge. Another judge decided that if the case involved injustices not dealt with by Jewish law, Muslim law should decide it. Such a lenient attitude on the part of Muslim legal authorities may have been influenced by the custom of Jews routinely appealing to Muslim courts.[51]

It was not unusual for Jews to turn to the Muslim authorities even in matters pertaining to religious observance. It turned out that the Jewish traditionalists of the time period shared one vital matter with the Muslim authorities: a respect for strict orthodoxy in religious practice. The Muslim Sultan was asked to rule on such religious issues as poetical insertions in the synagogue liturgy, matters pertaining to Jewish prayer on workdays and the *Sabbath*, and other topics concerning Jewish religious *bi'da* (innovations).

### Gaonate

This mutual assistance and understanding between Jewish and Muslim juristic scholarship and rulings was facilitated by the consolidation of the Jewish *Gaonate* (religious academy) in Baghdad (from earlier rural centers) in the 9th century. *Gaon* was the title of the leader of these religious academies, and they were regarded as the highest authority on religious and civil matters. The academies operated as centralizing forces for the Jewish religion – and Jews from around the world would send their social and religious questions to them. The *Gaons* then would issue *responsa*,[52] written answers to the legal and ritualistic questions.

> The *Gaon* was the highest authority on religious law [within medieval Judaism] and was entitled to expound on it in public lectures. He was the guardian of the religious and moral conduct of all the members of the community. He had the right to impose or cancel an excommunication. He appointed and dismissed preachers, cantors and religious slaughterers. He appointed and defined the competence of judges and supervised them, as well as the trustees of the courts. He could delegate his authority over a certain city or country to any person chosen by him.[53]

After the *Gaonate* was consolidated in Baghdad, the Muslim civilization influenced it in many ways. As S. D. Goitein notes in *A Mediterranean Society*, his groundbreaking study of medieval Jewish life under Islam, the *Gaons* would appeal to the Islamic authorities to help execute their decisions. The Jewish legal authority became so enmeshed with the Muslim power structure that in the early days of the Fatimid (969-1171) rule over Egypt, the Egyptian Caliphs granted substantial state-sponsored stipends to *Gaons*. Lastly, the Muslim rulers reserved the right to confirm the Jewish *Gaon* in his office – which led to the *Gaons* securing letters of "installment" from the Caliph, often with the help of influential Jews in the Egyptian capital.[54]

### Mutual Respect

Despite these areas of cooperation, Jewish citizens in Islamic lands never enjoyed equal legal status with the majority. In addition to safeguarding certain minority rights, Muslim law sometimes demanded segregation and subservience, conditions that were usually bearable but, under a weak or cruel government, could and did lead to situations bordering on lawlessness and even to outright persecution.[55] While this type of behavior wasn't the norm, it is important to recognize that neither was it unheard of.

Regardless of these occasional episodes however, many Muslims were deeply respectful of earlier Jewish thinkers. The Muslim biographer Abu Qasim ibn Sa'id (d. 1070, one of the world's first historians of science[56]) wrote a treatise on the history of sciences and religions, entitled *Kitab Tabakat al-Umam* (The Book of the Classification of Nations). He devoted an entire section to outlining the influence of Jewish scientists on the development of Islamic thought.[57] For instance, Ibn Sa'id relates the story of Hasdai ibn Shaprut (d. 970; Cordoba), a Jew who rose to become court physician and prime minister to the powerful Spanish Caliph 'Abd ar-Rahman III (d. 961; Cordoba):

> Hasdai [ibn Shaprut], who was in the service of Abd ar-Rahman, was interested in medicine, advanced in the legal sciences of the Jews, and was the first to open for his co-religionists the gates of the knowledge of the Talmud, chronology, etc. Up to this time, the Spanish Jews were dependent on the Jews of Baghdad for their law, chronology and dates of holidays … When Hasdai, however, became connected with ar-Rahman and gained his highest regard for himself by his superior mettle, perfection and culture, he succeeded, through the kind intervention of the Caliph, in procuring the works of the Jews of the East. Thus the Jews of Spain became informed about matters of which they were ignorant heretofore, and dispensed with an inconvenient transaction.[58]

In this short 11th-century passage, we see some of the most important themes of Jewish life under Islamic rule. First, that they enjoyed such stature that a Muslim biographer would mention many of them (there are dozens of Jews described in the book), and speak so highly about one who had risen to great heights in service to the Islamic Caliph. Also mentioned is the vital decentralization of Jewish law and *responsa* (religious edicts) from the *Gaon* in Baghdad to the West, initiated in the 10th century by Ibn Shaprut (with the aid of the Muslim leader), which reverberated down through the generations, allowing an Egyptian Jewish leader, Moses Maimonides, to become one of the most important Jewish thinkers since the fall of the Second Temple, in 70 C.E. (the Second Temple was destroyed in Jerusalem by the Roman Emperor Titus).

Far from unusual, Ibn Sa'id's work represented a not unusual note of appreciation from Islamic scholars toward their Jewish brethren. After all, written into the Koran are passages such as (45:16): "We [*Allah*] gave the Book [*Torah*] to the Israelites and bestowed on them wisdom and prophethood. We provided them with wholesome things and exalted them above the nations." Although contemporary enmities make it hard to believe, there is impetus for positive Jewish-Muslim relations written directly into the Muslim Holy Book.

Jews under Islamic rule returned the favor. Released from nearly one millennium of oppressive rule – first under the Romans, and then Christians – medieval Jews exalted in the new atmosphere of freedom. Whenever Muslim rulers were mentioned in letters – even private ones, between two Jews – they were fondly remembered for acts of kindness, generosity and justice, with wishes for success. The respect for the temporal Muslim leaders was such that "the person of the ruler was regarded as sacrosanct; [a Jewish supplicant] might even mention the *Torah* and the [Muslim] ruler in the same breath while making a public declaration in the synagogue."[59]

The Arabized Jew

The rise of Islam inspired a renewal for the Jewish people, supporting the social and cultural enrichment for the expansion of the Hebrew religion, the rise of a Jewish merchant class, the explosion of Jewish scholarship and poetry and expansion of the Hebrew language. It offered the Jewish people their first true experience of social and political possibility in the post-Second Temple era.

Arabized Jews quickly shed their ancient Aramaic language and adopted the Arabic tongue, which became central for the restructuring of their lifestyle, culture and even religion. As Professor Thomas Glick (Director of the Institute for Medieval History, Boston University) notes in *Islamic and Christian Spain in the Early Middle Ages*:

> *Andalusi* [Spanish] Jews substantially revitalized both Hebrew secular poetry and philology under the influence of Arabic poetry and grammar … The social status of scholarship was also influenced by the Islamic milieu, in which both scholarly and commercial pursuits conferred prestige and were frequently combined in the same person. The figure of the "learned merchant" as bearer and seeker of high culture on his far-ranging business trips was as characteristic of the Arabized Jew as of his Muslim counterpart.[60]

Along with the Arab language came an acceptance of Arab ways of thinking and seeing the world, their forms of literature, religious notions, grammar and other basic cultural underpinnings. "Arabic was used by Jews for all kinds of literary activities, not only for scientific and other secular purposes, but for expounding and translating the Bible or the *Mishna* [redaction of the oral law, c. 200],[61] for theological and philological treatises, for discussing Jewish law and ritual and even for the study of Hebrew grammar and lexicography."[62]

An open-minded, outward looking worldview formed during these first centuries of the Muslim era, which, in turn, affected the inner life and forms of expression for Jewish practitioners.[63] And it wasn't just the Muslims that were influencing these medieval Jews: as was already noted, Jews now had access to the work and thought of ancient sciences and methods of thinking. As S. D. Goitein notes in his *Jews and Arabs*, for the first time in their history, the Jewish people practiced systematic, scientific thinking such as that developed by the Greeks.[64]

### Arabic Influence on the Hebrew Language

The Hebrew language also underwent a renaissance, stimulated not only by Jews' introduction to the Arabic language, but also by a healthy, and not unfriendly, intellectual competition with their Muslim counterparts. Moses ibn Ezra (d. 1138), a Jewish poet and philosopher, observed that Jews studied Arabic grammar, which allowed them to make great strides in understanding Hebrew language and grammar. Over the first few centuries of Jewish-Muslim interaction, Arabic, as a cognate language to Hebrew, came to play an increasingly important role in the deepening comprehension of the Jewish idiom. Numerous obscure Hebrew words were explained on the basis of an Arabic equivalent.[65]

Ibn Ezra wrote a seminal work on the art of poetry, with which he hoped to pass on to Hebrew writers the lessons he had learned from Arabic. He states: "The art of correct expression had become the special prerogative of the Arab world as a whole. The Arabic language is to other languages as spring is to the other seasons."[66] Ibn Ezra's pronouncement was not so out of line with his contemporary Jewish poets and philosophers, who agreed with him to varying extents, and who used Arabic as a doorway to understanding their own Hebrew language and culture.

### Demise of the Golden Age

After about the 12th century, the Abbasid Caliphate slowly disintegrated – and the Islamic lands eventually shrank in geographical breadth and temporal power. As early as 1377, the great Muslim sociologist and philosopher of history Muhammad ibn Khaldun (d. 1406; Cairo), writes: "The realm of the Arabs has been wiped out completely; the power now rests in the hands of non-Arabs, such as the Turks in the East and the Franks [Europeans] in the North."[67] At the end of the 15th century, there were a spare one thousand Jews in what was left of Islamic Spain,[68] as compared with the 300,000 who were expelled along with many Muslims from Christian Spain in 1492.[69]

The situation continued to deteriorate for Arab-speaking lands over the centuries:

At the beginning of the First World War, not a single independent Arab state was in existence ... Concurrently, the Jews in Arabic-speaking countries, who at one time had formed both the majority of the Jewish people and its social and spiritual pivot, simply faded out of Jewish history. They were almost forgotten by the bulk of the nation [of Israel], which was now concentrated in the Christian countries ... There were still Jews in Arab-speaking territories, but their number was less than 10% of the total Jewish population of the world.[70]

Jewish demographics had completely reversed since the Golden Age one millennium before, when 90% of the Nation of Israel had lived under Islamic rule.

Throughout the long period of Muslim decline, however, familial relations and even mutual respect continued between the two People. Until the rise of European Zionism (an international political movement that calls for the existence of a sovereign, Jewish national homeland) in the late 19th century, and the creation of the State of Israel (1948) and the political tensions it spawned, Muslim lands were often more accepting of a Jewish minority than were Christian countries.[71] As Professor Abraham S. Halkin notes: "Islamic administrative policy was generally determined by practical considerations which led to toleration [for Jews] and, on occasion, even privilege."[72] More than one thousand years of often positive relations between Jews and Muslims have been swept away in the past century or so of political history.

Jewish-Muslim Spiritual Fraternity

The ease with which Jews operated in Islamic lands, and the intertwining of cultural influence between Jew and Muslim that this incubated, explains how even the most religious of Jews, those whom we will meet in the ensuing pages of this book, turned so easily and so fully to Islamic ideas for inspiration of how to create a Jewish spiritual life. With interactions between the two People so extensive – and Jews educated in everything Muslim from clothing to the Koran – it was only natural that they would look to their hosts for spiritual inspiration as well. And this is exactly what they did: medieval Jews inscribed a new, virtually unknown chapter in the extensive volume not only of the Jewish religion, but also in the annals of Jewish-Muslim relations.

It is also vital to note that this interaction has hardly been constrained to the geographic places and chronological times in which the interaction took place – it reverberates to this day. S. D. Goitein notes, concerning this period of Jewish growth:

> Every aspect that we regard today as Judaism – the synagogue service and prayer book, law and ritual, theology and ethics, the text of the Bible, the grammar and vocabulary of Hebrew – was formulated, consolidated and canonized in the first centuries of Islam.[73]

We are left to question how it can be that a relationship with so long, so positive and so decidedly intertwined a history, can have dissolved to the point that so many of our current world's political troubles seem to revolve, either directly or indirectly, around the Israeli-Palestinian conflict?

There are two responses, the first one being quite basic. With members of both religions claiming the same plot of earth in the Middle East – Israel/Palestine – the religious aspect of the relationship has become embroiled in political concerns. And as war is just a continuation of politics,[74] and perceived ethnic and religious differences are symbolically potent, the traditional distinctions between Jews and Muslims are used by political leaders as justification for hatreds, and laying a claim to a "divine right" in the conflict.

A second factor is suggested by the Muslim scholar al-Jahiz (d. 869; Babylonia):

> The Jews were immediate neighbors of the Muslims in al-Medina and other places, and hostility between neighbors is as strong and tenacious as that between relatives; for people hate only that which they know and are opposed to those who are like them, knowing the weaknesses of those with whom they are in daily contact.[75]

Jews and the Muslims, inextricably linked as far back as the Biblical Genesis narrative, simply know (and resemble) each other too well. After all, love and hate are both passionate sides of the same coin. As the love of the Golden Age waned, it was replaced with a seemingly unbounded revulsion.

If these two People, so similar and so desperately entangled spiritually, historically and *en terra* are ever to coexist in peace again, they must find a manner of overcoming the recent politically-based hatred and acknowledge the rich, varied and often positive history that they share. As we shall soon see, the story of a constructive relationship between Jews and Muslims at the deepest core of their religions is there, waiting to be rediscovered. It is just a matter of bringing it to light – and making it part of the contemporary narrative between these two Biblical cousins, so that their essential oneness on numerous doctrinal and spiritual facets can inspire a renewal of that marvelous time, when Jews and Muslims lived together peacefully for more than one thousand years, a rich period of mutual respect and shared growth.

## Endnotes

1. Goitein, S.D. *Jews and Arabs.* (New York: Schocken Books, 1964).

2. The story of Ishmael and Isaac is taken from *The Holy Scriptures.* (Philadelphia: The Jewish Publication Society, 1948), pp. 17-23 (Genesis 16-21).

3. Goitein, S. D. *Jews and Arabs*, p. 22.

4. Information in this paragraph taken from Ibid. p. 27.

5. Ibid. p. 130.

6. Quoted in Kister, M. J. "Haddithu 'an Bani Isra'ila wa-la Haraja: A Study of an Early Tradition." (*Israel Oriental Studies II,* 1972: 215-237), p. 239.

7. Roth, Cecil and Wigoder, Geoffrey (eds.). *Encyclopaedia Judaica 1st Edition, CD ROM.* (New York: MacMillan and Company, 1972), Editorial Staff.

8. Ibid. Editorial Staff.

9. Goitein, S. D. *Jews and Arabs*, p. 55.

10. Sells, Michael (ed.). *Early Islamic Mysticism: Sufi, Qu'ran, Mi'raj, Poetic and Theological Writings*. (Mahwah, NJ and New York: Paulist Press, 1996), p. 79.

11. Ibid. p. 58.

12. Wasserstrom, Steven. *Between Muslim and Jew: The Problem of Symbiosis Under Early Islam*. (Princeton, NJ: Princeton University Press, 1995), p. 173.

13. Ibid. p. 174.

14. Kister, M. J. *Israel Oriental Studies II*, p. 221-222.

15. Quoted in *Isra'iliyat in Tasfir: Sheikh Ahmad Shakir's View*, from his introduction to *'Umdah at-Tasfir 'an al-Hafiz ibn Kathir*, found at http://islamicsciences.wordpress.com/2006/09/03/israiliyat-in-tafsir-shaykh-ahmad-shakirs-view/ .

16. Ibid. footnote 3.

17. Kister, M. J. *Israel Oriental Studies II*, p. 231.

18. Rizvi, Sayyid Abul Hasan. *Middle East Studies Association Bulletin*, Summer 2002.

19. Goitein, S. D. *Jews and Arabs*, p. 194.

20. Quoted in Ariel, David S. "The Eastern Dawn of Wisdom: The Problem of the Relation Between Islamic and Jewish Mysticism." *Approaches to Judaism in Medieval Times*, vol. 2 (David Blumenthal, ed.). (Chico, CA: Scholars Press, 1985: 149-167), p.151.

21. Goitein, S. D. *Jews and Arabs*, p. 149.

22. Ibid. p. 150.

23. Ariel, David S. *Approaches to Judaism in Medieval Times II*, (David Blumenthal, ed.), p. 152.

24. Goitein, S. D. *Jews and Arabs*, pp. 149-150.

25. Ibid. p. 151.

26. Ben-Sasson, Menachem. "Varieties of Inter-Communal Relations in the Gaonic Period." *The Jews of Medieval Islam: Community, Society and Identity*, (Daniel Frank, ed.). (Leiden: E. J. Brill, 1995: 17-32), p. 17.

27. Information in this paragraph from Assis, Yom Tov. "The Judeo-Arabic Tradition in Christian Spain." Ibid. p. 112.

28. Goitein, S. D. *Jews and Arabs*, pp. 59-60.

29. Ibid. p. 194.

30. Ibid. p. 165.

31. Roth, Norman. *Jews, Visigoths and Muslims in Medieval Spain*. (New York: E.J. Brill, 1994), p. 178.

32. Ibid. p. 182.

33. *http://www.jewishencyclopedia.com/view.jsp?artid=171&letter=L&search=lekha%20dodi#540.*

34. Bendiner, Elmer. *The Rise and Fall of Paradise*. (New York: Putnam Books, 1983), p. 69.

35. Goitein, S.D. *A Mediterranean Society: The Jewish Communities of the Arab World as Portrayed in the Documents of the Cairo Geniza (An Abridgement in One Volume)*. (Berkeley, CA: University of California Press, 1967), p. 82.

36. Ibid. p. 82 "The family of the Exilarchs, which had been prominent for so long a time, was large and ramified; it is not surprising that some of its more ambitious members tried to make capital of their dignity as princes of the House of David. We find them everywhere, often trying to assume authority, even in faraway Yemen." pp. 82-83.

37. Lobel, Diana. *A Sufi-Jewish Dialogue: Philosophy and Mysticism in Bahya ibn Pakuda's "Duties of the Heart."* (Philadelphia: University of Pennsylvania Press, 2006), p. x.

38. Wasserstrom, Steven. "Sefer Yesira and Early Islam: A Reappraisal." (*Journal of Jewish Thought and Philosophy III*, 1993: 1-30), pp. 15-16.

39. Gabirol, Solomon ibn. *Selected Poems of Solomon ibn Gabirol* (Peter Cole, trans.). (Princeton, NJ: Princeton University Press, 2001), p. 8.

40. Roth, Norman. *Jews, Visigoths and Muslims in Medieval Spain*, p. 163.

41. Goitein, S. D. *A Mediterranean Society: An Abridgement in One Volume*, p. 252.

42. Halkin, A.S. "The Great Fusion." *Great Ages and Ideas of the Jewish People* (Leo Schwarz, ed.). (New York: Random House. 1956: 215-263), p. 219.

43. Roth, Norman. *Jews, Visigoths and Muslims in Medieval Spain*, p. 166.

44. Goitein, S. D. *A Mediterranean Society: An Abridgement in One Volume*, p. 215.

45. Quoted in Ibid. p. 179.

46. Ibid. p. 89.

47. Ibid. p. 299.

48. Roth, Norman. *Jews, Visigoths and Muslims in Medieval Spain*, p. 183.

49. Goitein, S. D. *A Mediterranean Society: An Abridgement in One Volume*, pp. 302-303 This was because written into the Koran (2:256) was the injunction: "There is no compulsion in Islam," and only when Islamic governments grew weak, or fundamental in nature, did the idea of forced conversion to Islam arise.

50. Glick, Thomas F. *Islamic and Christian Spain in the Early Middle Ages.* (Princeton, NJ: Princeton University Press, 1979), p. 3.

51. Roth, Norman. *Jews, Visigoths and Muslims in Medieval Spain*, p. 184.

52. Goitein, S. D. *Jews and Arabs*, pp. 121-123.

53. Goitein, S. D. *A Mediterranean Society: An Abridgement in One Volume*, p. 80, 81.

54. Ibid. pp. 80, 81.

55. Ibid, p. 297.

56. According to Dr. Ahmad Yousef Hassan, Rector, University of Aleppo, Syria, quoted at *http://www.unu.edu/unupress/unupbooks/uu39se/uu39se08.htm*.

57. Finkel, Joshua. "An Eleventh Century Source for the History of Jewish Scientists in Mohammedan Land (ibn Sa'id)." (*Jewish Quarterly Review 18*, 1927: 45-54), p. 49.

58. Abu Qasim ibn Sa'id quoted in Ibid. p. 51.

59. All information and quotes in the passage from Goitein, S. D. *A Mediterranean Society: An Abridgement in One Volume*, p. 164.

60. Glick, Thomas, F. *Islamic and Christian Spain in the Early Middle Ages*, p. 7.

61. "The oldest authoritative post-Biblical collection and codification of Jewish oral laws, systematically compiled by numerous scholars (called *tannaim*) over a

period of about two centuries. The codification was given final form early in the 3rd century AD by Judah ha-Nasi." *Encyclopedia Britannica.*

62. Goitein, S. D. *Jews and Arabs*, p. 131, 132.

63. Ross Brann quoted in McGaha, Michael. "The Sefer ha-Bahir and Andalusian Sufism," (*Medieval Encounters III,* 1997: 20-57), p. 44.

64. Goitein, S. D. *Jews and Arabs*, p. 141.

65. Roth, Norman. *Jews, Visigoths and Muslims in Medieval Spain*, pp. 171-172.

66. Zafrani, Haim. "The Routes of al-Andalus." (*http://unesdoc.unesco.org/images/0011/001144/114426Eo.pdf*), p. 13.

67. Quoted in Goitein, S. D. *Jews and Arabs*, p. 8.

68. Wasserstein, David J. "Jewish Elites in al-Andalus." *The Jews of Medieval Islam: Community, Society and Identity* (Daniel Frank, ed.). (Leiden: E. J. Brill, 1995: 101-110), p. 101.

69. *http://www.jewishgen.org/sephardic/popul.HTM.*

70. Goitein, S. D. *Jews and Arabs*, p. 8.

71. Halkin, A. S. *Great Ages and Ideas of the Jewish People*, (Leo Schwarz, ed.), p. 217.

72. Ibid. p. 217.

73. Quoted in Wasserstrom, Steven. *Between Muslim and Jew: The Problem of Symbiosis Under Early Islam*, p. 181.

74. A well-known sentiment from Karl Von Clausewitz (1780-1831). He was a German military officer.

75. Goitein, S. D. *Jews and Arabs*, p. 63.

# Chapter 2
# Sufism

Sufism means seizing realities and renouncing that which is between the hands of created beings.[1]

Ma'ruf al-Karkhi, d. 813,
considered to be the first to define Sufism.

For countless Muslims, Sufism is the heart and soul of Islam, the beating heart that pumps lifeblood into the *shari'a* (religious law) and five pillars of Islam. Sufis concern themselves with ultimate Truth, the Divine mystery (*sirr*) that lies veiled at the center of every human's experience. Islamic mystical practice leads the aspirant through a series of spiritual stations, to comprehension of the Divine. Like other aspects of the Muslim religion, Sufism grows directly out of God's Word, as it was revealed to the Prophet Muhammad.

All Sufi orders trace their lineage back to the Prophet Muhammad, and all Sufi teachings initially grew out of the Koranic revelation. Easily overlooked among the exoteric facets of the religion – and often denigrated within mainstream Islam as unorthodox and perhaps even heretical – this spiritual path represents, according to the Sufis themselves, the beautiful core of the Muslim faith. And, more importantly for this book, Sufism became the single most important regenerative impulse for Judaism in the post Talmudic era (c. 2$^{nd}$–5$^{th}$ centuries).

Muhammad and the Koran

According to Sufi scholar Martin Lings, the Sufis hold that the Prophet Muhammad was a Sufi master in all but name.[2] They look to his actions and words, as well as to the Koran itself, as the purest sources of knowledge concerning their practice. The Koran is the book of the whole Islamic community, but the "spiritual elect" believe that its esoteric, hidden meanings –which, as well as the exoteric, are of concern to Sufi practitioners – offer a deeper level of guidance and meaning to the *shari'a*, or Islamic law.[3]

The Koran is considered by Muslims to be the "uncreated word of God,"[4] the universal Truth revealed as a book. Each word, and even letter, is the visible representation of the Divine Essence; it is through the study and comprehension of this Book that the aspirant can empty himself* of all but the Divine. For normative Islam, it is the stories, and the laws that these propose, that guide the practicing Muslim. These are based on the Five Pillars of Islam, which are faith (*iman*), ritual prayer (*salat*), fasting (*sawm*), almsgiv-

---

* This book is gender neutral; however, in the interest of readability, the masculine signifier will be used throughout and stand for both genders.

ing (*zakat*) and pilgrimage (*hajj*).[5] Every Muslim must practice these Five Pillars, and for the great majority of Muslims, these define their worship.

These laws of Islam, however, do not represent all levels of devotion. Islamic mysticism is grounded in supererogatory (beyond what is due or asked) worship. Sufis look beneath the exoteric meaning of the Koran to the hidden, inner meaning. One example of the esoteric reading of the Book is that each letter has mystical import far beyond the meaning of the word they comprise, symbolizing a specific, spiritual reality. As Titus Burckhardt notes in his *Introduction to Sufi Doctrine*: "According to a saying of the Prophet, 'No verse of the Koran has been revealed which has not an external aspect and an inner aspect.'"[6] The goal of Sufism is to become immersed in the hidden meanings of the Koran, moving far beyond the simple adherence to the exoteric law (*shari'a*) toward extinction (*fana*) of the created (the sense of self, or ego) in the uncreated (the Divine Essence).[7]

### Emergence of Sufism

In the early days of Islam, the practice of Islamic esotericism was so closely associated with regular Islamic practice that there was no specific designation for it. All Muslims were "Sufis." All who practiced Islam appreciated both the outer laws and inner meanings of the Koran. The Muslim historian Muhammad ibn Khaldun (d. 1405) remarked that in the first three generations of Islam (c. 632-700), Islamic mysticism was too common to have a specific name. However, "when worldliness spread and men tended to become more and more bound up with the ties of this life, those who dedicated themselves to the worship of God were distinguished from the rest by the title, 'Sufis.'"[8]

The origin of this word has stimulated much discussion among historians and scholars. One reading has the word coming from the Arabic word for wool, "suf." Wool was the material of choice for early Sufi's vestments, as it represented the unadorned manner in which these gentle souls lived, in addition to echoing the simple clothing of the Prophet himself.

Another explanation held that the term became established because "Sufi" conjured up the homonym "safi" (purity), which represents the central goal of the Islamic mystic. Bishr al-Hafi (d. 840; Baghdad) states in explaining the term: "The Sufi is he who keeps his heart pure [*safi*]."[9] While it is unclear whether they named themselves "Sufi" or were called the term by others, the title became emblematic of those attempting to achieve complete humility for the sake of God.

Regardless of the derivation of the word, the meaning of it for Muslims is clear. As Titus Burckhardt notes:

Sufism is the esoteric, or inward (*batin*) aspect of Islam, distinguished from the exoteric or external (*zahir*) Islam ... whereas the ordinary way of believers is directed towards obtaining a state of blessedness after death, Sufism contains as its end the sense that it can give access to direct knowledge of the eternal.[10]

Sufism's growth followed closely the geographic expansion of Islamic believers, sweeping out of the deserts of Arabia with the Muslim traders and conquerors. During the ninth and tenth centuries, Sufism's influence exploded throughout the Arab world, in Arabia, Egypt, Syria and Iraq.[11] It was introduced into Spain at this time, as well, where it grew into a powerful mystical impetus, influencing both Judaism and Christianity. With the coming of the great Sufi theoreticians of the 10th-13th-centuries, such as Junayd al-Baghdadi (d. 910; Baghdad), Abu Hamid al-Ghazali (d. 1111; Persia) and Muhyiddin ibn Arabi (d. 1240; Damascus), Sufism took on its mature form, defining a rich spiritual path of love and meditation.

## Sufi Practice

Sufi practice leads towards one goal: to "know" God while still alive. The various prayer and meditation methods, terminology, hierarchy of mystical states and stations, all help lead the aspirant toward a complete awareness of the Divine Essence. The 14th-century Muslim historian Ibn Khaldun defined Sufism succinctly as: "The knowledge that comes directly from God."[12] The Sufi scholar Martin Lings states: "Sufism is necessary because it is to Islam what the heart is to the body."[13]

According to many observers, however, this knowledge cannot be accessed through study and intellectual learning. Titus Burckhardt points out in his *Introduction to Sufi Doctrine*:

> The Islamic doctrine is contained as a whole in the *tawhid*, the "affirmation of the Divine unity" … the further the mind of the contemplative penetrates into the apparent rational simplicity of the Divine unity, the more complex that simplicity will become; until a point is reached where its different aspects can no longer be reconciled by discursive thought alone. Meditation on these contrasts will in fact take the faculty of thought to its very furthest limits and the intelligence will in this way be opened to a synthesis lying beyond all formal conception.[14]

If this goal is reached, the adept achieves complete appreciation of God, through the annihilation of his or her own sense of self (*fana*) and subsistence (*baqa*) in the Truth, which is rooted in God. Martin Lings notes in *What is Sufism*: "The full grown Sufi is conscious of being like other people, a prisoner in the world of forms, but unlike them he is also conscious of being free, with a freedom which incomparably outweighs his imprisonment."[15] The freedom stems from the belief that the world of forms is nothing more than a mirage, and Truth lies in the silence at the heart of being.

### Al-Faqr

The term "Sufi," strictly speaking, cannot be applied to anyone who has not achieved complete emptiness of all but God;[16] therefore one who attempts this path would never call himself a "Sufi," but a "*matasawwuf*," or one who aims to be so. Islamic mystics refer to themselves as *fuqara*, or the "poor" in spirit. Burckhardt writes, "All virtues are contained in spiritual poverty and the term, *al-faqr*, is commonly used to designate spirituality as a whole. This poverty is nothing other than emptiness for God."[17]

This "poverty" represents the ultimate humility, whereby the aspirant is able to still the desires of the ego. The self is reduced to nothing, and the person's interior experience is directly in line with the "Divine Nought," since only "nought" can enter it.[18] *Al-faqr* represents an appreciation that all personal attributes stem from the ego, and hinder the Divine from entering the interior.

This conception of *faqr* is based in the Koran (35:15): "O mankind, you are the poor [*al-fuqara*] before God; He is the rich." As the French Islamic scholar Jean-Louis Michon notes:

> This verse contains an exhortation and a promise, because it is, in fact, in becoming aware of his impoverished condition and in drawing all the conclusions that this implies that man realizes the virtue of humility, that he empties himself of all pretensions, including that of existing "at the side" of God.[19]

This state of spiritual poverty is arduous to achieve, something that only the rare person can accomplish. These are the true "Sufis;" all the rest of the *fuqara* are arrayed along the path between ego-identification and complete spiritual poverty. Every residual aspect of the ego and human desire represents a "veil" between the searcher and God.

As Muhammad an-Niffari (d. 965; Egypt), an early Sufi *sheikh*, notes concerning the veils that stand between a seeker and the Divine (speaking in the first-person voice of God):

> Your veil is everything I make manifest; your veil is everything I keep secret; your veil is everything I affirm; your veil is everything I obliterate and your veil is what I unveil, just as your veil is what I curtain. Your veil is yourself ... You will not come out from your veil except through My Light. So My Light will pierce the veil, and you will see how it veils by what it veils.[20]

God can only be known when the human ego, which instinctively regards itself as a self-sufficient center, is extinguished before God. As Titus Burckhardt notes: "This does not mean that the immortal essence of the soul must be annihilated; what must be dissolved is that compound of ego-determined passions and imaginings, the tendency to restrict consciousness to the level of ephemeral appearances."[21] As Niffari states, even the wish to supercede the veils is yet another veil; true realization comes in the ultimate grace of the Divine light, which provides an "understanding" beyond cognition, a "Truth" that appears as utter perplexity, incomprehensible to the intellectual capabilities of the human mind.

### *Fana* and *Baqa*

Concomitant with the goal of achieving spiritual poverty are the Sufi ideals of *fana* (annihilation of self) and *baqa* (subsistence in God). These represent the specific manner in which *faqr* is experienced: *fana* signifying the adept's success at completely effacing his own ego, and *baqa* standing for the subsequent influx of the Divine Essence, whereby God fills the space vacated by the human ego.

Hardly incidental to Sufi practice, the double experience of *fana* and *baqa* is considered so essential to Islamic mysticism that the 9th-century master al-Junayd (d. 910) states that this experience alone defines the path: "Sufism is summed up thusly: the Real makes you die to yourself (*fana*), and causes you to come alive again through Him (*baqa*)."[22] This practice stems from the Koran (55:26-27): "Everything upon the earth is undergoing annihilation, but there subsists the face of your Lord …"[23]

This passing away to be reborn – also known in Sufi terminology as "dying before you die" – echoes Islam's fundamental declaration, the *Shahadah*: *Ashadu an la ilaha illa-llah, wa ashadu anna muhammadan rasulu-llah* (I testify that there is no god but God, and I testify that Muhammad is the messenger of God). The *Shahadah* (from *shahida*, to testify) is the Muslim affirmation of belief in the oneness of God (*tawhid*) and acceptance of Muhammad as God's final Prophet. Recitation of the *Shahadah* is the most important of the Five Pillars of Islam for Muslims, and is repeated numerous times during the five daily prayers.

For Sufis, however, the *Shahadah* represents the declaration of the ultimate goal, with the initial annihilation ("there is no God") followed by acknowledgement ("but God"). Sufis recite this testimony far more than prescribed by normative Islam, using it as a meditative vehicle to unlock the Divine secret (*sirr*) at the heart of the human experience. As Professor William Chittick, a leading translator and interpreter of classical Islamic philosophical and mystical texts, notes:

> In contrasting subsistence and annihilation, we need to remember that subsistence is real, not annihilation, for subsistence is the affirmation of an ancient reality, but annihilation is the negation of something that never truly was. "No God" (from the *Shahadah*) negates all the false realities, and "But God" affirms the subsistence of the Real.[24]

### Equanimity

An important corollary to *fana* and *baqa* is the Sufi ideal of "equanimity," or detachment from concern for the views of others, whether positive or negative. If a person is completely cognizant of the Divine *at all times*, and attains a state of indifference to all but God, then the approbation or reprobation of other humans becomes irrelevant. Someone who attains spiritual poverty (*faqr*) and annihilation of the personal ego (*fana*) has no emotion (other than love, in the sense of *agape*) toward others – as the "other" is viewed as but another manifestation of the Divine.

A Sufi tale illustrates this ideal of equanimity toward the actions and attitudes of others. The story was related about the early Sufi saint Ibrahim ibn Adham (d. 777; Syria):

> On one occasion, Ibrahim arrived at a village in the pouring rain, with his patched robe soaked through and his body chilled by the bitter cold. He went to a mosque, but was refused admittance, and at three others, failed to find shelter. Then in despair he entered a bathhouse, and sat close to the stove, the smoke from which blackened both his face and his clothes. Then he felt entirely satisfied.[25]

The unstated reason for his "satisfaction," is because he did not care how he was treated, or the reasons for this treatment. He had attained the Sufi ideal of equanimity. This represents a high mystical station, one that foreshadows *baqa*, or subsistence in God. If one has cleansed oneself of desire to the point where he does not care about what people think or how he is treated, then surely he has purified himself completely.

### *Sukr* and *Sahw*

Some of those who are able to empty themselves of all but God experience something so intense that they may become what has been termed "drunken mystics," inebriated on the experience of the Divine. Professor William Chittick notes: "Intoxication (*sukr*) followed upon being overcome by the presence of God. It designated the joy of the seekers in finding the eternal source of all beauty and love within themselves."[26] In Sufi lore, there are stories of mystics who achieve this goal of total awareness of God, only to remain spiritually "drunk," unable to return from this overwhelming experience of the Divine. A story told by the Persian Najib al-Din Buzghush (d. 1280) illustrates this state:

> Once someone told me that there was a strange Luri tribesman who had come to the city, named Jamal al-Din. He was overpowered by a strong divine attraction and was staying in the congregational mosque ... From the intensity of his state his eyes were like two cups filled with blood. I went up to him and greeted him, and he replied. Then he said, "I have

nothing to do with black and white makers," meaning that he had nothing to do with legal scholars, learned people and writers. "I am an illiterate Luri tribesman, and I don't know anything. I used to be happy taking care of the horses; one day I was sitting at the stable in front of the horses. Suddenly, a spiritual state was unveiled to me, and a divine attraction occurred. The veil of ego was taken away from me, and I became unconscious. I fell and rolled under the horses' hooves. When I regained consciousness, the whole divine unity was revealed to me."[27]

Within Sufism, there is admiration for these so-called "drunken mystics." Biographical collections sometimes contain long lists of "intoxicated" (*sukr*) saints, who had been overpowered with the force of their attraction to God.[28]

Sufi belief holds that an even higher state of realization is that of the "sober" (*sahw*) mystic. In this case, the practitioner ascends to the heights of the spiritually "drunken" adept, but then is able to reenter his ego and the world around him, remaining drunk within, but sober without. As Professor William Chittick states: "The true Sufi, having realized fully the pattern and model established by the Prophet, is inwardly drunk with God and outwardly sober with the world."[29] In this way, such masters can act as emissaries of God in this world. As al-Junayd defines the Sufi:

> He is existent in both himself and in God after having been existent in God and non-existent in himself. This is because he has left the drunkenness of God's overwhelming presence and come to the clarity of sobriety. Contemplation is once again restored to him, so that he can put everything in its right place and assess it correctly. Once more he assumes his individual attributes: After the "obliteration" his personal qualities persist in him and in his actions in this world, when he has reached the height of spiritual perfection granted by God, he becomes a pattern for his fellow men.[30]

### *Dhikr*

To achieve such profound states, Sufis developed a concentrated contemplative practice. *Dhikr* (remembrance of God) is intended to center the aspirant in the Divine presence, offering a "remembrance" of God at all times throughout the day, and often through the night. Like most Islamic mystical practices, this devotional method is derived from the Koran (29:45). "Assuredly prayer prevents passionate transgressions and grave sins, but the remembrance of God (*dhikr-Llah*) is greater." Other foundational passages for this practice include God saying, "Remember me and I will remember you" (2:152); "Verily, is it through the remembrance of God that their hearts find rest in security" (13:28) and many others.[31]

Sufis believe that the Divine Name, *Allah*, contains the Truth manifested as multiplicity in the world.[32]  Therefore, by repeating this Name over and over, as part of a group or in solitary meditation, as part of a ritual occasionally with music and dance, but usually while fingering prayer beads, the aspirant can approach the state of the true Sufi.  As the Name passes the lips, the novice begins to experience the Divine unity, existing beyond cognition.  As William Stoddart notes in *Sufism*: "The doctrine of *dhikr* is that the Divine Name (*Allah*) directly vehicles the Principle, and when the believer unifies himself with the Divine Name in fervent invocation, he inwardly frees himself from manifestation."[33]  Through repetition of the Divine Name, analogous to the original and limitless enunciation of the Word of God which underpins creation, the Sufi becomes aware of the undifferentiated knowledge superior to mere rational "knowing."[34]

*Dhikr* is a multi-tiered process, utilizing all of the faculties, beginning with the outermost shell of humans, as represented by the tongue, and then subsequently engaging the soul, the heart, the intellect, the spirit and the innermost conscience called the *sirr* (mystery).[35]  The fundamental component of *dhikr* is the *Shahadah*, the testimony *La ilaha illa 'Llah* or "There is no god but God."  This denotes the total renunciation of everything *except* God.  A passage from *Merton and Sufism: The Untold Story* gives a firsthand example of a *dhikr* litany through the eyes of an observing outsider:

> The Sufis developed *dhikr* connected with some sort of breath control ... every time one breathes out in recollecting the Lord, the breath is connected to Him ... the breathing was related to the witness that "there is no god except God."  The method of learning the *dhikr* was for the disciple to sit before his Sufi master and then they started breathing rhythmically together ... The exhaling breath turned everything out, and then he breathed in love, desire and total concentration on God.[36]

"According to the renowned scholar of Islamic mysticism, Annemarie Schimmel, not only are the tongue and heart filled with the name of God in the experience of *dhikr*, 'but the whole body of the meditating Sufi is permeated so that his blood and each of his limbs is replete with the name of God and practices, as it were, its own *dhikr*.'"[37]  By "remembering" one's own Divine core through this practice, eliminating the veils of ignorance or forgetfulness, the searcher draws ever closer to the Real.  Ali al-Hujwiri (d. 1073; Persia), who wrote *Kashf al-Manjub* (The Revelation of the Veiled) the oldest Persian treatise on Sufism, says: "All veils come from ignorance; when ignorance has passed away, the veils vanish and this life becomes one with the life to come."[38]

As the veils are pierced, the interior mirror becomes clearer, and God perceives Himself in man.  This is the original impetus for the act of creation: God's desire for Self-knowledge.  At the very end, as William Stoddart explains, "it is God Himself who invokes, God Himself who is invoked and God Himself who is the invocation. That this Divine act should pass through man is the mystery of salvation."[39]

## Khalwa

*Khalwa* (spiritual retreat) is central to Sufi methodology. Supervised by the spiritual advisor (*sheikh*), this practice can last from several hours up to 40 days, and includes prayer, fasting, nightly vigils and *dhikr* litanies. Retiring to a *zawiyya*, or private prayer cell, the aspirant separates himself from society and sensory input, spending all waking hours in prayer. At its most intense, *khalwa* may take place in the complete dark, and the senses become affected, growing dim as interior awareness expands to fill the void left by the lack of external stimuli.

This often marks a time when the aspirant opens up to new and higher spiritual stations (*maqamat*). It also may be undertaken by novices about to enter the Sufi Way, as a manner of inducing the necessary frame of mind for the life of devotion to follow.

It is said that the practice of *Khalwa* was inspired by a *hadith*, told to Ali ibn Ali Talib (d. 661), the cousin and son-in-law of the Prophet Muhammad. Jean-Louis Michon notes in "The Spiritual Practices of Sufism," that when Ali once asked the Prophet the shortest way to God, Muhammad answered: "Ali, always repeat the name of God in solitary places ..." Ali later initiated Hasan al-Basri (d. 728) into this method,[40] and from there it entered Sufi practice.

The Sufi master Abu Hamid al-Ghazali (d. 1111), known as the "Renewer of Islam" for the manner in which he reconciled the *shari'a* (religious law) with Islamic esotericism, explains the *khalwa* (spiritual retreat), at his own entrance into the practice of Sufism:

> When the intense desire to follow [Sufism] seized me, I consulted one of the main Sufis, a very famous man, on the ardent recitation of the Koran. He [said]: "The best method consists of completely cutting ties with the world, in such a way that your heart does not occupy itself with family, or with children, or with money, or with homeland, or with science, or with government – the existence or the non-existence of these things being for you of equal value. For you to be alone in a retreat [*khalwa*], it is necessary ... for you to concentrate your thought on *Allah*, without interior preoccupation ... The result will be a state in which you will feel this Name in the spontaneous movement of your tongue without any effort on your part."[41]

The master here makes reference to equanimity, when he states: "the existence or the non-existence of these things being for you of equal value." As noted above, this represents a basic tenet of Sufism.

Another scriptural foundation for the practice of *khalwa* is found in the

Koran (33:41): "Invoke *Allah* much and often." Sufis also looked into both the Jewish and Islamic prophetic past, basing this retreat on the sojourn of Moses on Mount Sinai, as well as that of the Prophet Muhammad in the cave on Mount Hira, following the visitation of the angel Gabriel.[42]

### *'Ilm al-Huruf*

The *dhikr* litanies and *khalwa* both are enhanced with specific prayers. The most common form of invocation is the *Shahadah*, as well as the repetition of one of the ninety-nine Names of God. However, other prayer techniques grew out of something called the *'Ilm al-Huruf* (Science, or Knowledge of the Letters).

For Sufis, the words and even letters of the ninety-nine Divine Names possess mystical import. Each of the ninety-nine Names of God represents a Divine quality or one particular aspect of God. These Names, according to Muhyiddin ibn Arabi (d. 1240), are the creative possibilities latent in the One. "In reality," the Sufi saint avers, "the whole cosmos is the locus for the manifestation of the Divine Names. There is nothing in existence but His Names."[43]

These Names are the central focus of invocatory prayer. Their sounds represent eternal archetypes existent in God before creation, and meditation on them through *dhikr* allows the aspirant to have access to a higher plane and, ultimately, to the Real. The idea of the vocalization of each letter relates to the symbolism of the Divine word, as do the different sounds of the letters from the Koran, which are analogous to the universal archetypes, reflected in the manifested universe. In this view, the human breath, which is the vehicle for the articulated sounds, echoes the Divine principle, the original act of creation.[44] Such ideas developed into the *'Ilm al-Huruf*.

Professor Carl Ernst (William R. Kenan, Jr. Distinguished Professor at UNC Chapel Hill) mentions the importance of the *letters* of the prayers and Koranic passages, suggesting the divine provenance of the Arabic language:

> The sound of the words, recited either aloud or sub-vocally, is an inextricable part of their meaning and texture. But the visual form of the words is also an important aspect of the Names of God. The form of the letters is an abstract depiction of the qualities of God ... Visualization of the actual form of the Arabic script in the Koran seems to have played an important role in Muslim religious experience from an early date ... Visual concentration on the Koran as the word of God was the closest approximation of seeing God face to face.[45]

Each letter or sound (Arabic writing is phonetic) corresponds to a determination of the primordial and undifferentiated sound, the substance of the perpetual Divine enunciation.[46] Building on this idea, that the forms and sounds of the individual letters have mystical qualities in and of themselves,

Islamic thinkers have looked for hidden meanings of the letters separated even from the words that they comprise. Esoteric treatises on the properties of the Arabic alphabet, based on the numerical values of letters, revealed profound conceptions of the prayers themselves. Professor Carl Ernst notes that some Sufi orders developed the isolated letters at the beginning of the Koranic chapters into mystical portraits, spiritual diagrams and even magical incantations[47] that could unlock the angelic and Godly powers hidden in the letters themselves.

> Intricate formulas based on the properties of the Divine Names, with instructions regarding how many hundreds (or thousands) of repetitions were required to obtain the desired results, appeared in popular handbooks ... It has to be recognized that [such] practices could be found in some of the most important Sufi teachings, such as the complex meditations of Muhyiddin ibn Arabi.[48]

The Science of the Letters – practices devoted to individual sounds of letters, and permutations of letters built around the sounds in one or another of the Names of God – became a technique for embodying and accessing various facets of God, and then employing them in prayer, all in service to achieving a complete awareness of the Divine Essence. Both *dhikr* and *khalwa* methods sometimes included these mystical repetitions.

### Sama'

*Dhikr* has taken many forms, such as prayers employing the aforementioned *'Ilm al-Huruf*, but the one practice most foreign to exoteric Islamic practitioners – one sometimes considered heretical – is *sama'* (listening). This spiritual practice combines music and movement into a sacred dance, often centered on recitation of the Divine Name of God. Jean-Louis Michon notes: "Few subjects have been debated or have raised as many contradictory emotions and opinions as music *vis-à-vis* religious law at the heart of Islamic society,"[49] as many *'ulema* (religious scholars) and normative practitioners have been against this practice. Yet no Koranic prescription explicitly forbids using music as a devotional tool,[50] and many Sufi orders utilize it to heighten spiritual awareness. Titus Burckhardt discusses the efficacy of music and dance as a prayer method:

> Just as the rhythm of the sacred words imposes itself on the movement of breathing, so the rhythm of breathing in its turn can impose itself on all the movements of the body. Herein lies the principle of the sacred dance practiced in Sufi communities. According to the *hadith* [saying of the Prophet Muhammad]: "He who does not vibrate at the remembrance of the Friend has no friend." This saying is one of the scriptural foundations of the dance of the dervishes.[51]

Due to the seductiveness of the sound and movement, however, *sama'* offers a tool that can be dangerous for the aspirant, who must be very careful not to fall into sense-based pleasure. As the early Sufi saint Dhu'l Nun al-Misri (d. 859; Cairo) states: "[*Sama'*] is an influx from God with which He stirs up the hearts and encourages them to search for Him. Whoever hears it through the Real finds the road to the Real, and whoever hears it through the self falls into heresy."[52]

A few Sufi orders include some manner of *sama'* in their Way. Pronouncing the Divine Name is considered a sacrament in the truest sense of the word – a supernatural act that affords the aspirant the possibility of leaving his human nature behind, and of being absorbed into the Divine Essence.[53] For those who partake in this spiritual concert, the music represents the sacred language of God's luminous, audible spheres, the sound of creation and being. According to Professor William Chittick, hearing such harmony, the soul may recall its original state, when nearness to God was its natural home.[54]

## The Sufi *Tariqah*

The way that traverses the infinite distance separating man from God is called *tariqah* (the way of poverty). On the one hand, it means the mystical journey in general – the sum of the teachings and the practical rules that had been drawn from the Koran, the Prophetic *sunnah* (the way of the Prophet) and the experience of the spiritual masters ... It also signifies a brotherhood or a particular order of Sufis, usually bearing a name derived from the founder.[55]

### Bay'ah

The decision to enter a Sufi order represents a lifelong commitment. The first stage on this path is the decision to become an aspirant in a specific Sufi *tariqah* (order). This indicates the novice's resolve to turn away from sensual desires and devote himself to the service of God. The initiation is then completed by "taking the hand," a pact (*bay'ah*) that implies submission to the master (*sheikh*) in all that concerns the spirit. The relationship, once sanctioned by the *bay'ah*, cannot be suspended unilaterally by the choice of the novice.[56]

The initiation rite takes varied forms. The prototype for the induction ceremony was an event that took place four years before the death of the Prophet Muhammad (c. 628) when, sitting beneath a tree, he asked his companions to pledge their allegiance to him with a handshake, over and above the vow they made at their entry into Islam.[57] Most often, the *sheikh* holds the neophyte's hand in his and recites from the Koran (48:10): "Those who swear fealty to thee swear fealty in truth to God; God's hand is over their hands. Then whosoever breaks this oath breaks it but to his own hurt;

and whoso fulfills this covenant made with God, God will give him mighty wage."[58] This vow underscores the supererogatory nature of Sufism.

Ali al-Hujwiri (d. 1073) wrote of the initiation rite:

> The adept then, who has attained the perfection of saintship, takes the right course when he invests the novice with the Sufi cloak [*khirqah*] after a period of three years during which the *sheikh* has educated the aspirant in the necessary discipline. In respect of the qualifications and demands, the Sufi cloak is comparable to a winding sheet: the wearer must resign all his hopes of the pleasures of life, purge his heart of all sensorial delights and devote his life entirely to the service of God.[59]

In many orders, the bestowal of the Sufi *khirqah* represents being accepted on the Sufi path, after the administration of the *bay'ah*. The donning of this cloak mirrors stories in the Koranic tradition. The Prophet Muhammad performed this ritual for an Ethiopian woman disciple, Umm Khalid, when he gave her a special shirt, with the admonishment to "wear it out." It also hearkens back to the story of Joseph and his "many-colored coat" (Genesis 37:2-11), a well-patched vestment, which, according to the Koran, had originally been provided to Abraham by Gabriel. Carl Ernst mentions: "As the stories of the shirts of the Prophets suggest, the shirt is a sign of the possibility of the presence of God; in the cloak, the disciple sees Divine mercy and grace."[60]

### *Murshid/Sheikh*

Once the novice has been initiated into the *tariqah*, he begins a life of devotion to God, represented by dedication to a specific master. Each teacher (known as a *murshid*, God-realized saint, or *sheikh*, elder) traces his authority back to the Prophet Muhammad, and may head a particular order, which usually is named after an originating master (for instance *Suhrawardiyya* for Abu Hafs al-Suhrawardi's [d. 1234] teachings, *Qadiriyya* for Abd al-Qadir al-Jilani [d. 1166] and *Shadhiliyya* for Abu'l-Hassan as-Shadhili [d. 1258]) who developed specific manners of working through the stations (*maqamat*) of the Sufi path.

The line of transmission through which the *sheikh* traces his spiritual lineage back through his teacher, his teacher's teacher etc. all the way to the Prophet Muhammad, is called a *silsilah* (chain). Each *silsilah* is built around the methodology of the original teacher, who may have readapted the original practices to his contemporary circumstances.[61] Aspirants may join a particular order with which they find a spiritual affinity.

For the *sheikh*, being a link of a *silsilah* does not imply a geographic specificity. Some orders extend throughout the Islamic world and, more recently, into the West. It is not uncommon for the leader of an order to authorize a *muqaddam* (a representative in the same order), to teach and receive disciples. As William Stoddart notes, "all Sufi orders are expressions of Islamic spirituality and are only differentiated in that each is 'perfumed' by the *baraka* [blessing] of its original founder."[62] In this manner, Sufi doctrine is continually manifested afresh for each new era.[63]

The role of the spiritual instructor should not be minimized. A Sufi saying holds that a novice without a master has Satan as his master. To attempt to delve into Islamic mystical practice without the aid of an expert is a dangerous affair. Professor William Chittick states: "The notion of not needing prophetic help [from a *sheikh*] is the fatal defect of the modern world. Modern science, technology and all of the other branches of learning – not to mention politics – are nothing but ignorance of the self masquerading as knowledge."[64]

Manuals of practice contain minute discussions of how the disciple is to behave in relation to his *sheikh*; obedience to the teacher is understood in the context of completely renouncing the lower self and aiming to replace it with the realized state of the *murshid*. As the 13th-century Sufi master Abu Hafs al-Suhrawardi (d. 1234; Persia) states:

> When the sincere disciple enters under obedience to the master, keeping his company and learning his manners, a spiritual state flows from within the master to within the disciple, like one lamp lighting another. The state is transferred from the master to the disciple by keeping company and by hearing speech. This only applies to the disciple who ... is annihilated in the master by giving up his own will.[65]

### *Maqam* and *Hal*

The *sheikh* leads the novice through a series of stations, which help to define the Sufi path. The fundamental stations have been enumerated as three, through which the novice moves in a systematic progression: fear (*makhafa*), love (*mahabba*) and knowledge (*ma'arifa*). These three, however, are subdivided into further smaller stages, each leading the aspirant closer to the ultimate goal.[66] According to Abu al-Qasim al-Qushayri (d. 1072; Persia) who wrote a central Sufi text, *Risalat at-Tasawwuf* (Epistle on Sufism), the list of stations reaches fifty, while Khwajah Abdullah Ansari (d. 1088; Persia), known as "Master of the Sufi Masters," provided a list of one hundred different rungs on the spiritual ladder. Ruzbehan Baqli (d. 1209) outlined 1001 different stations through which a seeker had to pass on the journey to union with the Divine.[67]

A *sheikh* determines the specific pathway for the novice. By reaching a "station," the aspirant accesses a more spiritually profound level from which to understand reality, and is one step closer to spiritual realization. The goal of the Islamic mystical path is "union" (*ittihad*) with God, or the full realization of human perfection, where the illusory sense of "self" has been negated and God alone affirmed.[68] As the Sufi saint Abu Hamid al-Ghazali (d. 1111) states: "Whoever belongs to God, God belongs to him." This formulation reaffirms the doctrine of *ittihad*, union between the Creator and the created.[69]

A more transitory experience than the spiritual station is termed a *hal* (state), which is an unexpected unveiling of Reality, conceived of as grace from God. This flash of awakening can come upon anyone and might last for only a few moments or, like the Luri tribesman from the previously recounted tale, may last a lifetime. It does not, however, necessarily come in response to the rigorous practice of the *tariqah* and often passes as quickly as it arises. "A 'state' (*hal*) is a passing immersion of the soul in the Divine light. A 'station' (*maqam*) is a 'state' that has become permanent."[70] The 11th-century Persian al-Hujwiri notes:

> "State" [*hal*] is something that descends from God into a man's heart, without his being able to repel it when it comes, or to attract it when it goes, by his own effort. Accordingly, while the term "station" [*maqam*] denotes the way of the seeker, and his progress in the field of exertion, and his rank before God in proportion to his merit, the term "state" denotes the favor and grace which God bestows upon the heart of His servant, and which are not connected with any mortification on the latter's part. "Station" belongs to the category of acts, "state" to the category of gifts.[71]

### Ihsan

Although early Sufi orders advocated ascetic practice, and some of the greatest early saints, like Jafar as-Sadiq (d. 765; Medina), Ibrahim ibn Adham (d. 777; Syria) and Rabi'a (d. 801; Babylonia) followed this path,[72] Islamic mysticism quickly moved away from self-abnegation as the center of its spiritual path. While Sufis might follow an ascetic approach for periods of time, such as during a meditative retreat (*khalwa*), the seeker usually found redemption within the world. This ideal of a socially involved spiritual practice was founded on a well-known *hadith* (saying of the Prophet Muhammad) that states: "There is no monasticism in Islam."[73]

In the Koran, three aspects of the religion reverberate: "submission" (*islam*), "faith" (*iman*) and "doing the beautiful" or "excellence" (*ihsan*). The first two categories are familiar to all exoteric Muslim practitioners, and correspond to the Five Pillars of the religion and *shari'a* (religious law). The last of the three, however, is the responsibility of those with a mystical aptitude, who take "doing the beautiful" as their own domain. In the most basic sense, this represents the transformation of the Muslim into someone who is in harmony with God, putting him in touch with the original goodness inherent in the human soul (*fitra*). "Doing the beautiful" represents acting not out of obligation or scholarly knowledge, but from the heart, the seat of *ma'arifa*, or direct knowledge of God.[74] As Jean Louis Michon writes:

> The man who is in a state of *ihsan* is truly the *khalifa*, the vice-regent of God on Earth. He rediscovers the "most beautiful form" in which he was created (Koran 95:4: "We molded man into the most noble image"), because his heart is like a pure, well-polished mirror in which the Divine can be reflected. Leading man back to this station is the goal of Sufi practices.[75]

*Ihsan* (doing the beautiful) keeps spiritual practice intimately involved with everyday life. Even most *sheikhs* have wives, and most novices hold normal jobs. Some mystics undoubtedly devote themselves entirely to their inner practice, living in Sufi *tekkes* or *khanaqahs* (lodges), but far more blend Sufi practice into their everyday existence in the world. Like most other aspects of Islamic mystical practice, this stems from the Koran and *hadith*. The Angel Gabriel said to the Prophet Muhammad: "*Ihsan* is that you worship God as if you see Him and while you see Him not, yet truly He sees you," meaning that one should always act as if in the presence of God.

### *Ihsan* and the Sensual

In many passages, the Koran speaks in imagery recalling pleasures of the senses, because these direct pleasures are reverberations of the universal archetypes, which are imbedded in the ground of all being, or God. In his *What is Sufism*, Martin Lings points out that the senses have the power to recall these symbols and facets imbedded in the Divine Essence; any aspect of the world can resonate with spiritual significance.[76]

As Baha'uddin Walad (d. 1231; Persia), the father of Jalalludin Rumi (d. 1273; Turkey, the 13th-century Persian mystic on whose thought was founded the *Mawlawiyya tariqah*), notes:

> Since the created thing derives from the Giver of Existence, how should God not be its intimate? Since God's desire, God's act, God's attribute, God's creativity and God's mercy are connected to the creatures, if they are not intimate with God, with whom will they be intimate? Are not all these appetites, loves and intimacies from God? All the words between lovers, their whispered secrets, their touching, and their intercourse – God brings all of this into existence. Since no one's will has any effect but God's, how should the Wanted not have intimacy with the wanter?[77]

*Ihsan* is considered a synthesis of all the virtues – the will itself transfigured by Divine attraction,[78] pointing all deeds toward one thing: God. The love expressed by the *fuqura* is simply a mirror of the Divine motive for the original act of creation. In one of the most important *hadith qudsi* (saying of God) for the Sufi Way, the adage describes what happens when the lovers of God devote themselves wholeheartedly to the Beloved: "My servant draws near to Me through nothing that I love more than what I have made obligatory for him. My servant never ceases drawing near unto Me through supererogatory works until I love him. Then when I love him, I am his hearing with which he hears, his sight with which he sees, his hand with which he grasps and his foot with which he walks."[79]

Thus arrives the completion of the Sufi path, when the aspirant has emptied himself of all but God. Or, as the Sufi martyr Mansur al-Hallaj (d. 922) averred, "I am He," meaning that the searcher and the Searched-for have become one.

### Al-Insan al-Kamil

Hearkening back to the story of Adam, humans are considered to be created in the image of God. After the Fall however, people "forgot" their God-nature, becoming mired in the individual ego and will. Sufi seekers, through the practice of *dhikr* (remembrance of God) in its various forms, attempt to return to their primal and undifferentiated state, when humans were close to the Divine. This is based on the saying of the Prophet: "He who knows himself knows his Lord." The seeker tries to strip away the layers of veils that stand between him and Him, uncovering the immutable self. When the rare individual attains the goal of mystical practice, he becomes a Perfect Man (*al-Insan al-Kamil*), and fulfills his function as God's Vice-regent (*khalifa*) here on earth.

Aspirants do this in two steps, first by recognizing their shortcomings and working toward their elimination, and then by seeing in themselves the reflection of the qualities and beauty of the Creator.[80]

> The term Universal Man [*al-Insan al-Kamil*] has two meanings that coincide or are distinct according to the point of view adopted. On the one hand this name is applied to all men who have realized Union or "the Supreme Identity," to men such as the great spiritual mediators and especially the prophets and the "poles" [*qutb*] among the saints. On the other hand this name designates the permanent and actual synthesis of all states of Being, a synthesis that is at the same time both an immediate aspect of the Principle and the totality of all relative and particular states of existence. This is the "clear prototype" spoken of in the Koran 36:12: "In truth, We have counted everything in a clear prototype."[81]

### Mirror

The *al-Insan al-Kamil* becomes a perfect mirror, reflecting the Divine through a soul purified of all personal attributes. As Abd Allah ibn Sina (d.

Sufism

1037; Persia), a Sufi adept who was known as the Leonardo da' Vinci of the
Muslim world for his breadth of knowledge, notes:

> [The soul becomes a] polished mirror facing the Truth. At this level, it
> apperceives both himself and Truth. He still hesitates between them;
> but then, becoming oblivious to himself, he is aware only of the Sacred
> Presence, or if he is at all aware of himself, it is only as one who gazes
> on the Truth. It is then that true union is achieved.[82]

The idea of the mirror image representing the human soul is reflected in
the *hadith*: "There is a polish for everything that becomes rusty, and the
polish for the heart is the remembrance of God (*dhikr*)."[83] Abu Hurayra (d.
678; Medina), a Companion of the Prophet Muhammad, from whom many
*hadith* (sayings and doings of the Prophet) have been passed along, further
clarifies this metaphor:

> Verily, when a true believer commits a fault, a black spot is created in
> his heart, and if his sins are increased, the black spot increases, so that
> it takes possession of the whole heart. For the spot is rust that God
> has mentioned in the revelation, "their hearts became rusty from their
> works (Koran 83:14)."[84]

When true believers are able to completely purify themselves through spiritual practice, they attain the goal of the Way, as they have emptied themselves of all but God.

## Poetry: Love and Wine

In our contemporary world, poetry is hardly at the vanguard of popular
expression. But in medieval times, when Sufism coalesced into a spiritual
method at the heart of Islam, poets stood at the forefront of both popular
and high culture. Poetry expressed salient contemporary ideas to the wid-
est possible audience. Its role in medieval Sufism – the lyrical expression
of ideas at the heart of mystical practice – inspired thousands of poetic
couplets.

Professor William Chittick notes:

> Sufis commonly call direct knowledge of God "unveiling." Partly be-
> cause unveiling often takes the form of a visionary, imagistic knowl-
> edge, they made frequent use of poetry to express their teachings about
> God, the world and the human soul. Many of them felt that poetry was
> the ideal medium for expressing the truths of the most intimate and
> mysterious relationship that human beings can achieve with God.[85]

Often, the language employed took great poetic license, imitating the Sufi
path, which transports the aspirant far beyond the mundane toward the
Real. Some Sufis went so far as to read the Koran as a love letter from the

Beloved.[86] According to William Chittick, in employing the language of intoxication and sensual love, Sufi writers explained that precedent found in some Koranic verses and *hadith* (sayings of the Prophet Muhammad) inspired them.[87]

Some of these mystical poets attempted to convey the experience of the Divine presence – though ineffable – with imagery that shocked the conventionally pious.[88] At times, this intense, spiritual love blinded these poets to all else, and they composed elegiac poems bursting with images of romantic liaisons: metaphors for the constant, overwhelming yearning to annihilate the personal ego in the Divine Essence. Believing that total dissolution of the self in God was virtually unattainable before death, much medieval Sufi poetry took on the melancholy characteristic of a longing for the impossible. As Abd ar-Rahman Jami (d. 1492; Persia), considered one of the last great Sufi poets, writes: "The heart that is free of love sickness isn't a heart at all. The body deprived of the pangs of love is nothing but clay and water."[89]

Imagery of Passion

Some Islamic mystical poets borrowed imagery and ideas from the existing literature of their cultural milieu. As Professor Carl Ernst notes, sensuality, young lovers, ecstatic inebriation – themes that had been existent in pre-Muslim Arabic and Persian poetry – were reinvigorated with allegorical and mystical meanings by Sufi poets.[90] Due to the graphic images employed, this poetry attracted the attention of the religious authorities, as the erotic and even idolatrous wordplay trod dangerously close to blasphemy.

Even the great *Andalusian* saint Muhyiddin ibn Arabi (d. 1240) was accused of heresy for his use of profane imagery in his mystical verse. Although he made it quite clear in the introduction to his spiritual masterpiece, *Futuhat al-Makkiyya* (The Meccan Revelations), that his verse was concerned only with the spirit, some of his followers were so disturbed by the imagery that they complained the great mystic must actually be conducting a love affair. To counter these concerns, Ibn Arabi wrote a commentary on the imagery to explain its mystical import. Among other things, he states:

> I indicate lordly knowledge, Divine illuminations, spiritual secrets, rational truths and religious admonitions, but I have expressed them in the style of the erotic lyric. This is because of the soul's passionate love of these expressions, so that they have abundant reasons for paying attention to them. This is the language of every cultivated writer and elevated spiritual person.[91]

Eventually a system of poetic imagery was developed using specific metaphors of human life and love to represent different stations of the wayfarer. In one particularly graphic example, Ayn al-Qudat (d. 1131; Persia), an ecstatic who was executed by the Muslim authorities, intoned:

> Last night my idol placed his hand upon my breast,
> He seized me hard and put a slave ring in my ear.
> I said, "My Beloved, I am crying from your love!"
> He pressed his lips on mine and silenced me.[92]

Thousands of sensual and love-based odes emanated from these poets. The best known in our times is the poetry of Jalalludin Rumi (d. 1273). His writing has been extensively translated into English, so much so that he currently is the best selling poet in contemporary America. Rumi stands out in 21st-century popular culture as *the* example of Sufi spirituality (though some of his work has been published without prominently noting that he was an Islamic mystic), and his poetry provides a fine example of the ecstatic and pining anguish of the lover for the Beloved.

> My soul is screaming in ecstasy
> Every fiber of my being is in love with you
> Your effulgence has lit a fire in my heart
> and you have made radiant for me the earth and sky.
> My arrow of love has arrived at the target
> I am in the house of mercy
> and my heart is a place of prayer.[93]

### Wine Imagery

Another highly charged sensual image is the use of "wine" as a spiritual metaphor. The use of wine as a mystical image became problematic for the Sufis, as did their reliance on eroticism to express the yearning for union with the Divine. The "wine" of which the Sufi spoke is not that of the vine, but of the intoxication of spiritual attainment (*sukr*). As Martin Lings notes:

> Owing to the frequent mention of wine in Sufi poetry, it is perhaps worth mentioning that the only wine that the Sufis allow themselves is that which the Koran allows, namely the wine of paradise. Umar ibn al-Far-id [d. 1235; Cairo], the author of the famous *Khamriyyah* [Wine Song], begins his work: "We have drunk to the remembrance of the Beloved a wine wherewith we were made drunk before wine was created."[94]

There are two important aspects concerning wine imagery. First, as noted earlier, intoxication on the wine of God (*sukr*) is not the goal of the Sufi. The novice must pass through this stage to arrive at the "sober" stage (*sahw*), whereby one who has experienced the spiritual "licentiousness" of inebriation with God returns to this world, God-awareness still intact, to conduct their lives within the world of the day-to-day.

Another aspect of some mystics' desire to be "drunk" with God is that no matter how much they "drink" from that cup, they always long for more. A story told about Bayazid Bistami (d. 874), an early "drunken mystic" and a revered Islamic saint, illustrates this point:

> Yahya b. Mu'adh wrote to Bistami: "What would you say of one who, from one drop of the ocean of love, becomes intoxicated?" Bayazid wrote in reply: "What would you say of one who, if all the oceans in the world were composed of the Wine of Love, could drink them all and yet cry aloud because of his consuming thirst?"[95]

## Conclusion

Much of what has been presented here concerning Islamic mysticism also appeared in medieval Jewish thought. General ideas of God and the mystic's path, specific aspects of mystical grammar, the Perfect Man, prayer techniques, *sama'*, the use of sensual poetry to express Divine love and other Sufi inspirations were woven into the Jewish mystical quilt, and Judaized by their attachment to purported Biblical antecedents. As we will see in the pages that follow, this influence was hardly peripheral to Jewish practice, and over the centuries changed Judaism to the point where many facets of contemporary Jewish worship can actually be traced back into Islam, via medieval Jewish-Sufi interactions.

## Endnotes

1. Ma'ruf al-Karkhi (d. 813), quoted in Michon, Jean-Louis. "The Spiritual Practices of Sufism." *Islamic Spirituality: Foundations* (S. H. Nasr, ed.). (New York: Crossroad,1987: 265-293), p. 269 Michon notes that al-Karkhi was probably the first to define Sufism.

2. Lings, Martin. *What is Sufism?* (Cambridge, England: The Islamic Texts Society, 1995), p. 101.

3. Ibid. p. 27.

4. Stoddart, William. *Sufism*. (Northamptonshire, England: The Aquarian Press, 1984), p. 26.

5. Ibid. p. 62.

6. Burckhardt, Titus. *Introduction to Sufi Doctrine*. (Bloomington, IN: World Wisdom, Inc., 2008), p. 31.

7. Lings, Martin. *What is Sufism?* p. 25.

8. Information and quote from Ibid. p. 45.

9. Information and quote from Ibid. p. 77.

10. Burckhardt, Titus. "Sufi Doctrine and Method." *Sufism: Love and Wisdom* (Jean-Louis Michon and Roger Gaetani, eds.). (Bloomington, IN: World Wisdom, Inc., 2006: 1-20), p. 1.

11. Esposito, John L. *Islam, The Straight Path*. (Oxford: Oxford University Press, 1991), p. 102.

12. Quoted in Geoffroy, Eric. "Approaching Sufism." *Sufism: Love and Wisdom* (Jean-Louis Michon and Roger Gaetani, eds.). (Bloomington, IN: World Wisdom, Inc., 2006: 49-62), p. 51.

13. Lings, Martin. *What is Sufism?* p. 107.

14. Burckhardt, Titus. *Introduction to Sufi Doctrine*, p. 43.

15. Lings, Martin. *What is Sufism?* p. 14.

16. Lings, Martin. *The Book of Certainty.* (Cambridge, England: The Islamic Texts Society, 1996), p. x.

17. Burckhardt, Titus. *Introduction to Sufi Doctrine*, p. 78.

18. Lings, Martin. *The Book of Certainty*, p. 4.

19. Michon, Jean-Louis. *Islamic Spirituality: Foundations*, (S. H. Nasr, ed.), pp. 266-267.

20. Quoted in Chittick, William. *Sufism: A Short Introduction.* (Oxford: Oneworld Publishers, 2000), p. 145.

21. Quoted in Stoddart, William. *Sufism*, p. 45.

22. Quoted in Geoffroy, Eric. *Sufism: Love and Wisdom*, (Jean-Louis Michon and Roger Gaetani, eds.), p. 60.

23. Quoted in Chittick, William. *Sufism: A Short Introduction*, p. 36.

24. Ibid. pp. 36-37.

25. Smith, Margaret. *Studies in Early Mysticism in the Near and Middle East.* (Oxford: Oneworld Publications, 1995), p. 182.

26. Chittick, William. *Sufism: A Short Introduction*, p. 26.

27. Quoted in Ernst, Carl. *The Shambhala Guide to Sufism.* (Boston and London: Shambhala Publishers, 1997), p. 116.

28. Information in this paragraph from Ibid. p. 115.

29. Chittick, William. *Sufism: A Short Introduction*, p. 37.

30. Quoted in Peters, F. E. (ed.). *Judaism, Christianity & Islam III.* (Princeton, NJ: Princeton University Press, 1990), p. 241.

31. Burckhardt, Titus. *Sufism: Love and Wisdom.* (Jean-Louis Michon and Roger Gaetani, eds.), p. 16.

32. Lings, Martin. *What is Sufism?* p. 63.

33. Stoddart, William. *Sufism*, p. 65.

34. Burckhardt, Titus. *Introduction to Sufi Doctrine*, p. 90.

35. Ernst, Carl. *Shambhala Guide to Sufism*, p. 93.

36. Dr. Burton Thurston in Baker, Rob and Henry, Gray (eds.). *Merton & Sufism: The Untold Story.* (Louisville, KY: Fons Vitae, 1999), p. 37.

37. Ibid. p. 45.

38. Smith, Margaret. *Studies in Early Mysticism in the Near and Middle East*, p. 210.

39. Stoddart, William. *Sufism*, p. 67.

40. Information in this paragraph from Michon, Jean-Louis. *Islamic Spirituality: Foundations* (S. H. Nasr, ed.), p. 287.

41. Schaya, Leo. "On the Name *Allah.*" *Sufism: Love and Wisdom* (Jean-Louis Michon and Roger Gaetani, eds.). (Bloomington, IN: World Wisdom, Inc., 2006: 207-216), pp. 214-215.

42. Gril, Denis. "The Prophetic Model of the Spiritual Master in Islam." *Sufism: Love and Wisdom* (Jean-Louis Michon and Roger Gaetani, eds.). (Bloomington, IN: World Wisdom, Inc., 2006: 63-88), p. 76.

43. Quoted in Chittick, William. *Sufism: A Short Introduction*, p. 76.

44. Information in this paragraph from Burckhardt, Titus. *Introduction to Sufi Doctrine*, p. 58.

45. Ernst, Carl. *Shambhala Guide to Sufism*, p. 81, 85.

46. Burckhardt, Titus. *Introduction to Sufi Doctrine*, p. 33.

47. Ernst, Carl. *Shambhala Guide to Sufism*, p. 91.

48. Ibid. pp. 91-92.

49. Michon, Jean-Louis. "Sacred Music and Dance in Islam." *Sufism: Love and Wisdom* (Jean-Louis Michon and Roger Gaetani, eds.). (Bloomington, IN: World Wisdom, Inc., 2006: 153-178), p. 153.

50. Ibid. p. 153.

51. Burckhardt, Titus. *Sufism: Love and Wisdom*, (Jean-Louis Michon and Roger Gaetani, eds.), p.18.

52. Quoted in Chittick, William. *Sufism: A Short Introduction*, p. 91.

53. Michon, Jean-Louis. *Islamic Spirituality: Foundations*, (S. H. Nasr, ed.), p. 281.

54. Chittick, William. *Sufism: A Short Introduction*, p. 89.

55. Michon, Jean-Louis. *Islamic Spirituality: Foundations*, (S. H. Nasr, ed.), p. 270.

56. Burckhardt, Titus. *Introduction to Sufi Doctrine*, p. 7.

57. Lings, Martin. *What is Sufism?* p. 39.

58. Information and quote from Michon, Jean-Louis. *Islamic Spirituality: Foundations*, (S. H. Nasr, ed.), p. 271.

59. Quoted in Peters, F. E. (ed.). *Judaism, Christianity and Islam*, p. 182.

60. Ernst, Carl. *Shambhala Guide to Sufism*, p. 144.

61. Danner, Victor. "The Early Development of Sufism." *Islamic Spirituality: Foundations* (S. H. Nasr, ed.). (New York: Crossroad, 1987: 239-264), p. 246.

62. Stoddart, William. *Sufism*, p. 61.

63. Burckhardt, Titus. *Introduction to Sufi Doctrine*, p. 7.

64. Chittick, William. *Sufism: A Short Introduction*, p. 50.

65. Quoted in Ernst, Carl. *The Shambhala Guide to Sufism*, p. 124.

66. Schuon, Frithjof. "The Quintessential Esotericism of Islam." *Sufism: Love and Wisdom* (Jean-Louis Michon and Roger Gaetani, eds.). (Bloomington, IN: World Wisdom, Inc., 2006: 251-275), p. 271.

67. Ernst, Carl. *Shambhala Guide to Sufism*, p. 103.

68. Chittick, William. *Sufism: A Short Introduction*, p. 17.

69. Quote and information from Michon, Jean-Louis. *Islamic Spirituality: Foundations*, (S. H. Nasr, ed.), p. 269.

70. Burckhardt, Titus. *Introduction to Sufi Doctrine*, p. 77.

71. Quoted in Baker, Rob and Henry, Gray (eds.). *Merton and Sufism: The Untold Story*, pp. 251-252.

72. Danner, Victor. *Islamic Spirituality: Foundations*, (S. H. Nasr, ed.), p. 249.

73. Quoted in Ernst, Carl. *The Shambhala Guide to Sufism*, p. 99.

74. Ibid. pp. 4-6.

75. Michon, Jean-Louis. *Islamic Spirituality: Foundations*, (S. H. Nasr, ed.), p. 266.

76. Lings, Martin. *What is Sufism?* p. 55.

77. Quoted in Chittick, William. *Sufism: A Short Introduction*, pp. 104-105.

78. Burckhardt, Titus. *Introduction to Sufi Doctrine*, p. 79.

79. Quoted in Chittick, William. *Sufism: A Short Introduction*, p. 38.

80. Michon, Jean-Louis. *Islamic Spirituality: Foundations*, (S. H. Nasr, ed.), p. 285.

81. Burckhardt, Titus. *Introduction to Sufi Doctrine*, p. 66.

82. Lobel, Diana. *Sufism and Philosophy in Muslim Spain and the Medieval Mediterranean World*, (Manuscript, 2001), p. 8.

83. Quoted in Smith, Margaret. *Studies in Early Mysticism in the Near and Middle East*, p. 147.

84. Ibid. p. 146.

85. Chittick, William. *Sufism: A Short Introduction*, p. 34.

86. Ibid. p. 112.

87. Ibid. p. 37.

88. Ibid. p. 27.

89. Quoted in Fadiman, James and Frager, Robert (eds.). *Essential Sufism*. (New York: HarperCollins, 1997), p. 121.

90. Ernst, Carl. *Shambhala Guide to Sufism*, p. 158.

91. Quoted in Ibid. p. 154-155 For further explication of the use of profane imagery in the expression of mystical states, see pp. 159-161.

92. Ibid. p. 157.

93. *http://www.spiritualawakeningradio.com/souloflove.html* (*The Love Poems of Rumi*, D. Chopra, Translations by Farsi scholar Fereydoun Kia, Harmony Books).

94. Lings, Martin. *What is Sufism?* p. 87.

95. Smith, Margaret. *Studies in Early Mysticism in the Near and Middle East*, p. 208.

# Chapter 3
# The Jewish-Sufis of Medieval Egypt

## The Maimonides' of Cairo

### Maimonides Family Tree[1]

All merged Jewish and Sufi ideas and practice.
Names on the left side operated as the *Rayyis al-Yahud* of Egyptian Jewry.

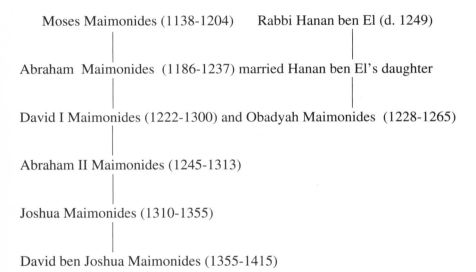

Moses Maimonides (1138-1204)      Rabbi Hanan ben El (d. 1249)

Abraham Maimonides (1186-1237) married Hanan ben El's daughter

David I Maimonides (1222-1300) and Obadyah Maimonides (1228-1265)

Abraham II Maimonides (1245-1313)

Joshua Maimonides (1310-1355)

David ben Joshua Maimonides (1355-1415)

Perhaps it should come as no surprise that this story of a virtually unknown mystical fraternity centers on the progeny of one of Judaism's most renowned and respected philosophers, Moses Maimonides. A story of labyrinthine relationships, hidden influences and propositions some even consider heretical, why shouldn't it also involve the family of the most important Jewish thinker of the past 2000 years?

Moses Maimonides (d. 1204; Egypt) viewed himself as one who could interpret and ultimately codify the whole of Jewish religious law in a definitive manner, allowing Jews to practice their religion without having to concern themselves with questions about the specific meaning of texts. And his self-assessment as one of the most important Jewish thinkers in the post-Second Temple era (beginning in 70 C.E.) wasn't far from the truth: he is considered by many historians to be the most important Jewish figure in the past two millennia. The *Encyclopaedia Judaica* states that without Maimonides, modern Judaism would have fractured into different sects and beliefs.[2]

While Moses Maimonides was certainly no Jewish-Sufi himself, though Islamic influence *did* run deep in his thought (which will be explored below), his son and spiritual heritor Abraham fused Judaism and Sufism into a unique amalgam, developing Jewish-Sufi ideas which would reverberate through Jewish practice down until our times. Perhaps no single figure so embodies the fusion of Islam and Judaism, as does Abraham. Of the many individuals we will explore, none inspires more agreement among scholars than Abraham, whose Sufi leanings are indisputable.

## Abraham Maimonides

No Jewish leader imported more Islamic mystical ideas into Egyptian Judaism than did Moses' only son, Abraham (d. 1237; Cairo). Following in his father's footsteps as *Rayyis al-Yahud* (head of the Egyptian-Jewish community), he rose by the end of his life to be viewed as the pre-eminent living scholar in Jewish thought and practice. His rulings were solicited from throughout the Arab-Jewish world, a population that defined 90% of Jewry in his lifetime. He unabashedly turned Jewish worship in the direction of the Sufis.

### A Born Leader

That Abraham followed in his father's footsteps as leader of Egyptian Jewry came as no surprise. When Abraham was only six years old, Moses could already say of his son:

> Of the affairs of this world I have no consolation save two things: preoccupation with my studies and the fact that God has bestowed upon my son Abraham, grace and blessings similar to those he gave to him whose name he bears [the Patriarch Abraham] ... May God give him strength and prolong his life, for he is meek and humble toward his fellow men, not to speak of the excellence of his virtues. He is endowed with subtle intelligence and a kind nature that ... will certainly gain renown among the great.[3]

In addition to taking over his father's duties as *Rayyis al-Yahud*, Abraham also became the physician to the Islamic Caliph in Cairo. Added to these duties, were all of the civil and administrative chores that are today divided among a phalanx of local and regional political leaders. According to Professor Paul Fenton (Sorbonne):

> [Abraham Maimonides] was the supreme legal and religious authority within the religious community itself and as such played a similar role to that of the Grand Mufti [within Islam] ... He had the authority to appoint chief judges and other community officials ... within his administrative district – which extended to the whole of Egypt and some-

times beyond. He would define their duties and privileges, censure their abuses and, when necessary, punish. Ultimately, he embodied the most powerful representation of medieval Jewish autocracy in the Islamic world.[4]

In addition to his temporal power, he was blessed with a unique personality that made his Sufi reforms more palatable to many of his contemporaries. According to Professor S. D. Goitein:

He combined the humility and meekness to be expected in an ascetic with the firmness and determination required in a communal leader. His fervent religiosity and his strictness in the enforcement of the [Jewish] law were paired with common sense and humane consideration for special circumstances.[5]

The combination of these special attributes allowed him to walk the fine line between his adoration for Islamic ideas and strict adherence to Jewish law and tradition.

### A Spiritless Religion

Abraham lived during a time of spiritual decline in the Jewish communities of North Africa. Like many today, Jews of 11th and 12th century Egypt enjoyed the "good life" far more than their moral and religious obligations. Additionally, there had developed a disturbing lack of respect for the synagogue rites due, perhaps, to concentration on worldly matters. As Samuel Rosenblatt relates, in his translator's introduction to Abraham's spiritual masterpiece, *Kifayat al-Abidin* (A Comprehensive Guide for the Servants of God):

He [Abraham Maimonides] called out with bitterness against the lack of decorum in the synagogues, against the disturbance of the services by continual quarrels about the presidency, by joking and general levity of mind, and declaimed against the unbecoming haughty demeanor of the leading officers in prayer and worship. Places where such outrages were perpetuated, he said, were the ones to which the prophets [of the Bible] referred to as being intolerable in the sight of God.[6]

### Jewish-Sufi Renewal

Hardly indifferent to these pressures, Abraham Maimonides and a growing coterie of like-minded spiritual leaders turned for guidance to the model for sincere holiness closest at hand – the Sufis. The Islamic mystics' stated goal was to react against the spiritual degeneration that had affected humanity since the creation of the world.[7] Abraham, noting this, turned to this model to help resuscitate his own contemporary Jewish practice.

Abraham's attraction to Sufism grew partly out of his conviction that they (Islamic mystics) had inherited their discipline from the ancient prophets of Israel – and that he and his group (Jewish-Sufis) were reclaiming an authentically Jewish doctrine from Islam. Abraham was hardly shy about this influence, trumpeting the borrowed Sufi ideas, even going so far as to contend:

> Thou art aware the ways of the ancient saints of Israel, which are not or but little practiced among our contemporaries, have now become the practice of the Sufis of Islam, on account of the iniquities of Israel … Observe then these wonderful traditions and sigh with regret over how they have been transferred from us and appeared amongst a nation other than ours … My soul shall weep because the pride of Israel was taken from them and bestowed upon the nations of the world.[8]

### Islamic Mysticism Leading to Jewish Prophecy

Abraham's fascination with Islamic mysticism didn't stop with lamentations, however. As Professor Paul Fenton notes, Abraham believed that the Jewish-Sufis were reviving a dormant Jewish doctrine that had originally been imparted to Adam and revealed by the Patriarchs, Abraham, Isaac and Jacob. Lost in successive generations, it resurfaced to Moses on Sinai, where he revealed the precepts of Sufism to Israel, in the Biblical story of Exodus.

According to Abraham, the Sufis dressed in rags, subsisted on alms and were organized as leaders and followers – all like the Hebrew Prophets of yore. Just like those Prophets, when a novice was initiated among them, the master threw a ragged cloak (*khirqah*) around his shoulders. The Sufis conquered sleep and fear through nightly vigils, and spent so much time in dark places praying that they actually injured their faculty of sight,[9] which allowed a powerful *inward* light to replace the sensorial experience of light on the retina. Abraham traced all of these Sufi ideas back to the Biblical saints.[10]

Samuel Rosenblatt went so far as to assert:

> [Abraham's] whole ethical system … appears to be Sufi from beginning to end in terminology and ideology … The parallels are so striking that it hard to assert anything less than identity of them. The special course which Abraham Maimonides prescribes for those who wish to reach "the goal" corresponds as a whole almost exactly to the path of the Sufi.[11]

### Sufis in the Synagogue

As Abraham was claiming Sufism for his own, and instituting minute aspects of Islamic mystical practice within Egyptian synagogue liturgy, it is not hard to discern specific Muslim influences. For instance, modeling his practice on the Sufis that surrounded him, Abraham advocated nightly vigils, a well-known Islamic spiritual practice, but one that had not been practiced within Judaism for at least a millennium. Abraham states:

> It is commendable to spend the night in prayer and to awaken in the middle thereof ... as David hath said: "At midnight do I rise up to give thanks to thee." Moreover he that pursueth this Path might not slumber at all during certain nights of his solitary retreats, as it is said: "Neither shall I give sleep unto mine eyes."[12]

Abraham assimilated other Sufi prayer methods. Practices that have been part of Islamic spirituality became attached to Jewish antecedents and wrapped into Egyptian Jewish services. "Abraham devotes a whole chapter of his *Kifaya* to the virtues of *khalwa*, which he considers the highest of the mystical paths."[13] Known as *'Arba'in* to the Sufis, the practice had been enshrined within Islamic mysticism. Paul Fenton notes that this form of retreat is still practiced by Sufis to this day, and until recently, Arab Jews. Twentieth century Jews living in the Levant, influenced by their Jewish-Sufi forbearers, practiced these retreats. In countries such as Morocco and Tunisia, Jews would retire to pray and meditate in particularly revered synagogues, some of which had hostels attached to them for the use of worshippers,[14] echoing the ancient Sufi prayer practice of *khalwa*.

### Jewish *Sheikh*

Abraham also called for novices to seek out a spiritual master to help them along the inner path. This spiritual master was a key element for the Sufis, called the *sheikh*. According to Abraham, this *sheikh* (and he used this exact term) "would initiate the novice into the intricacies of the mystical discipline before bestowing upon him the master's tunic, as Elijah had bestowed the cloak upon Elisha."[15] This "tunic," of course, was the Sufi *khirqah*, and represented acceptance of the Sufi path. As Professor Paul Fenton notes in *Jewish Mystical Leaders of the 13th Century*:

> It is possible that Abraham saw himself as this *sheikh*, in his position as spiritual leader of Egyptian Jewry ... Several letters addressed to him by his disciples are formulated in extremely reverential terms; one of his admirers goes so far as to address him as "the Divine presence dwelling among us" ... There are indications that he considered his own comportment exemplary as when, for example, after having discussed the property of Sufi attire, he mentions that he himself wore [Sufi] garments ... It is, in fact, tempting to apply to him the contemporary Sufi term "the Pole of his time" (*qutb zamanihi*).[16]

### Jewish *Sama'*

Abraham even likened Sufi music to the music of the Levites in the Bible, overlaying contemporary Sufi spiritual practice onto stories from the Jewish Scripture. Abraham notes:

> In order to attain inward solitude that unites one with God, the Prophets and their followers made use of musical instruments and melodies so as to arouse the impulsive part [of the soul] towards God and to empty their interiors of all else but Him ... [17]

Paul Fenton notes that Jews were known to have participated in Sufi *sama'* rituals since the inception of the Islamic mystical practice, leaving detailed explanations of these ceremonies, some of which were incorporated into the liturgy of Oriental Jewry. The fascination with Sufi musical rites continued deep into the 19th century, as an apology for the use of music in prayer written by Mordecai Abbadi (1873) states: "The ancient and contemporary poets borrowed the tunes of foreign (=Arabic) songs and composed for them holy words."[18]

The theory behind this prayer practice with musical accompaniment can most likely be traced back to al-Ghazali's (d. 1111) *Ihya'ulum ad-Din* (Revival of Religious Sciences), which was widely read by medieval Egyptian Jews and included a full chapter on *sama'*. Another important source for Abraham's ideas on the inclusion of music in prayer practice was the Muslim *Rasa'il Ikhwan as-Safa* (Epistles of the Brethren of Purity, Baghdad, 10th century), an Islamic compendium of all known sciences, including spirituality, which was heavily influenced by Sufi thought.[19]

As Paul Fenton notes:

> (Abraham Maimonides) associated the Biblical references to the music of the Levites, the Prophets and Saints (especially King David) with the musical usages of his Sufi contemporaries ... Traditional exegesis and Sufi notions are inextricably combined in the description of the musical instruments employed by the Biblical prophets and the Temple service ..."[20]

### Jewish *Ittihad*

When Abraham states: "the Prophets and their followers made use of musical instruments and melodies *so as empty their interiors of all else but Him*," (see above) he touched on one aspect of Sufi doctrine that was definitely not prefigured in the rites of ancient Jewish worship. That was his belief that man could experience a manner of union (*ittihad*), or ego identification with the Divine, through these practices. In another passage, Abraham claims: "Upon being thus moved [by *sama'*], the (soul) will submerge in the Divine ocean ..."[21] Abraham states that music could help in achieving this goal, fusion with God – an idea that ran directly counter to Jewish prayer practice and was almost certainly considered heretical by his more tradition contemporaries.

While his father had used the Sufi term *ittihad* to connote an intense spiritual closeness to God, Moses Maimonides had been clear that he believed man could never be "annihilated" in Him, as was advocated by the Islamic mystics. Abraham, however, accepted the Sufi ideal of personal ego identification with God, a first in the history of Jewish worship. Building on his father's vocabulary of union, Abraham was able to propose this as part of the Jewish religious path.

Abraham asserts: "By the union of his [i.e. the righteous person's] soul and intellect, with the Active Intellect [Divine], he and He became one entity."[22] As Professor Moshe Idel (Hebrew University) notes in his *Studies in Ecstatic Kabbalah*, Abraham's father Moses had specifically denied that man could actually fuse with the Divine: "Maimonides' *Guide* is based upon the assumption that *imitatio Dei* can be achieved in the practical domain, with human science being limited to the terrestrial realm. In other words, man *cannot* attain an accurate knowledge of the separate intellects, or of God's nature, *a fortiori* the union of his soul or his intellect with them while alive."[23] Abraham, however, did make just such a claim.

This Sufi ideal of mystical knowledge of God so captivated Jewish seekers in the generation after Moses Maimonides that even the translator of Maimonides' *Guide for the Perplexed*, one of his most important devotees, Rabbi Samuel ben Judah ibn Tibbon (d. 1230; Marseilles), states:

> The soul then unites with the Intellect [i.e., God] and they become one single thing for then the soul becomes divine, of a higher order, immortal, as is the Intellect with which it has united, the Intellect whose being is separate from matter.[24]

Professor Moshe Idel asserts: "The two greatest authorities on Maimonides' thought [Abraham Maimonides and Ibn Tibbon], preceding Abraham Abulafia [d. 1291; Sicily, who also accepted Divine union, Chapter 5], explicitly accepted non-Maimonidean [Sufi] conceptions of uniting *unio mystica* with the Active Intellect."[25]

### Jewish Law and Sufi Practice

What made Abraham so important for the dissemination of Islamic thought throughout the Jewish world was that he did not break with traditional Judaism to practice his Jewish brand of Sufism. In the first three sections of his opus, *Kifayat al-'Abidin*, he presented the letter of the law, as it was to be complied with by every Jew.[26] Here, he stayed close to Rabbinic Judaism, as he had learned it from his father. In fact, one would be hard-pressed to imagine a spiritual heir more dedicated to his predecessor than was Abraham to his father. In all of his writings, he quoted liberally from Moses Maimonides.[27]

At the same time that he proposed a scrupulous observance of Jewish law in the first part of his treatise, in the fourth chapter, Abraham veered far away from his contemporary Jewish practice. It was here that he assimilated beliefs and practices of the Sufis, proposing in minute detail how Islamic mystical practice should influence Jewish observance. He justified this paradoxical situation – believing that the Jewish law must be strictly adhered to while advocating Sufi-like reforms – by reading his own innovative reforms and Sufi attitudes *backwards* into Jewish history. He claimed to have "rediscovered the esoteric doctrines of ancient Israel,"[28] which still lived in the practice of the Sufis.

### *Kifayat al Abidin*

Abraham disseminated his Jewish-Sufi ideas to his local Jewish community, and through *responsa* (religious rulings) to Jews of the greater Islamic realm. However, it was his mystical treatise, the *Kifayat al-Abidin* (A Comprehensive Guide for The Servants of God)), a 2500-page tome, that had the greatest resonance within Jewish mysticism over the next several centuries. In the final section of the book, Abraham enumerated the specifics of Islamic mysticism, including sincerity, mercy, generosity, gentleness, humility, faith, contentedness, abstinence, mortification, equanimity and solitude, and attached them to the Jewish path.[29]

In this book, where the Jewish-Sufi Way took definitive form, Abraham demanded the punctilious observance of every commandment in the *Torah*[30] and then filled in his vision of Jewish observance with Islamic ideals. Many of the smallest details of religious observance outlined by Abraham were imported verbatim from the Muslim mystics. As Samuel Rosenblatt, translator of Abraham's *Kifayat*, states:

> There are correspondences [between Maimonides' *Kifayat* and the Sufis] in details such as the distinction made between external and internal pride; the recognition of various degrees of faith; the definition of what constitutes lack of faith; the assumption of the possibility of inner abstinence despite external wealth; the importance attached to contemplation as a method of rapprochement with God; the differentiation between prophet and saint; the acceptance of miracles as proof of holiness and the use of such expressions as "the shining of the Divine lights," "prophetic emanation," etc.[31]

### Further Specific Sufi Influences on the *Kifayat*

Concurrences with and outright borrowing from earlier Sufi tracts are not difficult to discern. According to Samuel Rosenblatt, Abraham shared much with the Islamic philosopher Mohammed Ben Hussein (d. 1271, Persia) on various ideas concerning anger, pride and humility, indicating that they both probably shared the same Sufi source. Anger and pride, of course, stood between a man and God, while humility (*faqr*) was a necessary precursor to remembrance of the Lord.[32]

Sufism influenced Abraham Maimonides on the nature of the soul – ideas that were of profound importance, as the soul was the part of man that could empty itself of all but God. Traditional Islamic sources such as al-Ghazali and the *Rasa'il Ikhwan as-Safa* (Epistles of the Brethren of Purity) described the soul as an organ that was devoted to the welfare of the body, but through training could work towards spiritual purification, as well. By strengthening the soul, much as a person trains a muscle, a permanent connection could be created between it and God, which would outlast corporeal death. However, if persons allowed themselves to spend their lives concentrating on worldly issues, the connection between the soul and God would atrophy and the soul would remain in a state of perpetual unrest. Abraham reiterated these ideas.[33]

It is important to note here that these ideas listed here, like so many ideas assimilated by medieval Jewish thinkers, did not initiate with the Sufis. In this particular case, many conceptions concerning the human soul can be traced back to the Roman philosopher Plotinus (d. 270). However, the immediate source of the ideas for medieval Jewish thinkers were Sufis, who had themselves re-discovered and then translated them into the medieval mystical vernacular. The fact that many scholars will point to the earlier genesis of a plethora of Sufi ideas – be it in Aristotle and Plato, neo-Platonism or even Roman texts – does not affect the actuality that the Jewish thinkers were *directly* influenced by their Islamic contemporaries.

Ultimately, there is little difference between Abraham Maimonides' Jewish spiritual path and the Sufi *tariqah*. Professor Paul Fenton asserts:

> The whole portion is imbued with Sufi ideology and terminology. The "special path" is none other than the Sufi *tariqah* and the stages are identical with some of the Sufi *maqamat*, or "stations," as can be ascertained by comparing them with the stages as described in classical Sufi manuals. The goal of the path (*wusul*) is identical in both cases, involving a sort of meeting with God and beholding the light of His certainty.[34]

### Abraham's Sufi Influence on Jewish Worship

Abraham infused not only his commentary with Sufi terminology and beliefs, but his correspondence as well. And it is important to remember just how far-reaching was his correspondence: supplicants contacted him from far and wide on questions of Jewish law, due to his position as *Rayyis al-Yahud* (Head of the Jewish Community). It is almost certain that he used these contacts to further spread his novel ideas. In fact, many of his Sufi inspirations found easy acceptance in the Holy Land, seeding the important mystical centers of Acre and Safed (Chapter 5) with the mystical ideas that would eventually help create the Kabbalistic system. Issakar ibn Susan, a 16th-century Jewish mystic in Safed, mentioned that Abraham's *Kifayat al-Abidin* was one of the Arabic books still read in that Kabbalistic center.[35]

In his own synagogue, where he was the head rabbi, Abraham introduced controversial new practices including ablutions prior to prayer, raising of the hands in supplication, standing in rows, profuse prostrations and other Islamic-inspired rituals, some of which could be traced back into Jews' Biblical past, and some which could not. Not all of his contemporaries meekly accepted his sometimes-extreme innovations. He was forced to address the concerns of his community, who could not always follow his line from ancient Israel, through the Sufis and into Judaism:

> Take heed ... not to confuse innovated doctrines and practices with ancient ones, which after having been neglected and forgotten, have been revived and restored, such as the question of prostration under discussion. Indeed, prostration is a *halakhic* obligation and ancient Jewish rite, which (because) of the Exile, has been abandoned for numerous years. Now that its obligatory nature has been realized and adopted by some [i.e. the Jewish-Sufis], it appears to the unversed and ignorant as a new religious practice, whereas in fact it is a renewal only in respect of the intermediate period, and not in relation to time of the original Jewish rite.[36]

He also endeavored to institute these reforms in other, more far-flung areas of the Egyptian community. Despite his assurances such as the one above, however, his measures were too obviously inspired by Islamic practice for many. Some in his community went so far as to condemn them as "imitations of heathen practices."[37] He was able to institute his reforms, however, because as *Rayyis al-Yahud*, he represented the final say in matters of the synagogue rites.

Perhaps one of the most surprising innovations, as it ran directly contrary to thousands of years of Jewish law and practice, was Abraham's advocacy of a celibate lifestyle, eschewing both wife and children. Abraham and the other Jewish-Sufis considered marriage and offspring impediments to spiritual fulfillment. If absolutely necessary, a wife should not be taken until the 40th birthday by which time presumably, an inwardly directed lifestyle would be securely established. As Paul Fenton notes, however:

> Such an attitude can only be explained in light of Sufi teaching, since the traditional Jewish stand is to encourage the early observance of the divine precept of procreation. Both Abraham Maimonides and his son Obadyah do "violence" to the scriptural text in an endeavor to find support for the delaying of marriage.[38]

### Heresy

As noted, the entire Jewish community in Egypt did not fall meekly into line behind this Jewish-Sufi innovator. Some of Egypt's most important Jewish leaders charged Abraham with *bi'da*, or "innovation," an accusation that could have led to his removal as *Rayyis al-Yahud* by the Muslim authorities. A group of prominent Jews went to the Sultan in the hope of denouncing the Sufi reforms, removing Abraham from his position and replacing him with a member of the aristocratic Jewish families that had been native to North Africa for centuries.

Abraham devised the successful defense of his innovations along the lines of Sufi theoreticians, using Sufi vocabulary and Islamic forms of apologia to rebut the charges, following the leads of such Muslim thinkers as Abu'l-Qasim al-Qushayri (d. 1074) and al-Ghazali. Rabbi Gerson Cohen (Chancellor of the Jewish Theological Seminary) relates that like these two Sufis, "Abraham acknowledged only one way to the mystical life, namely the one embodied in the laws and doctrines of traditional religion, which to him meant rabbinic Judaism [though in his case, strongly influenced by Sufism]."[39]

### Abraham's Legacy

Perhaps if Abraham Maimonides had been just another Jewish heretic, his Sufi beliefs would have been relegated to the dustbin of Jewish history – and Jewish mysticism would have remained just that: a purely Jewish response to this perplexing world. Abraham Maimonides, however, was one of the most-respected Jewish authorities of his era. The 13th century, when Abraham was active, was a time of tremendous fertility in Jewish thought – Rabbi Mark Verman (Zusman Chair of Judaic Studies, Wright State University) argues that it was the most creative epoch in the entire history of Jewish mysticism.[40] It was into this fertile loam that Abraham injected his ideas.

Not all contemporary scholars have made the leap that I am proposing – that Abraham Maimonides helped inspire a *lasting* influence on the direction of post 13th-century Judaism. Professor Paul Fenton states: "Although there would be some justification in saying that he [Abraham Maimonides] was the true founder of a mystical dynasty, it would seem excessive to conclude that the radical religious revival that Abraham had initiated exercised a profound and abiding effect on the destiny of Jewish spirituality."[41]

I must beg to differ. My own research in this area has convinced me that it would not be too far of a stretch to say that the Sufi leanings of Abraham not only influenced virtually all mystical writings in Judeo-Arabic over the next two hundred years – but also, as we shall see, helped lay the bases of an entirely new direction in Jewish mysticism, for the Kabbalah, the Baal Shem Tov's Hasidism and even contemporary Jewish worship and liturgy.

## Abraham's Jewish/Sufi Community

Abraham did not develop these beliefs in a vacuum; a vibrant Jewish-Sufi community surrounded him. He was not the founder of this coterie, but joined a fraternity of Hasidim ("Pietists," a code word for "Jewish-Sufi") that had already begun pushing for Sufi-style reforms in the Egyptian synagogue rites during his father's time.[42] Abraham did become the leader of this group, which included members from some of the most politically prominent families, with local, national and international ties. Many of the key rabbinical positions in Egypt were occupied by co-religionists.[43] Professor Paul Fenton relates:

> The Pietists ... viewed themselves, to varying degrees, as an elect, possessing special enlightenment, whose primary goal was "personal perfection," regardless of any social aims. They thus constituted, within the larger community, a distinctive elitist group, guided by its own leadership, which upheld a specific type of extremist religious worldview underpinned by a ritualized system of sacred symbols. Most probably they considered their system to be the true interpretation of the Divine message as encoded in the Scripture.[44]

Professor S. D. Goitein notes that these Hasidim attracted followers from distant countries[45] – contacts that undoubtedly carried the novel ideas back to their homelands after their travels. What began in Abraham Maimonides' time or even before, continued for several hundred years, as there is evidence of an unbroken chain of writings by Egyptian Jewish-Sufis, starting with Abraham Maimonides and his circle in the early 13th century and continuing into the 15th century.[46]

### Rabbi Hanan-El ben Samuel ha-Dayyan

Rabbi Hanan-el, who was Moses Maimonides' contemporary, had familial ties to the Maimonides: his daughter married Abraham Maimonides, making him Abraham's father-in-law. He also was a member of Abraham's circle, and stood by his side in defense of the Jewish-Sufi way.

Hanan-el utilized the usual methods of Jewish-Sufi apology to insist that the ways of the Sufis actually hearkened back to Biblical times. For instance, he claimed that the ancient prophets of Israel practiced *khalwa*, or solitary retreat, by identifying Mizpah [Judges 11:11 – "and Jephthah spoke all his words before the Lord in Mizpah"][47] as a "spiritual retreat in an 'elevated place,' where Jephthah practiced solitary meditation and attained divine inspiration."[48] Even a cursory reading of the text, however, shows that this is not explicitly stated.

He also referred to a Sufi practice called *tazayyuq*, which entails a specific meditation posture, as having come down to the Sufis from Jewish precursors. He points out the exact phrase in the Bible, "And Elijah went up to the top of Carmel, and he bowed himself down upon the earth and put his face between his knees" (1 Kings 18:42), which he considered the inspiration for this Sufi prayer method. Hanan-el writes, "The nations [i.e. Sufis] have taken this practice over from us and have adopted it and adorned themselves with it, whereby they sit in the position for a whole day. They call this *tazayyuq*, i.e. concealing of one's face in the collar, i.e. the hem of one's garment."[49]

While there is no way to know for sure, it might well be Hanan-el who helped influence Abraham Maimonides with Sufi conceptions. After all, given their familial relations and Hanan-el's position within the community – he was a Rabbinical judge (*dayyan*) of Moses' same generation – they undoubtedly found themselves often in social and professional company, as part of the same social circle in Fustat.

### Rabbi Abraham ben Abu Rabi'a he-Hasid

Another important figure around Abraham Maimonides was Rabbi Abraham ben Abu Rabi'a he-Hasid (d. 1223), a contemporary whom Abraham viewed as his mentor.[50] He-Hasid was a strong advocate of the Jewish-Sufi cause, proposing Sufic clarifications to spiritual problems, using preaching and writing to proselytize his ideas, as well as offering Sufi solutions to issues raised in Moses Maimonides' *Guide for the Perplexed*.[51] He-Hasid, along with Abraham Maimonides and Rabbi Hanan-el, occupied an official post in the Jewish governing body.

Dissatisfied with contemporary methods of Jewish worship, he-Hasid yearned for a more rigorous approach that would be conducive of the high mystical states to which he aspired. His innovations look similar to, if not being direct copies of, Islamic methods:

1) *Ablution*: Pietists instituted stringent laws of ablution before prayer.

2) *Prostration*: Prostrations, which had been abolished in Jewish custom, were restored.

3) *Kneeling*: In parts of the daily liturgy, worshippers kneeled, as in Muslim practice.

4) *Spreading of the hands*: The worshipper stretched forth his hands in Muslim fashion.

5) *Weeping*: The first Sufis were known as "weepers" because of the profusion of tears during prayer. Jewish-Sufis advocated weeping as a necessary expedient to prayer.

6) *Orientation*: To enhance decorum, worshippers stood in rows, in Muslim fashion.

7) *Vigils and Fasting*: Supererogatory supplication and nocturnal vigils were instituted.

8) *Solitude*: *Khalwa* was practiced in dark places to encourage an internal illumination, in accordance with Rabbi Abraham he-Hasid's interpretation of Isaiah 50:10.[52]

9) *Dhikr*: Abraham he-Hasid alluded to this Islamic mystical practice when he said: "One can attain to the spiritual world through the practice of outward and inward holiness, excessive love of God and the delight in His recollection (*dhikr*) and Holy Names."[53]

The solitary practice of *khalwa* was particularly remarkable as an addition to Jewish worship at this time, since it ran contrary to almost one millennium of community prayer as central to Jewish worship. This practice was of such importance to the Jewish-Sufis that Abraham Maimonides devoted a whole chapter of his *Kifayat* to it. In a letter addressed to Abraham he-Hasid and to he-Hasid's brother Joseph, Abraham Maimonides alludes to their practice of solitary prayer, as they were two who "spend their nights in vigils and their days in fasting as on the Day of Atonement, purging their souls and purifying their bodies ... and many are their followers." Paul Fenton notes: "This is an allusion to the common Sufi practice known as *al Qiyam wa-Siyam*, 'standing and fasting,' which the Pietists had adopted."[54]

Abraham he-Hasid also was instrumental in solidifying the central importance of the Biblical personage King Solomon for the Pietists. Solomon's *Canticles* ("Song of Songs") provides a clear example of Sufi-like worship in the Bible. In *Canticles*, the desperate love of God that inspired Solomon parallels the Islamic ideal of the lovesick mystic in search of communion with the "Beloved." A couple of verses provide an idea of why this would be so:

> Let him kiss me with kisses of his mouth –
> For thy love is better than wine.
> *Song of Songs*, 1:2

> By night on my bed I sought him whom my soul loveth;
> I sought him but I found him not.
> I will rise now, and go about the city,
> In the streets and in the broad ways,
> I will seek him whom my soul loveth.
> *Song of Songs*, 3:1-2[55]

Although Moses Maimonides had already explained King Solomon's *Canticles* in an allegorical manner, weaving in some Sufi interpretations, Abraham he-Hasid took the mystical aspects much further, bringing together ideas concerning the ancient Jewish king with Islamic mysticism. As Professor Paul Fenton writes: "[He-Hasid's] conception that *Canticles* expressed the rational soul's longing for union with the intelligible worlds, largely pervades the commentaries of subsequent Judeo-Arabic mystical philosophers, who use Sufi notions and vocabulary."[56]

Abraham he-Hasid was unabashed about his Sufi sources, copying into Hebrew Sufi writings from such sources as Abu al-Ma'ali al-Malik al Jili (d. 1100; Baghdad) and Abu Nuíaym al-Isfahani (d. 1038). The influence of these Islamic tracts became clear in Abraham's he-Hasid's own work, *Maqala fi-Salat* (Treatise on Prayer), which summarizes many of the Sufi ideals of approaching God, and finishes with such conceptions central to the Sufi *tariqah* as the purpose of prayer being to "polish the soul," and prayer being a "continuous turning towards God through permanent recollection of Him."[57] He also was careful to link his Sufi reforms to the Jewish Hasidim of the Talmudic period (c. 2nd-5th centuries). When advocating Muslim preparatory practices of bodily cleanliness and mental purity, for instance, he connected these to a passage in the *Mishna Berakot V* (the section of the 2nd-century Oral Law which deals with prayer).[58]

The Influence of Jewish-Sufism

While it might today be difficult today to imagine such forthright respect shown by leaders from one religion for theologians of another, these medieval Jews had no compunctions about their attraction to Islamic mysticism. Jewish libraries were replete with Islamic texts copied into the Hebrew script, including poems by the Sufi martyr al-Hallaj (d. 922), chapters from Abd Allah ibn Sina's (d. 1037) *Al-Isharat wa-'l-Tanbihat* (Remarks and Admonitions), works by Shihabuddin Yahya al-Suhrawardi (d. 1191) and above all the writings of Abu Hamid al-Ghazali (d. 1111).[59] The Jewish-Sufis colored much of Egyptian Jewish practice with the revivifying force of Islamic mysticism.

> The Pietists infused the religious precepts with their own teachings [drawn from Islamic inspiration]. Thus the *Sabbath* was instituted to curb worldly preoccupations in order to give oneself over to worship and seclusion [*khalwa*], "to delight in God's recollection [*dhikr*] and to fill one's thoughts with him." The Day of Atonement [*Yom Kippur*] was similarly "a moment of withdrawal from worldly pursuits in order to devote oneself to acts of purity [*ikhlas*] and to purge oneself of the impurity and veils of matter." Similar conceptions of the inner meaning of the festivals are exposed by the Jewish-Sufi author of the *Risalat al-Asrar* [Epistle of the Secrets].[60]

## Moses Maimonides

Before moving on to 14th- and 15th-century Egyptian Jewish thinkers who continued in the Pietist tradition, it is important to acknowledge the central role played by Moses Maimonides in turning Jewish mysticism towards the Sufi model. Though he never went as far as his son did, Moses was most definitely attracted to Islamic conceptions of spirituality, and wove many Sufi ideas discretely into his exegesis of the Jewish path.

It should also be noted how contentious a proposal this is. Many scholars and educated laypersons will grumble over some of the assertions in this book, but to bring the venerated Moses Maimonides into the story can appear sacrilegious. As my mentor, and a committed interfaith peacemaker himself, Abdallah Schleifer (Senior Fellow, Foreign Policy Research Institute, PA, as well as Professor Emeritus at the American University in Cairo) stated: "You know, Moses Maimonides is probably the most sensitive sticking point for even well meaning scholars, which I can appreciate. Joel Kraemer (in his biography, *Maimonides*, New York: Doubleday Publisher, 2008) acknowledges Maimonides' debt to Muslims in philosophy, jurisprudence, literary form, medicine etc. And on top of that, some might say, now you have to make him a Sufi! *Ganig Shauwn*!! ('Enough already,' in Yiddish)"[61]

While there might be few more contentious assertions to make than to claim Sufi influence on Abraham's father Moses, it is a line of thought that I am compelled to explore, as the evidence, to my mind, is as overwhelming as it is controversial. Moses Maimonides was one of the most learned men – Christian, Muslim or Jew – of his time and had virtually all of Western learning at his beck and call, synthesizing this vast compendium of human thought with his reading of traditional Judaism to create his own philosophy. Therefore, it is not difficult to find any manner of influences on his thought, ranging from ancient Greek through to his contemporary Muslims. Among these varied stimuli, Sufism was very important.

Many Jewish scholars have explored the Islamic influence on Maimonides, from the Stanford Encyclopedia of Philosophy, which includes an article entitled: "The Influence of Islamic Thought on Maimonides," to Joel Kraemer's aforementioned book, which proposed that Moses Maimonides actually converted to Islam for a time. However, almost none have explored the *Sufi* influence on the great master.

Part of the reason for this hesitation is that Moses Maimonides is considered as the pre-eminent *rational* thinker in Jewish history, hardly prone to mystical thinking. Therefore, the question of mystical influence on his thought runs contrary to the accepted scholarly narrative. However, the research I have undertaken indicates that there was a spiritual thread running through Maimonides' oeuvre. This aspect of his thought was often influenced by the Sufis.

A Far-Ranging Influence

The reach of Maimonides' work and thought must not be underestimated, which explains why the moderate Sufi influence that can be discerned therein is so important and far-reaching. In his own lifetime, his writing was so well respected that he illuminated not only the Jewish sphere, but the Muslim, as well. Muslims, who could read much of Maimonides' work in its original Arabic, were drawn to his ideas – though partly, as we shall see, because he was reconsidering many Islamic themes. He was held in such high esteem, that the Muslim poet and *qadi* (judge) Ibn Sana al-Mulk (d. 1211; Egypt), a personal friend, penned this paean:

> Galeno's art only cures the body,
> Whilst Abu Imram's [Maimonides'] cures body and soul.
> His knowledge made him the doctor of the century.
> With his knowledge he can cure the disease of ignorance.
> If the moon decided to put herself in his hands
> She would be freed of her spots at full moon.
> He would cure her of her monthly indispositions
> And prevent her waning in her moment of conjunction.[62]

To this day, Muslims will refer to "Maimun" as one of their own, a fact that I know personally from my travels to Cairo to deliver a paper at Al-Azhar University. When I handed my paper to the Arabic translator and he looked at the title of it: "The Maimonides of Cairo: Five Generations of Jewish-Sufis," his face lit up and he exclaimed: "Maimun! He's one of ours!" "He's one of *ours*, too," I responded.

That Moses Maimonides would be recognized in 21$^{st}$-century Cairo as important to both Jewish and Muslim practitioners represents how his renown has grown in the decades and centuries following his death, to the point where his once radical ideas are now thought of as traditional. He is a figure of such distinction that many a Jewish grandmother the world-over traces her lineage back to the Maimonides clan – and forward to her very own grandson. In fact, family lore has it that my great-grandmother herself would proudly announce at social gatherings that she, too, was descended from the great Eagle of the Synagogue.

What has become lost in Maimonides' narrative, however, is how very radical were some of his innovations in the interpretation of Jewish life and law – and from where some of these novelties actually stemmed. In my opinion, it was Maimonides himself who helped open the door for Sufi ideas to illuminate the Jewish path – a threshold that would be thrown wide in successive generations and, as we shall see, become completely permeable by the time of the composition of the Kabbalistic treatises, a century or so later.

### Sufis in the Synagogue

In Fustat (Old Cairo), Maimonides found himself in an open-minded community, one that allowed him to get to know Muslim customs in a warm and friendly environment. His well-known works on Jewish life and law, the *Guide for the Perplexed, Mishneh Torah* and other writings – many of which are still studied in *yeshivas* (Jewish religious schools) and synagogues today – were infused with Islamic ideas.

In the introduction to his *Eight Chapters,* Maimonides states, "One should accept the truth from whatever source it proceeds,"[63] including, of course, Islam. Being that he spoke fluent Arabic, studied with famous Muslim scholars and cited Islamic authorities frequently in his works, the cross-pollination seems only natural.

### Guide for the Perplexed

As Professor David Blumenthal (Emory University) noted in *Maimonides: Prayer, Worship and Mysticism*, Moses Maimonides reinterpreted Hebrew terms and metaphors, inspired by the Islamic beliefs that surrounded him.[64] It must be pointed out that not all scholars have accepted Professor Blumenthal's thesis; in fact, Professor Robert Eisen of George Washington University stated in a note to this author: "Blumenthal's Sufi reading of Maimonides has not been generally accepted by the scores of scholars who write on Maimonides." However, it is also important to point out how much scholarship in this area has been influenced by contemporary politics, historical, scholarly prejudices and other concerns that have little to do with the matter at hand. Although Professor Blumenthal's arguments fall outside of mainstream Maimonidean scholarship, it fits seamlessly into the narrative of this book, and the facts that I have found from various sources, as they have come together to weave the story of the Jewish-Sufi.

Maimonides' masterpiece, *The Guide for the Perplexed* (an exploration of God, humanity and the meaning of life), far from representing a point on the continuum of traditional Jewish theology, marked a turning point in the history of Jewish belief. The great 20th-century Islamic scholar S. D. Goitein notes: *"The Guide for the Perplexed* is a great monument of Arab-Jewish symbiosis, not merely because it is written in Arabic by an original Jewish thinker and was studied by Arabs, but because it developed and conveyed to large sections of the Jewish people ideas which had so long occupied the Arab mind."[65]

The *Guide* utilizes what became the typical Jewish-Sufi device of attaching new, Sufi-inspired ideas to the far-off Biblical and Talmudic past, thereby situating them within Judaism. Maimonides' explains in his introduction to the second part of the *Guide* his manner of "uncovering" ancient Jewish practice in the Sufi Way, "rediscovering" esoteric doctrines of ancient Israel, which he was then imparting to a new generation of Jews.[66] This flow of spiritual concepts – from ancient Jewish doctrine, through the Sufis and then on to medieval Jews – would be replayed time and time again, though some of the "rediscovered" ideas were in fact novel to Judaism.

Maimonides' hybrid work was such a perfect expression of the open-minded times in which he lived that it was studied closely and even taught by his contemporary Muslims, to both Jewish and Muslim students. Jews sought out Muslim teachers for the *Guide* because Jewish teachers were less familiar with the scientific thinking of the time, and therefore the Muslims could better interpret Maimonides' thought.

Sufism and the Jewish Guide

The title of *The Guide for the Perplexed* itself can be traced to Sufi antecedents. As Professor Diana Lobel of Boston University has shown, language that stemmed from earlier Sufi masters was appropriated by Moses Maimonides to express the Sufi ideal of "learned ignorance," the notion that the ultimate level of knowledge is to realize that one does not know.[67] The more one "knows" God, according to Islamic thinkers, the more one grows perplexed – and the title of this seminal Jewish work, *Guide for the Perplexed*, was drawn from a Sufi aphorism by Dhu'l Nun al-Misri (d. 859) to that effect.[68]

Maimonides' basic ideas concerning the flow of God's energy from an uncreated point, through descending levels of created spirituality and into the world of manifestation, where humans live, were based on Muslim precursors. Although this conception can be traced back to the ancient Greek philosopher Aristotle (d. 322 B. C. E.), Maimonides' immediate influences were Islamic thinkers. Specifically, Abd Allah ibn Sina (d. 1037) proposed that the Divine Essence had overflowed into a series of 10 different "intellects," each linked to its own celestial sphere, with the lowest of these being the "Active Intellect," or that aspect of God available to man.

The *Stanford Encyclopedia of Philosophy* notes: "Maimonides rehearses the idea, seen clearly in his Islamic predecessors, that there are a series of intellects which generate one another. Maimonides then goes on to mirror the idea, also found in Ibn Sina, that each intellect additionally generates the body of its sphere and that there is, furthermore, a set of influences which these spheres wield over the generation and corruption of terrestrial, corporeal beings on earth."[69] These ideas concerning the ten spheres of spiritual powers became the basic building blocks of the Kabbalah's Tree of Life and its ten *Sephirot* (spiritual stations), which has been central to Jewish spirituality since that time.

Other Sufi images are not difficult to discern in this work. In the introduction to the *Guide for the Perplexed*, Maimonides states:

We are like someone in a very dark night over whom lightning flashes again and again. Among us there is one for whom the lightning flashes time and time again, so that he is always, as it were, in unceasing light ... That is the degree of the great one among the prophets, to whom it was said: *But as for thee, stand thou here by Me* (Deuteronomy 5:28; referring to Moses) ... Among them there is one to whom the lightning flashes only once in the whole of his night; that is the rank of those of whom it is said: *They prophesied, but they did so no more* (Numbers 11:25). There are others between whose lightning flashes are of greater or shorter intervals ... It is in accord with these states that the degrees of the perfect vary.[70]

As Professor Shlomo Pines (Hebrew University) mentions: "the simile of the lightning flashes seems to be derived from Ibn Sina's *al-Isharat wa'l Tanbihat* [Remarks and Admonitions]. According to this work, experience of the *'arifun* [men of understanding] perceiving something of the light of truth may be likened to lightning that flashes momentarily and then is extinguished. These are called *awqat* [by Maimonides], a Sufi term."[71] This image represented the mystical enlightenment that comes to the searcher in greater or lesser degrees. At the very best, a mystic could attain a period of extended, or even permanent illumination.[72]

Prophecy

This lightning flash of mystical enlightenment led the aspirant toward the central goal of Maimonides' philosophy: prophecy. Maimonides assimilated novel ideas concerning prophecy from Islam. The prophet, according to Maimonides:

... was the person whose ability to receive the overflow from the Active Intellect [the aspect of God available to humankind] was especially superb ... There were different levels of prophecy, corresponding to different levels of engagement with the overflow from the Active Intellect.[73]

It is important to note how vital were conceptions of prophecy to Moses Maimonides and his contemporaries. They believed themselves to be fast approaching the time of the Messiah (Maimonides himself was said to have even speculated on a specific date for the return of the Savior[74]), an epoch during which prophetic souls would be needed. Maimonides' mixing of Islamic ideas with Jewish notions of prophecy forever changed this ideal within Judaism.

Abu Hamid al-Ghazali (d. 1111) had addressed issues concerning prophecy, utilizing the lightning flash of inspiration image that, nearly a century later, showed up in Moses Maimonides' *The Guide for the Perplexed*. The Muslim thinker fashioned a passage nearly identical to the one from the *Guide* (see above). While there is no direct record of influence of the one on the other, much of al-Ghazali's work has been found in medieval Egyptian Jewish libraries, both in its original Arabic and copied into

Hebrew, and it, as well as Ibn Sina's treatises, were almost certainly available to Maimonides as he worked through his ideas.

Al-Ghazali writes with regard to prophecy:

> Then, if the will of the Sufi has been sincere, the rays of truth will shine in his heart. At the outset this will be like a sudden lightning flash that does not last, then returns but slowly. If it does return, sometimes it remains and sometimes it is only passing. If it remains, sometimes its presence is extended and sometimes not. And at times, illuminations like the first appear, one following the other, at other times they are reduced to a single experience.[75]

From the idea of the "lightning flash" of mystical clarification came other Sufi ideas concerning prophecy and sainthood. The difference between prophecy, in which the adept is privy to revelation and is charged with disseminating the light of God to normative practitioners, and sainthood, which represents the drawing aside of the "veil" of ignorance, offering access to the ultimate Truth for one individual, became central to the understanding of Jewish mysticism, via earlier Sufi thinking. The Sufi al-Ghazali explains the difference:

> The knowledge which presents itself in the heart of a sudden and without striving, study or work on the part of the subject is of two types: the first is the kind that a man is unaware how it came to him or whence; the second carries with it an understanding of the means whereby it came ... the first type is called inspiration, and breathes in the depths of the heart; the second is called revelation and properly belongs to the prophets. As for the first, it is characteristic of the saints.[76]

Prophets work for the received primordial energy, and understand the necessary steps to prepare themselves for its influx. The inspired saint, on the other hand, has a personal experience of realization that he might not even be able to comprehend himself, beyond the actual encounter, having received a spiritual gift (*hal*, or state).

In Sufism, the preexistent "light" of God operates as the medium of prophecy – it represents the Divine spirit that God breathed into Adam, which was the first emanation from the One and which became incarnate in the prophets. This idea was developed by Ibn Sina and Shihabuddin Suhrawardi (d. 1191) into the Illuminist (*Ishraqi*) School, which posits that God is nothing but this pre-existent light. It then influenced later Islamic thinkers, becoming the ten spheres of luminescent emanations; ever-fainter Divine overflows which ultimately coalesce into the world of manifestation, where humans live.

This idea is based in part on the Koran (24:35), which states:

God is the Light of the heavens and the earth;
The similitude of His Light is as if there was a niche;
And within it a Lamp: the Lamp enclosed in Glass;
The glass, as it were, a glittering star;
Lit from a Blessed Tree;
An Olive, neither of the East nor of the West;
Whose oil is nigh luminous, though no fire has touched it;
Light upon Light; God guides to His Light whom He will.

Prophetic Legislation

Once the Sufi accesses this primordial light, he is charged with disseminating this understanding in such a manner that the exoteric practitioners of the religion can appreciate it. This represents the ideal of "prophetic legislation" which became central to Jewish practice due to Islamic influence, and may be traced back to Jafar as-Sadiq (d. 765), the Sixth Imam of Shi'a Islam. Jafar devised a schema for prophets that led from unconscious inspiration (what might be termed a "saint" by al-Ghazali or Maimonides) to a role as a prophetic legislator. Specifically:

> As early as Jafar as-Sadiq, the following categories of prophecy were set up: 1) the *nabi* (prophet) who receives signs and inspiration; 2) the *nabi* who hears an angel, but only in a dream and never awake; and 3) the *nabi* who hears an angel but is awake. The parallel socio-political scheme [obligation of the prophet] was developed by as-Sadiq: 1) the *nabi* who does not have to transmit that which he receives; 2) the *nabi mursal* who has a mission which is to support and to teach a previous revelation; and 3) the *nabi rasul* whose mission is to legislate. His prophecy is called *nubuwat al-tashri* [legislative prophecy].[77]

According to Professor David Blumenthal in *Approaches to Judaism in Medieval Times*, this conception influenced Maimonides:

> Drawing on Islamic political theory in which the prophet is separated from other ideal types by virtue of his being a "messenger," that is by virtue of his having a divinely ordained socio-political function, Maimonides ... set forth the role of the legislator/prophet ... The mixture of piety and politics, of religious awareness and socio-political mission, may sound strange to modern ears, but it is basic to Islam and hence to medieval Jewish thought.[78]

For Maimonides, the prophet/lawgiver not only is possessed of the perfect intellect, but also is a gifted rhetorician, leader and socio-religious guide. As the *Stanford Encyclopedia of Philosophy* notes, concerning Maimonides' prophet/lawgiver: "He is able to take the truths that he knows and, by imaginatively devising an effective system of concepts, images, rituals and stories, enable these Truths to work in the lives of ordinary people ... These words are impressed on the imagination of the listeners as they are themselves crafted in the imagination of the lawgiver."[79] Maimonides states that man is by nature a political animal, and that the prophet must operate in this sphere.[80]

Maimonides tied these Islamic-inspired ideas of prophetic action to the ancient Jewish past, and specifically to Moses. "The role of the legislator-prophet is clearly assigned to Moses, and Maimonides applied to him the Hebrew word *mehogeg* (legislator)."[81] Undoubtedly Maimonides also felt that he himself followed in Moses' line as a prophetic legislator.

### Al-Insan al-Kamil

The ideal of Maimonides' prophetic legislator became enmeshed with another central Sufi concept: *al-Insan al-Kamil*, or the Perfect Man. For Islamic mystics, this symbolizes the highest station on the mystical path, representing an aspirant who has achieved complete realization of the unmediated, primordial God, which lies latent in all humans. The Sufi becomes a vice-regent of God (*khalifa*) on Earth, a prophetic actor channeling the energy of the Divine for the good of all humankind. The model for the Islamic *al-Insan al-Kamil* is the Prophet Muhammad.

Maimonides developed a strikingly similar conception, even utilizing the Sufi term to describe the person who attains man's final cause. Replacing "Muhammad" with "Moses" as the most perfected human being,[82] Maimonides mixed Sufi conceptions of the *al-Insan al-Kamil* with Jewish antecedents.

Maimonides lashed these ideas to the Bible by explaining the notion of man's being created in the image of God (Genesis 1:26-27) in this manner: "It is because of this something, I mean because of the Divine Intellect (*aql al-Ilahi*) conjoined (*al-muttasil*) with man, that it is said of the latter that he is in the image of God and in His likeness."[83] It was the man who is "in the image of God," the *al-Insan al-Kamil* for Maimonides who played the role of the "prophetic legislator," the highest spiritual possibility within the human realm.

### Jewish-Sufi Prayer

Maimonides gently turned ideas of prayer away from traditional Jewish practice, toward Sufi ideals. He raised silence in importance within the pantheon of Jewish worship, an idea that ran counter to Jewish practice, though it was in line with his contemporary Muslims. The Prophet Muhammad reportedly stated: "The first stage of worship is silence,"[84] and Islamic mystics, building on this *hadith*, make silence a vital step along their spiritual path. As David Blumenthal notes in research into Maimonides' Sufic leanings, the Jewish thinker quotes directly from the Sufis when he explains the importance of silence, though like later Jewish-Sufis, he simply attributes this Islamic influence to a euphemistic "all philosophers," and attaches the idea to a Biblical passage:

> All philosophers say ... "Silence is praise to You," which interpreted signifies: silence with regard to You is praise. Accordingly, silence is preferable, and limiting oneself to the apprehension of the intellects [Divine emanations], just as the perfect ones have enjoined, "Commune with your own heart upon your bed and be still." (Psalm 4:4)[85]

The idea of "silence" as a necessary precursor to receiving the Divine Essence goes hand-in-hand with solitude as a form of prayer. This spiritual retreat (*khalwa*), based in silence, was an especially noteworthy Jewish innovation, as it ran directly counter not only to the practice of 12th-century Egyptian Jewry, but also to the Jewish tradition of community prayer rituals, specifically the idea of a *minyan*, or minimum of ten men being necessary to perform the synagogue rites. This idea of community prayer had underpinned Jewish worship for one thousand years prior to Maimonides.

Since the fall of the Second Temple (c. 70 C.E.), Jewish practitioners have known no central physical structure to unite the Nation, as has Islam, for instance, with the *Ka'ba* (in Mecca). In place of the Temple, Jews substituted the idea of community as the binding force of their people. The *minyan* replaced the physical presence of the Temple in Jerusalem, and hence to move prayer toward a solitary experience was viewed as heretical. As we will see, from Maimonides' proposing silence as central to Jewish prayer, there later arose some of the most important, and contentious, ideas of the Kabbalah and Hasidism.

### Sufi Terminology to Elucidate the Jewish Path

Maimonides utilized other Sufi conceptions and specific vocabulary, although he often subtly changed the meaning to keep the ideas in line with traditional Jewish thinking. As Professor David Blumenthal notes in *Philosophic Mysticism: The Ultimate Goal of Medieval Judaism*:

> Maimonides does use Sufi and Islamic philosophic mystical terms such as *ghibta* (bliss), *'ittihad* (union), *'ishq* (passionate love), *al-'inqita 'ilayhi* (total devotion) and *al-qurb minhu* (closeness to Him). He also uses phrases taken from Sufi literature such as: "The whole truth, together with the intensity of its brightness, is hidden from us;" "Then one advances to contemplating the holy divine Presence;" "He has dazzled us by His beauty and He is hidden from us by the intensity of His brightness;" and "Apprehension of Him consists in the inability to attain the ultimate apprehension of Him."[86]

This seeding of Sufi vocabulary into his work made it possible for subsequent Jewish thinkers to uncover deeper Sufi implications in Maimonides' thought. The words were there, though Maimonides may have shaded their meaning back toward rabbinical Judaism. Later Jewish philosophers, however, were able to see in Maimonides what they desired, which often were Sufi interpretations of the Jewish religion.

One example of the manner in which this subtle metamorphosis in meaning took place may be seen in Maimonides' use of the Sufi term for Divine union – *ittihad*. As Maimonidean scholar David Blumenthal has asserted, Maimonides co-opted this word, applying it to the far-off Biblical past,[87] using it to signify the highest *approach* a seeker could make in his appreciation of the ineffable. At no time did he use this term with its Islamic meaning, as Maimonides never thought it possible for humans to fuse their ego with the Active Intellect.

Later Egyptian Jewish-Sufis, including his son Abraham, grandson Obadyah and others, adopted the term with its full Sufi intent, and *did* posit that Jewish aspirants could attain the Sufi ideal of union with God. This became the primary goal of Jewish mysticism from the middle of the 13th century onward (termed *devequt* for Jews), influencing the Kabbalah, 18th-century Hasidism and even contemporary Jewish mysticism. And in every case, later Jewish thinkers could point back to Maimonides' use of this terminology, even though he never adopted the complete meaning of it from Islam. Medieval Jews could believe and/or claim that their ideas stemmed from the ancient Jewish prophets, via Moses Maimonides.

Equanimity

In most cases, Maimonides used Sufi terminology to expand Jewish ideas, without completely accepting the Islamic connotation implied by the vocabulary. However, in the case of "equanimity," I propose that he accepted completely the Sufi ideal, even though it was novel within Jewish worship, and according to Moshe Idel of Hebrew University, even ran contrary to some Talmudic teachings.[88] Maimonides advocated a "joyous equanimity in the face of the vicissitudes of life."[89] The concept of equanimity (*hishtawwut* for later Jews) is central to Muslim life, and became so for medieval Jewish mystics, as well. For Sufis, the attainment of disinterest in what other people think is a vital rung on the ladder of spiritual realization.

In a Hebrew translation (found in a medieval Egyptian Jewish library) of the great Sufi theologian al-Ghazali, the idea of "equanimity" is presented as a necessary precursor to acceptance of the Divine Essence:

> According to the Hebrew version of al-Ghazali, the Sufis have a fixed path by which they attain communion with God, which involves several clearly delimited stages: 1) separation from the world [*faqr*]; 2) indif-

ference or equanimity [*hishtawwut*]; 3) solitude [*khalwa*]; 4) repetition of God's name [*dhikr*] and 5) communion with God [*ittihad*].⁹⁰

Equanimity, as a station along the path of spiritual realization, was so respected by Moses Maimonides that he retold a story about a Sufi adept to illustrate its importance. As Abraham Halkin (Jewish Theological Seminary) revealed, Moses Maimonides relates the tale in a letter to a fellow rabbi, referencing "a sage and great philosopher."⁹¹ The story would be taken up by later Jewish thinkers to represent a new *Jewish* mystical ideal:

> And it happened once that a sage and a great philosopher was traveling on a ship and sat in the place of the refuse, until one, that is, one of the people of the ship, came and urinated on him on the place of the refuse, and he lifted his face and laughed. And they asked him: "Why do you laugh?" He answered them: "Because is it now absolutely clear to me that my soul is on the highest level, because I did not at all feel the disgrace of this thing" ... And the philosophers have said that it is very rare to find a man whole and complete in both ethical qualities and wisdom, and if he is to be found, he is called a divine man, and certainly such a one as this is on the highest level.⁹²

This story was also retold by Maimonides in his *Commentary on the Mishna*, as well as by his student Joseph ben Judah ibn Aknin (12ᵗʰ century) and by the 16ᵗʰ-century Safed Kabbalist Elijah da Vidas in his *Reshit Hokhmah* (Beginning of Wisdom).⁹³ The tale originally was related about the Islamic mystic Ibrahim ibn Adham (d. 777), in biographies by the Sufis al-Hujwiri (d. 1073) and Farid ad-Din Attar (d. 1221).

Seven Levels of Worship

In the *Guide for the Perplexed*, Maimonides outlines an extended metaphor for the seven levels of worship, each representing closer proximity to a king ensconced on his throne. The Sufis initially inspired this seven-palace motif, which would pass from Maimonides into Kabbalistic lore, and finally into 18ᵗʰ-century Hasidism. I contend that this movement of ideas, from the Islamic mystics to 12ᵗʰ- and 13ᵗʰ-century Mediterranean Jewish thought, through the Kabbalah and then into European Hasidism, was one of the most important revivifying impetuses in post Second Temple Judaism – a contention that few pure scholars would agree with, but one that this book attempts to make clear with its weave of historical influences.

According to Professor Luce Lopez Baralt, The earliest known reference to this particular symbol of seven spiritual levels in any religious writing took place in the work of the ninth century Sufi Abu-l-Hasan al-Nuri (d. 907; Baghdad), in his *Maqamat al-Qulub* (Stations of the Hearts). In his image, there were seven castles that referred to the various ascending stages that a mystic has to pass through on his way to complete knowledge of and union with God.

Although the metaphor used by Maimonides and the 10th-century Sufi were not exactly the same, the number of castles was the same, and many of the *stations* were similar. This "seven palace" image became common-place in medieval Sufi writing.[94] Professor Luce Lopez-Baralt notes that this seven concentric castle motif may be traced back to Muhammad, whose *Mi'raj* ("ascension" of the Prophet to meet with God, Koran 17:1[95]) became an Islamic metaphor for spiritual enlightenment:

> It is interesting to recall ... the paradisal heavens described in the *Mi'raj*, which are made of seven different metals and precious gems, and which sometimes are described in terms of castles.[96]

This image entered into the Jewish canon with Maimonides' work, later becoming central to Moses de Leon's Kabbalistic masterpiece *The Zohar* (The Book of Splendor; c. 1295, Chapter 5) and then to 18th-century Hasidism (Chapter 6). Michael McGaha (Professor Emeritus, Pomona College) notes its appearance in the *Zohar*:

> The thirteenth century *Zohar* speaks of seven palaces – corresponding to the seven lower *Sephirot* [stations of the Kabbalistic Tree of Life] through which the soul ascends in the mystic journey, stating that: "in the midst of a mighty rock, a most recondite firmament, there is set a palace which is called the palace of love. This is the region wherein the treasures of the King are stored, and all His love-kisses are there. All souls beloved of the Holy One enter into that palace." (3:293) The *Zohar* usually speaks of the palaces of being of hard, diamond-like sapphire.[97]

### A Central Role

Maimonides was certainly no Jewish-Sufi: he had a profound respect for the imagery and vocabulary of Islamic mysticism, while rejecting many of the more esoteric ideas and the specifics of Sufi practice. Nor was he the first Jew to be inspired by Islamic mysticism – we find Islamic-influenced Jewish thinkers as far back as the beginning of Islam (c. 630). But due to his unique position within Judaism, he was undoubtedly one of the more important Islamic-inspired Jewish thinkers.

We see, time and again, Egyptian and Spanish Jews, as well as Kabbal-ists and even later pre-modern Jewish thinkers, using Moses Maimonides as their lodestar for understanding Judaism, as well as to prove their own traditional Jewish orientation, even as they wove Sufism ever-more deeply into Jewish theology. As the *Encyclopaedia Judaica* points out, "the influ-ence of Maimonides on the future development of Judaism is incalculable.  No spiritual leader of the Jewish people in the post-Talmudic period has exercised such an influence both in his own and subsequent generations."[98]

Moses Maimonides may have been surprised to know what he had initiated by his acceptance of Islamic modes of thinking, as his son Abraham was followed by a succession of 150 years of Jewish-Sufi descendants.  He might be even more surprised to learn, however, that Abraham interpreted the family history as being comprised of a long line of Jewish-Sufis, though he uncovered this lineage on his mother's side, thereby leaving untouched his father's heritage.

Professor S. D. Goitein discovered among the folios preserved from this time period one which listed nine generations of Abraham Maimonides' ancestors, representing nearly 300 years of immediate forbearers.  It portrays most members of the family bearing the honorific "he-Hasid" ("the pious"), which was a code word for "Jewish-Sufi."  Goitein posited that either Abraham, or some member of his mother's family before him who had adopted the ways of the Jewish-Sufis, retroactively applied the pious tribute to this lineage,[99] providing further support for the Islamic-inspired reforms to medieval Jewish worship.

According to Paul Fenton, the tendency to fuse Sufi mysticism with elements of Moses Maimonides' ideology may be found in the writings of virtually all-subsequent Maimonidean descendants.[100]  And not only were these Maimonidean progeny Jewish-Sufis, but they also continued to act as the *Rayyis al-Yahud*, or temporal leaders of the Egyptian Jewry.  The family list of leaders – Moses Maimonides (d. 1204) to Abraham (d. 1237), then to his son David (d. 1300), to Abraham II (d. 1313), Joshua (d. 1355) and finally, the last Maimonides of whom we have record, David II (d. 1415), who served as *Rayyis al-Yahud* into the early 15th century[101]—all blended their temporal and religious duties with an overt fusion of Jewish-Sufi mystical principles.

## Four More Generations of Maimonidean Jewish-Sufis

### Obadyah Maimonides

Obadyah Maimonides (d.1265; Cairo), a white-robed mystic and the son of Abraham (though not the *Rayyis al-Yahud*; that role was reserved for his brother David), followed the Sufi manner of his father.  Though he did not rise to the temporal heights achieved by others in his family, he was very influential within the framework of the Egyptian Jews.  A letter of a contemporary identifies Obadyah in this manner:

> As for our glorious teacher and master Obadyah, the eminent Sage to whom mysteries are revealed, in whom "light, understanding and wisdom like the wisdom of the angels are to be found" (Daniel V:11) "no

secret mystifieth him, he lieth down and all is revealed to him" (Daniel IV:6). [102]

It also might be added that although his brother David was not remembered with ritual honor in the local Egyptian synagogues, after Obadyah's death, *his* name was added to the memorial list of particularly spiritual Jews, which was read out on *Kol Nidre*, the eve of Atonement, [103] the holiest day on the Jewish calendar.

### Al-Maqala al-Hawdiyya

Obadyah's most important work is a Sufi-inspired tract entitled *Al-Maqala al-Hawdiyya* (Treatise of the Pool). On the face of it, Obadyah remained loyal to his Jewish precursors. As Professor Paul Fenton notes in his translator's introduction to the tract:

> He [Obadyah] greatly relies on his father's and grandfather's works, whole sentences of which he incorporates into the texture of his own composition. Indeed [*Treatise of the Pool*] can be considered an enlargement of the concluding chapters of the *Guide for the Perplexed*, albeit with a markedly more mystical bent. Obadyah shows much more concern about how to obtain the constant "being-with-Reason" that Moses Maimonides had briefly outlined. Besides the *Guide*, Obadyah quotes from [Moses'] *Mishna Torah*, *Commentary on Abot* and [Abraham's] *Kifayat*. [104]

However, a closer study of the work shows that Obadyah continued to move interpretations of Jewish practice deeper into the Islamic realm. The central theme of this book is the Sufi idea that the heart, the seat of spiritual experience, resembles a pool (*al-hawdiyya*) that must be cleansed before the water of pure knowledge can be poured into it. Obadyah followed the Jewish-Sufi practice of claiming that the source for his Islamic innovations was actually Judaism's own Biblical past. Quotes from Genesis, Deuteronomy and other books of the *Torah* were interspersed with Sufi quotes and terms. For example, in one passage concerning the cleansing necessary before worship, he sounds particularly Sufic, though he claims to base his ideas on Biblical antecedents:

> It is for this reason that our pure and purifying Law hath cautioned us concerning all external and internal defilement … Thus Aaron and his descendents were enjoined "to wash their hands and feet, that they perish not" (Exodus 30:21), this being the reason for the act of purification (*ikhlas*). For through the conviction man's soul acquireth after immersion that all veils (*hijab*) have been lifted, there ensueth a state similar to spiritual predisposition (*tahayyu*) and communion (*ittisal*) with God. [105]

Removing the veils (*hijab*) that stand between the aspirant and God are a central Sufi theme. Purification (*ikhlas*) is a basic Sufi concept that under-pins the dissipation of intermediary forms between the ego and God. The idea of striving for purification, leading to communion with God, seemed to stem from Obadyah's contemporary Islamic practitioners.

An Interior Pool

The central theme of Obadyah's work mirrored a well-known passage that al-Ghazali (d. 1111) expounded on in his *Kimiya'yi Sa'adat* (The Alchemy of Happiness), concerning the Prophet Muhammad's "pool." The similari-ties become evident by comparing the passages from the Sufi and the Jew-ish mystic. In al-Ghazali's work, we read:

> The heart is like a pool, and the senses are like five streams by which water enters the pool from the outside. If you want limpid water to rise from the bottom of the pool, the way to do it is to remove all of the wa-ter from it ... The paths of all the streams must be blocked so the water does not come ... So long as the pool is busy with water that comes from the outside, water cannot rise up from within. In the same way, then knowledge that comes from within the heart will not be gained un-til the heart is emptied of everything that has come from the outside.[106]

As Obadyah Maimonides states in his *Treatise of the Pool*:

> Imagine a certain person who, possessing a very old pool, desireth to cleanse the latter of dirt and mire and to restore it ... he must occupy himself with its gradual cleansing until that the pool be completely pu-rified. Only after having ascertained that there remain therein no im-purity can the living waters that go forth from the house of God flow therein, concerning which it is said, "And a source from the House of God." (Joel 4:18) The foregoing is an allegory alluding to the purifica-tion, cleansing and purging of the heart, the correction of its defects and failings and its being emptied of all but the Most High.[107]

Any input from the outside is impure; only the spiritual effluence that arrives from within the soul comes from God. Much of the imagery, and even some of the specific language for Obadyah's idea, appear to stem directly from the great Sufi philosopher.

*Al-Lawh al-Mahfuz*

Another central Islamic image originating in the Koran showed up in Obadyah's treatise. In Chapter 10 of *Treatise of the Pool*, he states: "When thou will have persevered in this effort, thine imaginative faculty will be purified and all that is given graven on the 'well-guarded tablet' [*al-lawh al-mahfuz*] will be manifested to thee."[108] It seems that this image of the "well-guarded tablet" originated with the Prophet Muhammad's revelation. The Koran (85:21-22) states: "Indeed, it is a glorious Koran, in a preserved master tablet." For Muslims, this image of the "master tablet" became identified with the Active Intellect, that aspect of the Divine that can be accessed by humans.

As al-Ghazali, who died about 150 years before Obadyah, relates in his *Ihya'ulum ad-Din* (Revival of Religious Sciences):

> The truths contained in the mirror of the Tablet are revealed in the mirror of the heart, the forms of one mirror being reflected in the other ... when the veils [*hijab*] of the sensual world are lifted from the heart's vision, then something of what is inscribed in the "Well-Guarded Tablet" [*al-Lawh al-Mahfuz*] are revealed to it.[109]

Professor Paul Fenton notes:

> The correspondence between the two parables of the cleansing of the heart, the organ of divine knowledge, as well as between the vocabulary involved, is a clear indication that al-Ghazali was a major source of Sufi ideas to both Obadyah and the Jewish Pietists in general. It is noteworthy that the idea of the heart as the locus "of the Ark in which lie Two Tablets of the Testimony" is to be found in the *Chapter on Beatitude* [an un-attributed Jewish-Sufi work, perhaps by Obadyah] and in the apocryphal letter of Moses Maimonides to his own son, Abraham, *Musar na'eh*.[110]

### Divine Union

Obadyah based his idea for the prolongation of Divine union on terminology found in Moses Maimonides' work – although he subtly merged it with the Sufi Way. Moses Maimonides utilized the word *wusla* ("bond," though the Sufis use the associated word *ittisal* in this context) to mean the *approach* of humans to the Divine through prayer, without ever intimating that there could be a complete emptying of the one (human), allowing for entrance of the other (the Divine).

In Obadyah's work, however, the actual meaning of the phrase *wusla* took on significance more in keeping with the Sufis. Obadyah *did* imply an actual joining between man and God, a cessation of the differentiation between the two. For him, *wusla* defined the Sufi station of ego-identification with God, thereby reinterpreting the term borrowed from his grandfather.

As 20th-century French scholar George Vajda (University of Paris) notes in "The Mystical Doctrine of Rabbi Obadyah, Grandson of Moses Maimonides," Obadyah's conception of Divine union echoed the portrait of the Perfect Man (*al-Insan al-Kamil*) outlined in Ibn Sina's *Al-Isharat wa-'l-Tanbihat* (Remarks and Admonitions): "Purified knowers are able to attain the world of holiness and blessedness and become inscribed with the highest perfection" (3:96), and "Whoever wishes to know about it should train himself gradually to become one of the people of vision (*al-musha-hadah*) ... and one who has arrived (*al-wasilun*) instead of just one who has heard the report." (3:99-100)[111] The term for "bond" used by Obadyah (*wusl*) and that used for "those who have arrived" for Ibn Sina (*al-wasilun*) stemmed from the same root, *wsl*.[112] Vajda also notes that around this time, the Islamic proposition of Divine union appeared in Jewish mysticism, termed *devequt*.[113]

### Jewish *Sheikh*

Obadyah strongly advocated for the necessity of an aspirant finding a spiritual master, or *sheikh*, to help in the path towards Divine union. Though his father Abraham had already proposed the stipulation of following a spiritual master, the urgency with which Obadyah expounded on the idea raised its importance. Obadyah insists: "We are powerless to establish and maintain by our own efforts communion with God. The aspirant to perfection must have recourse to a mediator. 'It is clear that he who has no intercessor to tie the bond between himself and his Beloved, is considered as dead.'"[114]

The importance of a spiritual advisor is echoed time and again in the Sufi tradition, as the idea of embarking on the *tariqah* without a spiritual guide is considered dangerous. "Do not take a step on the path of love without a guide. I have tried it a hundred times and failed," writes the poet Hafiz (d. 1379; Persia). And the master-disciple relationship was seen as an essential facet of Sufism by al-Ghazali:

> The *murid* [disciple] must of necessity have recourse to a *sheikh* to guide him aright. For the way of faith is obscure, but the Devil's ways are many and patent, and he who has no *sheikh* to guide him will be led by the Devil into his ways. Therefore the *murid* must cling to his *sheikh* as a blind man on the edge of a river clings to his leader, confiding himself to him entirely, opposing him in no matter whatsoever and binding himself to follow him absolutely.[115]

Obadyah had much influence among his contemporary Jews concerning this novel Jewish necessity, as can be seen in an un-attributed tract from his circle, entitled *Waza-if al-Murshid* (Meditations of a Spiritual Leader). This book was a teaching document advising the Jewish *sheikh* how to guide his disciples along the Way. It bore a striking resemblance to a Sufi work by Abd al-Qahir al-Suhrawardi (d. 1168; a relative of the other Suhrawardis mentioned in this book) called *Adab al-Muridin* (A Sufi Rule for Novices). Paul Fenton notes that in the Jewish-Sufi work, "great emphasis is placed on the fact that the [Jewish *sheikh*] himself must shun all worldly gain, for in the words of a rabbinic saying, his role is even more important than that of the disciple's own father, since the latter brought him into the world, whereas the *sheikh's* purpose is to bring him safely to the next."[116]

Obadyah enjoyed the same success as his predecessors in reaching a large Jewish audience with his innovative views. While he was not the temporal leader of the Jewish community in Egypt, he was tremendously well respected, being referred to, along with his brother David, as "These masters, the two great luminaries, the two tablets of the law, the two princes of the host of Israel, the two eminent dignitaries, the two Cherubim, may their position be magnified."[117] Clearly, his Sufi leanings did not stand him in bad stead with at least some Egyptian Jews.

## David ben Joshua Maimonides

The final Maimonidean Jewish-Sufi of whom we take notice is David ben Joshua (d. 1415; Cairo), Obadyah's grandnephew. Testament to the ongoing importance of the family, David also held the position of *Rayyis al-Yahud*, continuing the family tradition of officially sanctioning Sufi practices within Jewish rites.

### A Jewish-Sufi Bridge

David was a vital conduit for bringing Jewish-Sufi ideas out of Egypt and into the Holy Land, where they would flower within Judaism afresh, in the 15th and 16th centuries. After two-decades of operating as *Rayyis al-Yahud* in Cairo, he left Egypt for Aleppo and then Damascus (Syria) from 1375 to 1386, continuing to act as the leader of the Egyptian Jewish community throughout those the years.[118] In Aleppo, he collected one of the largest libraries in the western Mediterranean that, in addition to Jewish books, included works by virtually all well-known Sufi writers up to his time. Although the most prominent influence on David Maimonides was the *Ishraqi* (Illuminist) school of Suhrawardi (d. 1191), other folios in his collection highlighted such central Islamic thinkers as al-Ghazali, al-Hallaj, Ibn Sina, Dhu'l Nun al-Misri, al-Qushayri and many others, all of whose ideas are found represented in David's extensive writings.[119]

The importance of this library alone should not be underestimated, as it brought together Jewish and Sufi tracts in the very locale where, within a century, the Safed Kabbalists would once again revivify Jewish practice, utilizing Islamic ideas (Chapter 5). Even after David's death, Jewish scholars and theologians continued to visit Aleppo in order to study from his library.[120] He also commissioned many manuscripts, including, most remarkably, an Islamic commentary on Moses Maimonides' *Mishna Torah*.[121] In addition to this commission, David continued the family legacy of having direct contact with Muslims. Like all Maimonides before him, these contacts hardly soured his image within the Jewish community, as his contemporaries referred to him as "our master and teacher, the saint, the pious one [*he-Hasid*]."[122]

A Vast Literary Output

Perhaps even more than his ancestors, David based his ideas in Sufi thought and practice. In his writings, he made wide use of seminal Sufi tracts from al-Hallaj (d. 922), Abu'l-Qasim al-Qushayri (d. 1074), Abu Talib al-Makki (d. 996; Baghdad), Ibn al-Arif (d. 1141), al-Ghazali (d. 1111), Shihabuddin Yahya al-Suhrawardi (d. 1191) and other Islamic thinkers. Like those who went before him, he attached these ideas to the far off Talmudic past. David wrote a book entitled *Al-Murshid ila al-Tafarrud* (The Guide to Detachment), the title of which echoes the Sufi ideal of divesting oneself of worldly attachments, to clear space for entry of the Divine.[123] This book's second part concentrated on humans as moral beings, and ended with the Sufi ideal of the Perfect Man (*al-Insan al-Kamil*).[124]

Overtly, however, he based the book's theme on a saying by the first century Rabbi, Pinhas ben Yair:

> Caution leads to industry, industry leads to cleanliness, cleanliness leads to detachment, detachment leads to purity, purity leads to holiness, holiness leads to fear of sin, fear of sin leads to piety, piety leads to prophecy, prophecy leads to resurrection, resurrection leads to the state of Elijah.[125]

As the translator of this work, Professor Paul Fenton notes:

> David Maimonides equates each of these stages with a station on the Sufi Path. He was particularly sympathetic to the illuminative *Ishraqi* School of as-Suhrawardi. For instance, he equates the stage *zehirut* (caution) with the Suhrawardian notion of illumination, taking it to be derived from the Hebrew root, *zhr*, "to be bright." Moreover, numerous extracts of Suhrawardi's *Kalimat at-Tasawwuf* are found in his treatise.[126]

Other writings show strong Sufi influence. David's *Maqalah fi-Derek ha-Hasidut* was a pietistic manual describing the Sufi path toward prophecy, in Jewish terms.[127] His commentary on the *Sefer ha-Madda* (a section of Moses Maimonides' *Mishna Torah*) was preceded by two laudatory poems dedicated to the Islamic thinker Ibn Sina.[128] His *Dhawqiyyat al-Tehillim* (Tastes of the Psalms), a commentary of the Book of Psalms, used a Sufi technical term in the title, "*dhawq*,"[129] which implied the direct apperception of God through the sensation of taste.

Like earlier Sufi-inspired Jews, he substituted the word "*hasid*" for "Sufi" throughout his works, thereby attempting to make his Sufi reforms palatable for normative Jewish readers of his work. Additionally, in a passage explicating Divine love, David deftly replaced Koranic verses with Biblical passages that had the same philosophical import, a Jewish-Sufi technique that may be traced back more than three centuries.[130]

He also borrowed the Sufi device of discussing the roots of the word "Sufi," substituting "*hasid*," and then providing an etymological review of the meaning of the Hebrew word for "Pietist." Whereas "Sufi" derives from "as-suf," which can be translated as "wool," the fabric sometimes worn as the *khirqah*, or its homonym *safi* (pure), David averred that "*hasid*" actually related to the word "hasida," or stork, and represented how the mystic (like the stork) remained aloof from society so that he could commune directly with the Creator. Additionally, the word *hasid* appeared often in the Psalms, a fact that David constantly emphasized.[131]

### Jewish *Sama'*

In the portion of his treatise, *Guide to Detachment*, devoted to music, David wove Sufi ideas in with his views. Such well-known Muslim authors as the *Ikhwan as-Safa* (Brethren of Purity, 10th century) and al-Ghazali, as well as Sufi-inspired Jews such as Joseph ibn Aknin (d. 1220; Morocco), Moses ibn Ezra (d. 1138; Spain) and Abraham ibn Ezra (d. 1167; France) all permeate his Jewish-Sufi concept of music as a meditation tool. He went so far as to adopt specific Sufi music and dancing rituals to aid his practice of *dhikr* (recollection of God) litanies.[132]

David ben Joshua Maimonides was as prolific and important to the development of medieval Judaism as the other members of Moses Maimonides' family. Judging from the number of his manuscripts that have been preserved, he seems to have enjoyed widespread celebrity in the 15th and 16th centuries,[133] in the exact place (the Holy Land) and exact time (the beginning of the Safed renewal – see Chapter 5) that his ideas would have maximum import on the further development of Jewish mysticism. He, his writings and his extensive library played a central role not only in continuing the strong Islamic mystical influence on Jewish worship, but also in deepening it for later thinkers.

In understanding why these leaders of the Jewish community over the period of more than 200 years were able to sustain their attraction to Islamic mysticism, it is important to remember that all of them remained completely loyal to Jewish law and tradition. Abraham, Obadyah and David all based their Sufi-inspired works in Moses Maimonides' thought and a strict adherence to *halakha* (Jewish law), while at the same time basing so much of their interpretations on Muslim thinkers. It was certainly a fine-line to walk, but the family was blessed with powerful minds, as well as important temporal positions, and succeeded in the delicate balance for more than two centuries.

As the 15th century drew to a close, Egyptian Jewry lost its place of importance in the Jewish world and the Maimonides family slipped into obscurity. By this time, however, 250 years after Moses Maimonides had serendipitously uncovered Sufi spirituality after he settled in Egypt (1160), Jewish spirituality had been irrevocably changed. From that time on, he and his descendants did as much to align Jewish and Islamic mysticism as any other group of people, Jews or Muslims, in these spiritual cousins' history. And the seeds that they had sown would continue to grow, weaving their roots into the development of the Kabbalah and later Jewish mysticism.

## Endnotes

1. Fenton, Paul. "The Literary Legacy of David Ben Joshua, last of the Maimonidean Negidim." (*Jewish Quarterly Review 75,* 1984: 1-56), p. 40.

2. Rabinowitz, Louis Isaac. *Encyclopaedia Judaica 1st Edition, CD ROM* (Cecil Roth and Geoffrey Wigoder, eds.) (New York: MacMillan and Company, 1972).

3. Fenton, Paul. "Abraham Maimonides: Founding a Mystical Dynasty." *Jewish Mystical Leaders and Leadership in the 13th Century* (Moshe Idel & M. Ostow, eds.) (New Jersey and Jerusalem Northvale Press, 1998: 127-159), p. 130-131.

4. Ibid. p. 131.

5. Goitein, S. D. "Abraham Maimonides and his Pietist Circle." *Jewish Medieval and Renaissance Studies* (Alexander Altmann, ed.). (Cambridge, MA: Harvard University Press, 1967: 145-164), p. 151.

6. Maimonides, Abraham. *The High Ways to Perfection of Abraham Maimonides.* (Samuel Rosenblatt, trans.) (New York: AMS Press, 1966), p. 45.

7. Geoffroy, Eric. "Approaching Sufism." *Sufism: Love and Wisdom* (Jean-Louis Michon and Roger Gaetani, eds.). (Bloomington, IN: World Wisdom, Inc., 2006: 49-62), p. 56.

8. Quoted in Maimonides, Obadyah. *Treatise of the Pool* (Paul Fenton, trans.). (London: Octagon Press, 1981), p. 8.

9. Maimonides, Abraham. *The High Ways to Perfection of Abraham Maimonides* (intro) (Samuel Rosenblatt trans.), p. 49.

10. Ibid. p. 49.

11. Ibid. p. 50.

12. Quoted in Maimonides, Obadyah. *Treatise of the Pool* (Paul Fenton, trans.), p. 14.

13. Ibid. p. 16.

14. Ibid. p. 16.

15. Fenton, Paul. *Jewish Mystical Leaders of the 13th Century* (Moshe Idel & M. Ostow, eds.), p. 143.

16. Ibid. p. 143.

17. "A Jewish Sufi on the Influence of Music." *YUVAL IV* (Israel Adler and Bathja Bayer, eds.). (Jerusalem: The Magnes Press,1982: 123-130), p. 126.

18. Information and quote in this paragraph from Ibid. p. 125.

19. Ibid. p. 126.

20. Ibid. p. 126.

21. Quoted in Ibid. p. 128.

22. Idel, Moshe. *Studies in Ecstatic Kabbalah* (Albany, NY: SUNY Press, 1988), pp. 4-5.

23. Ibid. p. 4.

24. Ibid. p. 5.

25. Ibid. p. 5.

26. Ibid. p. 30.

27. Goitein, S. D. *Jewish Medieval and Renaissance Studies* (Alexander Altmann, ed.), p. 145.

28. Fenton, Paul. *Jewish Mystical Leaders of the 13th Century* (Moshe Idel & M. Ostow, eds.), p. 136.

29. Maimonides, Abraham. *The High Ways of Perfection of Abraham Maimonides* (intro) (Samuel Rosenblatt trans.), p. 51.

30. Ibid. p. 41 "Right at the beginning [of his *Kifayat*], we are struck with [Abraham's] insistence on the punctilious observance of every commandment of the *Torah*, the fulfillment of which he looks on as a debt pure and simple and as the *sine qua non*, the indispensable prerequisite for those who pursue the path leading to '*the goal*' (i.e. prophecy)."

31. Ibid. p. 53.

32. Ibid. pp. 87-89.

33. Ibid. pp. 67-70.

34. Fenton, Paul. *Jewish Mystical Leaders of the 13th Century* (Moshe Idel & M. Ostow, eds.), p. 144.

35. Fenton, Paul. "Judeo-Arabic Mystical Writings of the XIIIth-XIVth Centuries." *Judeo-Arabic Studies: Proceedings of the Founding Conference of the Study of Judeo Arabic* (Norman Golb, ed.). (New York and Milton Park, England: Routledge, 1997: 87-101), p. 101.

36. Quoted in Fenton, Paul. *Jewish Mystical Leaders of the 13th Century* (Moshe Idel & M. Ostow, eds.), p. 148.

37. Ibid. p. 139.

38. Maimonides, Obadyah. *Treatise of the Pool* (Paul Fenton, trans.), p. 18.

39. Cohen, Gerson D. "The Soteriology of R. Abraham Maimuni." (*Proceedings of the American Academy of Jewish Research 36*, 1948: 75-98), p. 78.

40. Verman, Mark. *The Books of Contemplation*. (Albany, NY: SUNY Press, 1992), p. 8.

41. Fenton, Paul. *Jewish Mystical Leaders of the 13th Century* (Moshe Idel & M. Ostow, eds.), p. 153.

42. Cohen, Gerson D. *Proceedings of the American Academy of Jewish Research 36*, p. 76.

43. Fenton, Paul. *Jewish Mystical Leaders of the 13th Century* (Moshe Idel & M. Ostow, eds.), p. 138.

44. Ibid. p. 149.

45. Goitein, S. D. *Jewish Medieval and Renaissance Studies* (Alexander Altmann, ed.), p. 153.

46. Idel, Moshe. *Studies in Ecstatic Kabbalah*, p. 93.

47. *The Holy Scriptures*. (Philadelphia: The Jewish Publication Society, 1948), p. 309. "Then Jephthah went with the elders of Gilead, and the people made him head and chief over them; and Jephthah spoke all his words before the Lord in Mizpah."

48. Quoted in Fenton, Paul. "A Judeo-Arabic Commentary on the Haftarot by Hanan'el Ben Samuel, Abraham Maimonides' Father-in-Law." *Maimonidean Studies* (Arthur Hyman, ed.). (New York: Yeshiva University Press, 1990: 27-49), pp. 48-49.

49. All of the information and quotes in this paragraph come Ibid. pp. 48-49.

50. Fenton, Paul. *Jewish Mystical Leaders of the 13th Century* (Moshe Idel & M. Ostow, eds.), p. 137.

51. Maimonides, Obadyah. *Treatise of the Pool* (Paul Fenton, trans.), p. 19.

52. Ibid. pp. 15-16 "Who amongst you feareth the Lord, he who walketh in darkness and hath no light."

53. Ibid. pp. 13-17.

54. Ibid. p. 14.

55. *The Holy Scriptures*, pp. 966-972 (the complete *Song of Songs*).

56. Fenton, Paul. "Some Judeo-Arabic Fragments by Rabbi Abraham he-Hasid, the Jewish Sufi." (*Journal of Semitic Studies 26,* 1981: 47-72), p. 49, note 7.

57. All information from this paragraph comes from Fenton, Paul. "A Mystical Treatise on Prayer and the Spiritual Quest from the Pietist Circle." (*Jerusalem Studies in Arabic and Islam 16,* 1993: 137-175), pp. 138-142.

58. Ibid. pp. 141-142.

59. Maimonides, Obadyah. *Treatise of the Pool* (Paul Fenton, trans.), p. 5.

60. Ibid. p. 69.

61. From a personal letter to the author from Abdallah Schleifer, February 16, 2010.

62. Ventura, David Romano. *The Jews in Cordoba (X-XII Centuries).* (Jesus Peleaz de Rosal, ed.). (Cordoba, Spain: Ediciones El Almendro, 1985: 139-153), p. 140.

63. Maimonides, Moses. *Guide for the Perplexed* (intro). (M. Friedlander, trans.). (New Yoek: Dover, 1956), p. xviii.

64. Blumenthal, David. *Maimonides: Prayer, Worship and Mysticism.* (*www. js.emory.edu/blumenthal*), p. 9.

65. Goitein, S.D. *Jews and Arabs.* (New York: Schocken Books, 1964), p. 146.

66. Fenton, Paul. *Jewish Mystical Leaders and Leadership in the 13th Century* (Moshe Idel and M. Ostow, eds.), p. 136.

67. Lobel, Diana. *A Sufi-Jewish Dialogue: Philosophy and Mysticism in Bahya ibn Pakuda's "Duties of the Heart."* (Philadelphia: University of Pennsylvania Press, 2006), p. 11.

68. Ibid. pp. xiii-xiv.

69. Quoted in "The Influence of Islamic Thought on Maimonides," *Stanford Encyclopedia of Philosophy*, p. 14.

70. Quoted in Pines, Shlomo. "The Limitations of Human Knowledge According to Al-Farabi, ibn Bajja and Maimonides." *Studies in Medieval Jewish His-*

*tory and Literature* (Isadore Twersky, ed.). (Cambridge, MA and London: Harvard University Press, 1979: 82-109), p. 89.

71. Ibid. p. 89.

72. Ibid. p. 89.

73. "The Influence of Islamic Thought on Maimonides," *Stanford Encyclopedia of Philosophy*, p. 21.

74. Maimonides, Moses, *Guide for the Perplexed* (intro), (M. Friedlander trans.), p. xxi.

75. Quoted in Peters, F. E. (ed.). *Judaism, Christianity & Islam III*. (Princeton, NJ: Princeton University Press, 1990), pp. 323-324.

76. Quoted in Ibid. p. 321.

77. Blumenthal, David. "Maimonides Intellectualist Mysticism and the Superiority of the Prophecy of Moses." *Approaches to Judaism in Medieval Times* (David Blumenthal, ed.). (Chico, California: Scholars Press, 1984), p. 38.

78. Ibid. pp. 37-38.

79. "The Influence of Islamic Thought on Maimonides," *Stanford Encyclopedia of Philosophy*, p. 28.

80. Ibid. p. 25.

81. Blumenthal, David. *Approaches to Judaism in Medieval Times*, (David Blumenthal, ed.), p. 37.

82. Kiener, Ronald. "Ibn Arabi and the Qabbalah: A Study of Thirteenth Century Iberian Mysticism." (*Studies in Mystical Literature, Vol. 2, N. 2,* 1982: 26-50), p. 40.

83. Quoted in "The Influence of Islamic Thought on Maimonides," *Stanford Encyclopedia of Philosophy*, p. 17.

84. Quoted in Fadiman, James and Frager, Robert (eds.). *Essential Sufism*. (New York: HarperCollins, 1997), p. 89.

85. Blumenthal, David. "Maimonides: Prayer, Worship and Mysticism," p. 6.

86. Blumenthal, David. "Philosophic Mysticism: The Ultimate Goal of Medieval Judaism." (www.js.emory.edu/blumenthal ), p. 3.

87. Blumenthal, David. *Approaches to Judaism in Medieval Times*, (David Blumenthal, ed.), pp. 29, 34.

88. Idel, Moshe. *Studies in Ecstatic Kabbalah*. p. 124.

89. Blumenthal, David. "Maimonides: Prayer, Worship and Mysticism," p. 4.

90. Idel, Moshe. *Studies in Ecstatic Kabbalah*, p. 107.

91. Halkin, A.S. "Classical and Arabic Material in ibn Aknin's 'Hygiene of the Soul.'" (*Proceedings of the American Academy of Jewish Research 14,* 1944: 27-147), p. 67.

92. Quoted in Idel, Moshe. *Studies in Ecstatic Kabbalah*, p. 146.

93. Ibid. p. 146.

94. McGaha, Michael. "Naming the Nameless, Numbering the Infinite," (*YCGL 45/46,* 1997/1998: 37-53), p. 42.

95. Koran 17:1 "Most glorified is the One who summoned His servant (Muhammad) during the night, from the Sacred Majid (of Mecca) to the farthest place of prostration, whose surroundings we have blessed, in order to show him some of our signs. He is the Hearer, the Seer."

96. Baralt, Luce Lopez. *Islam in Spanish Literature: From the Middle Ages to the Present* (Andrew Hurley, trans.). (Leiden: E. J. Brill, 1992), p. 119.

97. McGaha, Michael. *YCGL 45/46*, p. 42.

98. Rabinowitz, Louis Isaac. *Encyclopaedia Judaica* (Cecil Roth and Geoffrey Wigoder, eds.).

99. Goitein, S. D. *Jewish Medieval and Renaissance Studies* (Alexander Altmann, ed.), p. 152.

100. Fenton, Paul. *Jewish Mystical Leaders of the 13th Century* (Moshe Idel & M. Ostow, eds.), p. 151.

101. Goitein, S.D. "A Jewish Addict to Sufism." (*Jewish Quarterly Review 44*, 1953: 37-49), p. 41.

102. Maimonides, Obadyah. *Treatise of the Pool* (Paul Fenton, trans.), p. 25.

103. Ibid. p. 24.

104. Ibid. pp. 27-28.

105. Ibid. p. 84.

106. Quoted in Chittick, William. *Sufism: A Short Introduction.* (Oxford: Oneworld Publishers, 2000), p. 143.

107. Quoted in Maimonides, Obadyah. *Treatise of the Pool* (Paul Fenton, trans.), p. 91.

108. Ibid. p. 92.

109. Quoted in Ibid. p. 71.

110. Ibid. p. 71.

111. Quoted in Fakhry, Majid. *Ethical Theories in Islam.* (Leiden: E. J. Brill, 1991), p. 213, note 19.

112. All information in this paragraph from Vajda, George. "The Mystical Doctrine of Rabbi Obadyah, Grandson of Moses Maimonides." (*Journal of Jewish Studies 6*, 1955: 213-225), pp. 223-224.

113. Ibid. pp. 223-224.

114. Ibid. p. 220.

115. Quoted in Miller, Elliot. "Sufis: The Mystical Muslims." (*Forward,* Spring-Summer 1986), p. 19.

116. Fenton, Paul. *Judeo-Arabic Studies: Proceedings of the Founding Conference of the Study of Judeo Arabic* (Norman Golb ed.), p. 100.

117. Quoted in Maimonides, Obadyah. *Treatise of the Pool* (Paul Fenton, trans.), p. 25.

118. Fenton, Paul. *Judeo-Arabic Studies: Proceedings of the Founding Conference of the Study of Judeo Arabic* (Norman Golb ed.), p. 95.

119. Information in this paragraph from Fenton, Paul. *Jewish Quarterly Review 75.*

120. Ibid. p. 41.

121. Ibid. p. 43.

122. Ibid. p. 45.

123. Fenton, Paul. *Jewish Mystical Leaders of the 13th Century* (Moshe Idel & M. Ostow, eds.), p. 153.

124. Fenton, Paul. *Jewish Quarterly Review 75*, p. 7.

125. Quoted in Fenton, Paul. *Judeo-Arabic Studies: Proceedings of the Founding Conference of the Study of Judeo Arabic* (Norman Golb ed.), p. 95.

126. Ibid. p. 95.

127. Fenton, Paul. *Jewish Quarterly Review 75*, p. 15.

128. Ibid. p. 9.

129. Ibid. p. 17.

130. Fenton, Paul. *Judeo-Arabic Studies: Proceedings of the Founding Conference of the Study of Judeo Arabic* (Norman Golb ed.), p. 96.

131. Ibid. p. 96.

132. Fenton, Paul. *Yuval IV*, pp. 124-126.

133. Fenton, Paul. *Jewish Quarterly Review 75*, p. 2.

# Chapter 4
# Sufi Influence on Spanish Jews

Of all the time periods and places covered in this book, the era of *al-Andalus* (Arab Spain, 8-15th centuries) is the age of Jewish-Muslim peace and respect that has been best dealt with by both scholars and popular writers. Recently, two movies ("Out of Cordoba," by Jacob Bender, 2010 and "Cities of Light," by the Unity Productions Foundation, 2007) have continued to move knowledge of this era of interfaith harmony into the consciousness of the general public.

In the atmosphere of mutual respect and cross-religious interactions of *al-Andalus*, the influence of Sufi mystics on Jewish thinkers was deep and prolonged. However, it is vital to note that this is but one piece of the puzzle – and though popular culture works have posited that this time period was discrete and lacked future resonance, in terms of this story of a mystical fraternity, the interactions in *al-Andalus* represent but one piece of a larger puzzle. Additionally, while some well-known Spanish Jewish thinkers' interest in Islamic mysticism have been extensively documented, such as Bahya ibn Pakuda (d. 1080), others outlined below are less known, such as Solomon ibn Gabirol (d. 1058). As such, even in this chapter, there is fodder for scholarly disagreement.

It is also important to note that the air of comity and mutual respect in Islamic Spain epitomized an atmosphere that was present to differing degrees throughout the whole of the Muslim world during this time period – from Baghdad to Jerusalem to Cairo to Cordoba – and the other aspects of this story must not become subsumed in the popular appreciation for what took place in Spain in medieval times.

### Al-Andalus

While the Maimonides clan enjoyed mostly positive relations with the Muslim authorities in Egypt, there sometimes was prejudice. Jews in Egypt during the early medieval period were well aware that they inhabited a different social sphere from their Muslim hosts – and the boundaries between the two, while porous at times, were well defined.

Simultaneously with and even predating the Jewish-Sufi movement in Egypt, Jews in *al-Andalus* enjoyed a Golden Age during which those same social boundaries were sometimes non-existent. Defined by astounding advances in virtually all social endeavors, from politics and economics to the arts and letters and religious education, this era allowed *"Sephardic"* Jews, as the Spanish Jews were known, to initiate a renaissance of Jewish culture unseen in the previous thousand years.

## Jews Arrive on the Iberian Peninsula

Jews had been present on the Iberian Peninsula as far back as 600 B.C.E. They arrived in that far-flung locale, a people banished from Arabia by Nebuchadnezzar (605–562 B.C.E.), the Babylonian King. By the second century of the Common Era, Jews had settled in great numbers around the western Mediterranean basin. For several hundred years, under pre-Christian Roman rule, Jewish life flourished.

Upon the Christianization of the Roman Empire (c. 325), Jewish life deteriorated and by the fourth century, the Jewish way of life was under tremendous pressure. After the Visigoth kings from northern Europe pushed the Romans out of Iberia in the 5th century, existence for the peninsula's Jews became tragically arduous. References to Jews at this time included such phrases as a "plague of Jews," the "leprosy of Jewish corruption" and a "contagious pestilence."[1]

## A Muslim Army of Liberation

The beleaguered Jewish population of Spain was happy to see Muslim invaders heading across the Straight of Gibraltar, to unseat the Visigoths in the early 8th century. For the Jews, they represented an army of liberation, not conquest. The Arabs trusted the thankful Jews so immediately that during the Muslim domination of Spain beginning in 711, Jewish citizens in newly subjugated territories were left as garrison forces to secure the conquered cities, as the victorious armies pushed north.[2] By 715, the yoke of Visigoth rule was lifted; the Muslim forces occupied most of the Iberian Peninsula.

The early willingness of the Spanish Muslims to entrust the most important facets of their government to Jewish citizens hardly flagged after these initial incidents. Officially, both Jews and Christians had a special designation under Islamic law – that of *dhimmi*, or protected people, due to their monotheistic beliefs. Both peoples, once subjugated to the temporal Muslim authority, needed only pay a monetary tax (*jizya*) to the ruling class, and then were under no further obligation.[3]

Jewish life under Muslim rule steadily improved for the first three centuries after the invasion. Jews were part of *Andalusian* society at every level, acting as tax collectors, police officers, secretaries of state and even prime ministers to Muslim rulers. They drew inspiration from Arabic poetry and the arts; read Arab treatises on everything from astronomy to medicine; studied the Koran and Arabic grammar, and spoke the language of their hosts fluently.

## A Jewish Golden Age

One of the first official acts undertaken by the Muslim authorities after their conquest of the Christian areas in Spain was to repeal the egregious laws passed by the Visigoths afflicting the Jews. Due to this sudden leavening of the life of their people, Jews flooded into Spain from North Africa to enjoy the new rights.[4] The Islamic milieu influenced Jewish life on all levels, creating a new conception of the Jewish intellectual as a member of the host society, in a manner unheard of in the annals of Jewish history. As Professor Michael McGaha notes in *The Jewish Mystics of Medieval Spain*:

> Of all the specific things that the Jews learned from the Spanish Arabs – including science, grammar, philosophy, poetry, forms of social organization – perhaps the one with the most sweeping effect was the ability to maintain two opposing sets of ideals: to belong to both Israel and the international class of intellectuals allowed for a universalism among the medieval *Sephardic* Jews [that was unheard of in prior epochs of the Diaspora]. These "courtier rabbis" were capable of a universalism that is inspiring to this day.[5]

By the middle of the 11th century, Jews were serving as prime ministers to Muslim kings – and Samuel ibn Naghrila, known as Samuel the *Nagid* (prince), rose to become general of the Granadan armies, fighting battles for the Muslim caliph over the course of 18 years (1038-1056) and never losing a military campaign. Ibn Naghrila was the first Jewish commander-in-chief since the time of Josephus' command, one thousand years before.[6]

Other Jewish princes serving Arab caliphs included Hasdai ibn Shaprut (d. 970, prime minister to Abd ar-Rahman III); Yehosef ibn Naghrila (d. 1066), son of Samuel in Granada; Isaac ibn Albalia (d. 1056) and Abraham ibn Muhajir (d. 1100) in Seville.[7] Ibn Naghrila's son, Yehosef, helped build the original Alhambra Palace in Granada,[8] the astounding, hilltop citadel that still captivates visitors to this day. Far from turning their back on the religion of their birth to facilitate their temporal gains, these highly placed Jews – the most powerful Israelites in the world for nearly one millennium on either side of the year 1000 C.E. – advocated on behalf of their co-religionists, both in Spain and abroad.

### Hasdai ibn Shaprut

Hasdai ibn Shaprut (d. 970; Cordoba) served as a senior physician, customs director and personal envoy for the Caliph.[9] From this position, he negotiated treaties for the Muslim crown with foreign embassies.[10] Ibn Shaprut used his position to further that of the Spanish Jews, receiving permission from the Caliph to bring Jewish books from the Talmudic academies of the East,[11] thereby allowing *Sephardic* Jews to interpret the Jewish religion for themselves, in light of their intellectual and scientific advances. Prior to that time, when Spanish Jews had questions of Jewish law and practice, they had had to request *responsa* (religious edicts) from the East, a process that might take years, and could yield responses out of keeping with their advanced culture. Ibn Shaprut also was able to have onerous tax laws – laws that penalized the minority population – removed from the books, lessening the burden on Jewish merchants.

Additionally, as physician and linguist for the Court, he translated a document from Greek that had been gifted from the Byzantine ruler to the Caliph, accomplishing what innumerable other medieval physicians had tried and failed to do – understand the recipe for synthesizing an ancient Greek wonder drug called *mithradate*, a compound of as many as 100 ingredients. Norman Roth notes in *Jews, Visigoths and Muslims in Medieval Spain* that this act was thought of as the single most important pharmaceutical accomplishment of the Middle Ages! The potion, as rediscovered by Ibn Shaprut, eventually included opium and survived as a viable pharmaceutical option into the 19th century.[12]

Like many great men of his age, Ibn Shaprut was also a poet and philosopher. Along with studying the Jewish manuscripts in his extensive library, Ibn Shaprut also found time to peruse the works of Arab scholars and mystics. Though he was primarily a statesman, his open-mindedness to Islamic culture set a precedent for later Spanish Jewish thinkers.

Finding Islam in the Torah

Much like the Jewish-Sufis of Egypt, who stated that they were hearkening back to Biblical ideas of spiritual worship with their Islamic innovations, the *Sephardic* Jews looked back into Judaism's past to justify their Muslim inspirations. These Arabized Jews took great pains to point out that far from mimicking their Muslim hosts, they were reclaiming ancient Jewish forms of worship that had, due to the Diaspora, become lost. As Professor Ross Brann (Milton R. Konvitz Professor of Judeo-Islamic Studies, Cornell University) states:

> The courtier-rabbis tried to justify the transformation of Jewish culture by identifying its sources as intrinsically Jewish rather than Arabic. Poets and thinkers argued that the substance, as well as the tenor, of their adapted Arabic culture actually was derived from Jewish tradition! To explain how this was possible, they reinvented the historical fiction that the cultural legacy of Biblical Israel, once complete, was lost through exile and dispersion; and they meticulously culled Biblical references to music, poetry and science and interpreted and embellished them in such a way as to warrant every one of their innovative intellectual and artistic endeavors.[13]

One of the most important facets of the host culture assimilated by the *Andalusian* Jews was the rich Arabic language, which came to define the Jewish verbal, literary and even religious spheres. Arabic poetry and grammar prompted Jewish writers, philosophers and mystics to completely rejuvenate their understanding of their own ancient tongue – and even look afresh at the "Hebrew Koran," or *Torah*. Everything Hebrew came to be understood through the newly acquired idiom that, as a cognate language to their own, offered an important manner of helping reconsider the ancient tongue of Israel. And along with these other facets of Islam that inspired Jews during this period, Sufism became central to helping Jews expand their own understanding of Jewish religious and spiritual possibility.

### Sufism Comes to Spain

The earliest avenue of Sufi inspiration for *Sephardic* worship was through Muhammad ibn Masarra (d. 931; Cordoba). According to Professor Miguel Asin Palacios in his *Mystical Philosophy of Ibn Masarra and His Followers*, Ibn Masarra introduced the practice of Sufism into southern Spain. There is no mention of Sufism *per se* prior to the return of this Islamic thinker from Mecca in the early 10th century.[14]

In addition to his introducing Islamic esotericism to Iberia, his ideas were a vital influence on the thought of many Spanish Jews. For instance, he was one of the most important inspirations on the Jewish-Sufi Solomon ibn Gabirol (d. 1058, see below). Specific Masarrian conceptions also are found in writings of 12th-century Jews such as Judah Halevi (d. 1141), Moses ibn Ezra (d. 1138), Samuel ibn Tibbon (d. 1190) and others. According to Asin Palacios:

> [These Jewish thinkers all] alluded with more or less precision to a supposed … book called *Of The Five Substances*, which must have contained the complete system of … Ibn Masarra's thought. Flagrant analogies were clearly indicated between the technical terms, symbols and ideas [of the Jewish writers] and Arabic fragments of [Masarrian inspiration] … Moreover, as the philological analysis of these rabbinic texts demonstrates that they are not original, but a literal version of an Arabic source, the dependency of these Spanish Jews on Ibn Masarra is indisputable.[15]

Following on Ibn Masarra's introduction of Sufism into Spain, hundreds of Islamic masters contributed to the development of this mystical system in *Andalusia*, culminating in the vast synthesis accomplished by the Spanish-born Muhyiddin ibn Arabi (d. 1240).[16] Spanish Jewish practice was deeply marked by this influence.

### Poetry

A central manner of expressing these novel spiritual ideas was through the newly assimilated Arabic language. And a primary inspiration for Jews of the Arabic language and grammar was through the elegant poetry of Muslims, both mystical and secular. As Ross Brann notes in *The Compunctious*

*Poet: Cultural Ambiguity and Hebrew Poetry in Muslim Spain*, Jewish poets responded to this literary influence by borrowing from it, translating it into a Jewish framework based on the Bible[17] – and then claiming that the new poetics stemmed from Jewish antecedents.[18] And these poets were hardly ancillary to medieval culture: In *Andalusia*, there was no greater calling than that of a poet – and these wordsmiths played a role similar to movie stars, politicians or other celebrity icons in our contemporary society.

The best poetry of the era was deeply sensual, often treating themes such as unrequited love, debauched gatherings and other profane and sometimes illegal pursuits. Mimicking the Sufi poetic device of using worldly images to capture the ideal of Divine love, medieval Jews "transformed the human impulse to cherish love and beauty into a sacred obligation to bless God."[19] While this device was novel within the recent Jewish literary vernacular, it had been known for centuries to the Sufis, for whom it had already caused problems, and the occasional charge of heresy. *Sephardic* Jews were so taken with the new poetics, Diana Lobel notes in *A Sufi-Jewish Dialogue: Philosophy and Mysticism in Bahya ibn Pakuda's "Duties of the Heart,"* that erotic Arabic wine-poetry found its way into the *Sephardic* synagogue liturgy, even on the holiest of days![20]

One of the earliest and most important Jewish thinkers to take over the Arabic style was Samuel ibn Naghrila, the *Nagid* (d. 1056), the statesman-poet. Due to his elevated social position, his status at the head of the early generations of Jewish poets in Spain and the quality of his work, he had a great influence on successive *Sephardic* poets. Here is a short example of his work:

> In the cup is my allotted share and portion, for it is
> my beloved whom I desire and who desires me.
> Wherever I find goblets I
> dwell and lodge, my heart merry.

As we have already seen in the chapter on Sufism, wine imagery was a central metaphor for Sufi poets, signifying the rarified air of true mystical worship, or being "drunk" on God (*sukr*), as opposed to settling for the "grapes" of exoteric religious observance. The idea of desiring the "beloved" (or God) was a central Islamic mystical theme, as well. As Professor Ross Brann notes, woven in with these Sufi images are Biblical references, bringing together allusions to a Psalm (16:5, "The Lord is the portion of my inheritance and of my cup") and the Song of Songs (3:1, "By my night on my bed, I sought him whom my soul loveth"), seamlessly with the Islamic-inspired imagery.[21] Although one recent scholar has referred to wine poetry such as this as a "lighthearted knocking at hell's gate,"[22] it was in keeping with Sufi spiritual imagery of the time – and the Jewish-Sufi leanings of *Sephardic* Jews.

Discomfort with the sensual imagery of this poetry also was present at the time that the poet-rabbis were active.

> Even during the heyday of the school, Yehosef ibn Naghrila [son of Samuel], who edited his father's *diwan* [poems], cautions readers that the Nagid's erotic poetry is to be interpreted allegorically. "Though some of [the poems] include erotic themes," opined Yehosef, "[my father] believed these to be metaphors for the community of Israel and the like, just as is found in the writing of the prophets. God will reward him for his intention. Anyone who interprets them in a way contrary to his intention will bear his own guilt."[23]

This echoes the problem encountered by the great Sufi saint Muhyiddin ibn Arabi, who was forced to write a commentary on his imagery to explain its mystical import, after his students accused him of having a licentious affair.

## Solomon ibn Gabirol

Perhaps no single *Sephardic* Jew did more to knit Islam and Judaism together at their cores than Solomon ibn Gabirol. This seminal Jewish mystic belongs to the breed of artists and writers who are better appreciated posthumously. A stunted, angry man with a life-long skin condition,[24] Ibn Gabirol skulked from town to town throughout Spain during his short life (1020-1058), alternately wooing benefactors with his pen and then turning them against him with his difficult personality. "Arrogant, irascible and a bit of a misanthrope,"[25] Ibn Gabirol so disgusted his contemporaries that his greatest philosophical work, *Meqor Hayyim* (The Source of Life), was consigned to obscurity among his contemporary Jews. Another work of his, however, *Keter Malkuth* (The King's Crown), had a profound effect on medieval Jewish thought, introducing Sufi ideas into medieval Judaism, and becoming one of the important building blocks of the nascent Kabbalistic system.

After Ibn Gabirol's death, his star rose. Within 100 years of his demise, he already was considered one of the greatest Jewish thinkers and poets of his age and by our day, some contemporary scholars have described him as the greatest Jewish poet of all time.

### A Jewish-Sufi

Ibn Gabirol assimilated ideas from a variety of Muslim influences. Professor Michael McGaha asserts that Ibn Gabirol borrowed ideas from the Muslim *Rasa'il Ikhwan as-Safa* (Epistles of the Brethren of Purity, Baghdad, 10th century) to such an extent that after the Bible, it was his primary source of inspiration.[26] Like most of the Sufi-leaning Jews to postdate him, Ibn Gabirol probably believed that he was, in fact, recovering ancient Jewish teachings that had fallen into disuse due to centuries in exile, and had been appropriated by Islam.[27]

In addition to being inspired by the *Ikhwan as-Safa*, Ibn Gabirol followed the teachings of the great Sufi mystic Muhammad ibn Masarra (d. 931). Miguel Asin Palacios states that Ibn Gabirol is one of two *Andalusian* mystics who further developed Ibn Masarra's thought – the other being the great Sufi philosopher Muhyiddin ibn Arabi (d. 1240). As Asin Palacios relates, the Jew Ibn Gabirol and the Muslim Ibn Arabi were:

> Two lights radiating from the same center, since their mystic and theosophical systems shared in the identical Masarrian orientation. For both, the beginning was the concept of God as an absolutely simple being, whose essence is unknowable. Both represent Him with the symbol of light. For both, the creation is an effect of the love or merciful will of the One. The same allegories of the mirror and the blowing of the divine breath are used to exemplify the production of the cosmos. Above all, the reality and concept of spiritual matter, which is the true key to the Masarrian system, are presented in the *Futuhat al-Makkiyya* [*Meccan Revelations of Ibn Arabi*] with the very same outline as that of the *Meqor Hayyim* [*Source of Life of Ibn Gabirol*].[28]

Divine Emanations

Many of the ideas and terms that Ibn Gabirol borrowed from his Islamic mentors became the basic building blocks of the Kabbalistic system.[29] Peter Cole (2007 MacArthur Fellow "Genius Award"), translator of Ibn Gabirol's poetry, explains Ibn Gabirol's theory of the movement of God's energy:

> The conjunction of Universal Form and Matter gives rise to the simple substances, including intellect, soul and nature, and the chain of emanation extends down into the corporeal world and all its parts. The emanation of divine energy Ibn Gabirol likens to light from the sun – but not to the sun itself; or to intelligent acting in the limbs of its body, [or] … to a fountain whose flow transcends all temporal and spatial dimension. In this way the process of creation is continuous and ongoing at all levels at all times in a universal chain of transformation reaching from that pure source to the lowest point of the cosmos and back up to its unknowable origin.[30]

In this brief paragraph we find explicated the inner workings of Kabbalistic theory. This exact sense of God's movement from an uncreated upper region, down through various created spiritual "substances" and then back again into the Godly sphere, defines the theological foundation upon which would be built the tomes of Kabbalistic thinking, including the *Sefer Bahir* (Book of Clarity, c. 1230), *Sefer Zohar* (Book of Splendor, c. 1295) and others.

Like so much else in Ibn Gabirol's thought, this conception can be traced to Ibn Masarra.  As Angus Macnab describes Ibn Masarra's ideas concerning the Divine emanations, in his "Sufism in Muslim Spain:"

> Ibn Masarra's doctrine has a cosmological starting point.  The creation of the world is explained as a series of "emanations" from God, which constitute the multiple "levels" of reality, themselves manifestations of the Supreme Reality, which Itself remains transcendent and un-mani-fested.[31]

From this general outline, Ibn Gabirol codifies the ten stations through which this Divine emanation passes, which coalesced a couple of hundred years later into the ten *Sephirot* of the Kabbalah.  While the "ten categories" may be traced back to Plotinus (d. 270), and often have been by scholars (or sometimes misattributed to Aristotle), Ibn Gabirol's direct influence stemmed from Islamic interpretations of the earlier thinker's ideas.  In addition to Ibn Masarra, Ibn Gabirol was influenced by the *Ikhwan as-Safa* (Brethren of Purity),[32] which translated ancient ideas into the Sufi and Islamic worldview a century before Ibn Gabirol worked.

Later Kabbalists quoted Ibn Gabirol's work verbatim, borrowing from his Jewish-Sufi language and imagery to describe the inner workings of God's mind.  There are so many similarities between the great poet and the Kabbalistic tract the *Zohar* that one 19th-century Jewish scholar even hypothesized (erroneously) that Ibn Gabirol's work and the *Zohar* both stemmed from the same ancient Jewish source.[33]  Ibn Gabirol's work most probably did affect Moses de Leon, author of the *Zohar* (who wrote more than 200 years after Ibn Gabirol's death), though the shared "source" was almost certainly the Sufis.

### *'Ilm al-Huruf* (Science of the Letters)

Another quote illustrates the manner in which Ibn Gabirol foreshadowed many ideas important to later Jewish mysticism.  The following paragraph from the *Meqor Hayyim* (The Source of Life) echoes Sufi conceptions concerning the "Science of the Letters" and influenced later Jewish prayer methods based on this Islamic mystical practice.

> One can compare creation to a word, which man utters with his mouth.  In man's expression of the word, its form and meaning are registered upon the hearing of the listener and in his mind.  Along the same lines it is said that the exalted and holy creator expresses His word, and its meaning is registered in the substantiality of matter, and matter pre-serves that meaning, in other words, that created form is imprinted in matter and registered upon it.[34]

The idea of creation being a "word," which becomes manifest in substance, may be traced to the Koran, where God states: "When We decree a thing,

We need only say 'Be!' and it is" (16:40). Professor William Chittick notes in *Sufism: A Short Introduction*:

> In other words, each thing in the universe comes into existence as a result of God's spoken word ... On God's part, speech only occurs through the divine Breath known as the "Spirit," the same spirit that was blown into Adam's clay.[35]

Muhyiddin ibn Arabi, Ibn Gabirol's Islamic spiritual counterpart, says in his *Futuhat al-Makkiyya* (Meccan Revelations):

> The Breath of the All-merciful bestows existence on the forms of the possible things, just as the human breath bestows existence on letters. So, the cosmos is God's words in respect of this Breath ... And He has reported that His words will not be spent, so His creatures never cease coming into existence, and He will never cease being a Creator.[36]

Here, Ibn Arabi references two Koranic passages:

> If the waters of the sea were ink with which to write the words of my Lord, the sea would surely be consumed before His words were finished, though we brought another sea to replenish it. (18:109) And: If all of the trees in the earth were pens, and the sea, with seven more seas to replenish it, were ink, the writing of Allah's words could never be finished. (31:27)

The idea that God's act of creation representing the speaking of a word ("God said ..." Genesis 1:3) hearkens back to the *Torah*, but the manner in which Sufis interpret this primal moment stems from the Prophet Muhammad's revelation. The idea of creation being a "word" continuously spoken became central to Sufi interpretations of the Koran, and to Islamic spiritual prayer methods, as well.

The Sufis believe that since creation is a "word" that also is written in the Koran, the letters that comprise the words of the holy book have tremendous mystical import. The esoteric meanings to the individual *letters* of the Holy Writ, separate from the words that they comprise, were revealed to Islamic sages through inspiration. As noted in Chapter 2, this dynamic led to the creation of the *'Ilm al-Huruf* (Science of the Letters), a grammatical/mystical manner of conceiving language, and using the sounds of the individual letters themselves as spiritual engines to help drive the Sufi through various spiritual stations (*maqamat*) on the way to complete ego annihilation (*fana*) and then subsistence in God (*baqa*).

Long before Ibn Gabirol lived, Islamic mystics were writing esoteric treatises on the properties of the Arabic alphabet. Muhammad ibn Masarra introduced this mystical doctrine into Spain, with his work *Kitab Khawass al-Huruf* (Book of the Characteristics of the Letters). His theory posited that the 14 esoteric letters (of the 28 total letters in the Arabic alphabet), each of which stood at the head of a Koranic *Surah* (chapter), represent the universe in its entirety. He drew his ideas from the work of the earlier Sufi thinker Sahl al-Tustari (d. 896).[37]

In terms of Jewish thought, these ideas already had been presented in another Sufi-inspired pre-Kabbalistic tract, *Sefer Yetzirah* (c. 9th century, Book of Creation, see Chapter 5). From that book, Ibn Gabirol took the following idea, which stands as a basis for the Jewish Science of the Letters: "It has been said that the construction of the world was made through the inscription of numbers and letters in the air." It should be noted that an earlier Jewish thinker, Saadia Gaon (d. 942), had been drawn to this idea in the *Sefer Yetzirah*, proposing that this Science of the Letters should be a fundamental Jewish doctrine.[38] Ibn Gabirol helped codify and disseminate these ideas, from both Sufi and Jewish-Sufi sources, helping to establish the Science of the Letters as central to the Kabbalistic system.

This mystical letter system had far-ranging influence on the development of Jewish meditation practice, inspiring novel Jewish prayer methods. Even American popular culture has felt the reverberations of this far off Jewish-Sufi nexus, as the novel "Bee Season" (Myra Goldberg, Anchor Books, 2000), portrays a Jewish father teaching his daughter "alphabetic meditations and permutations" based on Abraham Abulafia's (a 13th-century Jewish-Sufi thinker, Chapter 5) methods, to aid in her spelling bee practice. As a reviewer of the book notes:

> The 13th-century Kabbalist Abraham Abulafia even developed ecstatic alphabetic meditations and permutations. These are the subject of Prof. Naumann's doctoral thesis and form the basis of the spelling-bee methods he teaches his daughter.[39]

To get from the Muslim thinker Jafar as-Sadiq (d. 765), who first devised the esoteric mystical letter system, through the 11th-century Solomon ibn Gabirol and 13th-century Kabbalist, Abraham Abulafia to a fictional 20th-century Jewish professor is a long road, and it will become clearer over the next few chapters just how this road was traveled.

Professor Elliot Ginsburg (University of Michigan) describes the specific Jewish prayer practice inspired by the Sufi Science of the Letters in the *Jewish Quarterly Review*:

> The adept essentially "deconstructs" the Biblical text, atomizing the weave of sentences and words into their elemental letters. Indeed, only through this obliteration of social language – the exoteric aspect of Scripture – can the primal language of Divine Names, the pure essence of the *Torah*, be recovered. The mystic variously chants, writes and silently meditates on the letter combinations, reconstituting *Torah*

and uncovering its divine core.  The radical linguistic transformation creates a parallel transformation of the adept's consciousness.  As the ordinary cognition founded on social language is overcome, the mystic's mind is said to become receptive to higher knowing, the influx of divine inspiration.[40]

Although Ibn Gabirol is one of the early Jewish thinkers to take inspiration from this Islamic prayer method, he would certainly not be the last.

### Keter Malkuth

The Science of the Letters and the image of Divine emanation leading to the ten distinct levels of God's power (which helped create the *Sephirot* – stations – of the Kabbalah), as vital and far ranging as they were, do not define the boundaries of Islamic influence on Ibn Gabirol's thinking.  One work after another shows the unmistakable mark of earlier Sufi thinkers.  In Ibn Gabirol's greatest poem *Keter Malkuth* (*Keter*, or "crown," came to represent the highest rung on the Kabbalistic Tree of life and *Malkuth*, or "king," the lowest), in addition to the Masarrian influence, may be found swaths of material bearing a strong relationship to the work of Abu Muhammad Ali ibn Hazm (d. 1064), a contemporary to Ibn Gabirol, who was one of the most powerful Muslim thinkers of this fertile period.[41]

In this treatise, as well, the spiritual levels that Ibn Gabirol outlines for humans correspond directly to the Sufi Way.  As Michael McGaha notes in *The Jewish Mystics of Medieval Spain*:

> In *Keter Malkuth*, Ibn Gabirol writes that God has established "under the Throne of Glory a level for all who were righteous in spirit … a place of position and vision for souls that gaze into the mirrors of the palace's servants, before the Lord to see and be seen."  The word "place"… appears to correspond to the Sufi technical term *maqamat* – the levels through which the Sufi progressively returns to God through ever greater identification with the divine traits.[42]

While originally disdained by more traditional Jews contemporary with Ibn Gabirol for its "innovations," *Keter Malkuth* recently has been translated into English (on seven different occasions), German, French, Italian, Dutch, Yiddish, Latin, Persian and Arabic.  Additionally, selections from this treatise appear in prayer books of Jewish communities throughout the world, where it has become part of the liturgy of Yom Kippur, the holiest day on the Jewish calendar.[43]  How many contemporary Jewish worshippers realize that they spend part of this vital Jewish holiday reciting Sufi-inspired odes, as they plead with God for understanding and forgiveness?

*Meqor Hayyim*

In his spiritual masterpiece *Meqor Hayyim* (The Source of Life), Ibn Gabirol dispenses with the medieval Jewish device of lacing the text with quotes
from the Bible, and the work takes on a decidedly Sufi orientation. In looking at a few of the phrases from the book, we find clear Islamic influence:

> *Student*: What is the proof that the motion of matter and the other sub-
> stances is desire and love? *Master*: Because it is apparent that desire
> and love are nothing but an effort to join the beloved and be united with
> it, and matter makes an effort to join form.[44]

Here we see early echoes in medieval Jewish thought of the Sufi goal of
Divine union with God, more than a century before Moses Maimonides
would use the Sufi term *ittihad* to describe man's *approach* to God during
prayer. Ibn Gabirol is less circumspect about this Sufi ideal than was Maimonides, even though, as we have seen, the idea of a pure, unitive prayer ran
directly counter to Jewish tradition, and could even be considered heretical.

In *Meqor Hayyim*, Ibn Gabirol hints at the movement of the Divine
force that would come to underlie the Kabbalistic conception of this power,
using decidedly Sufi imagery:

> The creation of all things by the Creator, that is, the emanation of form
> from the first source, which is to say, the will, and its overflowing
> across matter resembles the upwelling of water flowing from a foun-
> tain and descending ... except that this flow is unceasing and entirely
> outside of motion and time ... And the imprinting of form in matter,
> when it reaches it from the will, is like the return of the form of one who
> is gazing in the mirror.[45]

Here we find central Islamic mystical images echoed by Ibn Gabirol. When
he says that the "emanation ... resembles an upwelling of water flowing
from a fountain," he is repeating the central Islamic theme of the interior
pool, which must be completely cleansed so that the pure waters of the
Creator can flow into it. We saw in the last chapter how Obadyah Maimonides (d. 1265) drew on earlier Islamic source material (and perhaps Ibn
Gabirol, as well) to utilize this exact image, in his mystical tract *Al-Maqala
al-Hawdiyya* (The Treatise of the Pool).

The mirror also is a central Sufi image, representing the light of true
understanding. According to Miguel Asin Palacios, for Ibn Masarra, Ibn
Arabi and Ibn Gabirol, "the same allegories of the mirror and the blowing
of the divine breath are used to exemplify the production of the cosmos."[46]

Further Sufi Inspirations

Ibn Gabirol's personal masterpiece *Ani ha'Ish* (I am the Man), a spiritual biography in the form of a poem, is almost completely based in Sufi themes, from the two central ideas down to the smallest image and concept in it.[47] And *Sefer Meshalim* (The Choice of Pearls), another ethical/philosophical text, shares so much with Sufi philosopher al-Ghazali's (d. 1111) *Ethics*[48] that the two authors almost assuredly drew on the same Islamic sources. Ibn Gabirol channels other Arabic/Sufi writers, to the extent that his writings are often unrecognizable as necessarily Jewish. His ethical treatise, *Tikkun Middot ha-Nefesh* (The Improvement of the Moral Qualities), written in Arabic when the poet was 24, is modeled on Arab ethical handbooks such as Abu Bakhr al-Razi's (d. 925; Persia) ninth century *Book of the Treatment of the Soul*.[49]

### Sensual Poetry

The Islamic mystics inspired Ibn Gabirol's poetic language as well. He utilizes sensual Sufi poetic devices, which then helped inspire Kabbalistic terminology, as well as later *piyyutim* (religious poems) of the synagogue liturgy.[50] He makes use of Sufi ideas of attraction between God and the universe, and between man and God, in passionate terms.[51] As we will see in the next chapter, the impetus for the sensual/spiritual love affair grew fervent in the works of subsequent Spanish Kabbalists.

A cursory look at an excerpt of Ibn Gabirol's poetry shows strong Sufi influence, as he uses mystical vocabulary that was quite common to Muslim writers:

Friend, lead me through the vineyards, give me wine,
And to the very brim shall joy be mine;
Perchance the love you pledge me with each cup
May rout the troops around my care's ensign.

And if, in love for me, eight toasts you drink,
Fourscore the toasts in love for you I link;
And should I pre-decease you friend, select
Some spot where vine-roots twist, my grave to sink.

In grape juice have my body laved, and take
With divers spices, grape pips – they shall make
All my embalming. Mourn me not, guitar
And pipe with music's sound shall cheer my wake,

And on the place that shall conceal my mould
Let not the Earth be heaped and rocks be rolled
To raise a monument; to mark the spot
Rather a pile of wine jars, new and old.

This is quite similar to a quatrain by the Sufi poet Omar Khayyam (d. 1131; Persia):

> Ah, with the grape my fading Light provide,
> And wash my Body whence the life has died,
> And in the Windingsheet of Vine-leaf wrapt
> So bury me by some sweet Gardenside.[52]

It is important to reiterate that this fixation on wine does *not* represent hedonistic trifles written as diversions between more important poems and works. The grape – and wine in particular – are two of the most important Sufi symbolic images, a fact that sometimes has been misunderstood by scholars as they interpret Jewish-Sufi wine poetry as light diversions. "Grapes" stand for the normative religion, unfermented by the fires of mystical love, while "wine" represents the "drunken" possibility of the true God experience, provided by Sufism.

Understood in this light, Ibn Gabirol's "wine" poetry may be seen as a Sufi verse touting the advantages of the Sufi Way. Professor Raphael Loewe, a prolific scholar of Medieval Hebrew and Judaica for over fifty years, notes: "In point of fact, almost all the motifs that Ibn Gabirol uses in this short poem are paralleled in Arabic wine-poems; the wine-jars in place of tombstones which form its climax are borrowed from Ibn al-Mu'tazz (d. 908)."[53] Ibn Gabirol's "wine jars" might well represent spiritual attainment, the "death" of desire for anything but God, or a "dying before you die," as the Sufis refer to it.

### A Far-Ranging Influence

Despite obvious problems with Ibn Gabirol's character (a misanthrope) and his philosophy (strongly Islamic), much of his poetry and mystical thought heavily affected later Jewish writers and thinkers. Once the immediate Muslim influences on his philosophy became lost in the sands of time, the beauty of his ideas and presentation attracted traditional Jews. In addition to the selections of *Keter Malkuth* that are recited during the Yom Kippur liturgy, his religious poetry forms part of the regular Jewish prayer service to this day. One of the most important of Ibn Gabirol's liturgical works, *Adon Olam* (Lord of the World), still is chanted the world over during both the Friday evening and Saturday morning *Sabbath* services. And his legacy within the Jewish community has grown to the point that an important downtown Tel Aviv avenue bears his name.

Almost all subsequent Jewish mystics working in Spain based some, or much, of their philosophy on Ibn Gabirol – which naturally helped to open their minds to Sufi ideas. As we shall see in the biographies of the following Jewish thinkers, Ibn Gabirol was the single person about whom nearly all could agree, and who was a vital basis for a new direction in their thought.

Perhaps the most unlikely outcome of Ibn Gabirol's work, however, is how it served as a conduit for Sufi ideas to enter into medieval Christian mysticism. Ibn Gabirol's *Meqor Hayyim* (The Source of Life) was translated into Latin (from the original Arabic)[54] about a century after his death, and published under the title *Fons Vitae* by the author "Avicebron," the name by which Ibn Gabirol became known in Christian Europe.[55] Medieval European scholars believed it to have been produced by an Arab or perhaps even a Spanish Christian.

The influence of this Jewish-Sufi work was not incidental: Ibn Gabirol became known as a seminal medieval *Christian* thinker. As the translator of Ibn Gabirol's poems, Peter Cole notes:

> One important French scholar has gone so far as to say that a knowledge of 13th-century European philosophy is impossible without an understanding of *Fons Vitae* and its influence. Guillaume d'Auvergne, the mid-13th-century Bishop of Paris, declared that the author of *Fons Vitae* was the "most exalted of all philosophers."[56]

## Bahya ibn Pakuda

Bahya ibn Pakuda (d. 1080, Spain), a *dayyan* (judge) at the rabbinical court in Saragossa, Spain, was everything that Ibn Gabirol wasn't: modest, gentle and affable, traits sorely missing in the personality of the misanthropic genius 20 years his senior. Born in the same town in northeast Spain as Solomon ibn Gabirol, Ibn Pakuda was as deeply influenced by Islamic writers as was his older contemporary. Both viewed the Sufi Way as a regenerative power for calcified 11th-century Judaism, and both penned works that had far-reaching implications for the development of medieval Jewish mysticism.

These two Saragossans shared the basic underpinnings of their mystical philosophy. The five main points of their ideology, all of which may be traced to the Islamic mystics, were identical. Professor Michael McGaha identifies these common fundamentals in his *Jewish Mystics of Medieval Spain*:

> 1) God in His essence is unknowable; 2) our knowledge of God is based on the scriptures and on contemplation of His "traces" in creation; 3) since man is the apex of creation and a microcosm [of God], self knowledge is the surest path to knowledge of God; 4) the intellect is man's noblest quality, and he must use it both to understand his religion and to control his physical desires; 5) the purpose of human life is to acquire knowledge of God and to purify oneself so as to merit the life of the world to come.[57]

### Jewish on the Outside, Sufi on the Inside

Like other Jewish-Sufis, Ibn Pakuda's writing offers a Jewish response to the mysteries of this world, while basing his ideas liberally on Islamic mentors. He urges followers to abide by the outward laws of the *Torah*, including the *Sabbath*, the giving of charity, repetition of Jewish liturgy, etc. However, for Ibn Pakuda, there was a second level of observance: the inner duties, and these followed quite literally the Sufi Way. His treatise, *Kitab al-Hidaya ila Farad al-Qulub* (The Guide to the Duties of the Heart), shared as much of the Sufi Way with Jewish practitioners, as it did Jewish Biblical prescriptions.

Well aware that many of his fellow Jews would be suspicious of the foreign influence on his work, he offered the usual Jewish-Sufi apologia, pointing out that his Sufi path was really a reclaimed Jewish tradition, completely informed by the Hebrew Scripture. Professor Paul Fenton states:

> Despite the pain that he takes to disguise all material which was too specifically Islamic, replacing the Koranic quotations with Biblical ones, Bahya's long preamble betrays his apprehension at introducing a novel kind of devotion into the Jewish fold ... He could not, however, have concealed his use of Sufi sources from cultivated Jewish readers whose disapproval he anticipates, justifying himself with the Talmudic adage (*Megillah* 16A): "He who pronounces a word of wisdom, even of the Gentiles, is called a wise man."[58]

In putting together this classic work, Ibn Pakuda virtually ignored Jewish predecessors, concentrating instead on the teachings of the Sufis. Professor Michael McGaha observes that Ibn Pakuda was "deeply embarrassed by the contrast between the piety and asceticism of the Sufis, whose writings revealed a profound sensitivity to the subtlest workings of the human heart in its relationship to God, and the worldliness, ignorance and complacency of his fellow Jews,"[59] thus he opted to base his masterpiece on earlier Islamic writings.

The basic concept in the treatise stemmed from the *Rasa'il Ikhwan as-Safa* (Epistles of the Brethren of Purity). Drawing from that source, Ibn Pakuda maintained that the soul, connected to God at the root, was placed by Divine decree within the body, where it runs the risk of forgetting its nature and mission.[60] He asserted that his teachings would help remedy this situation, providing the soul impetus to remember its true mission, and reclaim its nearness to God.

*Guide to the Duties of the Heart* is divided into ten chapters, each representing a "gate," or a specific Sufi virtue upon which Ibn Pakuda expounds. The final gate is the approach and even acceptance of the lover by the beloved, echoing the Islamic mystical ideal Divine union.[61] Ibn

Pakuda's pathways through the ten stations (*maqamat*), when correctly followed, lead the pious Jew to the Sufi prayer ideal: union with the Divine (*ittihad*).

Ibn Pakuda's ten stations, added to the similar conception of ten Divine powers developed by his earlier contemporary, Solomon ibn Gabirol, helped formulate the ten *Sephirot* of the Kabbalistic Tree of Life. When both Ibn Pakuda's and Ibn Gabirol's works were read by later thinkers, Jewish practitioners had good reason to believe that the ten spiritual stations of the *Sephirot* did, in fact, stem from Jewish antecedents.

Professor Diana Lobel notes in *A Sufi-Jewish Dialogue: Philosophy and Mysticism in Bahya ibn Pakuda's "Duties of the Heart,"* that Ibn Pakuda was aware of virtually all major Sufi writers up to the time when he lived, quoting them frequently, though anonymously, and using their works as the basis for his own seminal Jewish work. His work breathed the same personal, devotional flavor as Hasan al-Basri (d. 728), Rabi'a (d. 801) and Dhu'l Nun al Misri (d. 859).[62] These Sufi masters bequeathed to the Jewish thinker the aphoristic language with which to express the nature of God's unity, the importance of perplexity and the essentials of pietistic worship.[63]

### On the Lookout

Ibn Pakuda introduces a Sufi tale to describe how far the Jewish seeker could go on the mystical path – expressing spiritual knowledge as being beyond the comprehensible. This idea of "learned ignorance" representing the highest intellectual stage of mystical awareness entered the stream of Jewish thought at that time, helping to influence Moses Maimonides' conception of Jewish spirituality, 150 years later.

The Sufi tale concerning "learned ignorance," as related by Bahya:

> One of them [i.e. the Sufis] was asked about God. He said, "God is one."
> The questioner said to him, "And what is He like?"
> He answered, "A great king."
> He asked, "Where is he?"
> He answered, "On the lookout."
> The questioner said to him, "I didn't ask about that!"
> He said to him, "Your question in those terms entails characteristics pertaining to the created, not to the Creator. As for the characteristics that we must verify with regard to our creator they are what I already said to you, since there is no way for us to see anything other than these."[64]

Ibn Pakuda's story rehearses an earlier rendition told about the Sufi, Yahya ibn Mu'adh (d. 871), which was found in al-Sulami's (d. 1021) *Abaqit al-Sufiyya* (The Classes of the Sufis) and then in al-Qushayri's (d. 1074) *Al-*

*Risala al-Qushayriyya Fi 'ilm l-Tasawwuf* (Epistle on Sufism).[65] The story, as it appears in al-Sulami's work:

> It was said to Yahya ibn Muadh: Tell me about God. What is He? He said, God is one. What is He like? An all-powerful king. Where is he? On the lookout. It was said: I didn't ask you about that. Yahya said: *That* is the description of the created. As for the description of the Creator, it is what I told you.[66]

The inspiration for this passage, like many others that inform medieval Jewish-Sufi thought, originates in the Koran, expressing the idea that God is "on the lookout," or not existent at any fixed point. In 89:14, the transgressions of Aad and Thamoud, two tribes that were destroyed due to their sins, are described: "Therefore your Lord poured upon them diverse punishments; surely your Lord is on the lookout."[67]

Clearly, in this sense, the term has a moralizing connotation, as well, portraying God as watching over the affairs of humankind so that He can punish and reward accordingly. However, as Professor Diana Lobel points out in *On the Lookout: A Sufi Riddle in Sulami, Qushayri and Bahya ibn Pakuda*, there is another manner in which to understand "on the lookout," and one which appears to be more germane to Ibn Pakuda's presentation of the Koranic idea:

> The term is meant to emphasize that God watches human beings wherever they are. God is always "on the way," in whatever "way" you might walk. It is this aspect of "on the lookout" that interests the Sufi story. One cannot find God as an answer to the question "where;" Yahya's assertion that God is on the lookout does not lock God into a place. God is aware of the world, but the world cannot find the one who is aware.[68]

Ibn Pakuda, unable to assume that his Jewish audience would recognize the Koranic allusion, relies on the phrase "on the lookout," itself. In this manner, he implies that the creator is known only by watching for traces of Divine wisdom in the manifested world. God cannot be "found" using the normal faculties of logic and reason, being beyond time and space, that is "on the lookout," and therefore must be intuited.

### Mur'qaba

In another section, Bahya develops the idea of *mur'qaba* (the state of vigilant awareness, leading to the understanding of God). This concept originated in the Koran (33:52): "God knows what is in your hearts." The Sufi contemporary of Ibn Pakuda, al-Qushayri explains this Koranic phrase with the well-known *hadith* (saying of the Prophet Muhammad): "Worship God as if you see Him, for if you see Him not, yet He sees you." Al-Qushayri avers that this represents the state of *mur'qaba*, the highest level of self-mastery and the victory on all fronts of the interior battle.

Quoting al-Qushayri, Ibn Pakuda explains how an aspirant can increase his awareness of God, until the Divine Essence enters into the seeker's inner consciousness:[69]

> If this point is repeated in the mind of the believer, and he reflects on it in his soul, God will be always present with him in his inner consciousness, and he will see Him with the eyes of his intellect ... If he continues to do this ... He will acquaint him with the secrets of His wisdom and open the door of knowing Him.[70]

In another instance, Ibn Pakuda draws on a *hadith qudsi* (a saying of God). As Diana Lobel notes, one passage from *Guide to the Duties of the Heart* sounds nearly identical to an interpretation of this *hadith* by the Egyptian Dhu'l-Nun al-Misri (d. 859), indicating a possible lineage from the *hadith qudsi*, through the 9th-century Sufi and then on to the Jewish thinker. According to the Islamic prophetic tradition:

> My servant draws near to me through nothing more loved by me than the religious duty I require of him. And my servant continues to draw near me through free acts of devotion (*naw'fil* or supererogatory worship), until I love him. And when I love him, I am the eye with which he sees and the ear with which he hears and the hand with which he grasps and the leg with which he walks.[71]

According to the interpretation provided by Dhu'l-Nun al-Misri:

> The knower [of God] becomes more humble every hour, for every hour is drawing him nearer to God. The knowers see without knowledge, without sight, without information received and without observation, without description, without veiling and without veil.[72]

Ibn Pakuda states in *Duties of the Heart*, echoing the ninth century Sufi:

> He enters the highest ranks of the pious friends of God ... and he will see with no eye, and hear with no ear, and converse with no tongue, and feel things with no senses, and sense these things with no need of logic.[73]

### Mirror of the Soul

Another important Sufi image, that of the mirror, helps illuminate how God can be understood, in the context of His being "on the lookout."

> Commentators interpret "on the lookout" in light of the [Arabic] verbal root *r-q-b*, which has the sense of "observation with care," and from which the Sufi term *mur'qaba* is derived. *Mur'qaba* is a state of attentiveness; the Sufi is taught to be ever conscious that God is aware

of him or her. *Mur'qaba* is like looking in the mirror and seeing God watching you. The story thus adds a playful ambiguity. Where is God to be found? Through one's looking. On the lookout is not only where God is, but where you are.[74]

This passage helps us understand the importance of the Sufi "mirror" image – and of polishing and keeping it clean. For God sees the image of Himself in humans as a reflection in the "microcosm," which offers a mirror to the "macrocosm." Spiritual impurities not only cloud human vision of the "within" that is synonymous with the "above," but they also sully the vista God has of Himself, which is seen only as a reflection in a spiritually pure receptor. Ibn Pakuda states that "anything found in the imagination is other than God; we must efface all images from the mind to find the Un-manifest One."[75]

This statement echoes one by al-Qushayri, who states: "Whatever the imaginer imagines out of ignorance that He is like, the intellect indicates that He is other than that."[76] The assumption by Jewish mystics of the Sufi idea of the "mirror" as the purest spiritual receptor, as seen in Ibn Pakuda, Obadyah Maimonides and others, helped to move the Jewish conception of "perceiving" or understanding God toward that of the Islamic mystics.

### Devequt

Ibn Pakuda connects the Sufi language of spiritual attainment with the Biblical language of clinging (*deveqa*), the exact term which came for later Jewish thinkers to represent the ideal of Divine union. He explains that when Proverbs 18:24 declares: "There is a lover who is closer than a brother," it indicates that one should cling (*deveqa*) to God through true and pure love.[77] This saying is mirrored in the *hadith qudsi* (saying attributed by Muslims to God): "I am closer to you than your jugular vein."

Ibn Pakuda's use of the exact terminology that the Islamic mystics utilized to represent the goal of the spiritual search, as well as his linking it with Scriptural passages, helped later Jewish mystics in Spain and Egypt to close the circle between the Jewish and Islamic mystical cores. For Egyptian Jewish-Sufis and Kabbalistic theorists, *devequt* came to mirror the Sufi ideals of *fana* and *baqa*, building on the vernacular of the earlier Jewish thinkers such as Ibn Pakuda.

### Reliance on Specific Sufi Thinkers

Passage after passage of Ibn Pakuda' *Guide* can be traced back to individual Islamic writers. The work of Al-Harith al-Muhasibi (d. 857; Baghdad) is particularly well represented, with ideas and whole passages of the 9th-century Muslim's work being imported faithfully into the Jewish treatise. Esoteric conceptions concerning duty (*fard*), the obligations of the seven limbs (the first of which is the heart) and ideas of love and awe[78] which show up in Ibn Pakuda's work, may all be found word-for-word, or nearly so, in al-Muhasibi's writings.

Moreover, the duties of faith (*iman*), repentance (*tawba*), reliance on God (*tawakkul*) and particularly purity of action (*ikhlas*) not only are central to Ibn Pakuda, but were to Muhasibi, as well, showing the clear influence of the one on the other.[79] Even the title of Ibn Pakuda's work echoes a short treatise by the Islamic thinker, who had penned *Questions Concerning the Actions of the Hearts and Limbs* nearly 200 years before the Jewish theologian lived.[80]

Other specific concurrences between Ibn Pakuda's ideas and earlier Muslims may be found throughout the book. In his introduction, Ibn Pakuda introduces the idea of the duties of the heart by telling a story about a sage who, as soon as he discharged his public duties and found himself alone with his dearest friends, stated: "Now spread the light," indicating that they should now concentrate on interior worship, the "duty of the heart." The "sage" Ibn Pakuda quotes is none other than the father of Sufism, Hasan al-Basri (d. 728), and the anecdote is taken verbatim from the 10th-century Sufi manual *Qut al-Qulub* (The Nourishment of the Heart), by Abu Talib al-Makki (d. 996).[81]

In another anecdote, Ibn Pakuda quotes directly the Second Caliph of Islam, Umar I (d. 644), referring to him as "one of the pious," in relating this story:

> One of the virtuous ones described how he found one of the pious laying in a desert land. He said to him: "Don't you fear the lions in your lying down in a place like this?" The man replied: "I should be ashamed before my Lord that He should see me fearing anything but Him."[82]

This passage unites rabbinic discussions of love and awe with Islamic literature, underscoring the centrality of dedication to God for every aspect of an aspirant's life.

Ibn Pakuda even quotes a famous Sufi saying by the female saint Rabi'a (d. 801), referring to her only as a "pious man:"

> Verily, I am ashamed to worship my Lord for His reward and punishment, because then I would be like the bad slave, who does his job only when he fears something, or hopes for something, and when he neither fears nor hopes, does nothing. I worship my Lord rather because He is worthy.[83]

Rabi'a had stated:

> O my Lord, if I worship these for the fear of hell, burn me in hell; and if I worship Thee for the hope of paradise, exclude me thence; but if I worship thee for Thine own sake, withhold not from me Thine eternal beauty.[84]

## Muhammad and the Koran

Even sayings of the Prophet Muhammad, and stories and passages from the Koran, are sprinkled throughout this tract. He introduces the idea of "hidden association:" the association of God with anything outside of Him. A usual representation of this spiritual mistake is one who makes a spectacle of his religious observance in order to win praise from other people. It shows that a person is more interested in the approval of other people, than in the joy of the unadulterated veneration of the Beloved. This runs directly counter to the central Sufi goal of equanimity. Ibn Pakuda brings together this Islamic conception of "hidden association," or polytheism (as it represents the worship of more than God — since one cares about God *and* the views of others) with the rabbinic dictum that the alien god within oneself is the inclination to evil.[85]

The concept of "hidden association" may be traced back into the Islamic past via several *hadith*, including: "The hidden desire and pretense are association/polytheism" and "The thing I would fear for you the most is pretense and the hidden desire."[86]

Perhaps the most astounding instance of the Prophet Muhammad's influence within the Jewish treatise is the *hadith* that explicates *Jihad*, or Holy War. Bahya cites a story, attributing it only to a Hasid, but which is taken from the life and words of the Prophet Muhammad:

> It was told of a pious man [Hasid] that he met some people returning from a great battle with an enemy. He said to them, "You are returning, praise be God, from a smaller battle [lesser *Jihad*], carrying your booty. Now prepare yourself for the greater battle [greater *Jihad*]." They asked, "What is the greater battle?" And he answered, "The battle against the instinct and its armies."[87]

The *hadith* from which Ibn Pakuda's story stems runs thusly: "When the prophet was returning from battle he said 'we have returned from the lesser *Jihad* to the greater *Jihad*.'" Even more astounding than this Islamic inspiration on Ibn Pakuda is that the Jewish thinker's version showed up verbatim in the earliest Hasidic tract *Toledot Ya'akob Yosef* (Jacob Joseph's Story) by Rabbi Jacob Joseph Polonnoy (d. 1769), in which the Baal Shem Tov's (Chapter 6) teachings are codified in print for the first time. This represents a direct influence of the Prophet Muhammad on the thought of 18th-century European Judaism.

## Ibn Pakuda, Maimonides and *The Guide for the Perplexed*

Ibn Pakuda's work became important to later Jewish thinkers, including Moses Maimonides, the Spanish Jewish-Sufis, Kabbalists and even 18th-century Hasidic masters, providing a bridge between early Islamic teachings surrounding the Prophet Muhammad and later Jewish practice. For example, Professor Diana Lobel points out that early in his book Ibn Pakuda quotes a Sufi sage in a short aphorism that ends up inspiring the title of Moses Maimonides' greatest philosophical tract, the *Guide for the Perplexed*. In Ibn Pakuda's words: "One of the knowers [of God] said, 'The more one knows God, the more one is perplexed by Him.'"

This "knower of God" is none other than the Dhu'l Nun al-Misri, as related in a quote by the 11th-century Sufi, al-Qushayri. This embodies a well-known Sufi ideal, as the 10th-century al-Junayd explains the statement: "When the intellects of rational beings reach the farthest limits of unity, they reach perplexity." This idea may be traced back to the beginning of Islam through a Companion of the Prophet Muhammad, Abu Bakr (d. 634, childhood friend of Muhammad and the First Caliph after the Prophet's death), when he says: "Glorified is He who made no way for his creation to know Him other than being unable to know Him."[88]

Moses Maimonides, who read Ibn Pakuda's work and took many ideas and quotes from it, was inspired by this particular conception enough to base the central theory of his tract on the Islamic conception of "mystical perplexity."

### A Far-Ranging Influence

Ibn Pakuda's text played – and continues to play – a profound role in the world of Jewish spirituality. His revolutionary mystical vision inspired numerous other Jewish ethical works in the centuries that followed.[89] The *Guide to the Duties of the Heart* became one of the most important Jewish pietistic works produced in the last one thousand years – and was among the first books ever printed in Hebrew (Naples, 1489). As Professor Paul Fenton mentions in his article, "Jewish Attitudes Towards Islam: Israel Heeds Ishmael," it has remained important reading for Jewish devotees, a living example of the profound assimilation of Sufi doctrines by the religion of Israel.[90]

Lastly, it is interesting to note that one of the three poems that Ibn Pakuda wrote in conjunction with this text, *Tokehah* (Admonition), was so beloved that it was adopted by the medieval Jews of Spain and Italy as part of the Yom Kippur (Day of Atonement) liturgy.[91]

### Judah Halevi

Judah Halevi (d. 1141; Holy Land), one of the pre-eminent *Sephardic* poets and thinkers of the 12th century, looked to the Sufis for spiritual guidance, as well. Born into a middle class family in Granada, he won a poetry contest as a young man that introduced him to Moses ibn Ezra (d. 1138), another *Andalusian* poet strongly influenced by the Arabic language and Muslim ideas. Halevi was forced from southern Spain after the Almoravide invasion from Africa at the end of the 11th century.

After being driven from southern (Muslim) Spain, he settled for a time in the Christian city of Toledo, where he served the town's elite as a doctor. However, after the murder of his Jewish benefactor (1108), Halevi became worried that he might be next and moved on, traveling throughout Spain and North Africa. His fame as a poet and thinker spread further and faster than his person – and he had contact with Jewish courtiers in North Africa, Egypt and France. He died in the Holy Land, just after completing a long planned pilgrimage to *Eretz* Israel (land of Israel).

Poetry

Halevi was known primarily as a poet – and over 800 of his works are still extant. It is important to remember that in 12th-century Spain, there was no more honorable or noteworthy undertaking than that of the poet – and poets expressed the cutting edge religious, philosophical and cultural issues of their day. Almost half of his surviving poems deal with religious subjects and, like many other *Andalusian* Jews, he wrote *piyyutim*, or religious hymns, for use in the synagogue during various Jewish festivals.[92]

His writing shows the same Islamic influences, as does that of many of his contemporary Jewish thinkers. His work often takes on the Sufi manner of describing the spiritual path in terms of the forlorn lover – portraying the aspirant in one poem as "one who becomes passionately in love with God, willing to die rather than be without him, because of the greatness of his love of being with Him and his pain in being apart from Him."[93]

In another poem about Jewish prayer, we see the strong influence of his Muslim contemporaries:

> With all my heart – O Truth – and all my might
> I love You, with my limbs and with my mind.
> Your Name is with me: Can I walk alone?
> With It for lover, how can I be lorn?
> With It for lamp, how can my light go dim?
> How can I slip with it the stick by which I stand?
> They mock, who do not understand: The shame
> I bear because I bear Your Name is pride to me
> Source of my life, I bless You while I live;
> My Song I sing to You while yet I breathe.[94]

Two specific Sufi-inspired ideas stand out in this brief passage. When Halevi states: "The shame I bear because I bear Your Name is pride to me," he is touching on the Sufi ideal of equanimity. As has been variously noted, for Muslims, the attainment of disinterest in what other people think of oneself is a vital rung on the ladder of spiritual attainment. Concerning oneself with other people's opinions represents "hidden association" and pantheism (the worship of more than one god), as it exhibits the worship of something other than God (the opinion of others).

Halevi also states: "With It [Your Name] for lamp, how can my light go dim?" The Koranic Chapter *Nur* ("light" – *Surah* 24) is of central importance to the Sufis and, via them, for medieval Jews. The Koran (24:35) states: "God is the Light of the heavens and the earth; The similitude of His Light is as if there was a niche; And within it a Lamp ... Light upon Light; God guides to His Light whom He will." Undoubtedly, Halevi was influenced, either directly from the Muslim holy book or through Muslim poetry, by this central Koranic image.

*Sefer ha-Kuzari*

Though Halevi was not considered a theologian – he was a physician and merchant, in addition to being a preeminent poet – he affected the direction of Jewish spirituality through his masterpiece, *Sefer ha-Kuzari* (The Book of the Khazars). This book is a fictionalized account of the true story of how the Khazars (c. 740-1250) of the Black Sea region converted to Judaism in the 8th century. Jacob Marcus (founder and director of the American Jewish Archives at Hebrew Union College) explains in *The Jew in the Medieval World*:

> About the year 740, many of the Khazars, a powerful Turkish tribe occupying the steppes of southern Russia, became converts to Judaism. More than two centuries later, the report of the existence of this Jewish kingdom aroused the curiosity of Hasdai ibn Shaprut [d. 970]. To satisfy his curiosity, he wrote to the ruler of the Khazars in about 960 and some time later received a letter from the Khazar King, Joseph. Fragments of the Khazar kingdom persisted into the 13th century.[95]

Halevi wrote a fictionalized account of the conversion, weaving spirituality in with his fantasy of the dialogue between the Khazar King and four spiritual leaders vying for his allegiance, a Christian, Muslim, "philosopher" and the Jewish leader, the Haber. Halevi's stated purpose was to provide an "apologia" for the primacy of the Jewish religion over that of Christianity and Islam. His claims of supremacy for the Jewish religion, however, included so much Islamic source material that the contemporary scholar, Diana Lobel recently published a book entitled: *Between Mysticism and Philosophy: Sufi Language of Religious Experience in Judah Halevi's Kuzari*. Lobel points out:

> Halevi does not mention the Sufis by name, but makes extensive use of Sufi terminology, appropriating and refashioning it to show his Jewish audience that the spiritual fruits promised by Sufism exist foremost within the living Jewish tradition ... images and vocabulary from Islamic mysticism form a prominent subtext to the *Kuzari*.[96]

### Halevi and Al-Ghazali

Halevi based important aspects of his Jewish mystical philosophy on the teachings of the great Islamic scholar and Sufi, al-Ghazali. According to Haim Zafrani (head of the Department of Hebrew Language and Jewish civilization at the University of Paris), the Jew Halevi was one of the first of any religion to accept the precepts of the central Islamic thinker. Halevi was inspired by al-Ghazali's belief that immediate religious experience is superior to deductive reasoning. Not wanting to misrepresent the great Sufi theologian, Halevi quotes directly from his texts.[97] Additionally, Halevi's criticism of Aristotle's philosophical system is based on al-Ghazali's critique of philosophy in his *Tahafut al-Falasifa* (The Incoherence of the Philosophers).[98]

Halevi also was strongly influenced by al-Ghazali's ideas on prophecy. Halevi's passage on the subject echoes nearly verbatim this one from al-Ghazali's *al-Munqidh min al-Dalal* (Deliverance from Error):

> The prophetic power (*al-nubuwwa*) is an expression signifying a stage in which man receives an eye possessed of a light, and in its light the unknown and other phenomena not normally perceived by the intellect become visible. Doubt about prophecy touches either its possibility, its existence or its belonging to a specific individual ... The proof of its possibility is the existence in the world of knowledge which could not conceivably be obtained by the intellect alone ... for whoever examines such knowledge knows of necessity that it can be obtained only by a Divine inspiration (*ilham*) and special help (*tawfiq*) from God most High ... The properties of prophecy beyond those just mentioned can be perceived only by taste (*dhawq*) as a result of following the way of Sufism.[99]

As Diana Lobel notes:

> Almost every statement in [al-Ghazali's] passage finds a parallel in Halevi. Like al-Ghazali, the Haber describes the gift of prophecy as an inner eye that sees what the intellect cannot perceive. The prophet regards others who do not possess this eye as blind people whom he or she must guide [the Sufi ideal of prophetic legislation]. Halevi is adamant, moreover, that prophetic vision is self-validating ... The prophets could not deny what they witnessed with the inner eye ... Halevi, too, characterizes the unique prophetic way of knowing God as *dhawq* [taste].[100]

Rabbi and scholar Israel Efros (Rector of Tel Aviv University), in his article *Some Aspects of Judah Halevi's Mysticism*, outlines how deeply is the Sufi influence on Halevi's conceptions of prophecy:

> Halevi's discussion of prophetic experiences follows so closely Ara-

bian patterns that his Hebrew translator occasionally finds only vague equivalents for his terminology, and is sometimes inconsistent and even contradictory ... All [his] distinctions ... are standard Mohammedan doctrine except for the necessary change of the "Talmud" to the "*Sunnah*," the "Bible" to the "Bible and Koran" and "Israel" to the "prophets culminating in Muhammad."[101]

Halevi had passed through Egypt on his way to the Holy Land, a few decades before the Maimonides clan settled in Fustat. Given Halevi's fame, his writings certainly were well known in Egypt during Moses Maimonides' lifetime. Maimonides' work shows influence by the earlier Spanish Jew, as his conceptions of prophecy have much in common with both al-Ghazali and Halevi.

### Other Sufi Influence

Halevi's *Sefer ha-Kuzari* borrows a number of other Islamic mystical ideas from various sources. For instance, his book contains an early treatise copied verbatim from Abd Allah ibn Sina (d. 1037). As Professor Shlomo Pines (Hebrew University) notes in *Shi'ite Terms and Conceptions in Judah Halevi's Kuzari*:

> Book Five [of the *Kuzari*] expounds the system of Ibn Sina. It seems evident that Judah Halevi was greatly impressed with [Ibn Sina], and he may have tried ... to adapt his own ideas or his own terminology, at least to some extent, to this newly discovered framework.[102]

In another instance, Halevi employs the Jewish-Sufi strategy of reading Sufi ideas backwards into the *Torah*. He quotes Psalm 34:9: "Taste and see the Lord is good," stating that intellectual pursuit of God is pointless, and that the spirit longs for "taste and witness" of the Lord. The words that he uses in this context, however, are well-known Sufi terms, *dhawq* (taste) and *mushahada* (witness). Halevi reinterprets Psalm 34 in light of Sufi conceptions, linking the Hebrew verbs of the original, *ta'amu* (taste) and *re'v* (see), with the Sufi ideas *dhawq* (taste) and *mushadah* (witness).[103]

### An Important Influence

As the *Encyclopaedia Judaica* notes, Halevi's importance on the development of Jewish mysticism is irrefutable: a titan in his own time, he wrote poetry specifically for his most famous contemporaries, including Moses ibn Ezra (d. 1138), Joseph ibn Zaddik (d. 1149, a *dayyan* in Cordoba who shared an office with the father of Moses Maimonides), Judah ibn Gayyat (c. 12th century, head of the *yeshiva* in Cordoba) and other poets, philosophers, religious scholars and nobles. His *Sefer ha-Kuzari* was influential within Kabbalistic circles into the 15th century,[104] providing one of many

Sufi avenues of influence on the development of medieval Jewish thought.

Halevi's inspiration resonated with Jews long after the medieval period – the *Encyclopaedia Judaica* also notes that his work had a marked influence on the direction of 18th-century Hasidism (see Chapter 6).[105] Even 19th- and 20th-century Jewish thinkers like Samuel David Luzzatto (d. 1865; descended from 16th-century Safed Kabbalists) and Franz Rosenzweig (d. 1929; a collaborator with Martin Buber) saw in *Sefer ha-Kuzari* some of the most important medieval Jewish ideas. And Abraham Isaac Kook (d. 1935; chief rabbi for British Palestine) saw in Halevi's works "the most faithful description of the particular qualities of the Jewish religion."[106]

## Moses ibn Ezra

Moses ibn Ezra (d. 1138) was born in Granada, acquired a comprehensive Jewish and Arabic education and eventually held an important civil position in the city of his birth. An early supporter of Judah Halevi, he was able to act as his patron until 1090, when the Almoravides overran Granada and Ibn Ezra was forced to flee. He spent his later life as a broken man, wandering throughout a Christian Spain that he never understood, suffering delusions related to his niece and finally being obliged to seek the help of patrons, whom he had to lionize with his poetry in return for their aid.

Ibn Ezra was one of the most prolific poets of medieval Spain, and his work served as a model for later writers. Like so many other medieval poets, he wrote extensive numbers of liturgical works, *piyyutim* (liturgical songs) and *selihot* (prayers). And, like so many of his co-religionists, Ibn Ezra's sacred poetry includes ideas, images and wording directly influenced by Arabic literature.[107]

Two of the most important influences on Ibn Ezra's theological views were Solomon ibn Gabirol and one of Ibn Gabirol's main inspirations, the *Rasa'il Ikhawan as-Safa*. Ibn Ezra followed Ibn Gabirol in believing that man was microcosm to God's macrocosm, and that God was present as an "emanation," which cascaded from the unknowable into the manifested world.[108] He described a substance that became the ten "categories," foreshadowing the *Sephirot* of the Kabbalistic Tree of Life.[109] He was part of the generation of Jewish poets and thinkers that helped assimilate both of these Islamic mystical ideas.

As Moses ibn Ezra writes in his *Arugat ha-Bosem* (Garden of Aromatics):

> The Active Intellect is the first among the creatures of the Most High; it is a faculty emanating from the will, a simple, pure and scintillating substance that bears in itself the forms of all existence. The human intellect is a composite faculty, in affinity with the Active Intellect ... Man is called the Microcosm [Little World], and the universe, the Great

World [Macrocosm], because the Microcosm greatly resembles by its composition, derivation and creation, the Macrocosm ...

Many of these ideas came from the oft-cited *Rasa'il Ikhwan as-Safa.* Ibn Ezra's *Arugat ha-Bosem* is full of references and doctrine taken verbatim from the *Ikhwan*, with a recent study by Professor Paul Fenton noting 36 separate passages borrowed directly from the Islamic tract. For instance the paragraph above, concerning the microcosm-macrocosm make-up of the human relationship to God, is inspired directly by the Muslim treatise.[110]

As Norman Roth notes in his *Jews, Visigoths and Muslims in Medieval Spain*, in a passage referenced earlier but one worth mentioning again:

Ibn Ezra wrote that he did not disdain citing the Koran, and he "paid no attention to the hatred of some of the hypocrites of the sages of our community," since earlier Jewish thinkers such as Saadia Gaon and others used the Koran to clarify issues in the Jewish Bible. As for the "hypocrites," they look at men's actions, but neglect their own sins, "and on this our predecessors said, 'Everyone who says a wise thing, even among the nations of the world, is called wise' (*Megillah 16a*) for that which is kept of their words is the heart of the wisdom and not the shell of what is faulty."[111]

This same passage from the *Megillah* (c. 2nd century) shows up time and again to buttress medieval Jews' use of Islamic source material.

As he was one of the major innovators in medieval Spanish poetry, Ibn Ezra's work and ideas were widely read – and though he was not one of the major spiritual thinkers of his era, his influence was disseminated throughout medieval Jewry due to his success as a literary artist.[112]

## Abraham ibn Ezra

Abraham ibn Ezra (d. 1167, of no relation to Moses ibn Ezra) was a close friend of Judah Halevi's, and became his son-in-law. Living the life of a wandering scholar, he traveled throughout the Iberian Peninsula, to Italy, Provence and Northern France and perhaps, toward the end of his life, to the Holy Land. His most important legacy was bringing to France and the *Ashkenazi* (European) Jews the pearls of *Sephardic* Jewish learning – along with their Islamic leanings. He translated many Arabic texts into Hebrew, functioning as an important conduit between the two traditions.[113] His scholarly commentaries on the Bible are to this day an authoritative source for Jewish students.[114]

### Mystical Grammar

Ibn Ezra introduced Arabic grammatical innovations to the Jews of northern Europe, which influenced not only their study of the Hebrew language, but also their mystical interpretation of the Bible. He translated all of the works of the 10th-century Jewish grammarian Judah ben David Hayyuj (d. 1000; Cordoba) into Hebrew. Hayyuj, the seminal figure in the history of Hebrew grammatical scholarship, continues to influence Hebrew language study to this day. As the *Encyclopaedia Judaica* notes:

> Hayyuj developed the view that all Hebrew roots are made up of three letters, one of which, however, may be interchanged when conjugated with a weak letter, and may be elided or assimilated to a letter with a *dagesh*. This is a departure from the earlier view that recognized two-letter roots and even some one-letter roots. All the work on Hebrew language and Biblical exegesis since Hayyuj has been based on his ideas, and much of what he said, as well as his terminology in translation, is used to this day.[115]

What the *Encyclopaedia Judaica* fails to mention, however, is that he adopted many aspects of his philological work from the surrounding Arabic-speaking culture, and applied it directly to the Hebrew language.[116] And not only did Hayyuj study and internalize Arabic grammatical lessons, he actually wrote his books about the Hebrew Language in Arabic.

While Hayyuj's works – with such titles as *Kitab al Af'al Dhawat Huruf al-Lin* (The Book of Verbs Containing Weak Letters) and *Kitab al-Tanqit* (The Book of Punctuation) – might not appear to bear the titles of bestselling tomes, Hebrew language study was one of the most important intellectual and religious pursuits during the Jewish Golden Age. With Hebrew growing into a far richer mode of communication at this time, the work that Hayyuj undertook in codifying the Hebrew language was tremendously important.[117] Abraham ibn Ezra's translations of Hayyuj's work are still found throughout the Jewish Diaspora, from the Middle East to Europe.

### Microcosm/Macrocosm

In addition to being a major translator and disseminator of Hayyuj's seminal grammatical studies, Ibn Ezra based other aspects of his thought on the ubiquitous *Rasa'il Ikhwan as-Safa* (Epistles of the Brethren of Purity). Borrowing from that 10th-century encyclopedic tract, Ibn Ezra links self-knowledge to the love of God – a concept that would play a central role in later Kabbalistic thinking. Ibn Ezra states:

> It is the root principle of the commandments that one should love God with all his soul and cleave unto Him. A man will not be perfect unless he recognizes the work of God in the [higher] and lower worlds and he knows His ways ... and he will not be able to know God, unless he knows his own soul and his body and his intelligent soul; for one who does not know the essence of his soul, what wisdom does he possess?[118]

This reflects ideas propagated by the *Ikhwan*, which state: "One who regards the soul as a mere accident of mixture of the body 'knows neither his soul nor his true essence; how then should he know the true essence of things and their First Cause?'"[119] The idea of self-knowledge leading to understanding of God may be traced back to a *hadith* (saying of the Prophet Muhammad), reported by Yahya ibn Mu'adh (d. 871), stating: "He who knows himself knows his Lord."[120]

As with other ideas inspired by Islam, however, Ibn Ezra attributes it to a Biblical passage, in this case Job (19:26): "From my flesh I behold God." As Alexander Altmann (Harvard University Center for Jewish Studies) notes in *Studies in Religious Philosophy and Mysticism*, this Jewish scriptural attribution continued throughout medieval Judaism: "It occurs – still unconnected with the *hadith* formula – in such 12th-and 13th-century writers as Abraham bar Hiyya, Joseph ibn Zaddik, Samuel ben Nissim Masnut, Bahya ibn Asher and others."[121]

### The First European Jewish-Sufi

Ibn Ezra was the philosophical offspring of Ibn Gabirol and the *Ikhwan as-Safa*, accepting many of their propositions on God, form and matter. Echoing Ibn Gabirol's proto-Kabbalistic imagery, Abraham ibn Ezra describes God's relation to the world in the same cascading imagery, offering an almost pantheistic vision of Divine reach and using the same idea of creation as a process of speech that solidified within a century into the important Kabbalistic prayer ideal based on the Science of the Letters (*'Ilm al-Huruf*).[122]

While it would be very difficult to directly trace the lineage of Ibn Ezra's ideas from his sojourn in France to the development of Hasidism in Europe more than half a millennium later, there is little doubt that his inspiration reverberated in those communities. By introducing novel Arabic grammatical and mystical ideas into the world of the *Ashkenazi* Jews, he helped to prepare them for later influence by the Sufi-inspired Mediterranean Kabbalists and their mystical progeny.

There were many, many more Spanish thinkers who played an important role in melding Jewish and Islamic mysticism. Isaac ibn Latif (d. 1290), Shem Tob ibn Falaquera (d. 1295) and others knit the two religions together at their mystical cores, and then helped to seed these ideas into the growth of the Kabbalistic system. A full compendium of the specific personages is outside the scope of this study and must wait for another time, when that story can be told in its entirety.

It is also important to acknowledge that the deep influences that I outline, and their far-reaching consequences for the Jewish religion, can and will almost certainly be contested by academicians who are loathe to make such far-reaching claims. However, as was noted in the introduction, while it is difficult to find direct citations of Muslim sources in the works of medieval Jewish thinkers – as this would have been counterproductive to their goal of assimilating the Sufi ideas within Jewish practice – by looking at such factors as specific language and imagery, geographic proximity and the direction of Jewish thought immediately prior to and after these Sufi inspirations, we can posit with a fair degree of certainty the influence of the one (Islam) on the direction of the other (Jewish spirituality).

These *Sephardic* Jews, so comfortable with the Islamic culture, Arabic language and Sufi mystical insights, played a central role in turning later Jewish mysticism toward their Sufi mentors. Their openness to the new ideas paved the way for subsequent Jewish philosophers and, in particular, for the Kabbalists to absorb Sufi ideas, quite often without fully realizing just how much these medieval *Sephardim* were influenced by "foreign" thought.

## Endnotes

1. All this information regarding pre-Muslim Jewish life comes from Zolitor, Jeff. "The Jews of *Sepharad.*" *http://www.csjo.org/pages/essays/essaysephard. htm,* pp. 1-2.

2. Roth, Norman. *Jews, Visigoths and Muslims in Medieval Spain.* (New York: E.J. Brill, 1994), p. 73.

3. The information about the *dhimmis* comes from Zolitor, Jeff. "The Jews of *Sepharad,*" p. 3.

4. Bendiner, Elmer. *The Rise and Fall of Paradise.* (New York: Putnam Books, 1983), p. 41.

5. McGaha, Michael. *The Jewish Mystics of Medieval Spain.* (unpublished manuscript, 2001), p. 4.

6. Roth, Norman. *Jews, Visigoths and Muslims in Medieval Spain*, p. 92.

7. Brann, Ross. *The Compunctious Poet: Cultural Ambiguity and Hebrew Poetry in Muslim Spain.* (Baltimore, MD: Johns Hopkins University Press, 1991), p. 4.

8. Roth, Norman. *Jews, Visigoths and Muslims in Medieval Spain*, p. 105.

9. Gabirol, Solomon ibn. *Selected Poems of Solomon Ibn Gabirol* (Peter Cole, trans.). (Princeton, NJ: Princeton University Press, 2001), p. 7.

10. Roth, Norman. *Jews, Visigoths and Muslims in Medieval Spain*, p. 82.

11. Ibid. p. 79.

12. Ibid. p. 81.

13. Brann, Ross. *The Compunctious Poet: Cultural Ambiguity and Hebrew Poetry in Muslim Spain*, p. 38.

14. Palacios, Miguel Asin. *The Mystical Philosophy of ibn Masarra and His Followers.* (Leiden: E. J. Brill, 1978), p. 120.

15. Ibid. pp. 129-130.

16. Ibid. p. 37.

17. Brann, Ross. *The Compunctious Poet: Cultural Ambiguity and Hebrew Poetry in Muslim Spain*, p. 23.

18. Ibid. p. 37.

19. Ibid. p. 11 "As Raymond Scheindlin has put it, the courtier-rabbis simultaneously lived according to 'two opposing principles of life.' On the one hand, they were enamored of the world of material culture and its indulgent pleasures and beauty; and on the other, they were devoted to the world of religion with its emphasis on divine judgment and the life in the hereafter. The ideal man lived in both worlds and found the ambiguity most attractive."

20. Lobel, Diana. *A Sufi-Jewish Dialogue: Philosophy and Mysticism in Bahya ibn Pakuda's "Duties of the Heart."* (Philadelphia: University of Pennsylvania Press, 2006), pp. ix-x.

21. Both the Naghrila poem and information about Jewish Scripture referenced, from Brann, Ross. *The Compunctious Poet: Cultural Ambiguity and Hebrew Poetry in Muslim Spain*, p. 44.

22. Ibid. p. 43 (Hamori, *On the Art of Medieval Arabic Literature*, p. 53).

23. Ibid. pp. 30, 50.

24. It has been speculated that he had tuberculosis of the skin, or perhaps boils, either one of which would have been tremendously disfiguring. Loewe, Raphael. *Ibn Gabirol.* (New York: Grove Weidenfeld, 1989), p. 18.

25. McGaha, Michael. *The Jewish Mystics of Medieval Spain*, p. 70.

26. Ibid. p. 10.

27. Ibid. p. 12.

28. Palacios, Miguel Asin. *The Mystical Philosophy of ibn Masarra and His Followers*, p. 130.

29. McGaha, Michael. *The Jewish Mystics of Medieval Spain*, p. 65.

30. Gabirol, Solomon ibn. *Selected Poems of Solomon ibn Gabirol* (Peter Cole, trans.), p. 27.

31. Macnab, Angus. "Sufism in Muslim Spain." *Sufism: Love and Wisdom* (Jean-Louis Michon and Roger Gaetani, eds.). (Bloomington, IN: World Wisdom, Inc. 2006: 117-130), p. 121.

32. Loewe, Raphael. *Ibn Gabirol*, p. 113.

33. Myer, Isaac. *Qabbalah.* (New York: Samuel Weiser, 1970), p. 10.

34. Gabirol, Solomon ibn. *Selected Poems of Solomon ibn Gabirol* (Peter Cole, trans.), p. 16.

35. Chittick, William. *Sufism: A Short Introduction.* (Oxford: Oneworld Publishers, 2000), p. 77.

36. Quoted in Ibid. p. 78.

37. Information in this paragraph from *www.muslimphilosophy.com/ip/rep/ H032.*

38. All information and quotes taken from Myer, Isaac. *Qabbalah*, p. 159.

39. Kushner, Rabbi Lawrence. *www.beliefnet.com/story/179/story_17910_1.html,*

40. Ginsburg, Elliot. "Idel's 'Mystical Experience in Abraham Abulafia.'" (*Jewish Quarterly Review 82*, 1991: 207-214), p. 208.

41. Gabirol, Solomon ibn. *Selected Poems of Solomon ibn Gabirol* (Peter Cole, trans.), p. 6.

42. McGaha, Michael. *The Jewish Mystics of Medieval Spain*, p. 57.

43. Gabirol, Solomon ibn. *Selected Poems of Solomon ibn Gabirol* (Peter Cole, trans.), p. 21.

44. Ibid. p. 15.

45. Ibid. p. 15.

46. Palacios, Miguel Asin. *The Mystical Philosophy of Ibn Masarra*, p. 130.

47. McGaha, Michael. *The Jewish Mystics of Medieval Spain*, p. 19.

48. Ibid. p. 29.

49. Gabirol, Solomon ibn. *Selected Poems of Solomon ibn Gabirol* (Peter Cole, trans.), p. 33.

50. McGaha, Michael. *The Jewish Mystics of Medieval Spain*, p. 61.

51. Ibid. pp. 56, 61.

52. Loewe, Raphael. *Ibn Gabirol,* p. 62.

53. Ibid. pp. 62-63.

54. As Peter Cole relates it: "Ibn Gabirol's work had, a century after his death, been rendered into Latin by a team of two working in Archbishop Raymond's Toledo translation center. Sitting at a table in a room with other translators, the Jewish convert Ibn Daud, whose Christian name was Johannes Hispanus, read from the Arabic and translated orally into Spanish and then Dominicus Gundissalius, the Archdeacon of Segovia, translated from Hispanus' spoken Spanish into written Latin. The volume that came from that project was to play a key role in European intellectual history." Gabirol, Solomon ibn. *Selected Poems of Solomon ibn Gabirol* (Peter Cole, trans.), p. 14.

55. Ibid. p. 14.

56. Ibid. p. 14 "Guillaume D'Auvergne, the bishop of Paris, believed (Ibn Gabirol) to be an Arab, but as he had written a book *De Verbo Dei Agente Omnia*, believed that he had professed Christianity." Myer, Isaac. *Qabbalah*, p. 163.

57. McGaha, Michael. *The Jewish Mystics of Medieval Spain*, p. 69.

58. Maimonides, Obadyah. *Treatise of the Pool* (Paul Fenton trans.). (London, Octagon Press, 1981), pp. 2-3.

59. McGaha, Michael. *The Jewish Mystics of Medieval Spain*, p. 70.

60. Vajda, George. *Encyclopaedia Judaica 1st Edition, CD ROM* (Cecil Roth and Geoffrey Wigoder, eds.). (New York: MacMillan and Company, 1972).

61. Lobel, Diana. "Sufism and Philosophy in Muslim Spain and the Medieval Mediterranean World," (Manuscript, 2001), p. 20.

62. Lobel, Diana. *A Sufi-Jewish Dialogue: Philosophy and Mysticism in Bahya ibn Pakuda's "Duties of the Heart,"* p. 239.

63. Ibid. p. 95.

64. Lobel, Diana. "On the Lookout: A Sufi Riddle in Sulami, Qushayri and Bahya," (Manuscript, 2002), p. 11.

65. Ibid. p. 11.

66. Quoted in Ibid. pp. 13-14.

67. Quoted in Ibid. p. 14.

68. Ibid. pp. 15-16.

69. All information in the previous two paragraphs from Lobel, Diana. "Sufism and Philosophy in Muslim Spain and the Medieval Mediterranean World," p. 22.

70. Quoted in Ibid. pp. 22-23.

71. Quoted in Ibid. pp. 23-24.

72. Ibid. p. 24.

73. Quoted in Ibid. p. 25.

74. Ibid. p. 21.

75. Quoted in Ibid. p. 24.

76. Quoted in Ibid. p. 24.

77. Lobel, Diana. *A Sufi-Jewish Dialogue: Philosophy and Mysticism in Bahya ibn Pakuda's "Duties of the Heart,"* p. 222.

78. Ibid. p. 238.

79. Ibid. p. 197.

80. Ibid. p. xi.

81. Ibid. p. 200.

82. Quoted in Ibid. p. 237.

83. Ibid. p. 121.

84. Quoted in Fadiman, James and Frager, Robert (eds.). *Essential Sufism.* (New York: HarperCollins, 1997), p. 229.

85. All information for this paragraph from Lobel, Diana. *A Sufi-Jewish Dialogue: Philosophy and Mysticism in Bahya ibn Pakuda's "Duties of the Heart,"* p. 160.

86. Ibid. p. 160.

87. Ibid. p. ix The *hadith* usually reads "the lower self" in place of "the instinct and its armies."

88. All the quotes in this paragraph and the previous one, from Lobel, Diana. "On the Lookout: a Sufi Riddle in Sulami, Qushayri and Bahya ibn Pakuda," pp. 8-9.

89. *SephardicSages.com*, p. 1.

90. Fenton, Paul. "Jewish Attitudes Towards Islam: Israel Heeds Ishmael." (*Jerusalem Quarterly 29,* 1983: 93-102) p. 95.

91. McGaha, Michael. *The Jewish Mystics of Medieval Spain*, p. 125.

92. Biographical information from Encyclopaedia Hebraica. *Encyclopaedia Judaica* (Cecil Roth and Geoffrey Wigoder, eds.).

93. Lobel, Diana. "Sufism and Philosophy in Muslim Spain and the Medieval Mediterranean World," p. 19.

94. Quoted in Lobel, Diana. *Between Mysticism and Philosophy: Sufi Language of Religious Experience in Judah Halevi's Kuzari.* (Albany, NY: SUNY Press, 2000), p. 148.

95. Marcus, Jacob. *The Jew in the Medieval World.* (New York: Harper Torchbook, 1965), p. 227 The letter written from Hasdai Ibn Shaprut, as well as the response from Joseph, the King of the Khazars, are reprinted in this volume, pp. 227-232.

96. Lobel, Diana. *Between Mysticism and Philosophy: Sufi Language of Religious Experience in Judah Halevi's Kuzari*, p. 4.

97. Zafrani, Haim. "The Routes of al-Andalus: Spiritual Convergence and Intercultural Dialogue." *http://unesdoc.unesco.org/images/0011/001144/114426Eo. pdf*, p. 12.

98. Schweid, Eliezer. *Encyclopaedia Judaica* (Cecil Roth and Geoffrey Wigoder, eds.).

99. Quoted in Lobel, Diana. *Between Mysticism and Philosophy: Sufi Language of Religious Experience in Judah Halevi's Kuzari*, p. 174.

100. Ibid. p. 175.

101. Efros, Israel. "Some Aspects of Yehudah Halevi's Mysticism." (*Proceedings of the American Academy of Jewish Research 11,* 1941: 105-163), pp. 135-137.

102. Pines, Shlomo. "Shi'ite Terms and Conceptions in Judah Halevi's Kuzari." (*Jerusalem Studies in Arabic and Islam 2,* 1980: 165-247), p. 219.

103. Lobel, Diana. *Between Mysticism and Philosophy: Sufi Language of Religious Experience in Judah Halevi's Kuzari*, p. 91.

104. All information in the paragraph from Schweid, Eliezer. *Encyclopaedia Judaica* (Cecil Roth and Geoffrey Wigoder, eds.).

105. Ibid.

106. Ibid.

107. Biographical information on Ibn Ezra to this point taken from Encyclopaedia Hebraica. *Encyclopaedia Judaica* (Cecil Roth and Geoffrey Wigoder, eds.).

108. Editorial Staff. *Encyclopaedia Judaica* (Cecil Roth and Geoffrey Wigoder, eds.).

109. Myer, Isaac. *Qabbalah*, p. 160.

110. "Influence of Arabic and Islamic Philosophy on Judaic Thought." *Stanford Encyclopedia of Philosophy*, p. 6.

111. Roth, Norman. *Jews, Visigoths and Muslims in Medieval Spain*, p. 178.

112. Ibid. p. 178.

113. Hughes, Aaron. "Mi'raj and the Language of Legitimation in the Medieval Islamic and Jewish Philosophical Traditions." *Exploring Other Worlds: New Studies on Muhammad's Ascension* (Christiane Grubar and Fredrick S. Colby, eds.). (Bloomington, IN: Indiana University Press 2008), p. 9.

114. Bridger, David and Wolk, Samuel (eds.). *The New Jewish Encyclopedia.* (West Orange, NJ: Behrman House Publishers, 1976), p. 216.

115. Allony, Nehemiah. *Encyclopaedia Judaica* (Cecil Roth and Geoffrey Wigoder, eds.).

116. Poznanski, Samuel. "New Material on the History of Hebrew and Hebrew-Arabic Philology During the X-XII Centuries." (*Jewish Quarterly Review 16,* 1926: 237-266), p. 248.

117. Information taken from the *Jewish Encyclopedia,* (1901-1906).

118. Altmann, Alexander. *Studies in Religious Philosophy and Mysticism.* (Ithaca: Cornell University Press, 1969), p. 26.

119. Ibid. pp. 26-27.

120. Ibid. p. 1.

121. Ibid. pp. 3-4.

122. All of the specific information on Abraham Ibn Ezra from Assaf, S. et. al. *Encyclopaedia Judaica* (Cecil Roth and Geoffrey Wigoder, eds.).

# Chapter 5
# Sufi Influence on the Kabbalah

No mystical teaching is considered to define Jewish spirituality as does the Kabbalah. With its roots seemingly sunk in deepest Jewish history – by some accounts stretching all the way back to Moses, Abraham or even Adam – the Kabbalah has remained at the center of Jewish mysticism since its creation in the 13th century. It has been one of the most powerful forces ever to affect the inner development of Judaism; according to the *Encyclopaedia Judaica*, from the 16th through 19th centuries, it was widely considered to be *the* Jewish theology.[1]

Whether scholars believe it to have flowered into being with the Jewish spiritual renaissance of the 13th century, or that it is the recovered lore of second-century Talmudic elders or even older Biblical figures, one central idea has almost never been challenged by modern scholarship: that the Kabbalah is an entirely Jewish creation.

For this reason, linking it at its core with Islamic mysticism is problematic for many. Add to this the fact that sources of influence are often hundreds of years apart or, like other Sufi-Jewish interchanges, Kabbalists went out of their way to hide foreign impact on this most Jewish of mystical systems, and we are left with a confusing plethora of contributions, from which it can appear difficult to untangle one or the other specific inspiration. However, though the Kabbalah certainly grew from many roots – including Talmudic writings, Neo-Platonic and Gnostic teachings and other more obscure sources – I contend that many of these ideas came to Jewish thinkers via the Sufis, or earlier Jewish-Sufis. The vital, if not central role that Islamic mysticism played in forming the Kabbalah cannot, in my opinion, be denied.

### What is the Kabbalah?

"Kabbalah" literally means "tradition," and represents the reception of ancient teachings. It is not a single book or tract, but a collection of tomes and treatises, ideas and myths that grew over time, from the proto-Kabbalistic *Sefer Yetzirah* (The Book of Creation) in the 9th century through other works such as the *Sefer ha-Bahir* (c. 1230, Book of Clarity), the *Sefer Zohar* (c. 1295, Book of Splendor) and a flood of Kabbalistic works that followed upon these, down to our current era. Most of these texts are esoteric, symbol-filled books of obscure imagery and obtuse instruction that, it was said, only the initiate could truly understand. Until the explosion of Hasidism in the 18th century, Kabbalistic lore remained the purview of a small, scholarly elite.

A Jewish Mystical Response?

Some of the greatest Jewish scholars have held the exclusive Jewish provenance of the Kabbalah to be an inviolable fact. Professor Abraham S. Halkin of the Jewish Theological Seminary, writing in the middle of the 20th century, stated: "In all the vast literature of the Kabbalah, there is no trace of a non-Jewish source or influence."[2] The pre-eminent Kabbalistic scholar of the 20th century, Gershom Scholem (Hebrew University), addressed the specific issue of Sufi influence on the Jewish teachings, declaring that the Islamic mystics had *no* discernible effect on the development of the Kabbalah.[3]

At other times, Jewish scholars have appeared uncertain about the origins of the Kabbalah. For instance, Professor Joseph Dan (Hebrew University) notes in his introduction to *The Early Kabbalah*:

> When the first Kabbalistic circles began to appear in Provence and Spain in the Middle Ages, their symbols and terminology, as well as their concept of the Divine world, seemed to be completely novel. Though we do not have a clear understanding of the roots of the Kabbalah in the generation immediately preceding its appearance, we do have some evidence that what is characteristic of the first Kabbalists was not known to [Jewish] scholars living only a short time before them. The basic problem with the emergence of the Kabbalah is the difficulty in discovering a continuous line of development from Palestine and Babylonia in late antiquity to Southern Europe in the 12th century.[4]

He goes on to note: "This key question of Jewish mysticism is still quite obscure."

The reason that a "continuous line of development" from the Talmudic era (c. 2nd-5th centuries) to 12th-century Jewish mysticism cannot be found is because, in many instances, it does not exist. The Kabbalah emerged from, among other places, the inspiration of Sufi-oriented Jewish mystical exploration. The trends that we have explored in the preceding chapters hardly disappeared with the turning of the common calendar from the 12th to the 13th century. These earlier Jewish-Sufi thinkers helped pave the way for the profound change in Jewish mystical thinking – and the appearance of the Kabbalah. The Kabbalah, when correctly understood, is influenced by Sufi thought, with Jewish Kabbalistic thinkers sometimes discovering the essence of Biblical ideas in Islamic rituals, beliefs and terminology, and adopting the same.

A Sufi-Inspired Jewish Mystical Response

Sufis surrounded the early Kabbalistic philosophers as they had the Spanish and Egyptian Jews in the generations before. It was only natural that when the impetus for Jewish mystical thought burst forth in the 12$^{th}$ and 13$^{th}$ centuries, Jewish Kabbalists, like their immediate predecessors, would look to their spiritual cousins as well as earlier Sufi-inspired Jews for guidance and inspiration.

As Professor Michael McGaha points out in his *Sefer ha-Bahir and Andalusian Sufism*:

> It was no coincidence that the earliest Kabbalistic writings and the work of [Sufi philosopher] Ibn Arabi appeared around the same time [late 12$^{th}$-early 13$^{th}$-centuries]. Jewish refugees from Muslim Spain were breathing new life into the doctrines and imagery developed by the Sufis in Baghdad and later in *Andalusia*, creating the new system of mysticism known as the Kabbalah.[5]

This time period marked one of the most fecund epochs for Jewish mysticism in the history of post-Second Temple (c. 70 C.E.) Judaism. At the beginning of the 13$^{th}$ century, building on several hundred years of Islamic influence on Jewish thought, there was an explosion of creative spiritual energy. Lasting about a century, this dynamic process culminated in the creation of the Kabbalistic system, which persists at the center of Jewish mysticism to this day.

## The Early Books of the Kabbalah

### Sefer Yetzirah

The *Sefer Yetzirah* (Book of Creation) was one of those medieval Jewish mystical texts that have baffled scholars with its obscure imagery and unclear genesis. Originally thought to have been created between the second and sixth centuries, it has only recently been dated with more specificity to the ninth century, just before the *Rasa'il Ikhwan as-Safa* (Epistles of the Brethren of Purity) appeared. It predated – and foreshadowed – the other Kabbalistic works.

The small (it is only a few chapters long), anonymous treatise took on great importance for later Jewish thinkers. This tract introduces many of the terms and symbols that grew into the fully conceived Jewish spiritual system. Not surprisingly, its creators looked to the model of spiritual piety closest at hand to help define their ideas of Jewish worship: Islamic Mysticism.[6]

### Sephirot

The most important innovation introduced in this short work is the ten *Sephirot*, or spiritual way stations on the Jewish mystical path. As the pre-eminent scholar of the Kabbalah, Gershom Scholem notes in the *Encyclopaedia Judaica*: "The *Sephirot*, a term which first appears in this text ...

126

are described in a style full of mysterious solemnity almost without parallel in Jewish tradition."[7] Herein is described the exact number of mystical pathways (22) and stations (10) that define the Kabbalistic Tree of Life, with each of the 22 pathways represented by a different letter of the Hebrew alphabet, and the ten "primordial numbers" signified by the new expression: *Sephirot*.[8]

As Scholem, again, states, the word *Sephirot* derives from a Hebrew verb that means "to count." By introducing this new term, *Sephira*, in a place where the Hebrew word *mispar* normally would suffice, the *Sefer Yetzirah* indicates that the *Sephirot* concern the "building blocks and elements of the universe."[9] In the words of the 9th-century *Sefer Yetzirah*:

> The appearance of the *Sephirot* is like that of a flash of lightning and their goal is without end. His word is in them when they come forth [from Him] and when they return. They are the depths of all things: the depth of the beginning and the depth of the end, the depth of good and the depth of evil, the depth of above and the depth of below – and a single Master, God, the faithful king, rules over all of them from His holy abode.[10]

Farhana Mayer, of the Institute of Ismaili Studies in London, points out in a conference paper[11] that the word *Sephirot* shares linguistic properties with the Arabic word, *sifat*, which means "qualities" or "characteristics." While there is no direct record of influence of the Arabic term on the emergence of the word *Sephirot* in its novel Jewish conception, the similarity is close enough to posit that the Arabic-speaking, Jewish authors of the *Sefer Yetzirah* used the cognate word to help them develop this central Kabbalistic term.

The idea of ten stages of Divine emanation was fixed in this tract.[12] These ten Jewish mystical phases, however, did not originate here but, as Professor Eric Geoffroy (University of Strasbourg) notes in his article "Approaching Sufism," they can be traced into Islam's deepest past, to Ali ibn Abu Talib (d. 661; Babylonia), who was cousin and son-in-law of the Prophet Muhammad. Originally, the concept of ten Divine levels of Being goes back to Plotinus (d. 270), but it was the Sufi interpretation of these ideas that influenced medieval Jews. It is important to remember that Jewish thinkers had little knowledge of earlier philosophy until it was translated into Arabic and interpreted by Muslim thinkers.

The idea of spiritual stations within Islam comes from the Koran (37:164): "There is no one among us who has not a designated station [*maqam*]." Ali was the first Muslim to evoke a ten-stage gradation of these powers.[13] As Ali holds a high position in almost all Sufi orders, many of which trace their lineage back through him to the Prophet Muhammad, his proposition of ten specific gradations of the Divine emanation has much resonance within Sufi theory.

The *Sefer Yetzirah* offers an early translation of this idea into Judaism. It continued to develop independently within Islam, however, and later Muslim thinkers inspired Jews, who mixed ideas found in the *Yetzirah* with further Islamic conceptions. For instance, as Rabbi Mark Verman notes in *The Books of Contemplation*, Abd Allah ibn Sina (d. 1037) proposed a system of ten emanations that was quite similar to the *Sephirot* of the Kabbalah.[14]

The idea of ten different levels of God's powers is also present in the 10th-century *Rasa'il Ikhwan as-Safa* (Epistles of the Brethren of Purity). According to the *Ikhwan*, enumerating a theory from the Muslim philosopher al-Farabi (d. 950), who in turn absorbed it from Plotinus, the superabundance of the Supreme Being led to Its spilling over, and filled the nine successive levels with ever-weakening Divine overflow. The Sufis al-Ghazali (d. 1111) and as-Suhrawardi (d. 1191) added specific concepts of the Divine light, further clarifying how the emanation flowed throughout the ten "intellects."[15]

From these various Muslim motivations, the idea appeared in Jewish writings throughout the Diaspora starting in the 11th century, from Moses Maimonides and the Egyptian Jewish-Sufis to the Sephardic thinkers such as Solomon ibn Gabirol and Bahya ibn Pakuda. While the *Sefer Yetzirah* undoubtedly inspired these Jewish thinkers, in most cases they were mixing the Jewish influence, which itself appears to owe its provenance in many respects to Sufism, with more recent Islamic ideas.

### Mystical Language

The assimilation of Arabic grammatical/mystical ideas first took form in this short tract as well. As the *Encyclopaedia Judaica* notes, according to the *Sefer Yetzirah*:

> The whole work of creation was enacted through the combinations of the Hebrew letters that were inscribed on the sphere of heaven and engraved into the spirit of God. Every process in the world is a linguistic one, and the existence of every single thing depends on the combination of the letters that lies hidden within it. Perhaps this view can be seen as the ultimate conclusion of the theory that the world was created through the *Torah*, which is made up of letters and which contains these combinations in some mysterious way.[16]

As was noted in the previous chapter (See Solomon ibn Gabirol, *'Ilm al-Huruf*), the idea of creation being enacted through combinations of the letters in the Holy Book can be traced to Islamic influences. The *'Ilm al-Huruf* (Science of the Letters) developed in Islam in advance of the appearance of the *Sefer Yetzirah*. Some of the most important propositions in the Jewish tract translate the theories of the Arabic Science of the Letters into the

Hebrew grammatical and mystical vernacular.

Although specific concurrences between the Islamic and Jewish systems are numerous and highly esoteric, a single example of direct influence will suffice to show how closely the Jewish method follows the Muslim precursor. The three Hebrew letters in the *Sefer Yetzirah* with the strongest mystical significance stem directly from their linguistic counterparts in Arabic, where they hold similar import for Muslims. The so-called "Mother-letters" of the third chapter of the *Sefer Yetzirah, alef, mem* and *shin*, each representing a primordial element – ether, water and fire – are inspired by the earlier designation of the Islamic mystical triad taken from the Arabic letters, *'ayn, mim* and *sin*.[17]

For Shi'a Islam, the three Arabic letters *'ayn, mim and sin* stand for the three pillars of the Muslim religion – Ali, Muhammad and Salman Pak. As Professor Steven Wasserstrom (Moe and Izetta Tonkon Professor of Judaic Studies and the Humanities, Reed College) notes in *Sefer Yetzirah and Early Islam: A Reappraisal*:

> The triad *ain/mim/sin* designated the continuity of a certain form of Shi'a authority. This implication is encoded by the succession of *mim* (Muhammad) to *ain* (Ali) to *sin*, or Salman Pak, a mythical hero of the *ghulat* [a term used by mainstream to designate minority Islamic sects]. *Jafr*, or letter mysticism, was an essential feature in this *ghulat* argument for self-legitimation. This self-legitimation can be found in such eighth century Shi'a works as the cosmogony of Mughira ibn Sa'id [d. 737], or the semiotics of the *Umm al-Kitab* [Mother of the Book: The repository from which truth enters into our material universe and takes on the clothing of form, substance, space and time; representing the cosmic origination point of the Koran – as seen in 43:4: "It is in the Mother of the Book, in Our presence, high and full of wisdom."][18]

The concurrences between the Jewish and Muslim letter systems are too close to be explained away as coincidence. Wasserstrom continues: "The likelihood of these systems coincidentally hypostasizing the same three cognate letters in the same order is simply out of the question, on arithmetical grounds. There are [as calculated by Aryeh Kaplan, author of *Sefer Yetzirah: The Book of Creation in Theory and Practice*] approximately one sextillion possible permutations for the twenty-two letters of the Hebrew alphabet."[19]

As Islamic scholar Eliezer Paul Kraus (University of Cairo) states: "Insofar as there exists a relationship between the [Arabic] series *ain/mim/ sin* and that of the *Sefer Yetzirah* [*aleph/mem/shin*], the priority seems to go back to the Muslim system, where it is rooted in the religious history of Islam."[20] Even the term for the *aleph/mem/shin* triad in the Jewish mystical/grammatical system, *immot* (mothers), stems from the Muslim source, where it is termed as *unmahat* (mothers).[21]

Many other ideas behind the mystical meanings of the letters in the *Sefer Yetzirah* also have their genesis in Islamic thought. Wasserstrom notes:

> As [Islamic scholar Louis] Massignon stated the case: "It is useless to examine the works of Muslim mystics unless one has studied very closely the mechanism of Arabic grammar, lexicography, morphology and syntax ..." Less explicitly, but no less forcefully, such a case has been made for the similarly mystical utilization of grammatical concepts in *Sefer Yetzirah*. From Abraham Epstein to Nicholas Sed and Nehemiah Allony, scholars studying the *Sefer Yetzirah* have observed that the linguistic theory of the *Sefer Yetzirah* is closely related to that pioneered by the Arabic grammarians of the eighth and ninth centuries.[22]

Perhaps because early Jewish exegetes of the *Sefer Yetzirah* had to look to Muslim precursors to fully understand the new thinking, even their commentaries are intertwined with Islamic concepts. In Saadia Gaon's (d. 942, head of the Talmudic academy in Pumbedita, Babylonia) interpretation of this Jewish tract, specific concurrences between his ideas and those of Jabir ibn Hayyan (d. 815; Babylonia, the father of Islamic alchemy) are many:

> 1) The centrality of the permutation of the word roots [in ascertaining mystical meaning in the Scriptures].
> 2) The close similarity of terminology for this permutation.
> 3) Classification of the letters and their articulation in the mouth – [ideas that were] unknown in Talmudic times, but pioneered by early Arabic grammarians. [This concerned translating the written words into meditation vehicles to achieve specific mystical states.][23]

The complete system of later Kabbalistic meditation, ascendancy toward God, mystical interpretation of the Scriptures and other aspects of post-10th-century Jewish mysticism stem directly from the new understanding of the Hebrew language that Arabic grammar brought to medieval Rabbis. The linguistic theory of the *Sefer Yetzirah* is a vital conduit in moving the ideas from Islam into Jewish spiritual thinking.

### *Sefer ha-Bahir*

The *Sefer ha-Bahir* (c. 1230, The Book of Clarity), written a few hundred years after the *Sefer Yetzirah*, is commonly thought of as the first complete Kabbalistic text, one in which ideas of the mystical system are fleshed out in more or less their final form. Attributed to an ancient Talmudic scholar, Rabbi Nehuniah ben ha-Qanah (c. 2nd century), it is written in classic Kabbalistic style, replete with the mystical doubletalk and the numerology common to these obscure mystical texts.

The stimulus for this tract, however, cannot be found solely among ancient Jewish thinkers. While the earliest Kabbalists themselves spoke of such influences as the appearance of the Holy Spirit, the revelation of the Prophet Elijah and unspeakable celestial mysteries,[24] the truth is more banal. Many of the "novel" Jewish concepts illuminating the *Sefer ha-Bahir* were actually imported, disguised in Hebrew and mixed with older Jewish ideas, from Islam and Sufi-inspired Jews that had come before.

The Blueprint of Creation

The author of the *Sefer ha-Bahir* bases some of his most fundamental ideas on earlier Muslim thought. For instance, the anonymous Jewish author borrows verbatim from Sufi sources, the idea that the Holy Book represents a "blueprint of creation," simply changing the name of the holy book from "Koran" to "*Torah.*" This idea, which first had been proposed in the *Sefer Yetzirah*, helped complete the new manner in which to understand Jewish scripture, as a second, and hidden aspect became more important than the exoteric story of the nation of Israel.

> The *Bahir* agrees with the Sufi teaching that the Qu'ran (or *Torah*, for the Jews), the "blueprint of creation," which begins with the letter *ba* (Hebrew: *beth*), symbolizing *baraka* (Hebrew: *berakhah*), is like an infinite ocean, which at the moment of creation, overflowed, filling the world with knowledge of God.[25]

The theory that the Holy Book provides a "blueprint of creation" continued the assimilation of the Sufi Science of the Letters, as the *Bahir* posits that the letters of the Holy Book, and even spaces between the letters, are all symbols of God's power and thought. It is the letters of the text that are the engine of creation – the very breath of God as He exhales being into a previously non-existent universe. As Professor Michael McGaha notes in *Sefer ha-Bahir and Andalusian Sufism*: "In its treatment of the symbolism of the letters of the Hebrew alphabet, the *Bahir* is remarkably consistent with the Sufi Science of the Letters."[26]

Islamic *'Ilm al-Huruf*

These concepts coalesce beliefs that the words themselves are formed according to the same laws that correspond to the physical and spiritual worlds. The ideas *represented* by the words are imbedded in the letters of the words themselves. As Islamic scholar Denis Gril (Université de Provence) notes concerning this symbolism: "The words of language were formed according to principles rigorously corresponding to those that governed the physical and spiritual constitution of the realities signified by the words. The simple elements of language [are] the key to all knowledge."[27]

Jewish interest in the Sufi *'Ilm al-Huruf* (Science of the Letters) predated the appearance of the *Sefer ha-Bahir* by several centuries. One early medieval Jewish thinker to garner inspiration from this Islamic mystical system was Hai Gaon (d. 1038, head of the Talmudic Academy in Pumbedita, Babylonia). He borrowed extensively from the Islamic concepts underpinning the Science of the Letters, though like virtually all other Sufi-inspired Jews, he attributed his novel ideas to a Biblical prophet, in his case, Ezekial. Hai Gaon's use of the "tradition of the forms of the Holy letters," however, exhibits specific concurrences with Arabic mystical/calligraphic techniques known in Baghdad and Damascus during the period in which he was active, and represents the fusion between Islamic ideas, the *Sefer Yetzirah* and early medieval Jewish thinkers. As David Ariel notes in *Approaches to Judaism in Medieval Times*:

> Ibn Washiyya, a ninth century Damascene composed *The Book of Longing for Participation in Knowledge of the Symbols of Languages* in which he presented a catalogue of ancient symbols. His writings were widely disseminated throughout the ancient Middle East and were even known among Jews, such as Maimonides, who quoted him in the late 12th century. In this book we find a pointillistic technique of calligraphy ascribed to the ancient Nabateans. This technique is reproduced identically in the second Hebrew passage [attributed to Hai Gaon] as a method for the writing of the Tetragrammaton [*YHVH*, the unpronounceable name of God, known as "Yahweh" among contemporary Christian fundamentalists]. The technique of magical and mystical calligraphy current among Muslims around Damascus and Baghdad beginning in the ninth century found its way into Jewish mystical traditions in the 12th and 13th centuries. This technique of mystical calligraphy in Islam was based on Sufi teachings on divine names.[28]

Ariel also notes that the Kabbalistic theory of Divine language stems directly from the earlier Sufi mystical technique:

> The Kabbalistic theory of Divine language maintains that emanation is a linguistic process in which the means of Divine expression is the medium of language. Kabbalists explain this process whereby the *Sephirot* are the linguistic expressions of God since speech is a process of auto-representation [or the creation of the approachable God by the ineffable God]. Each individual *Sephira* constitutes a stage in the process of the unfolding of Divine thought and speech. As the intellectual process of emanation continues, God's wisdom culminates in the linguistic expression of wisdom in the *Torah*. Divine language finally becomes the language of Scripture so that the *Torah* is ultimately the repository of Divine wisdom and the final stage in the process of auto-

representation ... The *Sephirot* are the Divine names and these names are essential names, inseparable from the essence of God. This concept parallels Islamic teachings of Divine names and represents a Jewish variation of the Sufi doctrine of mystical names.[29]

Jewish Science of the Letters

These Arabic grammatical ideas helped to recast the Jewish concept of the Hebrew language and the *Torah*. The Science of the Letters emerged as one of the most important "revelations" of medieval Jewish mysticism, leading to comprehensive changes in the methods and goal of Jewish prayer, reverberations that are evident still within contemporary Jewish meditation practice.

As Professor Michael McGaha notes in *Sefer ha-Bahir and Andalusian Sufism*, in its specifics, the *Sefer ha-Bahir* is remarkably consistent with the Islamic grammatical science.[30] The Kabbalistic tract expands the concurrences between specific Arabic and Hebrew letters, first outlined in the *Sefer Yetzirah*, by concentrating its attention on 14 consonants (out of 22 possibilities in the Hebrew alphabet) – paralleling exactly the Sufi theory of dividing the 28-letter Arabic alphabet into two segments of 14 letters each, with 14 representing esoteric truths, and the other 14, exoteric truths. Those representing the interior truths correspond to the letters found at the beginning of the *Surat* (chapters) of the Koran. In addition, seven of the 14 letters upon which the *Sefer ha-Bahir* concentrates attention correspond directly to those described by earlier Muslim thinkers as the "noblest ones."[31]

*Sheckinah*

Another innovation of the *Sefer ha-Bahir* was a novel concept of approaching the *Sheckinah* which, again, appears to have been imported into Judaism via Sufism. The *Sheckinah* was an idea well known in medieval Jewish mystical circles and, dating from Talmudic times, had been identified with the *presence* of God. This "presence," however, often seemed heretical, as it could be taken to represent a literal aspect of God "present" in a time and place.

Jewish thinkers wanted to steer clear of anthropomorphizing – attributing human attributes to – God, and therefore they created another, variable meaning of the *Sheckinah*. According to Saadia Gaon, the *Sheckinah* was an intermediary created by God that was approachable by humankind.[32] This not only solved the problem of not wanting to "humanize" God, as the *Sheckinah* was now an expression of God that was not God Itself, but also opened up a novel avenue of approach for mystics.

One important Sufi idea that inspired notions of approaching the *Sheckinah* in the *Sefer ha-Bahir* was the passionate imagery of union. As already noted in the section on *Sephardic* poets (Chapter 4), the application of romantic symbolism to the mystic's relationship with God had recently re-entered Jewish mysticism via the Sufis. Joseph Dan notes in *The Early Kabbalah* that the *Sefer ha-Bahir* was the first Jewish mystical text to give this idea a theological basis,[33] echoing the Sufi concept that sensual symbolism was appropriate for the description of the Divine realm. Divine union – as firstly proposed by the Sufis and then adopted by Jewish philosophers – came to be defined as an ecstatic experience between "lover" and the "beloved," or the Jewish mystic and the *Sheckinah*. Joseph Dan explains in *The Early Kabbalah*:

> The *Bahir* was the first Jewish mystical work to introduce the idea that sexual and familial symbolism was appropriate for the description of the essence of the Divine realm. This sexual motif was to become one of the most central and distinctive themes of the Kabbalah.[34]

### *Ishraqi* (Illuminationist School)

The *Bahir* also built on ideas concerning Divine light from Sufi antecedents, specifically Shihabuddin Yahya al-Suhrawardi (d. 1191; Persia):

> Suhrawardi elaborated a system of "light mysticism," according to which the deity is "pure light" beyond all positive determination and is causative of all existent things which are themselves constituted as light. A Hebrew passage [in the *Sefer ha-Bahir*] ... describes the Divine realm as a pleroma of "spiritual lights" that are interposed between the absolute deity and the world. These lights – "the internal, primordial light" (*or penimi qadmon*), "the clear light" (*or sah*), and the "polished light" (*or mehsuhsah*) – generate subsequent "spiritual, pure and internal lights." This elaborate scheme of Divine light mysticism entered the Kabbalah through Suhrawardian sources.[35]

The *Sefer ha-Bahir*, considered by the pre-eminent Kabbalistic scholar Gershom Scholem as the first true book of the Kabbalah, as well as being untouched by "foreign" content, in fact continued to solidify Sufi influence on Jewish mystical theory. There were few *Sephardic* Jewish Kabbalists whose work postdated the *Sefer ha-Bahir* who did not base their ideas, at least to some extent, on the symbolism found in this seminal treatise.

### *Sefer Zohar*

The *Sefer Zohar* (c. 1295, Book of Splendor) appeared about 65 years after the *Sefer ha-Bahir* and immediately supplanted it as the most important Kabbalistic work. Written under a pseudonym in northern Spain, the *Zohar* expanded on the ideas of the earlier tracts, running some 2400 tightly written pages.[36] While not a conventional book, in that it lacks a specific beginning, middle and end, its collection of commentary, stories, anecdotes and fragments of ideas all are held together by one common thread: they purport to represent the sayings and beliefs of the second century Rabbi Simeon ben Yohai (c. 150), a historical figure who is buried not far from Safed, in the Holy Land.

While the *Zohar* was said to be the "rediscovered" lore from the legendary Talmudic age, the treatise actually was written by Moses de Leon (d. 1305; Spain).[37] His specific influences, well hidden beneath the double-talk, historical allusions and mystical patina of ben Yohai's circle, comprise the usual collection of medieval Jewish sources, some of which had been strongly influenced by the Sufis themselves. Abraham ibn Ezra, Moses Maimonides, sections taken from Judah Halevi's *Sefer ha-Kuzari*, Bahya ibn Pakuda, Solomon ibn Gabirol, the *Sefer Yetzirah* and the *Sefer Bahir* all play important roles in the formation of the seminal tome.[38] Add in a bit here and a few pinches there of direct Muslim inspiration, and the *Zohar* takes on that particular Jewish-Sufi sheen which colors much of medieval Judaism.

For the period leading up to and including the beginning of Hasidism (c. 1740), the *Zohar* ranked with the Bible and the Talmud as one of the canonical Jewish texts. As Gershom Scholem suggests in *Major Trends in Jewish Mysticism*, it stands out as the expression of all that is most deeply hidden in the innermost recesses of the Jewish soul.[39]

### Muhyiddin ibn Arabi and the *Zohar*

At times Moses de Leon appeared to work directly from Islamic thinkers. For instance, the Sufi thinker Muhyiddin ibn Arabi (who was born in Spain, and died about 50 years before de Leon wrote his treatise) foreshadowed many of the concepts that became central to the Kabbalistic tract. As Rabbi Ariel Bension notes in *The Zohar in Moslem and Christian Spain*, both Ibn Arabi and de Leon:

1. Used the same poetic style and mystical imagery to detail the spiritual quest.
2. Considered mystical revelation as superior to all other oral religious tradition.
3. Posited that light is the symbol of God and His Divine manifestations, while darkness is the symbol of matter.
4. Continued to develop a system whereby letters and their numerical value [Science of the Letters] had mystical values.
5. Believed that dreams offered a window into the mystery of death and spiritual realization.
6. Believed that creation took place from a point or a circle emanating from the Infinite, and from this point all other circles or creations

emanate in turn. Herein lay the genesis of the Kabbalistic idea of *"Ein Sof,"* the ineffable power of God from which spilled forth the ten *Sephirot* of the Tree of Life.

       7. Considered that stars exert an influence on human life.[40]

Another aspect that the *Zohar* shares with Ibn Arabi concerns the Perfect or Primordial man (*al-Insan al-Kamil*), that aspect of the "microcosm" which reflects the "macrocosm." This idea became vital for later Jewish mystics, and had a deep influence on the concept of the Hasidic leader (18th century), known as the *tzaddik*.

    As Gershom Scholem describes in the *Encyclopaedia Judaica*, for the Kabbalah, the creative process involves the emanation of the One from an uncreated point, through a series of stations (the *Sephirot*) to the manifested world and then back again. The crucial turning point in this cycle takes place within man, at the moment that he begins to develop an awareness of the Divine Essence that lies dormant within him. At this time, he develops a yearning to retrace the path from the multiplicity of human nature to the Oneness from which he originates. A complete self-awareness of the Divine aspect of oneself represents the Perfect Man, or the microcosm that encompasses within his being the totality of the universe, and often is represented within Sufism by the image of a totally cleansed mirror, reflecting God to God.[41]

    These ideas are central to Ibn Arabi's concept of human nature. The emphasis throughout much of this Islamic thinker's work is on the true potential of the human being and the path to realizing this potential, and becoming the Perfect or complete man (*al-Insan al-Kamil*). There are specific aspects of the theory of the Perfect Man that the *Zohar* shares with the Islamic thinker. According to Professor Ronald Kiener (Director, Jewish Studies Program, Trinity College, CT) in his article *Ibn Arabi and the Qabbalah*, the similarities are striking:

> [For Ibn Arabi], a perfect man on the human level is a perfected rationalist who, by perception of the microcosmic status of his being, is granted by God mystical intuition into the essential unity of man the many and God the One. At the same moment, the Perfect Man is a Logos, the collected, revealed Self by which God Knows Himself and creates the world. The *Zohar* contains all of these functions [of the "Perfect Man"]. [According to the Jewish mystical tract], a Perfect Man is one who has fulfilled worldly creation by bringing into corporeality male and female. The Primordial Man is both microcosm and Logos, the "image" by which man knows the revealed God and by which the hidden God creates the sublunar world. In Ibn Arabi, all three functions coincide.[42]

Ibn Arabi's ideas of the Perfect Man may be traced back to a *hadith*: "He who knows himself knows his Lord,"[43] thereby situating this central Kabbalistic tenet not in the Talmudic past, but within the heart of Islamic thinking.

Solomon ibn Gabirol and the *Zohar*

De Leon also was inspired by Islamic thought through the works of the 11th-century Jewish-Sufi Solomon ibn Gabirol, whose writing was well known in northern Spain when de Leon was working. It is important to remember that the Jew Ibn Gabirol and the Sufi Ibn Arabi were referred to as "two lights radiating from the same center, since their mystic and theosophical systems shared in the identical Masarrian orientation."[44] Whether de Leon took his inspiration from Ibn Gabirol or Ibn Arabi, the result often was the same: to thread ideas from the 10th-century Sufi Muhammad ibn Masarra into this canonical Jewish text.

The influences of Ibn Gabirol on de Leon are so profound that the 19th-century scholar, Isaac Myer, wrote a book entitled *Qabbalah: The Philosophical Writings of Solomon ibn Gabirol and their Connection to the Sepher ha-Zohar*, which posits that the two systems are so similar in concept, that they stem from the same ancient source. Scholarship has shown, however, that there is no "ancient" Jewish source, and that most probably the concurrences come from the influence of Ibn Gabirol and Ibn Arabi on the later Moses de Leon.

Specific inspirations drawn from Ibn Gabirol's work are sprinkled throughout the Kabbalistic text. According to Professor Jochanan Wijnhoven (a Jewish scholar who was the first non-Protestant member of Smith College's Department of Religion) in his "Mysticism of Solomon ibn Gabirol," the *Zohar's* doctrine of Divine will, in which all forms are hidden awaiting the Divine emanation to be revealed, may be traced back to the 11th-century Spanish Jewish-Sufi.[45] The central Kabbalistic term *ein sof* ("no end," which refers to the uncreated creator who sits atop the Tree of Life, represented by three lightning bolts) also first appears in Ibn Gabirol's work. As Joshua Abelson (an early Kabbalistic scholar, working in the late 19th century) notes in *Jewish Mysticism: An Introduction to the Kabbalah*, the *ein sof* in the *Zohar* echoes Ibn Gabirol's theology, when de Leon states: "Before having created any shape in the world, before having produced any form, He was alone, without form, resembling nothing. Who could comprehend Him as He then was, before creation, since He had no form?"[46] This concept of God as "no-thing" tracks quite closely Sufi ideas of the deity.

The microcosm-macrocosm motif, so important in the *Zohar*, is found prefigured in Ibn Gabirol's writings as well, bringing together the Bible, Talmud, ancient philosophers and Islamic inspirations[47] in helping to set the foundation for what would become this central tenet of Jewish mysticism. Additionally, the Science of the Letters, and specifically the notion that the creation of the world was made through the inscription of numbers and letters in the air (an idea which first appears in Judaism in the *Sefer Yetzirah*) passes from that earlier text, through Ibn Gabirol and then to Moses de Leon.[48]

### Seven Castles

In the *Zohar*, de Leon describes a vision of the aspirant moving through seven successive castles, arranged in concentric circles, one above the next, with each higher one being defined by ever more precious substances. These palaces represent products of God's emanative flux, and as Gershom Scholem notes, this image has little in common with earlier Jewish mysticism[49] – but may be traced to the Sufis. De Leon was not the first to utilize this imagery – it is also found in the work of Moses Maimonides (Chapter 3). The Sufis, however, inspired de Leon's descriptions, as they did Maimonides.

In his "castle" motif, de Leon describes the different stages through which a mystic passes on his way toward realization, linking these stations to the seven lower *Sephirot* of the Kabbalistic Tree of Life. This image is inspired almost completely by the Islamic mystics. As Professor Michael McGaha notes in *Spanish Sufism, Kabbalah and Catholic Mysticism*:

> The earliest known example [of the seven castle motif] ... occurs in the ninth century Sufi writer Abu-l Hasan al-Nuri's [d. 907, Baghdad] treatise *Maqamat al-Qulub* [Stations of the Heart]. Abu-l Hasan describes seven concentric circles, beginning with the central one and proceeding outward, each successive castle being made of a mineral less hard or precious than the preceding one ... The castles of course refer to the various stages through which the believer moves toward the mystical knowledge of God ... the image was commonplace in medieval Sufi writing. The 13th-century *Zohar* speaks of seven palaces – corresponding to the seven lower *Sephirot* – through which the soul ascends in the mystic journey, stating that "in the midst of a mighty rock, a most recondite firmament, there is set a palace which is called the Palace of Love. This is the region wherein the treasures of the King are stored, and all His love-kisses are there. All souls beloved of the Holy One enter into that Palace." [3:293][50]

### Poverty

The *Zohar*, for the first time in the history of Rabbinic Judaism, lays special stress on the glorification of poverty as a religious value. Gershom Scholem states in *Major Trends in Jewish Mysticism*:

> This spiritualistic identification of the poor and the devotee finds further expression in the fact that Moses de Leon, in his Hebrew writ-

ings, uses the same term for the poor which in the *Zohar* he very often employs for the mystics, the true devotees ... The *Zohar* contains an interpretation of theosophic thoughts in which the quality of poverty is attributed to the *Sheckinah*, in other words to God himself in the last of his manifestations: The *Sheckinah* is poor because "she has nothing from herself," but only what she receives from the stream of the *Sephirot*. The alms from which the poor live symbolically reflect this mystical state of the *Sheckinah*.[51]

While this is clearly a central belief for the Sufis, who were known as "the poor" (*fuqara*), it was novel to medieval Jewish mysticism, though it hearkened back to the prototype of the Prophets. It is quite possible that the Hebrew word that de Leon used to denote the "true devotees" had been directly translated from the Islamic word for Sufi aspirant.

### Joseph Gikatilla and the *Zohar*

Another important avenue of Sufi influence on the *Zohar* was Rabbi Joseph Gikatilla (d. 1305; Spain), a zealous student of the Sufi-inspired Abraham Abulafia[52] (a central Jewish-Sufi Kabbalist who will be introduced a bit further along). Abulafia averred that Gikatilla was his most accomplished pupil – and Gikatilla met Moses de Leon in the 1270s, having a strong influence on that Kabbalist's thought. Gikatilla showed a particular affinity for the ecstatic, prophetic aspects of Abulafia's teachings[53] that were heavily inspired by Sufi ideas, thereby helping to influence Moses de Leon with Islamic sources.

We cannot know for sure the exact relationship between Joseph Gikatilla's Sufi-leaning masterpiece, *Sha'arei 'Orah* (Gates of Light), and Moses de Leon's *Zohar*, but the similarities are clear, with many of the same teachings, ideas and terminology cropping up in both. These two worked in close contact during the gestation period of both books – and many of the views undoubtedly sprouted from the fertile relationship between the two.[54]

The Sufi influence on Gikatilla's work is undeniable.

The basic underlying principle of Gikatilla's *Sha'arei 'Orah* is also one of the fundamental tenets of Sufism: "It is vitally important to be thoroughly familiar with the 'most beautiful' Names of God so that one can invoke the appropriate Name – the one that is most likely to provide effective aid – in a particular situation."[55]

Here we see another thread of the important Sufi doctrine of Divine Names and the Science of the Letters being woven directly into the Kabbalah. Reciting the 99 Names of God is a central Islamic practice, and underpins the *dhikr* (litany of remembrance) of the Sufis.[56]

In his *Ginnat Egoz* (Nut Orchard), written in 1274, Gikatilla spends much time fleshing out a Jewish version of the Science of the Letters, working through the mystical symbolism of the alphabet, vowel points and the Divine Names. By this time the Science of the Letters had become almost completely internalized by Jewish thinkers. Later works of Gikatilla's deal further with these grammatical/mystical concepts, as well as with various ideas concerning the ten *Sephirot* of the Tree of Life that stem from earlier, Sufi-leaning Jews. Joseph Gikatilla was able to point to recent Jewish influences (instead of the far-off Biblical past, as was necessary for the first generations of Jewish-Sufis), linking them to Moses Maimonides, and thereby to traditional Jewish beliefs.[57]

Gikatilla's works became vital reading for later Kabbalists, as well as 18th-century Hasidism, as testified by this statement of Rabbi Meshullam Phoebus of Zbarazh (d. 1775): "You shall study *Sefer Sha'arei Orah* and *Ginnat Egoz*, and, mostly, the book of the *Zohar*..."[58] This passage also exhibits how closely intertwined remained Gikatilla (who wrote the *Sefer Sha'arei Orah* and *Ginnat Egoz*) and Moses de Leon (author of the *Zohar*) half a millennium after they worked together in Spain. Gikatilla's work also was studied by Rabbi Shneur Zalman of Lyady (d. 1813) at the court of one of the most important early Hasidic leaders, Rabbi Dov Baer, the Maggid of Mezhirech.[59]

## Early Kabbalists Under Sufi Influence

### Abraham Abulafia

In addition to the earliest Kabbalistic texts' influence by Sufi precursors, individual Jewish theologians continued to be inspired by Islamic ideas. These thinkers searched out and inserted some Sufi material directly from Muslim sources, deepening the Sufi impact on Jewish spirituality.

One of the most important of these figures – whose impact reverberates within Jewish spirituality to this day – is Abraham Abulafia, who played a profound role in the ongoing Islamicization of Jewish worship. If Sufism was an inspirational agent of medieval Jewish mysticism, then Abraham Abulafia was an important vector, moving to and fro around the Mediterranean Basin, from Spain to Italy to Sicily, from the Holy Land to Greece and back again to Sicily, leaving Sufi-inspired Jews in his wake. Much like earlier Jewish-Sufis in Egypt and Spain, he hardly demanded that his followers break with traditional Jewish teaching, believing that his system was a continuation and elaboration of Moses Maimonides' *Guide for the Perplexed*,[60] overlaying that seminal Jewish text with further Islamic philosophical ideas.[61]

Even his dedication to Maimonides could not indemnify this genius, however. By the end of Abulafia's lifetime, his megalomaniac, Sufi-inspired activities attracted the attention of one of the leading rabbinic authorities of his time, Rabbi Solomon ben Abraham ibn Adret (d. 1310), who excommunicated him, forcing him into exile on a small island off the coast of Sicily, where he died in 1291.

A Self-Appointed Prophet

Throughout his wanderings, Abulafia wrote copiously, bringing together his Sufi-inspired prophetic visions with the Kabbalah and the teachings of his philosophical mentor, Moses Maimonides. He was one of the first commentators on the great sage's *Guide for the Perplexed*, making his living for a time teaching the *Guide* to students.[62] Like those Jewish-Sufis who came before him, it was his reliance on Jewish tradition in general and Moses Maimonides specifically, that helped his foreign influences to be digested into the heart of Jewish worship.

Abraham Abulafia's self-image as a prophetic voice was an important impetus for his gravitation to Sufi ideas. As he must have known (through disseminated writings of Abraham Maimonides and others), the earlier Jewish-Sufis of Egypt and Spain felt that Sufism represented a Jewish-inspired worship dating to the time of the Biblical prophets, which had been assimilated by the ancients as a manner of leading Jews to their prophetic heritage. As preeminent contemporary Kabbalistic scholar Moshe Idel (Hebrew University) points out in his *Studies in Ecstatic Kabbalah*: "As one who saw himself as a prophet and Messiah, he believed that this particular form of the Kabbalah [the Sufi-inspired version] paved the way for mystical experience for all who would follow his path. For this reason [unlike virtually all other medieval Kabbalists], the tone of his writing is clearly practical; his writings are intended as guides to 'prophecy' for his contemporaries."[63]

All Jews had prophetic revelation within their reach, and Abulafia wanted to provide a specific manual to aid the nation of Israel in achieving this necessary state. It was the lucidity of expression that allowed his writings to become so widely read – and followed – by Jewish practitioners over the next several centuries, becoming a primary influence on the development of 18th-century European Hasidism and even contemporary Jewish practice.

*Dhikr*

Perhaps no single medieval Jewish mystic has colored *contemporary* Jewish spiritual practice, as has Abraham Abulafia. Much of his meditation and prayer system is still practiced in Jewish prayer retreats and synagogues around the world (see Epilogue). And as much of his particular model for achieving spiritual purity is based on Sufi *dhikr* litanies, his influence is of particular interest to this story, and represents a specific manner in which Islamic and Sufi material continues to influence Judaism to this day.

Many aspects of Abulafia's meditation system appear to stem from interactions with Sufi prayer methods. Professor Harvey Hames (Ben Gurion University) discusses in his article, "A Seal Within a Seal: The Imprint of Sufism in Abraham Abulafia's Teachings," specific facets of Muslim prayer practice that influenced the Jewish mystic:

> It is worth considering a passage contained in the work of a disciple of Abulafia's which expressly mentions Sufi practices, the *dhikr*, or enunciation of the Divine names, which is a central part of Sufi discipline ... [after a discussion of the *dhikr*, the student] relates his own personal experience with his teacher, Abulafia, who teaches him to combine letters.[64]

Abulafia's letter combinations of the Tetragrammaton (the Hebrew letters *YHVH*, which represent the unpronounceable name of God) were his method of "remembrance," or *dhikr*. He deconstructed the four letters, combining them in complicated permutations that completely occupied the mind to the point that the aspirant could think of nothing else but his act of remembrance, and the spirit of God thus filled the one who prayed. This method played the same role for Abulafia as did the repetition of the prayers during Sufi *dhikr*, which typically involve the repetition of the Names of God.

Hames continues to explain how Abulafia tracks the Sufi saint Muhyiddin ibn Arabi's (d.1240) ideas concerning the Sufi prayer practice:

> In the *Fabulous Gryphon* and in other places, Ibn Arabi describes the name Allah as the name in which all the other Divine names take refuge and calls it: "the Greatest Name and the Most-Excellent Mighty First Principle." In addition, Allah is the only name referred to as a "Proper Noun," whilst all other names are adjectives by which God can be addressed. Abulafia refers to the Tetragrammaton [the unpronounceable Name of God] as the "perfect noun," whilst all the other names are clearly lesser names to be seen as stepping-stones toward the most perfect name ... Abulafia's disciple clearly studied with him before moving to Palestine; his reference to the annihilation of the self when repeating the name of Allah, the "Greatest Name," coupled together with his description of his own mystical rapture when combining the Tetragrammaton, may be a reflection of Abulafia's integrating Ibn Arabi's methods of practicing *dhikr* into his own Kabbalistic praxis.[65]

Further Islamic influence on Abulafia's prayer methods is not difficult to uncover. As Paul Fenton notes in the *Cambridge Companion to Medieval Jewish Philosophy*, the focal point of Abulafia's spiritual discipline was *hazkara* (memorial service), a term that is strikingly reminiscent of the Muslim term *dhikr* (according to al-Ghazali, a meditation on one's own death[66]). Fenton notes:

Independently of canonical prayer, the purpose of this activity was to prepare the devotee for prophetic inspiration. The meditative ritual, practiced in an isolated and dark place, as set out in Abulafia's writings, obviously involves Sufi techniques. After preliminary preparations, the devotee, arrayed in white, adopts a special posture and proceeds to pronounce the divine name accompanied with respiratory control and movements of the head.[67]

Science of the Letters

Abulafia's meditation method depended heavily on the Sufi *'Ilm al-Huruf* (Science of the Letters), a central aspect of the practice of *dhikr*. He accepted the Islamic conception that Divine language is the substance of reality – and that all things garner their true existence from the manner in which the letters representing them participate in the Names of God. Abulafia's prayer technique offered a detailed curriculum for the meditation practice predicated on the Islamic concept of the letters of words representing a Divine language.[68] Gershom Scholem notes:

> The science of the combination of letters and the practice of controlled meditation was, according to Abulafia, nothing less than "mystical logic" that corresponded to the inner harmony of thought in its movement towards God. Every letter represented a whole world to the mystic who abandoned him or herself to contemplation. Every spoken word consists of sacred letters, and the combination, separation and reunion of letters reveal profound mysteries ... Abulafia's great manuals, such as "The Book of Eternal Life," "The Light of Intellect," "The Words of Beauty" and "The Book of Combination" are systematic reference guides to the theory and practice of this system of mystical counterpoint. Through its methodical exercise the soul is accustomed to the perception of higher forms with which it gradually saturates itself.[69]

Abulafia's system includes specific pronunciations of the Divine Names, complex theories of breathing and bodily movements, singing, bobbing of the head and other techniques that have nothing to do with traditional Jewish prayer methods[70] – but much in common with Sufi *dhikr* ceremonies.

*Hitbodedut* (Jewish *Khalwa*)

Abulafia played a central role in codifying *hitbodedut* (*khalwa* to the Sufis, or solitary retreat) as a practice central to the path of the Kabbalist. Although Jewish thinkers such as Abraham ibn Ezra (d. 1167), Moses Maimonides (d. 1204)[71] and others had used the term *hitbodedut* in their writings, and tentatively expressed admiration for the method, it wasn't until Abulafia (d. 1291) attached it to the heart of his interpretation of Judaism, that the Sufi-inspired prayer method became a central aspect of the Kabbalah.

*Hitbodedut* had two meanings for Abulafia, which, as Moshe Idel notes, were novel to Judaism with his work, because he proposed them as part of the living religion, instead of simply a relic of ancient Judaism's prophetic history.[72] On one hand, it represented the intense mental concentration required to achieve *devequt* (Divine union). It also implied the solitary nature of this activity and the necessity to separate oneself from a community of worshipers to pray. Abulafia was the first Kabbalist to connect *hitbodedut* with a practical, detailed system of prayer, including the combination of the letters and various vocalizations associated with them.[73] Perhaps the single most important innovation of medieval Jewry, this prayer method became central to Hasidism, and has completely reconfigured Jewish meditation practice to this day.

Abulafia's solitary retreat, when combined with the Science of the Letters, bears a striking resemblance to Sufi *khalwa*, where the individual separates himself for up to 40 days of intense, private prayer, undertaken with aid of a teacher, or *sheikh*. As to the direct Sufi influence on Abraham Abulafia's system, Moshe Idel notes:

> The connection between pronouncing the Name of God and *hitbodedut*, in the sense of seclusion in a special place, is already present in Sufism. The similarity between Rabbi Abraham Abulafia's approach to the subject and the Sufi system is well known ... Sufism may also have influenced Abulafia directly.[74]

This relationship between *hitbodedut* and Sufi prayer methods was acknowledged by Kabbalists of Abulafia's era, and discussions of *hitbodedut* over the next two centuries included material from Islamic texts, including works by Ibn Bajjah (d. 1138; Morocco) and Abu Bakr ibn Tufail (d. 1185; Morocco). These Muslim-inspired concepts later influenced the Safed Kabbalists (c. 15th-16th centuries).[75]

One passage in Abulafia's writing references various Islamic techniques and even a *hadith* in explaining a specific prayer method that takes place during *hitbodedut*:

> According to our tradition [Kabbalah], inspiration pours forth upon the Perfect Man (*ha-Adam ha-Shalem*) the moment he arrives at the end of the first series of chants ... Thereupon, he will visualize the form of a young boy or a *sheikh*, for this is the Arabic word for "old man," who is none other than Metatron, who is also a young man who is Enoch or Hermes.[76]

Professor Paul Fenton notes that the mention of the young boy is reminiscent of a *hadith* often quoted by the Sufis, "I saw my Lord in the form of a beardless youth." Additionally, the mention of the *sheikh* might be a reference to the Sufi ritual of *tawajjuh*, conjuring up the mental image of one's spiritual master prior to meditation.[77]

Orthodox Rabbi and scholar Aryeh Kaplan, writing in *Meditation and Kabbalah*, explains the importance of *hitbodedut* within Judaism, without noting its novelty:

> There is one word that is consistently used as a term for meditation by the commentators, philosophers and Kabbalists: *hitbodedut* ... When discussed in a Kabbalistic context, *hitbodedut* ... refers to a state of internal isolation, where the individual mentally secludes his essence from his thoughts ... This state of mental seclusion is very important to the prophetic experience.[78]

Heretical Propositions

These various solitary prayer methods ran contrary to traditional Jewish practice up to that point in time. A passage from Moshe Idel's *Studies in Ecstatic Kabbalah* notes how revolutionary were Abulafia's innovations within Jewish practice:

> Rabbinic Judaism, more than as a religion of a people, took shape as the religion of Jewish communities ... The most significant religious-social framework that remained – and was even strengthened – following the destruction of the Temple [c. 70 C.E.] was the community, whose focus was the synagogue. The common Divine worship – prayer – was transformed into the center of religious life; it required the assembling of ten men [*minyan*] as a precondition for the performance of many of its most important components. *Halakhic* [Jewish law] thought made the gathering of the community a more and more essential part of the religious cult and rejected, directly or indirectly, tendencies towards individualistic separatism ... The individual was no longer able to achieve perfection by the separation from the company of other men.[79]

While Judaism certainly had a history of solitude among its prophets and saints, it is just that: A sacred history. The normative practice of 13th-century Jews demanded that the binding of the community of Israel took precedence over personal salvation – medieval Judaism rejected tendencies toward individual worship.

This underscores the radical innovation of the prayer practice of the Jewish-Sufis – and why practitioners such as Abraham Maimonides in Egypt, who was accused of heresy, and Abraham Abulafia, who was convicted of it, ran into so much resistance from mainstream practitioners of their faith. To appreciate the difference between Abulafia's ideas and those of more traditional Jews, one need only look to other early authors of the Kabbalah in Provence, France, who were untouched by the Sufi inspiration. Those rabbis remained loyal to the proscription against individual worship, shying away from personal methods of prayer.[80]

*Devequt*

Abulafia was one of the first medieval Jewish practitioners to devote his full attention to the ideal of union (*devequt*) with God, a Jewish prayer ideal that even recently hasn't been fully acknowledged as central to medieval practice by some of Judaism's greatest scholars. As Professor Moshe Idel notes in *The Mystical Experience of Abraham Abulafia*: "The idea of unity between man and God which, according to Gershom Scholem is foreign to Jewish mysticism, nevertheless appears in Abulafia."[81] Abulafia believed in the ability of human beings to "disintegrate the human composition and unite its highest component with its source through the use of mystical techniques, such as respiratory exercises and permutation of the letters."[82]

Abulafia's writings are rife with such heretical claims of *unio mystica*. In his *Or ha-Sekel* (The Light of Reason), Abulafia avers:

Since between two lovers there are two parts of love which turn to be one entity, when it (the love) is actualized, the (Divine) Name is composed of two parts, which (point to) the connection of Divine intellectual love with human intellectual love, and it (the love) is one, just as His Name comprises *ehad ehad*, because of the attachment of human existence with Divine existence at the time of comprehension, equal with the intellect, until they both become one entity.[83]

There can be little doubt about Abulafia's meaning here, as he clearly states: "they both become one entity;" the fusion of he and He is complete. While it is virtually impossible to find precedence for this kind of view in Judaism before a few of the more extreme Jewish-Sufis that predated Abulafia, this exact conception of prayer was central to Sufism from the inception of that discipline. As al-Hujwiri (d. 1077; Pakistan) states:

It is impossible for the servant, when he sees the grace of God, not to love Him, and when he has loved, he will feel fellowship, because awe of the beloved is estrangement and fellowship is oneness.[84]

Abulafia completes the transformation of earlier Jewish ideas of *devequt* from Moses Maimonides' concept of *approaching* God, to a perpetual being-with-God, a melting of the individual into the infinite sea of the Divine Essence. The themes of spiritual love leading to oneness, central to Islamic mystical practice, were to become codified within Judaism with Abulafia and, as we shall see, influence Jewish spiritual practice from that time until our present day.

Abulafia's path to *devequt* was often based in the Sufi Way. To express the transformation from the personal experience of a human ego to subsistence in God, Abulafia utilized a Sufi *shath*, or ecstatic utterance: "he [the mystic] is He [God]," implying that the subject and the object are one, in the end.[85] Abulafia explains this idea:

> If [a man] has felt the Divine touch and perceived its nature, it seems right and proper to me ... that he should be called "master," because his name is like the Name of his Master. For now he is no longer separated from his Master, and behold he is in his Master and his Master is he; for he is so intimately adhering to Him [through *devequt*], that he cannot by any means be separated from Him, for *he is He*.[86] (Italics mine)

This statement was profoundly offensive and even heretical to more traditional Jews, as it implied a sinful pride in likening the human intellect to that of the Divine. The Sufi originator of this *shath*, the 9th-century Islamic mystic Mansur al-Hallaj (d. 922), was condemned as a heretic for a similar statement ("I am the Truth") and hung, flayed, crucified, drawn and quartered, burned and then drowned by Muslim authorities. Abulafia at least fared better.

It is interesting to note here how Abulafia's acceptance of Sufi conceptions of Divine union influenced later Jewish practice. A teaching story told in the 18th century about Aaron of Karlin (d. 1772; Belarus) shows not only the direct lineage of Abulafian conceptions of Divine union, but also the story itself originated in the Sufi tradition, with Mansur al-Hallaj.

> A fellow disciple, returning from Mezhrich, came about midnight to Karlin, desiring to greet his friend Aaron. He at once went to Aaron's house and knocked on the lighted window.
>
> "Who are you?" asked a voice from within and, certain that Rabbi Aaron would recognize his voice, the friend answered, "I."
>
> No reply came, and the door was not opened, although he knocked again and again. At last he cried, "Aaron, why do you not open to me?" Then he heard from within, "Who is it that is so bold as to say, 'I,' as God alone may do?"
>
> Then Aaron's friend said in his heart, "I have not yet learned my lesson," and returned immediately to his teacher.[87]

The same story as it was told of al-Hallaj, by the 13th-century Sufi saint Jalaluddin Rumi:

> A man knocks at his friend's door. The friend asks, "Who is there?" He answers, "I." The friend sends him away. For a full year, the grief of separation burns within him, and then he comes and knocks again. To his friend's question, "Who is it?" he replies, "Thou." And at once the room is opened to him, wherein there is no space for two "I's," that of God [the "friend"] and that of the man.[88]

Here we can see that Abulafia's conceptions of Divine union have become accepted as traditionally Jewish, and were attached to the founder of one of the great Hasidic lineages (see Chapter 6). For the Hasidic *tzaddik* (spiritual leader), the Sufi standard offered the goal of contemplative prayer – an ideal that became central to *Hasidism*.

The Moment of Inversion

Further, esoteric Islamic ideas concerning mystical attainment influenced Abulafia. According to the Sufis, the experience of union (the effacement of all but God) is a moment of inversion, when one's innermost essence is experienced as if projected outside of oneself. The overlap between Sufi ideas and Abraham Abulafia's thought can be seen by comparing texts of Muhyiddin Ibn Arabi (d. 1240), and a 13ᵗʰ-century Jewish mystic and follower of Abraham Abulafia. In Ibn Arabi's text (taken from the *Risalat al-Anwar*, Treatise on the Lights):

> He reveals forms of the sons of Adam, and veils are lifted, and veils descend. They have a special praise, which upon hearing you recognize, and you are not overcome. You see your form among them, and from it you recognize the moment that you are in … You will know your destination and place and the limit of your degree, and which divine name is your lord and where your portion of gnosis and sainthood exists – the form of your uniqueness. And if you do not stop with this, you are eradicated, then withdrawn, then effaced, then crushed, then obliterated. When the effects of eradication and what follows are terminated, you are affirmed …[89]

As Professor Michael Sells (University of Chicago) notes in *Mystical Union in Judaism, Christianity and Islam*:

> The moment (of union) is aligned with the "moment of truth," or the eschatological revelation of one's destiny and true self. This moment of inversion, in which one's inner essence or self is seen as projected outside, recalls later Sufi theories of afterlife in which what is manifest and apparent in this world becomes interiorized and what is interior and secret in this world becomes manifest.[90]

The overlap between Sufi ideas and Abraham Abulafia's thought may be seen in the writing of a late-13ᵗʰ-century Jewish mystic and follower of Abraham Abulafia.

> Through sheer force that stage is reached where you do not speak nor can you speak. And if sufficient strength remains to face oneself even further, then that which is within will manifest itself without and through the power of sheer imagination will take on the form of a polished mirror … Whereupon one sees that his inmost being is something outside of himself.[91]

### A Mystic Devoted to Spreading the Word

One central reason for the profound effect that Abulafia had on the development of later Jewish practice was his presentation of a detailed and methodical approach to his prayer techniques, in an easy-to-understand language. He succinctly translated various esoteric concepts of ultimate reality found in both Jewish and Islamic thought into an easily understood handbook for the personal experience of his followers.[92] Abulafia spent much of his life explicating the exact manners in which a searcher could move beyond the veils of ego that stand between humans and the Divine.

The specific progression of the aspirant through various prayer stages as explained by Abulafia, however, may often be traced directly back to Sufi inspirations. For instance, his representation of the mystic's path echoes that proposed by the Sufi al-Ghazali (d. 1111):

> According to the Hebrew version of al-Ghazali [translated by Abraham ibn Hasdai, c. 1230], the Sufis had a fixed path by which they attained communion with God, which involved several clearly delimited stages: 1) separation from the world; 2) indifference or equanimity; 3) solitude [*hitbodedut* or *khalwa*]; 4) repetition of God's name; and 5) communion with God ... The similarity of Abulafia's approach to this subject to the Sufi system is well known.[93]

Although there are some differences in interpretation of specific aspects of this path toward union with God, a major impetus for Abulafia's ideas undoubtedly rested with the Sufis, and perhaps even with specific passages translated from al-Ghazali.

### A Far-Ranging Influence

Abulafia's Islamic influences were hardly a secret to his immediate followers – indeed, many of them were drawn to the ideas and methodology of the Muslim mystics as well. Abulafia headed a school of Jewish-Sufis in the Holy Land, which sprang up in the latter half of the 13th century. By the time of his death in 1291, virtually all Kabbalistic writings emanating from the Holy Land bore conspicuous traces of Abulafia's ideas, most clearly those stemming from Sufism.[94] As stated by Moshe Idel, the foremost scholar studying Sufi influence on Abraham Abulafia's work:

> In my view, the repercussions of this synthesis [between the Kabbalah and Abulafia's Sufi inspirations] for the later development of Jewish mysticism were tremendous: the overemphasis on the importance of *devequt* [mystical union], of *hitbodedut* [either as seclusion, *khalwa*, or mental concentration] and the introduction of *hishtawwut* [equanimity] as having a paramount mystical value, restructured the bosom of Jew-

ish medieval mysticism ... and later on, led to the formation of Hasidism as a mystical phenomenon.[95]

Abulafia's manuscripts themselves were well known in Eastern Europe as late as the 18th century,[96] at the exact time that the Baal Shem Tov was formulating Hasidism (Chapter 6).

## Rabbi Nathan ben Se'adya

Abraham Abulafia was a powerful teacher, and he left numerous students who expanded his ideas. One recently discovered 13th-century Jewish-Sufi under Abulafia's influence was Rabbi Nathan ben Se'adya, who made a deep impression on the next generation of Kabbalists in the Holy Land. Rabbi Nathan left us with one of the masterpieces of this era, *Sha'arei Tzedek* (c. 1295, Gates of Justice), which contains much of Abulafia's teachings, mixed with, among other things, further Sufi inspirations.

We find in this tract a detailed description of the Muslim *dhikr* ritual, in which Rabbi Nathan not only outlines the steps of that Islamic litany, but also implies that Jews can get more out of this prayer ritual than Muslims, due to their understanding of the Kabbalah:

> The common type of ecstasy consists in the Islamic mystics divesting their souls of all natural forms by various procedures to such a degree, so they claim, that if any spiritual form were to enter their soul, it is singled out in their imagination and this enables them to foretell coming events prior to their occurrence. Some are not sufficiently capable of such a degree of revelation and are uplifted by a spiritual revelation commensurate with their essence. I inquired as to how they achieve this and was informed that they do so by repeating the Divine name, which in the Arabic tongue is *Allah* ... After having repeated the letters thereof and entirely divesting their thoughts of all other natural forms, the letters of the name *Allah* take effect on them, each in accordance with his nature and the intensity of his devotions. They eventually enter into ecstasy but they know not wherefore, since they do not possess the esoteric tradition [Kabbalah].[97]

It is interesting to note that Rabbi Nathan had direct access to Sufis and their most important spiritual exercises, so that he could directly ask them "how they achieve this," underscoring yet again the porous relations and personal respect among practitioners of both religions at this time.

*Sha'are Tzedek* illustrates the path of *hitbodedut* by use of a story from the Muslim philosopher Abd Allah ibn Sina (d. 1037), stating unabashedly that this Sufi was the source. According to Rabbi Nathan:

> I found in the words of one of the great philosophers of his generation, namely, Ibn Sina, in which he said that he would concentrate while

composing his great works, and when a certain subject or matter would be difficult for him, he would contemplate its intermediate proposition and draw his thought to it.[98]

*Sha'arei Tzedek* also is one of the important texts that brought Sufi ideas to later Jews, while appearing completely loyal to ancient Jewish practice. The book traces the origins of the Science of the Letters back to Moses, thereby further grounding this concept in the Biblical past:

> With the revelation at Sinai, God Himself introduced Moses into "the inmost secrets of the Science of the Letters," and with this understanding, Moses arranged the *Torah*: "as a continuum of letters which [corresponds to] the path of [Divine] names, which reflects the structure of the letters on high; and he divided [the text of the Torah] in accordance with the reading of the commandments, which reflects the essence of the structure of the lower entities."[99]

## Rabbi Isaac of Acre

The next generation of Jewish mystics in the Holy Land embraced and expanded the Islamic mystical ideas and practices of Abulafia, Nathan and the other Jewish-Sufis. Rabbi Isaac ben Samuel of Acre (d. 1350, Spain) provided a bridge between the eccentric, personal (and officially vilified) vision of Abraham Abulafia and later mainstream Kabbalistic thinkers. He ended up being an important influence on European Hasidism.

### Hitbodedut

Rabbi Isaac expanded on Abulafia's ideas concerning *hitbodedut* (solitary prayer), aligning his concept of it more closely with the traditional Islamic definition of this technique. He posited that those practicing solitary contemplation should attempt to quiet their senses and cease their thoughts about all sensible objects, getting in touch, instead, with the spirituality of their reason.[100] This involved secluding oneself in a dark, silent place, where the adept focused his entire attention inward, utilizing various meditation methods developed by Sufi-leaning Jews.[101]

To further the quest for the spiritual ideal of *devequt* (Divine union), Isaac popularized Abulafia's Sufi-inspired combination of the letters. He also included other esoteric ideas appropriated from his Islamic contemporaries. Paul Fenton notes in *Solitary Meditation in Jewish and Islamic Mysticism*:

> According to Isaac ... cleaving with God is obtained by constant visualization of the Divine Name, "as if they were written before him in Hebrew script, each letter appearing before him in gigantic dimensions." This specific manner in which the letters were visualized is also attested

in Sufi sources. Here is the testimony of a modern mystic, *Sheikh* al-Alawi: "The way practiced most often by the Master and to which we also resorted, consisted in having the disciple practice the *dhikr* of the Unique Name [i.e. *Allah*] while concentrating on the letters until they became engraved in his imagination. He then recommended of the disciple to extend them and enlarge them until they filled the whole horizon."[102]

Isaac had a significant influence in moving these ideas into later versions of the Kabbalah.[103]

### Hishtawwut

Along with *hitbodedut*, Isaac solidified the Sufi ideal of *hishtawwut* (equanimity or detachment) as central to Jewish spiritual practice.

> According to Rabbi Isaac, a condition of *ataraxia* ["absence of passion," a term used in the Cynic and Stoic tradition] is necessary for concentration, which leads, as in the case of Abulafia, to the Holy Spirit and even to prophecy. One should note here the introduction into the context of Kabbalistic thought of equanimity as a precursor of *hitbodedut* ... Its appearance in Rabbi Isaac is another important addition based on Sufi influence.[104]

As Rabbi Isaac himself states: "He who merits the secret of communion [with the Divine] will merit the secret of equanimity [*hishtawwut*], and if he receives this secret, then he will also know the secret of *hitbodedut,* and once he has known the secret of *hitbodedut*, he will receive the Holy Spirit."[105]

Although Moses Maimonides had been attracted to this idea, including a Sufi story about equanimity in his letters and writing (Chapter 3), he did not conceive of it as a necessary precursor to Jewish prayer practice, and by means of meditation, to Divine union. This is another example of how Moses Maimonides' ideas were greatly expanded by later Jewish thinkers, who could point back to the venerable master as including the notions in his exegeses of Jewish practice.

### Ruhaniyyut

Isaac held that the purpose of meditation and letter permutations was to cause God's power to descend and cling to the human soul,[106] bringing the *ruhaniyyut* (Divine spirit) into the heart of the devoted. As Isaac states, "the wise man comes to isolate himself, and to concentrate to bring down into his soul the Divine spirit."[107]

This theory – inspired at least in part by Muslim mystics – posited that the supplicant could cause God's power (the *ruhaniy*) to descend and cling to him. We get an idea of one source of this concept by looking at the Muslim al-Shahrastani's (d. 1153) *Kitab al-Milal wa'l-Nihal* (The Book of

Sects and Creeds), which discusses the term in this way:

> Intermediaries between God and the other created beings and the plan-
> ets, called the supernal temples, are in relation to them, as it were, bod-
> ies and individual persons. These supernal beings receive an influx
> from the *ruhaniyyut* that set them in motion with a view to order and
> to the good; they in turn are the causes of everything that happens [in
> the sublunar world]. Men honor each of these "temples" with various
> kinds of observance and worship ... for addressing oneself to the *ru-
> haniy* to which it pertains and, beyond that, to the Lord of Lords.[108]

Isaac posited that the 22 letters of the Hebrew alphabet incorporate *ruhaniyyut*, thereby allowing correct meditation on them to bring this energy
down into the intellect of the mystic. As Isaac states: "When man separates
himself from the objects of sensation and concentrates [*hitbodedut*] and
removes all the powers of his intellective soul from them ... his thoughts
shall draw down the abundance [*ruhaniyyut*] from above and it shall come
to reside in his soul [*devequt*]."[109]

This represents another subtle change in Jewish mysticism, as in Judaism's most recent past, even Sufi-inspired unitive prayer had offered a one-
way path to God, with the adept ascending on high to achieve proximity
or, at the very best, communion with the Divine Essence. Isaac's concepts
helped to round out ideas of prophecy that originated with Jafar as-Sadiq
(d. 765). With the Divine power being represented as an essence that could
be not only be accessed but also brought into the world through the meditation of the mystic, the dissemination of this Power through prophetic action
became clearer.

Moshe Idel notes in *Mystical Union in Judaism, Christianity and
Islam*:

> It is important to point out the profound influence of the Islamic con-
> cept of *ruhaniyyut* on Jewish mysticism. The sources of this term are
> [Arabic] texts, which use *ruhaniyyut* in order to designate the supernal
> forces or lights. Union with the Divine was portrayed as a spiritual
> force (Hebrew: *Ruhaniyt*) that descends upon the mystic during *de-
> vequt*. This way of understanding unitive experiences is widespread in
> Jewish mysticism, though predominant in Hasidism.[110]

### Profane and Spiritual Eroticism

Continuing to refine another idea taken over from medieval Sufis, Isaac
gave the romantic symbolism of the Kabbalah a human twist. In Rabbi
Isaac's words, "he who hath not loved a woman hath no phenomenal model
for worship of God." The experience of human love provides a model for
spiritual experience. We see this idea played out time and again in the

Kabbalists and, especially, in Hasidism, for whom every experience in the world becomes a metaphor for, and even a stairway to, true knowledge of the Divine. This concept parallels a proposition found in Muhyiddin ibn Arabi's *Fusus al-Hikam* (Bezels of Wisdom): "The contemplation of God through woman is the most perfect of contemplations."[111]

While this certainly appears to be a contradiction to the idea of removing oneself from all sensory experience for prayer practice, it is important to remember that by the early 14th century, the ascetic element within Sufism was no longer as accentuated as before, and Sufis and their Jewish protégés were discovering the balance between interior experience and the exterior world. Both Islamic and Jewish mystics found separation for discrete periods of time (*khalwa*) vital to spiritual enlightenment, but a complete removal from the world into a monastic asceticism was unusual during this era in either tradition.

### From the Holy Land to Spain

Circumstances lifted Rabbi Isaac, and his Sufi-inspired vision of Jewish mysticism, from obscurity to a central role in the development of Jewish mysticism. Hearing of the Kabbalistic masterpiece, the *Zohar*, Isaac traveled from the Holy Land to northern Spain, hoping to meet the spiritual mastermind who had compiled the magnum opus.[112] There, much to his disappointment, he discovered that his contemporary had written the mystical masterpiece, rather than "assembling" it from ancient sources.

> Isaac met Moses [de Leon] in Valladolid and was informed under oath that he [Moses de Leon] was in possession of the "ancient book written by Simeon ben Yohai" and would show it to him in his house at Avila. Subsequently, after Moses de Leon's death when Isaac came to Avila ... both the widow of the deceased and his daughter denied the existence of such an original. According to them, Moses de Leon had written the *Zohar* all by himself and, to his wife's question as to why he did not claim the authorship of the work, he had replied: "If I told people that I am the author, they would pay no attention nor spend a farthing on the book, for they would say that these are but the workings of my own imagination. But now that they hear that I am copying from the book *Zohar* which Simeon ben Yohai wrote under the inspiration of the Holy Spirit, they are paying a high price for it as you know."[113]

All was not lost, however, as Isaac found his way to Barcelona, a center of Kabbalistic and Sufi studies in Spain (where Sufism had inspired Kabbalistic thought some 100 years earlier).[114] There, he introduced his Sufi-inspired ideas to a new generation of *Sephardic* Kabbalists, this time in Christian Spain. After the Jews were expelled from Spain in 1492, the Sufic strands threaded by Isaac into the Spanish Kabbalah would be reintroduced into the Holy Land, as the greatest thinkers of this Diaspora settled in Safed, north of Jerusalem.

### Further Jewish-Sufis in Isaac's Circle

There were many other Jewish practitioners during this time who were inspired by Abraham Abulafia, or directly by the Sufis. Rabbi Moses Narboni (d. 1362; Spain) quoted extensively from Abulafia's *Sefer 'Or ha-Sekel* (Book of Light of the Mind);[115] Rabbi Solomon ben Moses (c. 1290) sought out Abulafia specifically because he was teaching the Sufi-inspired Kabbalah – an interest of Solomon's which pre-dated his knowing Abulafia;[116] Rabbi Shem Tov ibn Gaon (d. 1330; Spain),[117] Rabbi Judah Albotini (d. 1520, see below), Rabbi David ibn Zimra (d. 1573; Safed), Rabbi Joseph ibn Zaiah (c. 16th century) and some of the greatest Kabbalists in the 15th-and 16th-century mystical center of Safed were greatly attracted to the work of the itinerant, prophetic luminaries, Abraham Abulafia and Rabbi Isaac of Acre.

## Later Kabbalists Under Sufi Influence

### Safed

Fast forward a couple hundred years and we come to another group of Kabbalists living in the Holy Land who still were deeply inspired by Sufism, and who would have a direct influence on the flowering of Hasidism in the 18th century. The lineage of Spanish Kabbalists who had inherited their ideas from Abraham Abulafia and Rabbi Isaac of Acre in late 13th-century Spain, returned to the Holy Land two centuries later after being expelled from the Iberian Peninsula. In addition to submerging the Spanish economy, the decision of King Ferdinand and Queen Isabella to evict the Jews from Spain in 1492 succeeded, once again, in scattering the influence of Sufi-inspired Jews throughout the world.

By this time, however, much of the Sufi influence had gone underground. For the first time in the development of the Kabbalah, most Jewish mystics who were building on earlier thought might not have realized that they were utilizing Sufi concepts. The original surge of Sufi discovery by Jewish thinkers that the Golden Age had inspired had run its course. Although echoes of the positive interpersonal relations between Jewish and Muslim mystics continued, in many instances, the Safed Kabbalists who built on the Jewish-Sufi works of their predecessors may have been unaware of the exact provenance of the ideas that so attracted them.

The small town of Safed, in the Upper Galilee in the Holy Land, emerged as the center of Kabbalistic studies about 40 years after the expulsion of the Spanish Jews. Jewish legend held that all the souls of the righteous dead passed through Safed on their way to the Cave of Macpelah, the first door of Paradise on Earth[118] – so perhaps some of the more righteous living figured that they would get a head start. In addition, the little town was close to Meron, the birthplace and tomb of the supposed author of the *Zohar*, Simeon ben Yohai (c. 2nd century). From the late 15th century onward, Jewish mystics from far and wide gathered in the small hill town. Recent exiles from Spain, wanderers from Poland and Germany, rabbis from Egypt and other North African countries and even a few stragglers from Yemen filtered into Safed to study and continue to expand the Kabbalah. The convergence of these many strains of Judaism precipitated a revival in the small town, bursting into spiritual flame between 1540-1570.[119]

### Sufis in Safed

Not only did the greatest Kabbalistic minds concentrate in the village, but a thriving community of Sufi mystics also was in residence there, providing the Jewish thinkers with a firsthand look at Islamic mysticism. For instance, the important Kabbalistic practice of seclusion (*hitbodedut*) mirrored similar activity by the Rifai Sufis who used seclusion cells, or *zawiyyas*, on the mountainside across from the town to practice *khalwa*.[120] Undoubtedly, this provided the Jewish mystics with an immediate view of the practice.[121]

Although not as widespread as it had been earlier in Spain, Egypt and the Holy Land, congenial relations between followers of the two religious paths certainly were not unheard of. Rabbi Hayyim Vital (d. 1620; Damascus), an important source of Kabbalistic lore for the Baal Shem Tov (d. 1760, founder of Hasidism), related that his theological discussions with Islamic dignitaries prompted him to study the Arabic tongue, so that he could better appreciate the nuances of their ideas.[122]

The Middle Eastern Sufi as-Sha'rani (d. 1565), operating a few decades prior to Vital, noted that not only did Jews come and study with him, but also that many found so much worth in his Islamic mystical teachings that they often embraced Islam.[123] His claim can hardly be dismissed, as half-a-century later, Rabbi Abraham Gavison of Tlemcen (c. 1605; Algeria) concluded his Hebrew translation of the Sufi al-Ghazali's mystical poetry with these words: "I have translated the poetry of this sage, for even though he be not of the Children of Israel, it is accepted that the pious of the gentiles have a share in the world to come and surely heaven will not withhold from him the reward of his faith."[124] As late as the 18th century, Kabbalists still had regular contact with the Sufis, such as the Moroccan Rabbi Halifa ibn Malka (c. 1750).[125]

### Abulafian Influence

The Sufi-inspired tracts of Abraham Abulafia, whose ideas had been smoldering in the Holy Land for two centuries, spread like wildfire among these

Kabbalists.[126] The greatest Jewish thinkers of Safed, such as Rabbi Judah Albotini (d. 1520), Rabbi Solomon ben Moses Alkabez (c. 1550), Rabbi Moshe Cordovero (d. 1570) and Rabbi Hayyim Vital (d. 1620) were directly influenced by Abulafia's works. As Moshe Idel notes: "*Sulam ha'Aliyah* [Ladder of Ascent], written by Judah Albotini in Jerusalem in the early 16th century, is based entirely on Abraham Abulafia's *Hayyei Ha'Olam HaBa* [The Life of the World to Come] and on Rabbi Nathan ben Se'adyah's *Sha'arei Tzedek* [Gates of Justice, another Jewish-Sufi tract]. Abulafia's influence is visible as well in *'Even HaShoham* by R. Joseph ibn Zaiah (d. 1539)."[127]

Traces of the Jewish-Sufi synthesis found in Abulafia's writings also were apparent in the theology of R. Elijah de Vidas' (d. 1592) work, *Reshit Hokhmah* (The Beginning of Wisdom).[128] All of these Jewish thinkers became important influences on the continuing growth of the Kabbalistic sciences – and, later on, Hasidism.

## Judah Albotini

Rabbi Judah Albotini (d. 1520; Jerusalem) was Chief Rabbi of Jerusalem, where he became known as a commentator on the writings of Moses Maimonides. He continued the centuries' old tradition of combining Sufi inspirations with an expertise in Maimonidean studies – a tradition which began with the great master Moses Maimonides himself. Albotini expended much effort explaining and defending the master, thereby strengthening his credentials as a traditional Jewish practitioner, while continuing to thread Sufi-inspired innovations into his Jewish exegesis. Like many other Sufi-inspired Jews, he held an important temporal position, rising to be head of the Jerusalem *Yeshiva* and of the Jerusalem rabbis, lending further credence to his ideas.

### *Hishtawwut*

In his book *Marot Elohim* (Visions of God), Albotini discusses the "Secret of the Chariot" (*Ma'aseh Merkabah*), the 1200-year-old Jewish mystical symbol, overlaying concepts borrowed from Islamic mysticism atop this ancient lore. In place of the necessary preconditions to approaching God mentioned in the Talmud, of which wisdom was primary, Albotini stresses *hishtawwut*, or equanimity. In the book, he relates a story exemplifying the necessity of reaching equanimity prior to achieving the level of *hitbodedut* that had appeared in Isaac of Acre's work. According to Albotini's story:

> By this he shall ascend to the level of equanimity, as that sage said to his student, who asked him: "Will you teach us the secret of the Chariot?" He answered: "Have you achieved equanimity?" And the student did not understand what he was saying to him, until he explained the

157

matter to him, namely that all attributes are equal to him. And this was what he said to him: "If a man insulted you, and took away that which was yours, would you be angry and strict with him over this? And if he did the opposite, namely, to honor you and give you many gifts, would you rejoice over this and feel it? And would you feel in your soul that you were affected by these two opposites?" Then this master said to him, "If so, then you have not yet acquired the quality of equanimity, that is, that it should be equal to you whether it should be honor or its opposite. And since such is the case, how can you ascend to the level of *hitbodedut*, which comes after you have achieved equanimity?"[129]

This anecdote originated in al-Makki's (d. 996) Sufi manual *Qut al-Qulub* (The Nourishment of the Hearts), which had a strong influence on Bahya ibn Pakuda's (d. 1080) *Guide to the Duties of the Heart*. The "master" described in his story is none other than the Prophet Mohammad.[130] Gershom Scholem notes: "There is nothing in this Kabbalistic or Sufi anecdote that is not entirely in harmony with the spirit of Hasidism."[131] Albotini's use of this tale was related to the tendency of Sufis to diminish or even negate completely the value of scholarly learning,[132] something that was still primary for Jewish traditionalists.

### *Sulam ha'Aliyah*

In another book, the *Sulam ha'Aliyah* (The Ladder of Ascent), Albotini went so far as to incorporate a Talmudic saying in the discussion of *hitbodedut* and *hishtawwut*, thereby attempting to give these Sufi ideas an honored place within the pantheon of Jewish prayer practice. Here is yet another example of a Sufi-inspired Jewish mystic reinterpreting ancient Jewish tradition in light of Sufi concepts.[133] As Moshe Idel notes, while important Kabbalists such as Albotini continued using Sufi interpretations of ancient Jewish scripture, in this case, the idea of *hishtawwut* opposed central Jewish attitudes.[134]

The name of Albotini's treatise, *Ladder of Ascent*, stems directly from Islamic precursors. This is a particularly fascinating example of Islamic influence, coming as it does from a central story concerning the Prophet Muhammad in the Koran, so it merits detailed discussion. The *Mi'raj* (night journey of the Prophet Muhammad) is a story from the Prophet's life and related in the Koran, which outlines a voyage that Muhammad took from Mecca to Jerusalem on a magic steed, and then via a "ladder of ascent" to the "farthest throne" and into the presence of God. Muhammad's "ladder of ascent" came to represent for Sufis and, through them, for some medieval Jews, the spiritual path that mystics followed to achieve the goal of Divine union. This metaphor had been referred to by Islamic thinkers as early as the eighth century, and became important to Jews starting in the 13th century, helping them to reinterpret the Biblical story of Jacob's Ladder (Genesis 28:10–15), as well as giving them another tool for representing the mystic's path.

The *Mi'raj* is not depicted with any specificity in the Koran; rather, it is based on passages from two different chapters (17:1, 60; 53:13-18, 70). The portrayals of this event expanded along with the Islamic tradition, growing into ever more elaborate accounts, outlining various aspects of the Prophet's voyage through the seven heavens.[135] The anniversary of this event now defines one of the two holiest nights of the Muslim calendar, the *Lay'lat al-Mi'raj* (The Night of the Ascent).

As the 20th-century scholar of Jewish mysticism, Rabbi Alexander Altmann describes the Sufi interpretation of the *Mi'raj*, in his article *The Ladder of Ascension*:

> The ladder motif is already found in Ibn Ishaq [d. 767; Muhammad's biographer], drawing on *Surah* 70 of the Koran, which bears the title "The Stairways" (*al-Ma'arij*) and *Allah* is there called *Dhu'l Ma'arij* (Lord of the Stairways) ... In Islamic mysticism, the story of the Prophet's Night Journey and of his ascension became the archetypal pattern of the soul's itinerary to God. Hasan al-Basri [d. 728] was probably the first to interpret the *Mi'raj* as a vision of the Divine essence. Al-Hallaj [d. 922] makes the theme one of mystical contemplation. The Persian Sufi Bayazid Bistami [d. 874] was several times banned from his native city because he attributed a *Mi'raj* similar to the Prophet's, to himself. Al-Hujwiri [d. 1076] speaks of Bayazid's mystical voyage as "the *Mi'raj* of Bayazid; and the term *Mi'raj* denotes proximity to God." The popularity of the theme among the Sufis is attested by the collection of the entire material in al-Qushayri's [d. 1072] *Kitab al-Mi'raj* [Book of the Ascent].[136]

There were two specific Islamic accounts of the *Mi'raj* that influenced medieval Jews. One was from Abd Allah ibn Sina (d. 1037), who wrote an account of the *Mi'raj* entitled, "Book of the Prophet Muhammad's Ascent to Heaven." Another important influence on Jewish thinkers was the account of the *Mi'raj* codified by the Spanish Muslim philosopher Ibn al-Sid al-Batalyawsi (d. 1127), in his *Kitab al Hada'iq* (Book of Circles/Gardens).

Al-Batalyawsi's book became popular among medieval Jews. There were at least three Hebrew translations of the treatise, as well as Hebrew translations of other Islamic works that treated the *Mi'raj* as allegory. Moses ibn Tibbon (d. 1283; Provence) translated al-Batalyawsi's work in its entirety, while Samuel ibn Motot (c. late 14th century; Spain) included al-Batalyawsi's section on the Prophet Muhammad's ascent in his commentary on the 9th-century proto-Kabbalistic work, *Sefer Yetzirah* (Book of

Creation).[137] Through these works, the Muslim interpretation of the spiritual path as a "ladder of ascension" (*Sulam ha-Aliyah*) along a "straight path" (*Khatt al-Mustaqim*) entered into the Jewish mystical lexicon.

One of the most important Jewish thinkers to incorporate this idea was Moses Maimonides, who reinterpreted the Biblical story of Jacob's Ladder in light of ideas proposed by the Sufi al-Batalyawsi. The Maimonidean interpretation of Jacob's Dream, and prophecy in general, reflected the newer Sufi concepts of a "spiritual ladder" by which saints moved toward their revelations. As Alexander Altmann notes:

> In Maimonides' references to the subject [the ascent towards God], the angels ascending the ladder [in Jacob's Dream] are said to denote the prophets, since they achieve a knowledge of God by moving up toward God who is "stably and permanently atop the ladder." They first ascend and having attained the degree of prophecy granted them, they descend in order to govern and teach the people in light of their prophetic inspiration. This interpretation of Jacob's Dream re-echoes al-Batalyawsi's view of the "ladder of ascent" ... and it reflects, in particular, the Sufi concept of the "spiritual ladder" by which the saints rise towards their ecstatic visions.[138]

By the time that Moses de Leon wrote the *Zohar* (c. 1295), he might not have known that the "ladder of ascension" motif that he utilized stemmed from Muhammad's *Mi'raj*. Regardless, de Leon incorporates the model of the "straight line" (*Khatt al-Mustaqim*), inserting it as an idea central to the Kabbalistic Tree of Life. "The decisive proof that Moses de Leon took this term from al-Batalyawsi lies in the fact that he links it with the ladder motif and the concept of the ascent of the souls of the departed to the supernal world. This is exactly what we find in al-Batalyawsi."[139] Altmann continues:

> All the essential elements of the specific configuration of the [Ladder of Ascent] motif found in al-Batalyawsi and in the *Ikhwan* (*as-Safa*, 10th century) ... are found [in the *Zohar*] re-assembled ... Since the *Sephirotic* diagram employs the symbol of a middle line leading straight from *Kether* down to *Tipheret*, *Yesod*, and *Malkuth*, and since the characteristic symbol of *Tipheret* is the linear [Hebrew] letter *vav*, it is not difficult to connect this line with the [Islamic] concept of the *Khatt al-Mustaqim*.

The fact that these ideas were based on the Islamic precursor was born out by the use of the specific term, *Khatt al-Mustaqim* (straight line), which the Jewish mystics utilized to denote the movement of energy from the highest level of the Tree of Life to the center of the lowest, in the tenth *Sephira* of *Malkuth*, which mirrors exactly the vocabulary of earlier Sufis.[140]

At the time that Judah Albotini was naming his Kabbalistic tract after the second most important holy day in the Muslim calendar, he might not have known that the central concept for his *Sulam ha-Aliyah* originated in Sufi precursors.

### Science of the Letters

Albotini also incorporated Abulafia's Sufi-inspired Science of the Letters into his system. Much of *Sulam ha-Aliyah* is based on Abulafia's work, as well as Rabbi Nathan's Jewish-Sufi tract *Sha'arei Tzedek* (Gates of Justice). He models his method of climbing the "Ladder of Ascent" toward union with the Divine spirit on the Abulafian permutation of the letters.[141]

Albotini might not have been aware that he was introducing Sufi-inspired ideas into his Jewish worship, as he based much of his work on Jewish precursors such as Moses Maimonides, Abraham Abulafia and Isaac of Acre. One can assume, however, that he had some idea that these "Jewish" methods mirrored Sufi practice, as the Islamic mystics were well represented throughout the Holy Land at the time that he worked.

## Moshe Cordovero

Moshe Cordovero (d. 1570; Safed) was one of the most important Sufi-inspired Kabbalists to work between the 14th century and the dawn of Hasidism, in the 18th century. It was in his influential text, *Pardes Rimmonim* (An Orchard of Pomegranates) that Abulafia's Sufi-inspired ideas fused with the more traditional, non-Islamic aspects of the Kabbalah and then were disseminated to a wider audience, spilling outside of the Holy Land and eventually reaching the parlors and prayer halls of Eastern Europe. While Cordovero almost certainly did not think of any of his innovations as "Sufic," the Islamic mystical provenance of some of them cannot be denied – and his inclusion of Islamic-inspired material from earlier Jewish-Sufis had a profound effect on succeeding generations of Jewish mystics.

### Abulafian Influence

Cordovero's *Pardes Rimmonim* borrows liberally from Abraham Abulafia's texts, including many passages taken verbatim from his works. Abulafia's pronunciations of the Divine Names are included in the book, as well as the cryptic "tables" (more like drawings) of the specific combinations of the letters to be followed during *hitbodedut*, plus Abulafia's explanations of how to apply his system. As Moshe Idel notes in his *Studies in Ecstatic Kabbalah*, so inspired was Cordovero by the heretical Jewish-Sufi that he considered Abulafia's Kabbalah to be the words of a "celestial messenger," superior even to the canonical text, the *Zohar*![142] Cordovero proposed that the Sufi-inspired idea of the union of the human intellect with the Divine could be achieved through Abulafia's combination of the letters.[143]

Cordovero also was attracted to other aspects of Abraham Abulafia's work that came directly from Islam. For instance Moshe Idel notes, concerning the importance of *hitbodedut* in Cordovero's work:

> The inclusion of the concept of *hitbodedut* in Cordovero's writings was an important step toward its appreciation by a far wider public ... *Hitbodedut* continued, together with Rabbi Bahya ibn Pakuda's views on the subject, to constitute a source of inspiration for the guidance of Jewish mystics. The influence of [these] views may be traced through the writings of the Hasidic mystics ...[144]

That Cordovero was basing many of his ideas on Abulafia and the 13th-century Jewish-Sufi Kabbalists of the Holy Land is clear, as he mentions both Abraham Abulafia and Rabbi Nathan's *Sha'arei Tzedek* (Gates of Justice) by name.[145]

Cordovero followed the time-honored manner of combining his Jewish-Sufi inspirations seamlessly with purported ancient Jewish lore. Echoing the *Sha'arei Tzedek*, he asserted that the "ecstatic Kabbalah" – i.e. Abulafia's Sufi-inspired version – was actually the vocation of the ancient Prophets of Israel.[146] He stated that the Prophets had used the Science of the Letters to acquire the *spirit* embodied in the letters. In *Pardes Rimmonim*, Cordovero brings together these ideas with the *Torah*:

> Several of the early ones explained that by the combination and transmutation of the 72-letter Holy Name or other names, after great *hitbodedut*, the righteous man, who is worthy and enlightened in such matters, will have a portion of the Divine voice [*bat qol*] revealed to him, in the sense of: "The spirit of God spoke in me, and His word was on my lips." [II Samuel 23:2][147]

Mirroring Muslim ideas, he held that *hitbodedut* defines a process whereby the soul migrates from the world of matter to the world of spirit – and through contemplation on the letters, sensory data is stripped away and the searcher empties himself of all but the Divine Essence.[148]

*Ruhaniyyut*

In combination with the idea of approaching God through *hitbodedut*, Cordovero proposed that the mystic can draw down the essence of God's power (*ruhaniyyut*) into his own soul, thereby acting as a prophetic agent for God in this world, reprising medieval Islamic ideas of prophetic legislation. Cordovero intones:

> For he combines together the potencies and unites them and arouses desire in them, each to its brother, as the *membrum virile* of man and his companion [i.e. the female], until there is poured upon him a spirit of abundance – on the condition that he be engaged in this thing, as a vessel prepared to and worthy of receiving the spirit [*ruhaniyyut*] ...[149]

This rejuvenation of Abulafia and Isaac of Acre's Sufi-inspired concepts of *ruhaniyyut* became of central importance to the Hasidic understanding of *devequt*.[150]

### Jewish *Sheikh*

Moshe Cordovero elaborates on this Divine influx achieved through union:

> The drawing down of spiritual force [*ruhaniyyut*] and influx from the top of the degrees [*Sephirot*] to *Malkuth* [the lowest *Sephira*, where humans live], the reservoir where the influx is gathered [i.e., in human-kind] ... and from there it comes down to the lower [entities] ... When there is a blessing after a commandment or an act ... that act is a vessel and a bucket, by means of which the waters of the influx are drawn.[151]

This concept of drawing down the spiritual effluence through a "command-ment or an act" led directly to later Hasidic ideas of the *tzaddik*, the Jewish equivalent of a *sheikh* who was at the center of the 18th-century Jewish spiritual system. While various Sufi-oriented Jewish mystics, most notably Abraham Maimonides, Obadyah Maimonides and Abraham Abulafia, had proposed the necessity of a spiritual teacher in earlier times, the concept of the Jewish *tzaddik* wasn't completely institutionalized until the life of the Baal Shem Tov (d. 1760, the founder of Hasidism), though no doubt it existed prior to that in actuality. Hasidic thinkers based many of their ideas on Cordovero's concepts of the drawing down and dissemination of the spiritual force. As Cordovero himself avers:

> Everything depends upon the spiritual force, the influx, which flows by means of the *tzaddik* and of his proper deeds ... The world is blessed by the spiritual force flowing because of the merit [of the *tzaddiks*] ... and all the worlds and things are subject to the *tzaddik*.[152]

Here we also get a sense of how Jewish mysticism, while strongly inspired by Sufism, extrapolates from it, and at the same time differentiates itself. In Cordovero and, as we shall see in Hasidism (Chapter 6), the *tzaddik* has magical powers that often go beyond those of the Sufi *sheikh* – and the role of the *tzaddik* as God's agent extends so far as to make this Jewish mystical leader responsible for God's spiritual health! The Sufi *sheikh*, on the other hand, operates mostly as an agent of personal salvation for his student.

### *Devequt*

Cordovero proposes a definition of *devequt*, which echoes Sufi ideas:

> Assuming that by pronouncing the letters of the Divine Name in each and every moment, one is clinging to God; the more precise meaning

of this cleaving to God is to sustain an uninterrupted awareness of the Divine in one's mind. The ideal of oneness with God obliterates the distance between the human and the Divine through a continuous act of remembering.[153]

"Continuous act of remembering" is the exact definition of the Sufi *dhikr*. Cordovero helped to institutionalize this radical, and even heretical, meaning of Jewish prayer to the extent that *today* it is considered the epitome of traditional Judaic practice!

## Rabbi Eliezer Azikri

Rabbi Eliezer Azikri (d. 1600) spent his life immersed in spiritual practice, ultimately achieving complete acceptance of the Divine Essence. Finally, far along on this path, he drew up a "deed of association" with God, in the form of a legal document, his witnesses being "Heaven" and "Earth." To achieve these lofty goals, Azikri folded Sufi ideas into his practice, sprinkling his seminal work *Sefer Haredim* (Book of the Pious) with Islamic mystical inspirations.[154]

In this work, Azikri discusses the practical aspects of *hitbodedut*, mentioning Rabbi Isaac of Acre by name. Elsewhere in *Sefer Haredim*, Azikri quotes the Safed Rabbi Isaac Luria (d. 1572; Safed, see below) as stating that *hitbodedut* "is helpful to the soul seven times more than study, and ... a man should concentrate and meditate one day a week." This sentiment paraphrased a statement by the Sufi adept, Abu al-Najib al-Suhrawardi (d. 1168), who said "contemplation for one hour is better than ritual worship for a whole year."[155]

This ideal may be traced all the way back to the Prophet Muhammad, who is quoted in a *hadith*: "One hour of meditation is worth more than the good works accomplished by the two species endowed with weight [humans and *jinn*]."[156] As we have seen, separation and contemplation for prayer run directly contrary to traditional rabbinic practice, which demands a gathering of at least ten men (*minyan*) for the performance of most important prayers.

Moshe Idel notes in his *Studies in Ecstatic Kabbalah*:

[Writings such as Azriki's and his contemporary Safed Kabbalists] constituted the final stage in a process of penetration of *hitbodedut* into Jewish culture as a practical teaching. Abulafia's writings constituted the beginning of the process of absorption of the Sufi outlook within Kabbalah ... The influence of the views sketched above may be traced through the writings of the Hasidic mystics.[157]

## Hayyim Vital and Isaac Luria

Rabbi Hayyim Vital (d. 1620; Damascus) was an important bridge for

Safed Sufi-inspired Jewish thought to enter later European Hasidism for two distinct reasons. Primarily, he translated the almost incomprehensible Kabbalah of his mentor, Isaac Luria (d. 1572; Safed), into more readily understandable language. Additionally, he was personally attracted to the Sufi Way, going so far as to study Arabic so he could more easily discourse with Islamic thinkers. The Islamic path influenced his interpretation of Isaac Luria's Kabbalah.

To understand Vital, it is necessary first to get a sense of Isaac Luria. Twelve years younger than Moshe Cordovero, Luria studied with Cordovero for two years before developing a profoundly personal and esoteric Kabbalistic vision. His version of the Kabbalah was *too* arcane even for many steeped in Jewish esotericism and, though he was a revered mystical thinker, he did not personally have the central influence on later Hasidic thought, as did Moshe Cordovero. As Moshe Idel notes in *Hasidism: Between Ecstasy and Magic*:

> Even the illustrious Kabbalist Rabbi Eliyahu, the Gaon of Vilna [d. 1797] is reported to have been uneasy with the authoritative Kabbalah of Luria; Rabbi Shneur Zalman of Lyady [d. 1813] maintained: "It is known to us for sure that the pious Gaon does not believe in the Kabbalah of Rabbi Isaac Luria ... in its entirety, that it was [received] from the mouth of Elijah [as Luria had claimed] ... and the remaining part was from [Luria's] great wisdom, and we are not obliged to believe in it ... and [his] writings are very corrupt."[158]

Luria's power as a mystical thinker and, via Vital, his influence on some of the greatest Hasidic thinkers, however, cannot be denied.

Lurianic Kabbalah

Although he committed virtually nothing to paper, Isaac Luria was fortunate enough to have a few supporters who translated his concepts from the almost incomprehensible expression of his own voice into the poetic language of the greatest Jewish mystics. Luria's ideas, as summarized by Professor Michael McGaha:

> Reacting to the catastrophe of the expulsion from Spain, Luria used the text of the *Zohar* as a pretext for creating a radical new interpretation of Judaism as a cosmic struggle between the forces of light and darkness that would ultimately triumph in the "repair" [*tikkun*] and redemption of the universe, which had been damaged or "broken" since the time of creation.[159]

The idea that the world was broken and had to be fixed and, specifically, that it was the Jewish mystic's obligation to take part in this healing, became central to Hasidic practice and belief, leading to the role of the *tzaddik* as

God's healer. In the Lurianic system, the world came into being when the Divine effluence was being poured into the universe from atop the highest *Sephira* of the Tree of Life. However, this energy became so heavy that the universal vessels (the *Sephirot*) meant to hold it "broke," spilling the Divine power into all matter, where God's energy became imprisoned. Therefore, all of the physical matter in man's world actually has a spark of the Divine within it. Humanity's task is to restore these sparks to the Divine Essence atop the Tree of Life, through prayer and correct action.

The genesis for some of these ideas may be traced back into Islam, though Luria almost certainly did not rely directly on Sufi mentors. The concept underpinning the *tzaddik's* role in healing the world may be seen as an expansion of Jafar as-Sadiq's prophetic legislative model, and the emanation of the Divine effluence as the engine of creation initially comes as well from Muslim precursors, who had translated Neo-Platonic ideas into the Islamic vernacular. Luria's model, however, uses many novel concepts, which separates his Kabbalistic system from the mainstream Jewish-Sufi one proposed by Abulafia, Cordovero and others who were to become more important to later Jewish practice.

Hayyim Vital

The bulk of Isaac Luria's teachings became known through the works of his student, Hayyim Vital. Not only did this loyal pupil write down the vast majority of the master's ideas so that they would be preserved, but he also "deepened, broadened and beautified them, [turning] them into an entirely new creation."[160] Insodoing, Vital added some Islamic content.

*Sha'arei Kedushah*

Vital authored an important text of his own, *Sha'arei Kedushah* (The Gates of Holiness), a handbook for the mystical way of life, which after his death was oft printed and widely circulated. It consisted of four chapters, of which the first three were well known, while a fourth section was rarely published. One medieval printer inserted these lines in place of that final segment: "Thus speaks the printer: This fourth part will not be printed, for it is all holy names and secret mysteries which it would be unseemly to publish."[161]

However, it is this fourth chapter that is most pertinent here. In the unpublished (though circulated) section of *Sha'arei Kedushah*, Vital sets out in detail, using copious quotes from earlier Kabbalistic authors, various methods of attaining prophetic wisdom and achieving union with the Divine spirit. This final section contains extensive material concerning *hitbodedut* and is filled with quotations from the writings of Abraham Abulafia and Isaac of Acre.[162] This progression, from the traditional Jewish worship in the first section to the end of the book, which includes much

166

Jewish-Sufi material, mirrors earlier mystical treatises, such as Abraham Maimonides' *A Comprehensive Guide for the Servants of God* (13th century) and Obadyah Maimonides *Treatise of the Pool* (13th century).

In a particularly striking case representing the direct line of Kabbalistic material traveling from Sufi sources to later Jewish readers, Vital relates a story concerning humility (*hishtawwut* or equanimity) that may well have come to him through the writings of Isaac of Acre. Isaac had copied this tale from the Sufi al-Ghazali. The story as related by Vital:

> The story is told of a man who fasted most of his days, and who did many righteous deeds and married off several orphans, but who pursued honor. And he came to those who practice *hitbodedut*, who had reached the level of prophecy, and said to the greatest among them: "Sir, in your kindness let me know the reason why it is that, after I have performed all these good deeds, that I have not yet merited the level of prophecy, to tell the future as you do." He answered him: "Take a purse full of figs and nuts and hang it around your neck, and go to the main street of the city before the great and honorable people, and gather together some youths and say: 'Do you wish that I should give you figs and nuts? Then hit me with your hand on my neck and on my cheek.' And after you have done this many times return to me, and I will guide you in the way of prophecy." He replied: "Sir, how can an honorable man such as myself do such a thing?" He answered: "Is this a great thing in your eyes? This is naught but the lightest task that you must perform if you wish that your soul see the light of truth." Then he stood up and left with downcast soul.[163]

The explanation of *hishtawwut* is clear: If the "honorable" man cares about what people think of him as he undertakes this exercise, then he has not achieved equanimity, which is a necessary precondition to prophecy, according to the Jewish-Sufis.

The Sufi tale told by al-Ghazali (who lived five centuries before Vital), concerning Bayazid Bistami (d. 874):

> One day a man came to the teacher Bayazid and said, "I have fasted and prayed for thirty years and have found none of the spiritual joy of which you speak." "If you fasted and prayed for three hundred years, you would never find it," answered the sage. "How is that?" asked the man. "Your selfishness is acting as a veil between you and God." "Tell me the cure." "It is a cure you cannot carry out," said Bayazid. Those around him pressed him to reveal it. After a time he spoke: "Go to the nearest barbershop and have your head shaved; strip yourself of your clothes except for a loincloth. Take a nosebag full of walnuts, hang it around your neck. Go into the market and cry out – 'Anybody who gives

me a slap on the neck shall have a walnut.' Then proceed to the law courts and do the same thing." "I can't do that," said the man, "Suggest some other remedy." "This is the indispensable preliminary to the cure," answered Bayazid. "But as I told you, you are incurable."[164]

### Hitbodedut

Vital was well aware of the Sufi practice that surrounded him in Safed and Damascus. Therefore, it is not surprising to find esoteric facets of Islamic mystical practice sprinkled through *Sha'arei Kedushah*. As Paul Fenton notes in his article "Solitary Meditation in Jewish and Islamic Mysticism in Light of a Recent Archeological Discovery," one aspect of Vital's presentation of *hitbodedut* comes quite close to the Sufi notion of *istihdar* (calling forth the *sheikh's* presence), which consists of concentrating on the mental image of the spiritual guide, usually as a preliminary to *dhikr*. Like many other ideas in medieval Judaism, this may be traced back to the Koran (9:119), which recommends: "be with the *saddiqin* [truthful]."[165] This technique is closely related to another Sufi inspiration on the Jewish Kabbalists, *tawajjuh*, in which the aspirant conjures up the image of the master prior to *hitbodedut* (see above, Abraham Abulafia).

Vital, like so many Jewish thinkers before him, ascribes the practice of *hitbodedut* to the ancient Talmudic masters, while in Islam, the genesis for *khalwa* as a model for Muslims is attributed to the Prophet Muhammad. Paul Fenton notes that attempts such as Vital's to tie innovations (especially those taken from another religion) to ancient masters often are made in cases of ritual revival or enhancement.[166]

In one section describing prayer, Vital echoes Abulafia in sounding very much like a Sufi *sheikh* describing *khalwa*, or separation for prayer:

> Meditate in a secluded house and close your eyes and if you wrap yourself in a *tallit* [prayer shawl] and wear *tfillin* [phylacteries or prayer wrap] and sit and close your eyes and remove yourself from the material world, as if your soul had left your body, and ascended to the heavens ... After you turn your thoughts completely and purify them, then do combinations in your thoughts, using any word that you wish in all its combinations.[167]

We see the blending of Jewish tradition (the *tallit* and *teffilin*) with the Sufi inspiration of a "secluded house" and the combination of the letters. Vital's extensive treatment of the ideal of *hitbodedut* indicates the impressive penetration of Abulafia's ideas into the Safed Kabbalah.

### Safed's Far-Ranging Influence

According to Gershom Scholem, the mystical systems developed by Cordovero, Luria, Vital and other Safed Kabbalists influenced the direction of

Jewish history no less than Maimonides' *Guide for the Perplexed*.[168] Virtually all of the moral and ethical treatises written after the middle of the 16th century came from the pens of Abulafia-inspired Kabbalists[169] – bringing his Islamic-influenced Kabbalah into the living rooms of Jewish homes the world over. By the time of this wide dissemination of earlier Sufi-inspired Jewish thought, however, it is almost certain that few people in those Jewish parlors were aware that they were reading ideas often originating with Muslim thinkers, sometimes even inspired by the Koran!

## Tree of Life and the *Sephirot*

This discourse thus far has been concerned with the little-known historical affinities between Sufism and individual Jewish thinkers. The importance of these similarities was amplified by the attraction to further Islamic doctrine, which then influenced the heart of Jewish mystical practice. The Kabbalistic Tree of Life owes much to earlier Islamic ideas. To appreciate just how important the Tree of Life and its ten *Sephirot* became to Jewish mysticism – and the post-13th-century concept of the Jewish religion in general – we need only look at this passage from Professor Michael McGaha's *The Jewish Mystics of Medieval Spain*:

> The *Sephirot* are emanations that bridge the gulf between the unknowable infinite [*Ein Sof*] and Its creation, between absolute unity and the diversity of creation. In the words of Leo Schaya: "The *Sephirot*, the metaphysical 'numbers' or 'numerations' of the Divine aspects, are the principle keys to the mysteries of the *Torah*. They form a tenfold hierarchy. The *Sephirot* in their totality constitute the doctrinal basis of Jewish esotericism." According to Elliot Wolfson, the ten *Sephirot* are not merely instruments in the hand of God, but constitute the very form of the Divine as imagined by human consciousness.[170]

As noted earlier, this specific concept first appeared in the Jewish spiritual lexicon in the *Sefer Yetzirah* (9th century, Book of Creation), and then in the writings of Moses Maimonides (12th century) and the *Sefer ha-Bahir* (c. 1230, Book of Clarity). Joseph Dan states in *The Early Kabbalah* regarding the term *Sephirot*: "This strange and untranslatable term first appears in the *Sefer Yetzirah* – its cosmology and terminology have no prior source in Hebrew literature."[171]

### An Inner Meaning

The emergence of the Tree of Life and its *Sephirot* as central religious tools helped coalesce a complete revision of Jewish mystical thought. Believing that the important books of the Jewish religion – first and foremost the *Torah* – were written in a symbolic language hiding a deeper truth (represented by the Tree of Life), the Kabbalists reinterpreted the whole of Jewish spiritual history in a new light. They saw in the Bible an enormous library of mystical ciphers that expressed the true function and interrelationship of the ten Sephirot[172] and, by extension, the world. As Professor Daniel Matt (Center for Jewish Studies, Graduate Theological Union, Berkeley, CA) states in *The Essential Kabbalah*:

> By penetrating the literal surface of the *Torah*, the mystical commentators transform the Biblical narrative into a biography of God. The entire *Torah* is read as a Divine Name, expressing Divine Being. Even a seemingly insignificant verse can reveal the inner dynamics of the *Sephirot* – how God feels, responds and acts …[173]

Each verb, every noun, all of the letters of the *Torah* provide entrée into a more profound meaning of the Jewish text, a peek into the gears of the Divine machinery. Even the physical world – spilled forth from the Divine Essence – contains hidden kernels of Truth. "All existence underwent a complete transformation in Kabbalistic literature, where literal meaning was supplanted by a wealth of mystical symbolism."[174]

But this idea, that the Jewish sacred texts has dual meanings – an inner and an outer one – is adopted from Muslim mysticism, which has long stressed the esoteric meaning of the Koran, as opposed to its literal meaning. For Islamic thinkers operating at the highest stages of spiritual realization, the literal meaning of the Koran becomes secondary, supplanted by the allegorical. This concept stems from Jafar as-Sadiq (d. 765).[175] As Carl Ernst notes in his *Shambhala Guide to Sufism*, as-Sadiq influenced later Muslim thinkers like Dhu'l-Nun al-Misri (d. 859), al-Qushayri (d. 1072) and Ruzbihan Baqli (d. 1209), all of whom expanded on these commentaries and seeded the idea of "hidden levels" of the Holy Book deeper into mainstream Islamic spirituality.[176]

Arabized Jewish mystics were so taken with this idea of hidden meanings that they wrapped it into their concept of the *Torah* and the Kabbalah. This allowed Jewish thinkers to expand on the literal meanings of the Hebrew Scriptures – which can be contradictory and violent – to search for esoteric aspects of God's meaning, as they were revealed through meanings hidden in the letters and words of the Holy Book. Gershom Scholem notes in *On the Kabbalah and Its Symbolism*:

> The Kabbalists adopted a line of thought that they found in Jewish philosophers of the Middle Ages, who in turn had taken it from the philosophical tradition of the Arabs. I am referring to the idea of the two levels of meaning – inward and outward – in the sacred texts … It is interesting to note that the terms used by many Jewish philosophers to denote these two levels of meaning (*hitson* and *penimi*, outward and inward) never occur in this context in older Jewish sources, but are

literal translations of the corresponding Arabic terms.[177]

This Islamic-inspired concept of dual worlds, which began influencing Jewish mysticism in the early Middle Ages, ended by coloring the totality of Jewish esoteric thought, influencing the manner in which *all* physical reality has been viewed by Jewish spiritual thinkers since this time.

### Prayer Methods

Specific meditation techniques defining Kabbalistic practice are foreshadowed in earlier, Sufi devotional methods as well. As the Jewish mystic worked his way up through the 22 pathways and ten stations of the Tree of Life through prayer and meditation, he had to be very careful in the forms of visualization that he imagined, or "happened upon." It is a grave sin to anthropomorphize God. Instead, the aspirant approached these mystical stations via their "shell" – visualizing the color of each individual *Sephira*. This technique, first introduced into Jewish thought in the 13th century, became important for the Safed Kabbalists (16th century). Concerning the power of the colors of the *Sephirot*, Moshe Cordovero (d. 1570) states:

> There is no doubt that the colors can introduce you to the operations of the *Sephirot* and the drawing down of their overflow. Thus, when a person needs to draw down the overflow of Mercy from the attribute of Grace, let him imagine the name of the *Sephira* with the color that is appropriate to what he needs, in front of him. If he applies to Supreme *Hesed* [let him imagine] the outermost white ... Likewise, when he undertakes a certain operation and is in need of the overflow of [the attribute of Judgment], let him then dress in red clothes and imagine the form [of the letters] of the Tetragrammaton [*YHVH* – the unpronounceable name of God] in red, and so on in the case of all the operations causing the descent of the overflows.[178]

This assertion of the centrality of colors as part of the mystical appearance of the *Sephirot* mirrors aspects of Islamic *dhikr* practice found in Sufism. As Jean Louis Michon states in *The Spiritual Practices of Islam*:

> The seven names [of *Allah*] correspond to the celestial spheres, to the colors emanated by the celestial light and to the stages of the soul on the path to perfection. A very similar teaching is found in the *Suhrawardiyyah* order ... whose *dhikr* also includes seven names ... and is practiced during retreats, whose normal duration is 40 days, and is accompanied by the visualization of the seven symbolic colors – blue, yellow, red, white, green, black and undifferentiated – which correspond to the various levels or worlds of universal manifestation.[179]

Moshe Idel notes the Islamic provenance of this Jewish prayer technique:

The fact that an alien technique, and this is my evaluation of the origin of color visualization, was adopted by Kabbalists only demonstrates the readiness, at the end of the 13th century, to expand the Kabbalah. It was exactly at this period that we can also detect other influences of Sufi views among the Kabbalists, as attested by the appearance of the concepts of *olam hademut* [world of imagination], *hishtawwut* [equanimity],[180] *hitbodedut* [separation for prayer] and others.

## Kabbalah: A Jewish-Sufi Amalgam

It would be wrong to claim that the Kabbalah is simply a mirror image of Sufi theology, cloaked in the Hebrew language and Biblical sources and then placed into the mouths of ancient Jewish sources. However, there is enough Islamic mystical thought cradled in the bosom of the Kabbalah to bring into question the pure "Jewishness" of this most Jewish of mystical systems.

By the time the center of the Jewish world moved north from the Mediterranean Basin into the *shtetls* and villages of Eastern Europe, Sufism had so completely permeated Jewish mysticism, that later Jews built it into their own spiritual concepts without giving it a second thought. As the Middle Ages gave way to the Age of Enlightenment and, soon thereafter, to our own frantic era of technological progress, the mystical fraternity between Muslims and Jews was virtually complete. It was left to 18th-century Hasidism to, albeit unknowingly, complete the fusion that had begun nearly one millennium before.

## Endnotes

1. Scholem, Gershom. *Encyclopaedia Judaica 1st Edition, CD ROM* (Cecil Roth and Geoffrey Wigoder, eds.). (New York: MacMillan and Company, 1972).

2. Halkin, A. S. "The Great Fusion." *Great Ages and Ideas of the Jewish People* (Leo W. Schwarz, ed.). (New York: Random House,1956: 215-263), p. 258.

3. Scholem, Gershom. *Origins of the Kabbalah*. (Philadelphia: The Jewish Publication Society, 1987), p. 6.

4. Dan, Joseph (ed.). *The Early Kabbalah* (Mahweh, NJ: Paulist Press, 1986), p. 4.

5. McGaha, Michael. "The Sefer ha-Bahir and Andalusian Sufism." (*Medieval Encounters III*, 1997: 20-57), p. 57.

6. See Wasserstrom, Steven. "Sefer Yesira and Early Islam: A Reappraisal." (*Journal of Jewish Thought and Philosophy III*, 1993: 1-30), pp. 1-30.

7. Scholem, Gershom. *Encyclopaedia Judaica* (Cecil Roth and Geoffrey Wigoder, eds.).

8. Dan, Joseph (ed.). *The Early Kabbalah*, p. 7.

9. Scholem, Gershom. *Origins of the Kabbalah*, pp. 25-27.

10. Quoted in ibid. p. 28.

11. Mayer, Farhana. "Alchemy of the Angelic Self in the Mystical Qur'an Commentary Attributed to Ja'far as-Sadiq; with Reference to the Verses on the Prophets Abraham, Joseph, and Moses," *Patristic, Medieval and Renaissance Studies Conference*, Villanova University (Philadelphia, PA), October 10, 2008.

12. Scholem, Gershom. *Encyclopaedia Judaica* (Cecil Roth and Geoffrey Wigoder, eds.).

13. Quote and information from Geoffroy, Eric. "Approaching Sufism." *Sufism: Love and Wisdom* (Jean-Louis Michon and Roger Gaetani, eds.). (Bloomington, IN: World Wisdom, Inc., 2006: 49-62), p. 54.

14. Verman, Mark. *The Books of Contemplation.* (Albany, NY: SUNY Press, 1992), p. 129.

15. McGaha, Michael. *The Jewish Mystics of Medieval Spain.* (unpublished manuscript, 2001), p. 379.

16. Scholem, Gershom. *Encyclopaedia Judaica* (Cecil Roth and Geoffrey Wigoder, eds.).

17. Scholem, Gershom. *Origins of the Kabbalah*, p. 30.

18. Wasserstrom, Steven. *Journal of Jewish Thought and Philosophy III*, pp. 3-4.

19. Ibid. p. 7.

20. Quoted in Ibid. p. 3.

21. Ibid, p. 3, note 3.

22. Ibid. p. 14.

23. Ibid. p. 11.

24. Scholem, Gershom. *Origins of the Kabbalah*, p. 35.

25. McGaha, Michael. *Medieval Encounters III*, pp. 50, 52.

26. Ibid. p. 53.

27. Quoted in ibid. p. 36 The understanding of corresponding realities arrayed in an ontological hierarchy is thus applied to the symbolism of the letters. (Editor's note: This is the nature of reality – corresponding realities at different levels of the ontological hierarchy. The Sufi explication, that is, the making explicit of this emanational nature of the Creation was read and absorbed by Jews and thus this reality within their own faith – for true faith traditions must necessarily encompass all Truth. And, according to Muslims, because Islam is simply a return to the "Religion of Abraham," it is different from Judaism in form only, not in Essence. This essential truth is what allowed for and made natural fluidity between the two Abrahamic mysticisms.)

28. Ariel, David S. "The Eastern Dawn of Wisdom: The Problem of the Relation Between Islamic and Jewish Mysticism." *Approaches to Judaism in Medieval Times, Vol. 2* (David R. Blumenthal, ed.). (Chico, CA: Scholars Press, 1985: 149-167), pp. 158-159.

29. Ibid. pp. 159-160.

30. McGaha, Michael. *Medieval Encounters III*, p. 53.

31. Ibid. p. 55.

32. Unterman, Alan. *Encyclopaedia Judaica* (Cecil Roth and Geoffrey Wigoder, eds.).

33. Dan, Joseph (ed.). *The Early Kabbalah*, p. 29.

34. Ibid. pp. 29-30.

35. Ariel, David. *Approaches to Judaism in Medieval Times II*, (David Blumenthal, ed.), pp. 160-161.

36. Scholem, Gershom. *Major Trends in Jewish Mysticism.* (New York: Schocken Books, 1971), p. 162.

37. Ibid. p. 29.

38. Scholem, Gershom. *Encyclopaedia Judaica* (Cecil Roth and Geoffrey Wigoder, eds.), with a couple of additions (Ibn Gabirol and Ibn Pakuda) that have stemmed from the studies represented in this book.

39. Scholem, Gershom. *Major Trends in Jewish Mysticism*, p. 156.

40. Bension, Ariel. *The Zohar in Moslem and Christian Spain.* (New York: Hermon Press, 1974), pp. 68-69.

41. Information in this paragraph from Scholem, Gershom. *Encyclopaedia Judaica* (Cecil Roth and Geoffrey Wigoder, eds.).

42. Kiener, Ronald. "Ibn Arabi and the Qabbalah: A Study of Thirteenth Century Iberian Mysticism." (*Studies in Mystical Literature, Vol. 2, N. 2, 1982: 26-50*), p. 45.

43. Quoted in Altmann, Alexander. *Studies in Religious Philosophy and Mysticism.* (Ithaca: Cornell University Press, 1969), p. 1.

44. Palacios, Miguel Asin. *The Mystical Philosophy of ibn Masarra and His Followers.* (Leiden: E. J. Brill, 1978), p. 130.

45. Information in this paragraph from Wijnhoven, Jochanan. "The Mysticism of Solomon ibn Gabirol." (*The Journal of Religion 45, 1965: 137-152*), pp. 147-148.

46. Quote and information about *ein sof* from Abelson, Joshua. *Jewish Mysticism: An Introduction to the Kabbalah.* (Mineola, NY: Dover Publications, 2001), pp. 129-130.

47. Myer, Isaac. *Qabbalah.* (New York: Samuel Weiser, 1970), p. 4.

48. Ibid. p. 159.

49. Scholem, Gershom. *Encyclopaedia Judaica* (Cecil Roth and Geoffrey Wigoder, eds.).

50. All information about the seven castles comes from McGaha, Michael. "Naming the Nameless, Numbering the Infinite." (*YCGL 45/46, 1997/1998: 37-53*), p. 42.

51. Scholem, Gershom. *Major Trends in Jewish Mysticism*, p. 234.

52. Idel, Moshe. *The Mystical Experience in Abraham Abulafia.* (Albany, NY: SUNY Press, 1988), p. 3.

53. Scholem, Gershom. *Encyclopaedia Judaica* (Cecil Roth and Geoffrey Wigoder, eds.).

54. McGaha, Michael. *The Jewish Mystics of Medieval Spain*, p. 470.

55. Ibid. p. 471.

56. Chittick, William. *Sufism: A Short Introduction.* (Oxford: Oneworld Publishers, 2000), p. 24, 53.

57. Scholem, Gershom. *Encyclopaedia Judaica* (Cecil Roth and Geoffrey Wigoder, eds.).

58. Quoted in Idel, Moshe. *Hasidism: Between Ecstasy and Magic.* (Albany, NY: SUNY Press, 1995), p. 11.

59. McGaha, Michael. *The Jewish Mystics of Medieval Spain*, 472.

60. Scholem, Gershom. *Encyclopaedia Judaica* (Cecil Roth and Geoffrey Wigoder, eds.).

61. Idel, Moshe. *Studies in Ecstatic Kabbalah*. (Albany, NY: SUNY Press, 1988), p. 16.

62. Ibid. p. 1.

63. Ibid. p. 108.

64. Hames, Harvey J. "A Seal within a Seal: The imprint of Sufism in Abraham Abulafia's Teachings." (*Medieval Encounters 12.2*, 2006: 153-172), p. 169.

65. Ibid. p. 170.

66. Nakamura, Kojiro, "Makki and Ghazali on Mystical Practices." (*Orient XX*, 1984: 83-91), g. 88.

67. Fenton, Paul. "Judaism and Sufism." *The Cambridge Companion to Medieval Jewish Philosophy* (Daniel Frank and Oliver Leaman, editors) (Cambridge, England: Cambridge University Press, 2003), p. 214.

68. Ideas and wording from Scholem, Gershom. *Major Trends in Jewish Mysticism*, p. 133-134.

69. Ibid. pp. 134-135.

70. Idel, Moshe. *The Mystical Experience in Abraham Abulafia*, pp. 8-9.

71. Fenton, Paul. "Solitary Meditation in Jewish and Islamic Mysticism in Light of a Recent Archeological Discovery." (*Medieval Encounters I*, 1995: 271-296), p. 274.

72. Idel, Moshe. *Studies in Ecstatic Kabbalah*, p. 108.

73. Ibid. p. 110.

74. Ibid. p. 106.

75. Information in this paragraph from Ibid. p. 111.

76. Fenton, Paul. *Medieval Encounters I*, p. 277.

77. Ibid. p. 277.

78. Kaplan, Aryeh. *Meditation and Kabbalah*. (York Beach, ME: Red Wheel/ Reiser, 1982), p. 16, 17.

79. Idel, Moshe. *Studies in Ecstatic Kabbalah*, p. 103.

80. Ibid. p. 104.

81. Idel, Moshe. *The Mystical Experience in Abraham Abulafia*, p. 131.

82. Fenton, Paul. "Idel 'Studies in Ecstatic Kabbalah.'" (*Jewish Quarterly Review 82*, 1991: 525-527), p. 525.

83. Idel, Moshe. *The Mystical Experience in Abraham Abulafia*, p. 129.

84. Quoted in Smith, Margaret. *Studies in Early Mysticism in the Near and Middle East* (Oxford: Oneworld Publications, 1995), p. 203.

85. Sells, Michael. "Meaning and Authority in Sufi Literature around the year 1240 CE: Literary Perspectives." *Jewish Mystical Leaders and Leadership in the 13th Century* (Moshe Idel and M. Ostow, editors). (New Jersey and Jerusalem: Northvale Press, 1998: 187-198), p. 194.

86. Quoted in Scholem, Gershom. *Major Trends in Jewish Mysticism*, pp. 140-141.

87. Buber, Martin. *Tales of the Hasidim I, II* (New York: Schocken Books, 1991), p. 199.

88. Buber, Martin. *Hasidism* (New York: Philosophical Library, 1948), pp. 185-186.

89. Quoted in Sells, Michael. "Bewildered Tongue: The Semantics of Mystical Union in Islam." *Mystical Union in Judaism, Christianity and Islam* (Moshe Idel and Bernard McGinn, eds.). (New York: Continuum Press, 1996: 87-124), p. 106.

90. Ibid. p. 106.

91. Ibid. p. 106. The full text can be found in Scholem, Gershom. *Major Trends in Jewish Mysticism*, pp. 154-155.

92. Idel, Moshe. *The Mystical Experience in Abraham Abulafia*, p. 13.

93. Idel, Moshe. *Studies in Ecstatic Kabbalah*, pp. 106-107 A long selection from al-Ghazali's description of the Sufi path was copied out by Rabbi Abraham ibn Hasdai (c. 13th century), one of Moses Maimonides staunches adherents.

94. Ibid. p. viii.

95. Ibid. pp. viii-ix.

96. Idel, Moshe. *Hasidism: Between Ecstasy and Magic*, p. 55.

97. Quoted in Maimonides, Obadyah. *Treatise of the Pool* (Paul Fenton, trans.). (London: Octagon Press, 1981), pp. 21-22.

98. Idel, Moshe. *Studies in Ecstatic Kabbalah*, pp. 111-112.

99. Quoted in Idel, Moshe. "Allegory and Divine Names in Ecstatic Kabbalah." *Interpretation and Allegory: Antiquity to the Modern Period* (Patricia Gauch & Jon Whitman, editors). (Leiden: E. J. Brill, 2003: 317-348), p. 340.

100. Maimonides, Obadyah. *Treatise of the Pool* (Paul Fenton, trans.), p. 63.

101. Idel, Moshe. *Studies in Ecstatic Kabbalah*, pp. 114-115.

102. Fenton, Paul. *Medieval Encounters I*, pp. 284-285.

103. Idel, Moshe. *Studies in Ecstatic Kabbalah*, p. 113.

104. Ibid. p. 113.

105. Quoted in Ibid. p. 112.

106. Ibid. p. 115.

107. Quoted in Ibid. p. 115.

108. Idel, Moshe. *Hasidism: Between Ecstasy and Magic*, pp. 156-157.

109. Quoted in Idel, Moshe. *Studies in Ecstatic Kabbalah*, pp. 118-119.

110. Idel, Moshe. "Universalization and Integration: Two Concepts of Mystical Union in Jewish Mysticism." *Mystical Union in Judaism, Christianity and Islam* (Moshe Idel and Bernard McGinn, eds.). (New York: Continuum Publishing, 1996: 27-58), p. 160.

111. These two quotes come from Maimonides, Obadyah. *Treatise of the Pool* (Paul Fenton, trans.), pp. 63-64.

112. Verman, Mark. *The Books of Contemplation*, p. 25.

113. Scholem, Gershom. *Major Trends in Jewish Mysticism*, pp. 190-191.

114. Idel, Moshe. *Studies in Ecstatic Kabbalah*, pp. 95, 99.

115. See Ibid. pp. 63-71 for specific instances.

116. Ibid. p. 93.

117. See Ibid. pp. 119-122.

118. Bension, Ariel. *The Zohar in Moslem and Christian Spain*, p. 228.

119. Idel, Moshe. *Messianic Mystics*. (New Haven, CT: Yale University Press, 1998), p. 164.

120. See Fenton, Paul. *Medieval Encounters I*, pp. 271-296.

121. It is interesting to note that the great Kabbalistic Scholar Gershom Scholem, writing in his *Major Trends in Jewish Mysticism* (p. 251), states that "strange as it may seem, the religious ideas of the mystics of Safed, which had such an immense influence, have to this day not been properly explored."

122. Maimonides, Obadyah. *Treatise of the Pool* (Paul Fenton, trans.), p. 64.

123. Goitein, S.D. "A Jewish Addict to Sufism." (*Jewish Quarterly Review 44*, 1953: 37-49), pp. 38-39.

124. Maimonides, Obadyah. *Treatise of the Pool* (Paul Fenton, trans.), p. 22.

125. Ibid. p. 64.

126. Idel, Moshe. *Studies in Ecstatic Kabbalah*, p. 95.

127. Ibid. p. 95.

128. Ibid. p. 95.

129. Ibid. p. 123.

130. Maimonides, Obadyah. *Treatise of the Pool* (Paul Fenton, trans.), p. 63.

131. Scholem, Gershom. *Major Trends in Jewish Mysticism*, p. 97.

132. Idel. Moshe. *Studies in Ecstatic Kabbalah*, p. 123.

133. Ibid. p. 124.

134. Ibid. p. 124.

135. Sells, Michael (ed.). *Early Islamic Mysticism: Sufi, Qu'ran, Mi'raj, Poetic and Theological Writings*. (Mahwah, NJ and New York: Paulist Press, 1996), pp. 47-48.

136. Altmann, Alexander. *Studies in Religious Philosophy and Mysticism*. (Ithaca: Cornell University Press, 1969), pp. 43-44.

137. Ibid. pp. 49-50.

138. Ibid. pp. 57-58.

139. Ibid. pp. 67-68.

140. Ibid. pp. 67-68.

141. Idel, Moshe. *Studies in Ecstatic Kabbalah*, p. 125.

142. Ibid. p. 101.

143. Ibid. p. 101.

144. Ibid. p. 133.

145. Ibid. p. 127.

146. Ibid. p. 128.

147. Quoted in Ibid. p. 128.

148. Ibid. p. 129.

149. Quoted in Ibid. p. 128.

150. Idel, Moshe. *Kabbalah: New Perspectives*. (New Haven, CT: Yale University Press, 1988), p. 101.

151. Quoted in Idel, Moshe. *Hasidism: Between Ecstasy and Magic*, p. 71.

152. Ibid. p. 70. For more on the *tzaddik* in Cordovero's thought, see pp. 190-193.

153. Ibid. pp. 86-87.

154. Idel, Moshe. *Studies in Ecstatic Kabbalah*, p. 143.

155. Quoted in Ibid. p. 165.

156. Burckhardt, Titus. *Introduction to Sufi Doctrine*. (Bloomington, IN: World Wisdom, Inc., 2008), p. 95.

157. Idel, Moshe. *Studies in Ecstatic Kabbalah*, p. 133.

158. Idel, Moshe. *Hasidism: Between Ecstasy and Magic*, p. 37.

159. McGaha, Michael. *The Jewish Mystics of Medieval Spain*, p. 496.

160. Bension, Ariel. *The Zohar in Moslem and Christian Spain*, p. 231.

161. Quoted in Scholem, Gershom. *Major Trends in Jewish Mysticism*, p. 122.

162. Idel, Moshe. *Studies in Ecstatic Kabbalah*, p. 132.

163. Ibid. p. 147.

164. Fadiman, James and Frager, Robert (eds.). *Essential Sufism*. (New York: HarperCollins, 1997), pp. 175-176.

165. Information about this influence and Koranic quote from Fenton, Paul. *Medieval Encounters I*, p. 292.

166. Ibid. p. 292.

167. Idel, Moshe. *Studies in Ecstatic Kabbalah*, p. 136.

168. Scholem, Gershom. *Major Trends in Jewish Mysticism*, p. 251.

169. Ibid. p. 251.

170. McGaha, Michael. *The Jewish Mystics of Medieval Spain*, p. 49.

171. Dan, Joseph (ed.). *The Early Kabbalah*, p. 7.

172. Ibid. p. 11.

173. Matt, Daniel. *The Essential Kabbalah*. (Edison, NJ: Castle Books, 1997), p. 7.

174. Dan, Joseph (ed.). *The Early Kabbalah*, p. 11.

175. Sells, Michael (ed.). *Early Islamic Mysticism: Sufi, Qu'ran, Mi'raj, Poetic and Theological Writings*, p. 77.

176. Information on the hidden meaning of the Koran from Ernst, Carl. *The Shambhala Guide to Sufism*. (Boston and London: Shambhala Publishers, 1997), pp. 40-41.

177. Scholem, Gershom. *On the Kabbalah and its Symbolism*. (New York: Schocken Books, 1996), p. 51.

178. Idel, Moshe. *Hasidism: Between Ecstasy and Magic*, pp. 67-68.

179. Michon, Jean-Louis. "The Spiritual Practices of Sufism." *Islamic Spirituality: Foundations* (S. H. Nasr, ed.). (New York: Crossroad, 1987: 265-293), pp. 287-288.

180. Idel, Moshe. *Kabbalah: New Perspectives*, p. 111.

# Chapter 6
# Hasidism and the Continuing Influence
# of Sufism

Hasidism emerged in the middle of the 18th century, an impassioned response to another spiritually trying era in Jewish history. Jewish thinkers had turned inward at the beginning of the 17th century; as Islamic lands contracted, the strong, direct interaction between Jewish and Muslim thinkers came to an end. The Golden Age of the Arabized Jew (c. 8-11th centuries) had long since passed. The majority of Jews now lived under Christianity, in Europe and Russia. It was a time of tremendous exterior pressure, as the northern lands were inhospitable to the Jewish minority. The threat of pogroms (directed riots), expulsions and other arbitrary violence was ever present.

These strains led to an increasingly desperate population, one that turned away from the spiritual paths that had been central to medieval Judaism. The religiously orthodox leaders tightened their control over synagogues and houses of study, sometimes proposing that the bleak era was retribution for Jewish iniquity. During this period, the latent esoteric impulse occasionally burst forth in messianic fervor, focused on a charlatan claiming to be the deliverer of Israel. Inevitably, after a brief time of great excitement, the dreams of the Jewish people were quashed, and their spirits sank to even lower depths.

Appearing in this Jewish world roiled by false prophets, oppressed by external forces and smothered by the stultified orthodox religious traditions, Hasidism offered a sincere, available antidote for the bruised soul of the 18th-century Jew. And unlike earlier incarnations of the Jewish mystical path, Hasidism made itself available to *all* Jews, no matter how learned or, conversely, how uneducated. Its gentle, democratic appeal helped it to gain a wide following in a short period of time.

## Shabbetai Zevi: False Messiah

To understand the emergence of Hasidism, one first must appreciate an aborted messianic disaster that preceded it. Shabbetai Zevi (d. 1676; Turkey) thrust himself upon the nation of Israel as its savior – and virtually the whole Jewish community followed along. The Diaspora society was turned upside down, first with the fevered excitement of the coming of the Messiah, and then with an overwhelming sense of hurt and loss, as Shabbetai Zevi was unmasked as a fraud.

Zevi's movement was important to the emergence of Hasidism in a specific way. The average Jew, as well as the spiritual elite, experienced an intense spiritual awakening due to the passion that Zevi's movement engendered. Gershom Scholem notes in *Major Trends in Jewish Mysticism* that for nearly two years at the height of the messianic hysteria (1665-1666), the Jewish community enjoyed a vibrant, living mystical reality that had been unavailable to it since Biblical times.[1] The experience of a living God – accessed outside of study and learning – that Zevi brought to the general population did not simply fade when his messianic dream shattered; it led to a deepened sense of religious possibility in the Jewish *shtetls* and villages, and helped to pave the way for the emergence of Hasidism.

This grandiose manic-genius happened upon fertile times for a false messiah. The Safed Kabbalah, which by 1660 had become an important influence among the mystical elite of European Jewry, had created a climate favorable for the release of the pent up messianic energies of the Jewish people. While the idea of waiting and hoping for the Messiah was hardly a novel idea for Jews, Messianism recently had taken on a new urgency, due to the apocalyptic bent of the Safed teachings.[2]

For nearly two years, Judaism experienced the most ecstatic messianic movement that the ancient people have lived through during the past two millennia.[3] Wealthy merchants sold their businesses, purchased boats and prepared to transport hundreds of less-fortunate co-religionists across the waters to the Holy Land. Jews from all over Europe and the East secured passage to Jerusalem on the phantom ships of swindlers, fully expecting the meet the Messiah and be borne "home" on wings of angels. Jewish commerce around the world ground to a virtual halt, as all energy was funneled into preparing for the momentous occasion.

In 1666, however, the Sultan of Turkey, where Shabbetai Zevi's activities were then taking place, wearied of the game and incarcerated the self-appointed Messiah. Shabbetai Zevi was given a stark choice: convert to Islam or meet his maker alone. Enjoying a period of lucidity, he chose the former option, and took Islam as his stated religion. The messianic dreams of the Jewish people were shattered.

### The Last Medieval Jewish-Sufi

The story does not end there, however. It was the post-conversion Shabbetai Zevi who had a direct influence on the Baal Shem Tov. Despite Zevi's apostasy, many Jews around the world continued to believe in him, proposing that there was a grand plan to his acceptance of Islam. These crypto-Shabbateans, as they were called, continued to follow his precepts, operating as a secret society within Judaism.

Shabbetai Zevi himself did not abandon his aspirations, and he created a hybrid religion, Islam on the outside and his own vision of Judaism on the inside. Hundreds of families followed his spurious (though convincing) conversion to Islam, and he lived in Salonika, Turkey like a petty king, surrounded by all the sycophants and followers of a royal retinue, who called themselves "Doenmeh"[4] (from Turkish *dön-*, "to convert to"). These Doenmeh melded Islam and Judaism in a manner reminiscent of the Egyptian Jewish-Sufis, half a millennium earlier.[5] Shabbetai Zevi participated in Sufi prayer rituals, including *sama'* (spiritual singing and dancing) and *dhikr* (prayer litanies), becoming personally acquainted with the Sufi poet Niyazi al-Misri (d. 1694).[6] Later Shabbateans included Sufi poems in their mystical practice, which often took place to music culled from *sama'* observances.[7]

Shabbetai Zevi's own utterances marked him as a Sufi mystic, showing how completely he assimilated the spiritual forms of his new religion. His assurance, stated in a Sufi *shath* (ecstatic utterance) that: "There is no God but Me," underscored how close his mysticism drew to Sufism, and to the Koranic passage from which this ideal came ("There is no God but me. Therefore serve me." 21:25).[8] These comments also implied that, in his opinion, at least, he had achieved the final station of the Sufi adept: complete acceptance of the Divine.[9]

### A Far-Ranging Influence

Post-conversion Shabbetai Zevi inspired numerous late 17th-century *Jewish* leaders. These hidden Shabbateans spread his Sufi innovations throughout the Diaspora. This offered the final direct impulse of Islamic spiritual teachings on Judaism, in many cases reaffirming earlier Kabbalistic ideas that had originated in Islam. As Paul Fenton notes:

> The writings of these Shabbatean sectarians exhibited by far the most radical and enlightened attitudes towards Islam. Shabbetai Zevi himself was said, following his capture by the Sultan of the Ottoman Empire, to study in his prison cell with the *Zohar* in one hand and the Koran in the other. Ultimately, a large number of his followers converted to Islam ...[10]

Many men who studied Shabbatean ideas and then outwardly turned away from him (only to guard Shabbateanism in their hearts) ended up in important religious positions. The head rabbis of Amsterdam, London and Ancona, Italy interspersed more traditional Jewish beliefs with Shabbetai Zevi's teachings. Gershom Sholem writes that Jewish leaders across Germany, into Italy and Poland and as far away as Lithuania, Hungary and Romania all exhibited Shabbatean leanings.[11] Lastly, many mystics and religious leaders emerging from the Holy Land during 1680-1740 were "tainted" with Shabbatean ideas.[12] An important center for crypto-Shabbateans became Galicia and Podolia in Poland,[13] the exact geographical area where the Baal Shem Tov, the founder of Hasidism, began his activities, and from which Hasidism spread.

## Baal Shem Tov

Rabbi Israel ben Eliezer, the Baal Shem Tov (d. 1760; Ukraine), developed Hasidism to soothe and uplift an emotionally bruised Jewish world. Born in 1698 in the small village of Okup on the Russian-Polish border, a spare third of a century after the apostasy of Shabbetai Zevi, the Baal Shem Tov (Master of the Good Name) became aware of his own mystical powers when in his twenties. He chose to go into hiding in the Carpathian Mountains (Poland), to properly prepare himself for his role as spiritual leader. Finally, in the mid-1730s – Hasidic tradition fixes it on his 36th birthday – Israel ben Eliezer revealed himself to the world as a healer and leader, acquiring the honorific "Baal Shem Tov," or "Master of the Good Name."

### The Emergence of Hasidism

The Baal Shem Tov steered clear of any messianic pretensions for himself, all too aware of the open wound left on the Jewish psyche by the Shabbatean and other recent messianic affairs. He did, nonetheless, believe strongly in the ultimate arrival of the Messiah, some time in the far-off future. The Baal Shem Tov emphasized the salvation of each individual, which had to precede the coming of the Messiah and the redemption of the world.

Hasidism removed the veils of secrecy and inaccessibility from the Kabbalah. While the Kabbalistic system had been shut off from the average Jewish practitioner since its inception in Spain in the 13th century – it had been well-guarded by a secretive elite – the Baal Shem Tov followed Shabbetai Zevi's democratizing impulse, sharing its mystical power with the general Jewish population. The Hasidic leader's open-minded practice based in joy and devotion, acknowledged the mystical impulse unleashed by Zevi, and swept through the huddled ghettos of 18th-century Europe.

Hasidism eschewed rabbinic study as the sole gateway to spiritual realization, relying instead on the visceral experience of the living God. All Jews were equal in the eyes of the Baal Shem Tov – and, more importantly, all had the ability to reach *in their own manner* some form of God-consciousness.

### Kabbalah and Hasidism

As Hasidic scholar Martin Buber notes, for the Baal Shem Tov, Hasidism was an amplification of the Kabbalistic path, a way to continue and perfect it as well as disseminate the heart of its teachings to a wider public. He borrowed much from that system, taking over its concepts, its style and on some points even its methods of instruction.[14] The relationship between Hasidism and the Kabbalah was unique in one important way: the manner in which the Baal Shem Tov broke with that centuries-old mystical practice. Prior to Hasidism, the masses of Jewish worshipers were offered the exoteric reading of the *Torah*, while the esoteric teachings were reserved for the spiritual elite.

The Baal Shem Tov, however, did not believe that his mystical practice formed a "fraternity, a separate order, which guarded an esoteric teaching, apart from public life."[15] Rather, Hasidism fashioned a heart and soul for the *whole* Jewish community. The Baal Shem Tov's teachings were about healing wounds – those within each human being and even those between the lettered "elite" and the masses of Jewish practitioners.[16]

## Sufi Echoes within Hasidism

By the 18th century, the earlier influence of Sufism that recast Judaism had become mixed in with more specifically Jewish tenets. Ideas concerning prayer practices, Divine union, ecstasy and many other mystical doctrines, which had been assimilated in the 10th through 16th centuries, had been linked back into the Biblical past, and presented to 18th-century Jewry as seamlessly Jewish in lineage. In many cases, however, their origination point in Islam is indisputable. Moshe Idel notes in *Hasidism: Between Ecstasy and Magic*:

> It is probable that the main, and perhaps single channel of information available to Jewish medieval authors was Muslim culture ... In general, the magical and mystical models [of Hasidism] owe much to the vigorous Muslim culture that existed between the 10th and 14th centuries ... these models, significantly affected by Muslim culture, were transmitted to Jews in Europe through various channels and were formative in the emergence of Hasidism.[17]

The Sufi and Islamic influence on 18th-century European Jewry is perhaps the most controversial aspect of this study – and one that has been overlooked by many 20th-century academicians. While oftentimes scholars have been willing to accept the Sufi influence on *Sephardic* (Spanish) Jewish thought, few have made the leap, as suggested by Moshe Idel, to *Ashkenazi* (European) Judaism and, through it, into contemporary Jewish practice.

What many have chosen to do, instead, is simply to reference Jewish ideas that "appeared" in medieval times, and which influenced the development of Hasidism. Even today, many books concerning Jewish mystical history contain not a single citation of either Islam or Sufism! Other books have one, two or three spare references, hardly indicating the deep impact that the Muslim spiritual path had on the development of Jewish mysticism and worship.

This book hopes to right this wrong. The following section provides the impetus for a new direction in scholarship and understanding of the Jewish religion, as it has developed in modern times. The following pages trace many Hasidic concepts back through the Kabbalah, to their original impetus: in medieval Sufism. In so doing, I hope to show how deeply inter-dependent Judaism and Islam continued to be throughout history and into today, at their mystical cores.

The Purpose of Creation

Hasidic thinkers developed a concept of the fundamental purpose of cre-ation that bore a striking similarity to Sufi thought. Earlier Kabbalists had believed that the reason God created the universe was because God, as a unitary experience, could have no consciousness or experience of the Divine. God "desired" an "independent otherness" that could perceive the Creator – and thereby bring God a sense of existence and love that was lacking when God alone pre-existed as an uncreated force, beyond being.

This concept of auto-representation, manifested through language, started with Sufi thinkers, and then became Judaized through its inclusion in the *Sefer Zohar* (c. 1295).[18] As was noted earlier, for the Kabbalah, the process of creation involved the emanation of the One from an uncreated point, through a series of stations (the *Sephirot*) to the manifested world, and then back again. The crucial turning point in this cycle took place within man, at the moment that he began to develop an awareness of his own true essence.[19] The process of man's unfolding awareness became central to the purpose of creation, and the self-awareness of God.

As Martin Buber relates, concerning Hasidic theory:

> God contracted Himself because He, non-dual and relation-less unity, wanted to allow relation to emerge; because He wanted to be known, loved, wanted; because He wanted to allow to arise from his primal one Being, in which thinking and thought are one, the otherness that strives toward unity. So there radiated from Him the spheres [*Sephirot*]: sepa-ration, creation, formation, making, the world of ideas, the forces, the forms, the material, the kingdom of genius, of spirit, of soul, of life.[20]

Islam had expressed a similar idea nearly one thousand years before the Baal Shem Tov was born, captured in the holy tradition: "I was a hidden treasure, and I loved to be known, and so I created the world."[21] Muhyiddin ibn Arabi (d. 1240) states:

> The soul sees that it sees Him only through Him, not through itself, and that it loves Him only through Him, not through itself. So He it is who loves Himself … None loves Him but He. He is the lover and the beloved, the seeker and the sought.[22]

According to both the Sufi and Hasidic traditions, human love of God represents an act of self-knowledge for God. This is the true purpose of humankind, to bring knowledge *of* God *to* God, fully realizing his function as the microcosm to the universal macrocosm.

Perfect Man

Achieving the ideal of the Hasidic Perfect Man (*al-Insan al-Kamil*, for Islam) became the ultimate goal for the European Jewish practitioner. For Muslim and later Jewish spiritual wayfarers, humans represented the turning point where God's self knowledge can come to fruition. The more that mystical awareness unfolds within the aspirant, the more God is reflected in the pure receptacle of the living human soul, and the further is God's ultimate purpose for creation realized.

Islam had initially developed this conception of the *al-Insam al-Kamil*, or God's vice-regent (*khalifa*), from the life of the Prophet Muhammad, as represented in the Koran. Titus Burckhardt explains the importance of this Sufi ideal in his *Introduction to Sufi Doctrine*:

> The "global meaning" of human nature is actualized only in one who has effectively realized all the universal Truths reflected in his terrestrial form and who is thus identified with the "Perfect Man" (*al-Insam al-Kamil*). Practically speaking, such a man will have his human individuality as his "external" form, but ... all other forms and all states of existence belong to him because his "inward reality" is identified with that of the whole universe. The term "Universal Man" is applied to all who have realized Union.[23]

In this state, the Sufi adept has emptied himself completely of his "self," becoming a "polished mirror," scrubbed of the impurities of the human ego, reflecting the universal essence back to itself. As was noted in chapter two, reflecting the genesis of this idea in a Koranic passage:

> The man who is in a state of *ihsan* is truly the *khalifa*, the vice-regent of God on Earth. He rediscovers the "most beautiful form" in which he was created (Koran 95:4, "We molded man into the most noble image"), because his heart is like a pure, well-polished mirror in which the Divine can be reflected. Leading man back to this station is the goal of Sufi practices.[24]

As we have seen, this Sufi image of the well-polished reflector appears in the work of many medieval Jewish mystics, from Solomon ibn Gabirol (11th century) to Obadyah Maimonides (13th century).

From there, the image of the human who becomes a pure receptor reflecting the Divine, appears in the *Zohar*, a central text for Hasidic thinkers. Gershom Scholem notes in the *Encyclopaedia Judaica*:

> Whereas God contains all, by virtue of being its Creator and Initiator in whom everything is rooted and all potency hidden, man's role is to complete this process by being the agent through whom all the powers of creation are fully activated and made manifest ... The key formu-

lations can already be found in the *Zohar*... The process of creation involves the departure of all from the One and its return to the One, and the crucial turning point in this cycle takes place within man, at the moment he develops an awareness of his own true essence ...[25]

Professor Rachel Elior (Hebrew University), writing in *The Mystical Origins of Hasidism*, echoes Scholem's contention, unwittingly utilizing language that echoes Sufi concepts of the realized spiritual adept:

> Both the early Hasidic masters and their successors regarded themselves as divinely appointed messengers and as emissaries of the congregation by virtue of being blessed with divine grace. They conceived of themselves as being in the image of Moses "the man of God" attached to the higher worlds from which he brought spiritual abundance ...[26]

The Sufi scholar Frithjof Schuon, writing in the *Quintessential Esotericism of Islam*, echoes Elior's language concerning the Hasidic ideal:

> The word *Rasul*, "messenger," indicates a "descent" of God toward the world; it also implies an "ascent" of man toward God ... The microcosmic aspect of *Rasul* ... is the immanent universal Intellect, and the purpose is to awaken within us the heart-intellect in the twofold relationship of receptivity and enlightenment.[27]

It is vital to note, once again, that this spiritual concept stems from the life of the Prophet Muhammad, the original *rasul* or divinely appointed messenger.

### Jewish *Sheikh*

Once cleansed of all spiritual impurities, the spiritual leader took on a role as intercessor in both Sufism and Hasidism. Although present in Islam from the outset, with the Prophet Muhammad standing at the head of all Sufi orders as the original *sheikh*, the idea of a spiritual teacher who has completely lost himself in God and then returns to act as an emissary and necessary teacher for aspirants originally was introduced into Jewish mysticism via the work of Abraham (d. 1237) and Obadyah Maimonides (d.1265). Both of these teachers had insisted on the necessity of a *sheikh* (they used this exact word) to help a novice along their spiritual path.

Obadyah, in particular, built his conception on earlier ideas outlined by the Muslim philosopher Abd Allah ibn Sina (d. 1037). As George Vajda (University of Paris) notes in the *Journal of Jewish Studies*:

> The concept of the "perfect man" according to Obadyah has definite forerunners in Bahya ibn Pakuda, Judah Halevi and Moses Maimonides, but here it takes on a rather special hue, owing to the fact that the "righteous man" enjoys pneumatic and thaumaturgic privileges that are

far more marked than in those authors. We might be put in mind of the Mohammedan philosophical influences, as for instance, the portrait of the Perfect One outlined by Ibn Sina in the last pages of the *Isharat*, or mystical influences from the same quarter.[28]

Obadyah went on to add another Sufi tenet, new to Judaism as well, which was reprised by the Hasidic *tzaddik* five centuries later.

> The most striking feature of the doctrine of R. Obadyah is unquestionably the renunciation, after a painful discussion, of conquest and above all of the personal retention of the mystical union, with the obligation arising therefrom, of recourse to the somewhat enigmatical "intercessor" or spiritual director [*sheikh*], who is even more a quasi-messianic figure. I am unable to say whether previous Jewish mysticism, of no matter what tendency, affords an exact or even approximate parallel … In Sufism, the spiritual master is sometimes termed a "road leading to God;" and even for ancient Mohammedan tradition, it is not inconceivable that, besides the Prophet [Muhammad], holy individuals interceded in favor of the faithful.[29]

Obadyah himself states: "It is clear that he who has no intercessor to tie the bond between himself and his Beloved, is considered as dead."[30] This echoes Sufi tradition, which he undoubtedly knew, stating: "Whoever has no master has Satan as his master."[31] We find strong echoes of Obadyah's conception in the words of Hasidic Rabbi Aharon Kohen of Apt (c. 1800), who states:

> The issue of prophecy is: It is impossible, by and large, to prophesy suddenly, without a certain preparation and holiness, but if the person who wants to prepare himself to prophesy sanctifies and purifies himself and concentrates mentally and utterly separates himself from the delights of this world, and he serves the sages, including his rabbi, the prophet … and when the rabbi, the prophet, understands that his disciple is already prepared for prophecy, then his rabbi gives him the topic of the recitations of the holy names, which are the keys for the supernal gates.[32]

The Islamic influence on this brief passage runs deep – from the role of the spiritual master in offering the "keys for the supernal gates," to the process by which the adept "sanctifies and purifies himself and concentrates mentally and utterly separates himself from the delights of this world," which sounds remarkably similar to *khalwa* (spiritual retreat). The "recitations of the holy names" also echoes the Islamic *'Ilm al-Huruf*, or Science of the Letters.

Social Role

Obadyah's ideas concerning the Jewish spiritual leader became interspersed with Islamic conceptions of prophecy. Taken together, these defined the role of the *tzaddik*: to act as the intercessor between God and the searcher, as well as disseminate through social action the Divine power that only the *tzaddik* could access.

The socially involved prophetic ideal within Judaism had been strongly influenced by Islamic ideas stretching back to Jafar as-Sadiq (d. 765), the Sixth Imam of Shi'a Islam, who in turn had based his ideas on the life of the Prophet Muhammad (see Chapter 3). As-Sadiq, we will remember, offered a hierarchy of prophetic realization, the highest stage being the prophetic "legislator," or one who was bathed completely in God's light, and charged with transforming this ineffable energy into a religious and legislative language that could be understood by the normative Muslim practitioner.

Starting with medieval thinkers such as Judah Halevi (d. 1141) and Moses Maimonides (d. 1204), Judaism was influenced by these Islamic concepts of prophecy. This change in the Jewish prophetic ideal added a strong social and even political role to the agenda of the medieval spiritual leader.

What has been less noted, however, is how this Islamic prophetic conception became central to later *Ashkenazi* Judaism and, specifically, to the social and spiritual role of the Hasidic *tzaddik*. For instance, here is a recent comment by Professor Rachel Elior on the development of leadership within Hasidic circles:

> Since the late 18th century, the most distinctive and probably most famous feature of Hasidic communities has been the leadership of the *tzaddik* ... the leadership of the *tzaddik* has continued to be a key feature of Hasidism into the 21st century ... The mystical concepts underlying the *tzaddik's* leadership and its spiritual and social significance are less well known, however. The doctrine was first articulated in the circle of the Maggid of Mezhrich in the 1760s and early 1770s ... and further articulated in the works published by Jacob Joseph of Polonnoy from 1780 on. The spiritual and social implications of these teachings were to have a profound effect in the various Hasidic circles. Leadership by a *tzaddik* is perhaps the main religious innovation of Hasidism. As a revolutionary rethinking of the relationship between man and God, it engendered a totally new view of the world.[33]

Elior overlooks the Islamic genesis of many of these ideas, however. Kabbalistic thinkers such as Moses de Leon (d. 1305) and Isaac of Acre (d. 1350) expanded on Moses Maimonides' Muslim-inspired concept of prophetic leadership, which informed the Hasidic "revolutionary rethinking of the relationship between man and God."

This leadership ideal did not become systematized within Jewish esotericism during medieval times. The organized application of this style of guidance didn't take place until the 17th century, when Shabbetai Zevi accepted the literal role of Messiah and, therefore, spiritual intercessor and social guide for the Jewish people. It was here, in the life of the disgraced Jewish leader, that Hasidism found its most salient representation of this new model of social and spiritual leader.

> There is a further and very important point in which Shabbateanism and Hasidism join in departing from the rabbinical scale of values, namely their conception of the ideal type of man to which they ascribe the function of leadership ... In place of the teachers of the Law, the new movements gave birth to a new type of leader, the illuminate, the man whose heart had been touched and changed by God, in a word, the prophet.[34]

### Living Saint

Much like the Sufi "sober mystic," the *tzaddik* is an ecstatic spiritualist who is able to control his experience by coming back from complete ego-dissolution in God, to function as a temporal leader. It is in this return, that the bond is cemented between the Islamic concept of the realized "Perfect Man" and the Hasidic *tzaddik*.

> The [Hasidic] mystic first has to negate the ego in order to be able to identify himself with the Nought, while by returning to the world he becomes helpful to the community ... The momentary, or more constant obliteration of the ego serves as a powerful tool for the quasi-prophetic mission of the Hasidic *tzaddik*. He is able to escape time, in his ascent to a-temporal perfection, but he is also able to return in order to act in time. This concept of the *tzaddik*, therefore, implies that he is not only a mystic who acquires powers, but also an ecstatic who is able to control his experience by coming back to function as a communal leader.[35]

Or, as Martin Buber notes:

> When a disciple once remarked that a *tzaddik* had "grown cold" and censored him for it, he was instructed by another, "There is a very high holiness; if one enters it, one becomes detached from all being and can no longer become inflamed." Thus ecstasy completes itself in its own suspension.[36]

This ideal is nearly identical to the Sufi *sheikh*, who for one thousand years before the foundation of Hasidism had been fulfilling a like role within

Islamic esotericism. As noted earlier, the 10th-century Sufi master al-Junayd (d. 910) thus defines the Sufi adept:

> He is existent in both himself and in God after having been existent in God and non-existent in himself. This is because he has left the drunkenness of God's overwhelming presence and come to the clarity of sobriety ... when he has reached the height of spiritual perfection granted by God, he becomes a pattern for his fellow men.[37]

And so it is that three different facets that help define the *tzaddik* can be traced back into Sufism. Perhaps the manner in which they are combined is not exactly how the Sufis originally conceived of these ideas, but specific facets of how Hasidism interprets the ascent toward union with the Divine, the attraction of the Divine Power into the being of the *tzaddik* and then the prophetic social role all stem, in part, from medieval Islamic inspirations.[38]

### Prayer

The way toward perfection for the Hasidic leader is not based in study, but in prayer. This in itself echoes Sufi and Jewish-Sufi antecedents. Hasidic *tzaddiks* were hardly unaware that they were distancing themselves from the Jewish tradition of study and learning as the highest form of worship with this change in emphasis. They, like earlier Jewish-Sufis, attempted to tie their innovations backwards into Judaic history. Hasidic Rabbi Kalonymus Kalman Epstein (d. 1827) made the point explicitly:

> When the Jew draws near to the form of worship that is prayer it is to the greatest thing in the whole world that he draws near, as the holy book tells us. In our generation, especially, the chief method by which a man can refine his character, so as to approach the divine and serve God, is prayer. From the time of his coming, the holy Baal Shem Tov caused the tremendous sanctity of prayer to illuminate the world for whoever wishes to draw near to God's service.[39]

Scholar Rabbi Louis Jacobs assures that the Hasidic elevation of prayer over the study of *Torah* was not in keeping with Jewish tradition. In the Talmud, one rabbi could rebuke another who prolonged his prayers unduly; Rabbi Simoen ben Yohai (c. 150) would never interrupt his studies in order to pray. As Jacobs notes, concerning the above quote from the Hasidic rabbi:

> Here we clearly see how an influential Hasidic author strives to reconcile the traditional view of the supremacy of *Torah* study with the new Hasidic emphasis on the supremacy of prayer ... In another passage, Rabbi Kalonymus Kalman Epstein, commenting on Jacob's dream, notes that Jacob awoke from his learning ("his sleep"). The *Midrash*

[commentary on the *Torah*], of course, suggests that Jacob saw his vision of the divine because he was learned in the *Torah*. But Rabbi Kalonymus boldly turns the *Midrash* on its head to suggest that, on the contrary, once Jacob has experienced true prayer he saw that his learning was only a dream insofar as he had imagined that by it he could come to love God.[40]

This trans-valuation of prayer and study follows the now-familiar lineage within Judaism, as do so many other Islamic ideas that influenced Hasidism: from the Koran and the life of the Prophet Muhammad to Sufism, then medieval Jewry, the Safed Kabbalists and finally into 18th-and 19th-century European Hasidism.

In this case, we can tease out the thread of this seemingly heretical proposition by looking at the work of Eliezer Azikri (d. 1600), who quoted the Safed Rabbi Isaac Luria (d. 1572) as stating that *hitbodedut* "is helpful to the soul seven times more than study, and ... a man should concentrate and meditate one day a week."[41] At the time, this was a highly unusual statement, and as it described a valuation so completely at odds with traditional Jewish practice, it could only be attributed to foreign influence.

Working backwards, we find the genesis for this ideal in earlier Sufi texts. As noted in the last chapter, this appreciation for the primacy of prayer echoed the Sufi adept, Abu al-Najib al-Suhrawardi (d. 1168), who said "contemplation (i.e. *hitbodedut*) for one hour is better than ritual worship for a whole year."[42] This also referenced al-Ghazali (d. 1111), and even the Prophet Muhammad, who was quoted in a *hadith* as saying: "One hour of meditation is worth more than the good works accomplished by the two species endowed with weight (humans and *jinn*)."[43]

Moshe Idel notes that writings such as Azriki's and his contemporary Safed Kabbalists "constituted the final stage in a process of penetration of (contemplative prayer) into Jewish culture as a practical teaching. Abulafia's (c. 13th century) writings constituted the beginning of the process of absorption of the Sufi outlook within Kabbalah ... The influence of the views sketched above may be traced through the writings of the Hasidic mystics."[44]

*Hitbodedut*

One of the most important additions to Jewish prayer, and one that has influenced Judaism since the 11th century, is *hitbodedut*. As we by now well know, this form of solitary meditation runs contrary to traditional rabbinic ethics, which call for the community to be the center of Jewish prayer life. By the time Hasidic authors were penning their treatises, they could point to nearly 800 years of Jewish tradition in solitary prayer, dating back to Bahya ibn Pakuda (d. 1080), Judah Halevi (d. 1141) and the 13th-century Egyptian Jewish-Sufis, thereby believing that they were simply reinvigorating a Hebraic prayer practice.

*Hitbodedut* was a central part of the mystical path for the Hasid,[45] one that was necessary to achieve the ultimate prayer goal of *devequt* (Divine union). In describing Hasidic prayer, Rachel Elior elucidates a practice that sounds nearly identical to Sufi *khalwa*:

> In order to be liberated from the subjugation to the constraints of physical existence and to become a free soul sustained in the expanses of nothingness, one must distance oneself from this world, alienate oneself from social concerns, withdraw from corporeality, and shut one's consciousness to external stimuli and routine modes of thought.[46]

To appreciate how closely this tracks medieval Sufi prayer ideals, we need only compare Elior's late-20th-century interpretation of Hasidic prayer with the 11th-century Sufi al-Ghazali's teacher, who enumerated the importance of solitude and separation for the realization of the Islamic mystical path:

> The best method consists of completely cutting ties with the world, in such a way that your heart does not occupy itself with family, nor with children, nor with money, nor with homeland, nor with science, nor with government – the existence or non-existence of these things being of equal value. In addition, for you to be alone in retreat, it is necessary ... to concentrate your thought on *Allah*, without other interior occupation.[47]

### Prayer as Love for the Divine

Another of the central aspects of Hasidic prayer that was derived in part from Islamic mysticism was the employment of the symbolism of the lover and the beloved for the contemplative act. For Hasidism, earthly and profane love may stand not only as a metaphor for Divine love, but also as a doorway: the appreciation of physical beauty and the sexual act itself become spiritual symbols, when properly understood. *Leqatim Yekarim*, a collection of sayings from the Baal Shem Tov, notes in a particularly graphic passage:

> Prayer is copulation with the *Sheckinah*. Just as there is a swaying when copulation begins so, too, a man must sway at first and then he can remain immobile and attached to the *Sheckinah* with great attachment ... Why do I sway my body? Presumably it is because the *Sheckinah* stands over against me. And as a result he [the aspirant] will attain to the stage of great enthusiasm.[48]

The usage of this symbolism for the spiritual quest may be traced back to the *Sefer ha-Bahir* (c. 1230), where it became systemized within medieval Jewish thought. The *Bahir*, however, is hardly the only medieval Jewish source that utilizes this imagery. Even so austere a thinker as Moses Maimonides (d. 1204) employs this trope:

> And what is the proper love? That one love God with great, excessive and mighty love until one's soul becomes permanently bound in the love of God like one who is sick of love and cannot distract his mind from the beloved woman but always thinks of her – when lying down or rising up, when eating or drinking.[49]

Louis Jacobs notes that the *Zohar*, a central text for 18th-century Jewish mystics, has many passages in which sex is used as metaphor for the love of God, including a passage where the Biblical Moses states that he had intercourse with the *Sheckinah*. In another instance, the *Zohar* notes that when a man cannot lie with his wife, due to travel or her monthly menstruation, then the *Sheckinah* is with him so that he can be "male and female."[50] Other Jewish-Sufi thinkers such as Bahya ibn Pakuda, Solomon ibn Gabirol and Judah Halevi incorporated the use of romantic imagery to describe the human relationship with God, which had been dormant in Jewish literature for almost 1000 years prior to their time.

From these medieval thinkers, this motif became important within the Safed Kabbalah. As Zwi Werblowsky (Martin Buber Professor Emeritus of Comparative Religion, Hebrew University) notes in *The Kabbalists in Sixteenth-Century Safed*:

> The life intended here was the *vita contemplative* of communion with God (*devequt*) which, in sixteenth-century Safed, acquired an erotic quality reminiscent of many ways of Sufi piety ... Eliezer Azikri [d. 1600] accepts all the consequences of violent love: sleeplessness, calling God fond names and singing to the Beloved: "It is the custom of passionate lovers to sing, and since the love of our Creator is 'wonderful, passing the love of women' (II Samuel 1:26), therefore he who loves Him with all of his heart should sing before Him" ... The best known, and in Schechter's phrase, most "vividly erotic" of these mystic bards was Israel Nagara [d. 1581], whose hymns have found their way into many a prayer book.[51]

The specific manner in which this ideal entered Hasidism may be teased out, by following the influence backward. In addition to the *Zohar*, the work of Elijah de Vidas (d. 1592), a student of Moshe Cordovero's in Safed, inspired this concept of contemplating God while considering human beauty. De Vidas quoted a story of human love leading to an understanding and realization for the Divine, from a lost treatise of Isaac of Acre (d. 1350).[52] Rabbi Isaac was hardly shy about his contention for the effectiveness of using sensual love as a metaphor, stating: "From the sensual, one must understand the nature of divine service" in the context of "lust for a woman."[53] The Sufis originally told the parable that helped to influence Hasidism![54]

Moshe Idel notes that the contemplation of beauty was a Sufi mystical technique. Isaac of Acre's story, of a deeply erotic love that could become the basis for the love of God, had a strong impact on Jacob Joseph of Polonnoy (d. 1782) and other Hasidic masters.[55] Like virtually all Islamic-inspired Jews before them, the Hasids tied their innovations back into Jewish scripture. Hence, we read in words of Rabbi Aharon Kohen of Apta (c. 1800):

> The intention of Sarah in all her adornments and embellishments was only for the sake of heaven, as someone who embellishes the image of the King ... so [one] must think of the case where someone sees a beautiful and adorned person. This person is in the image of God, and he shall think that he sees the beauty and adornment of the image of the King. And this was the intention of Sarah when she embellished herself.[56]

This Hasidic utilization of the profane as a doorway into the spiritual, while undoubtedly present in the Bible, specifically Solomon's *Song of Songs*, was inspired within 18th-century Judaism via the earlier Jewish-Sufi interactions, and may be tied back to Koranic origins. As previously noted, Sufi scholar Martin Lings states that in many passages, the Koran speaks in imagery recalling pleasures of the senses, because these direct pleasures are reverberations of the universal archetypes. The pleasures of the senses have the power to recall these very aspects imbedded in the Divine essence: according to Islam, any aspect of the world can vibrate with mystical significance.[57]

### Ruhaniyyut

*Ruhaniyyut* is the Divine power that the Hasidic *tzaddik* brings into the world. This underpins his role as social prophet – it is this energy that he distributes through his actions, the manner in which he brings God-consciousness to the general public. This idea of *ruhaniyyut* as the force that represents God's power may be traced back to Islamic origins.

> *Ruhaniyyut* entered some 14th-century Jewish texts, some belonging to Abulafia's Kabbalistic school. Rabbi Isaac of Acre, whose affinity to Abulafia's school is indisputable, describes the process of permutating letters in the "chamber of seclusion" as intended to draw down the Divine intellect ... *Ruhaniyyut* is tantamount to the Divine intellect that is caused to descend by the permutation of letters and their pronunciation ... in the late 14th century, the term *ruhaniyyut* as a designation for spiritual forces superior to the astral bodies became widespread.[58]

Before continuing, it is important to note two other specific Sufi influences mentioned in this passage, which became central aspects of Hasidic practice. The "chamber of seclusion" (known as a *zawiyya* to the Sufis) was absolutely a Muslim innovation adopted by medieval Jews, based on the Sufi practice of *khalwa*. Additionally, the method of drawing down the spiritual force, using prayer methods based in "permutating the letters," stems from the Sufi Science of the Letters.

At the end of the 15th century, the term *ruhaniyyut* appeared in the work of Rabbi Yohanan Alemanno (d. 1505), who was influenced by Abraham Abulafia.[59] From there, the idea passed on to the 16th-century Kabbalists. As Moshe Cordovero (d. 1570) says in his *Pardes Rimmonim*:

> A worshipper using *kavvanah* [devotional intent] has to draw the [*ruhaniyyut*] from the supernal levels onto the letters he is pronouncing so as to be able to elevate those letters up to that supernal level, in order to hasten his request.[60]

This exact passage from Cordovero's work ended up being cited in the text *Toledot Ya'aqov Yosef* by the Hasidic Rabbi Jacob Joseph of Polonnoy. And this book was hardly peripheral to 18th-century Jewish mystical practice, being the first work to express the basic teachings of Hasidism.[61]

The Baal Shem Tov almost certainly never saw any of the Islamic texts. He came to know these ideas through various Judaized avenues, including the Safed Kabbalists, and perhaps even copies of Isaac of Acre or Abraham Abulafia's manuscripts. As Moshe Idel notes in *Mystical Union in Judaism, Christianity and Islam*:

> It is important to point out the profound influence of the Islamic concept of *ruhaniyyut* on Jewish mysticism. The sources of this term are Sabian [a pre-Islamic Arabic sect] texts, which use *ruhaniyyut* in order to designate the supernal forces or lights. Union with the Divine was portrayed as a spiritual force [Hebrew: *Ruhaniyt*] that descends upon the mystic during *devequt*. This way of understanding unitive experiences is widespread in Jewish mysticism, though predominant in Hasidism.[62]

This Islamic idea would ultimately become so important to Hasidism that it defined the highest purpose of the *tzaddik* – to go forth into the "temples" of the *Sephirot* and glean from them the spiritual lifeblood, the power of God, and to bring it back to Earth. We can posit that to this day, no Hasidic *tzaddik* has any idea that his prayer practice – centered in drawing down *ruhaniyyut* – may be in some cases traced in a direct line back to medieval Muslim masters.

*Bittul ha-Yesh* or Annihilation of Self

The Baal Shem Tov proposed a concept of contemplative prayer comprised of two aspects, which would lead to drawing down the *ruhaniyyut*. Most importantly, the aspirant attempts to achieve *bittul ha-yesh* (annihilation of somethingness). In this manner, the interior psychic space is completely emptied of all impurities, such as personal ego and desire, and prepared to accept the Divine effluence.

This Hasidic concept of the "annihilation of somethingness" mirrors almost exactly earlier Sufi ideals of emptying oneself to the point of complete spiritual poverty (*faqr*), achieving *fana* (annihilation of the ego), and then acceptance of the Divine, *baqa* (subsistence in God). This self-effacement was considered heretical to traditional Jews due to its assertion that man could obliterate the separation between him and Him, allowing humans to merge their personal ego with the Divine essence.

> The concept [of annihilation] is crucial for many of the Hasidic discussions of mystical experience and may be considered one of the most important components of the mystical technique in Hasidism. The emphasis should be placed on the existence of a directive to imitate God by self-effacement, as well as on the practices of solitude and mental concentration.[63]

By the time that the Hasids were expounding on these ideals, there had been enough Jewish precedent in *bittul ha-yesh*, that the 18th-century mystics thought themselves to be employing a Jewish prayer ideal. The Baal Shem Tov states:

> Whoever wishes that the Godhead should dwell upon him should consider himself to be *ayin* [nothing], and the most important thing is to know that within him there is *but* Godhead, and this is a preparation for the dwelling of the Godhead on him.[64]

We remember the *hadith qudsi* (saying of God) that underpins the Sufi concept of *fana*, or annihilation of self: God "becomes the ear with which he [the realized adept] hears, the sight through which he sees, the hand with which he grasps, and the foot with which he walks." This experience of emptying oneself completely of the "self," so that God could fill the interior space was so essential to Sufism, that the early Sufi practitioner Junayd (d. 910) explained that this experience alone defined it.[65]

The idea of emptying oneself in this manner initially entered Judaism through well-worn medieval pathways, and is seen by example in Obadyah Maimonides' *Treatise of the Pool*:

> "And a source from the House of God." (Joel 4:18) The foregoing is an allegory alluding to the purification, cleansing and purging of the heart, the correction of its defects and failings and its being emptied of all but the Most High.[66]

The Baal Shem Tov is hardly the only 18th-century Jewish thinker to assimilate this central Sufi tenet. Another important *tzaddik*, Rabbi Menahem Mendel of Vitebsk (d. 1788), states:

> One should oneself be as one does not exist, to completely disown one's body and soul, [that it may be] obliterated for the sanctification of the Name from this world and the next … For he has already abnegated himself completely, because of his meditation upon the greatness of the Creator.[67]

Again, according to the Sufis: "When the self is annihilated [at the moment of *fana*], the divine fills its psychic space."[68] Or, as the Hasidic Rabbi Yitzhak of Radzivilow (c. 1800) explains, echoing the Sufi *hadith qudsi* noted above: "In the final stage of spiritualization, man discovers that he – that is, his soul – is identical with God's self knowledge."[69]

A small book could be compiled of sayings from Sufis concerning the *baqa* that follows *fana* and Hasids describing *bittul ha-yesh*,[70] all of which appear to stem from the exact same source: the *hadith qudsi* of earliest Islamic tradition, which enjoined the mystic to allow God to completely permeate his psychic space, becoming for God "the eyes through which He sees …"

### Science of the Letters

The Islamic *'Ilm al-Huruf* (Science of the Letters) exercised a vital impact on Hasidic prayer practice. Medieval Kabbalists were strongly influenced by changes in the perception of the mystical qualities of the Hebrew language and grammar. From there, the ideas passed easily into European Judaism. Of course, within Hasidic tradition, the *Sefer Yetzirah* was considered the originator of this mystical idea. Rachel Elior notes in *The Mystical Origins of Hasidism*:

> In the ancient mystical text *Sefer Yetzirah* written by an anonymous author in the early centuries of the Common Era, the process of creation is explicitly linked to the letters of the Hebrew language. The transition from abstract, creative divine power to the creative reality of enduring creation sustained by "divine breath" is effected through letters and ciphers … Jewish mystical tradition therefore has a distinctive attitude to the Hebrew language in all its aspects … the Hebrew letters are seen as the physical manifestation of divine speech, as the creative force that perpetually engenders and sustains the universe … God creates the world through the utterance and permutation of letters, by inscribing, carving and combining them as recorded in the *Sefer Yetzirah* …[71]

The Baal Shem Tov is remembered as echoing these ideas:

> It is from the holy letters that the root and animation of man derive.

For whatever is, gets its being and existence only from the letters out of which heaven and earth and all they contain were created. The Baal Shem Tov explained the verse: "Forever, O God, Your word stands in heaven" (Psalm 119:89) to mean that even now the entire life of creation and all existence springs from the holy letters that are God's word standing always in heaven to give them life.[72]

From the Baal Shem Tov, the ancient Sufi art of letter mysticism entered Hasidic theology. The compiler of much of the Baal Shem Tov's thought, Rabbi Jacob Joseph of Polonnoy (d. 1782), echoes specific aspects of the *Sefer Yetzirah,* stating:

For just as there are 22 letters of speech and *Torah* and prayer, so in all material and all physical affairs in the world there are 22 letters through which the world and all that is in it was created. Within these letters dwells the Divine spirit, for His glory fills all the earth and all that it contains ...[73]

A later Hasidic master, Ze'ev Wolf of Zhitomir (d. 1800), seeded letter mysticism more deeply into Hasidic practice: "For in truth, the entire *Torah* is only letters and each and every Jew, according to his standing and value, engenders permutations of the individual letters."[74]

This Islamic concept of viewing creation as language influenced Hasidic prayer in much the same way that it had Jewish prayer from the earliest Kabbalistic treatises. The unbroken path from 8th-and 9th-century Baghdad through Golden Age era Jewish thinkers, into the Kabbalah and, specifically Abraham Abulafia (d. 1291), to Hasidic thought is not difficult to trace.

Moshe Idel notes, drawing the line from Abulafia through to the Hasidic masters:

The same text by Abulafia, as copied by Cordovero, informs a statement found in Rabbi Kalonymus Kalman Epstein's [d. 1823] *Ma'or va-Shemesh* [Light and Sun], where the creation of the world by means of the 22 letters and combination of divine names is related to the notion of the Tetragrammaton [*YHVH,* the unpronounceable name of God], which is combined with each and every letter ... There is a description of the tables found in Abulafia's *Or ha-Sekhel* and Cordovero's *Pardes Rimmonim.* Thus we have [an] example of the direct acquaintance of the Baal Shem Tov with a crucial discussion of Abulafia's combination of the letters ...[75]

Abulafia also helped to provide the impetus for the supposed ancient Hebraic provenance of the "lore of the combination of the letters." Hasidic Rabbi Yeheil Mikhal of Zlotchov (d. 1786), in talking about the Baal Shem

Tov, states:

> If he is strongly united to the holiness, he is able to elevate profane things to holiness by means of the lore of the combination of the letters which is known to the holy and divine Baal Shem Tov, blessed be his memory, and to his disciples... the *Tannaim* [c. 70-200] were in possession of the divine spirit and they possessed the wisdom in a perfect manner, [namely] the combination of the letters ...[76]

The fallacious attribution of the "lore of the combination of the letters" to the ancient Jewish figures stems from Abraham Abulafia. A statement similar to that of the Maggid of Zlotchov appeared in *Sefer ha Peliyah* (c. 1400), and has been traced back to the 13th-century Jewish heretic. In *Sefer ha Peliyah*, Abulafia is quoted as stating: "Our sages, blessed be their memory, were experts in the combination of the letters," which was preceded by a supposed Talmudic discussion that interpreted a Biblical phrase in light of the combination of the letters.[77]

### *Devequt*

All of these prayer methods pointed toward one goal for the Hasids: *devequt*, or Divine union. While individual Jewish mystics had been working toward this goal since the earliest Jewish-Sufi interactions in the 12th and 13th centuries, it became institutionalized within Jewish practice only with 18th-century Hasidism. Jewish thinkers since the earliest Jewish-Sufi interactions had been pointing to Solomon's *Song of Songs* (and other Biblical passages) as precedence for many of their more extreme ideas, but in traditional Jewish practice, the Scriptures had not been interpreted as offering a manner to dissolve the personal ego completely in the Divine essence. As has been variously noted, the concept of union with the Divine not only was unprecedented within Judaism prior to Sufi influence, but it also was heretical, making its importance to 18th-century Jewish practice all the more surprising.

The centrality of this prayer ideal to Hasidic practice cannot be denied, however. As Moshe Idel notes in *Hasidism: Between Ecstasy and Magic*: "One of the most cherished values of Hasidism is that of cleaving to God. Indeed, the term *devequt*, the most recurrent designation for this spiritual value, appears thousands of times in Hasidic literature."[78]

The Hasidic concept of Divine union followed closely the Sufi ideal, going so far beyond traditional Jewish prayer goals that even the seminal 20th-century Jewish scholar, Gershom Scholem, was uncomfortable acknowledging how completely it broke with Jewish teaching!

> *Devequt* signifies "adhesion" or "being joined" *viz.* God. This is regarded as the ultimate goal of religious perfection ... Yet even the rap-

turous descriptions of this state of mind that abound in later Hasidic literature retain a proper sense of distance or, if you will, incommensurateness.[79]

One needn't look too deeply into Hasidic thought, however, to find that Scholem's analysis is incorrect: Jewish thinkers of this era did conceive of *devequt* as obliterating the distance between man and God, mirroring the Sufi goal. For instance, here is the presentation of the prayer ideal, as related by Rabbi Shneur Zalman of Lyady (d. 1813):

> That is the true *devequt*, to become one substance with divinity, to be swallowed up within Him, that it might be considered impossible to be a separate entity on his own at all. That is truly the injunction of cleaving unto God.[80]

This quote from the Hasidic Rabbi Levi Yitzhak of Berdichev (d. 1810) elucidates further the Hasidic doctrine:

> There are those whose gaze is fixed as if on Nought, and this is impossible without Divine help ... He who is granted this supreme degree, with divine help, to contemplate the Nought, his intellect is effaced and he is like a dumb man ... but when he returns from such a contemplation to the essence of his intellect, he finds it full of influx.[81]

The similarities between the Sufi doctrine and the Hasidic are clear: the *tzaddik* empties himself to where his intellect is "effaced," which echoes *fana* and then experiences an "influx," which mirrors *baqa*, becoming filled with God. Additionally, the necessity for Divine help to attain the goal of prayer echoes Sufi ideas, where prayer ultimately is a passive activity of preparing oneself for Divine favor. As Sufi scholar Titus Burckhardt notes, "The Sufi's ... individual human nature will always remain passive in relation to Divine Reality or Truth ... and in this relationship, the Divine Presence will always manifest itself as grace."[82]

It is not difficult to find the avenues through which the ideas of Divine union flowed into Europe. An early explanation of *devequt* comes from an anonymous adept of Abraham Maimonides' Jewish-Sufi circle (c. 13th century):

> Man's purpose concerning his personal perfection, is the pursuit of knowledge whose objective is in turn twofold: a) the soul's felicity (*tawfiq*) through obedience to God (Deuteronomy 11:13) and b) love of God (Deuteronomy 6:5), leading to "attachment" to Him (*deviqah*). This attachment involves two goals: First, the soul's edification through the continuous (benefits bestowed by) the divine effluence (*ruhaniyyut*) throughout life in this world (Deuteronomy 4:4) and second, the soul's enjoyment of God's intimacy (*qurb*) after leaving the body, and its eter-

nal delight in His Presence. (I Samuel 25:29)[83]

Like so many Sufi-inspired Jewish thinkers of his era, this anonymous 13th-century Jewish-Sufi uses Islamic terminology, but ties the ideas back to Biblical antecedents, through referencing specific passages in the *Torah*.

Early Kabbalists like Isaac of Acre and the ubiquitous Abraham Abulafia, as well as the 16th-century Safed Kabbalists accepted the Islamic view of *devequt*. Of Abraham Abulafia, Moshe Idel notes: "The idea of unity between man and God which, according to Gershom Scholem is foreign to Jewish mysticism, nevertheless appears in Abulafia."[84] Abulafia believed in the ability of human beings to "disintegrate the human composition and unite its highest component with its source through the use of mystical techniques, such as respiratory exercises and permutation of the letters."[85]

From Abulafia, it was an easy jump to Safed, where Moshe Cordovero disseminated the ideal:

> [Cordovero] propagated the view that the union of the human and divine minds was to be achieved through [Abulafia's letter combination], which, as Abulafia put it, "draws down the supernal force in order to cause it to be united with you." This Hermetical understanding of Abulafia's technique had an important influence on the Hasidic perception of *devequt* ...[86]

Concerning the Sufi influence on the Jewish ideal of *devequt*, Daniel Merkur states in his article "Unitive Experience and the State of Trance:"

> The Kabbalistic doctrine of the universalization of God – or the ability of an adept to join with the power of God – was imported from Islam in the 12th century. The Jewish version was based in, among other things, Sufism. Beginning with Moses Maimonides and his offspring, the Jewish-Sufis of Egypt, it was then passed through Abraham Abulafia and finally popularized by, among other people, Joseph Karo's 16th-century codification of Jewish law, *Shulchan Aruch*. The tradition then passed into Hasidism, where it survives to this day as a living practice.[87]

*Hishtawwut*

In Hasidism, *Hishtawwut* (equanimity) is a necessary corollary to achieving *devequt*. Any personal ego retained during prayer comes between the seeker and union with the Divine; the Divine Essence cannot suffuse the heart of the aspirant, unless he turns his soul into a vacant vessel. The realization of *hishtawwut* signals a state of total acceptance of God. As the Baal Shem Tov states:

> It says: "I have set God before me always" (Psalm 26:8) "Set" implies equanimity [*hishtawwut*]. Whatever occurs should be equal to him,

whether people praise him or despise him, and so too with all other matters ... let him not consider at all the affairs of this world, and let him not think about them at all, in order to separate himself from corporeality ... Thus, it should be equal in his eyes if he is loved or hated, for their love and hatred is nothing.[88]

It should be noted that the Jewish leader ties this ideal back to the Psalms. However, as we have seen, it stems from medieval Jewish-Sufi interactions. Moses Maimonides was so influenced by this spiritual ideal that he told (and re-told) a story illustrating it, which originally concerned the 8th-century Sufi ascetic Ibrahim ibn Adham (see Chapter 3). The 13th-century Kabbalist Isaac of Acre included *hishtawwut* as a necessary precursor to *devequt*. In fact, it was Isaac who solidified this idea within Kabbalistic thought, representing an "important addition based on Sufi influence."[89]

From Isaac and other earlier Jewish-Sufis, the spiritual ideal influenced the Safed mystics, and it is here that we can find the subtle change of the concept from a precursor of divine union, to an effect of *devequt*. Perhaps this minor change allowed the 18th-century Hasids to find *hishtawwut* in Biblical antecedents, though the idea emerged quite clearly from medieval Islamic influence.

It also is important to note again that many other Sufi ideas underwent a similar evolution over the centuries, inspiring Jewish thought, but not completely retaining their original form. Perhaps these deviations made it easier for later Jewish mystics to accept the material, relying on the proffered historical antecedents (added by medieval Jews) as definitive. It also might help to provide some explanation as to why, until recently, so few scholars have traced these ideas back through Judaism into medieval Islam and, from there, into the Koran, where many of them began.

Rabbi Judah Albotini (d. 1520, Chief Rabbi of Jerusalem) mixes the ideal of equanimity with his reading of Talmudic tradition. In this passage, he describes *hishtawwut*:

For the welfare of the body, that is, solitude [*hitbodedut*] brings about purity of the potencies and cleanness of qualities. Equanimity brings one to concentration of the soul, and concentration brings about the Holy Spirit, which brings one to prophecy, which is the highest level. If so, one of the necessary prerequisites for your path in concentration is that you first have the quality of equanimity, that you not become excited by anything.[90]

Perhaps the most astounding aspect of this statement concerning equanimity, beyond its simple inclusion as a Jewish spiritual necessity, is that it misreads historic Judaic thought. Moshe Idel notes that this reading of equanimity runs directly counter to the esoteric teachings of the Talmud:

We find here another case in which a Talmudic saying is incorporated into the discussion of *hitbodedut* [meditative prayer]; this use gives the two spiritual levels *hishtawwut* [equanimity] and *hitbodedut* [solitude] – a privileged place within the sequence of stages bringing about the Holy Spirit in the *Talmudic* tradition, and it indicates that these Sufi concepts were understood as matching – and even explaining and interpreting – the ancient Jewish tradition. However, this harmonistic claim has a harsh ring, from the standpoint of the Talmudic tradition. Although *hishtawwut* is claimed to fit a certain statement in the Talmud, at the same time it opposes central Jewish attitudes.[91]

From Albotini, the ideal influenced later Safed Kabbalists. The 16th-century Kabbalist and compiler of Isaac Luria's thought, Hayyim Vital (d. 1620), proposes about a century after Albotini:

> *Hishtawwut* will come about because of the attachment of the thought to God, blessed be He, which is called the "secret of *devequt*," because the attachment of his thought to God envelops that man, so that he will not look at one who honors him, nor at insults.[92]

Here, we see the shift from *hishtawwut* being a precursor and cause of Divine union, to an effect. From Albotini, Vital and others, it was a short step into the European spiritual vernacular. Looking at another quote from the Baal Shem Tov, we see how these ideas are echoed:

> Equanimity is a great principle ... What causes this is regular *devequt* in the Creator, may His name be blessed, so that because of his preoccupation with *devequt* he has no time to think about these matters, in so far as he is always preoccupied with attaching himself on high, to him.[93]

As Moshe Idel notes in *Hasidism: Between Ecstasy and Magic*:

> *Hishtawwut*: This term is precisely that used by the Hasidic masters in order to express the idea of equanimity. It should be mentioned that this represents the deep influence of the Sufi concept on Hasidism, by the mediation of Isaac of Acre.[94]

### Jewish Silsilah

A Hasidic or Sufi leader is more than an individual of special spiritual attainment, practicing the prescribed meditation methods. He operates at the head of a "school," teaching in a specific manner, often utilizing methods developed by an earlier master. In both cases, the head of the spiritual chain receives authority in some part from his forerunners, and the current master is known not only for his own abilities, but also those of his mentors, and the manners in which they had taught.

Perhaps coincidentally, perhaps due to underlying similarities in the impetuses that helped inspire the two paths, this leadership tradition emerged in both Sufism and Hasidism at about the same time in their respective developments. For the Islamic mystics, around the third generation after their practice coalesced as distinct within Islam (in the 10th and 11th centuries), mystical lineages of *sheikhs* began to form, sometimes following a hereditary line, known as a *silsilah*. Those who adhered to the teachings of the same master began to identify themselves as a single spiritual family.[95] Sufi *sheikhs* received their style of teaching and authority from their predecessors, forming a spiritual bloodline, which led through a series of mentors back to the Prophet Muhammad, who stands at the head of all Sufi teaching orders.[96] As Professor Carl Ernst notes in his *Shambhala Guide to Sufism*:

> Most Sufi orders are named after a famous figure that is viewed in effect as the founder. The founders are generally those masters who codified and institutionalized the distinctive teachings and practices of their order. The orders expanded as teaching networks based on initiatic genealogy; each master's authority derived from that of his predecessor in a chain going back to the Prophet Muhammad.[97]

Though written about a Sufi *sheikh*, these few lines could just as easily be referring to the *tzaddik*. The Hasidic idea of leadership evolved in a similar manner, and each Jewish master developed his particular method of Jewish worship. Like Sufism, the idea of the *tzaddik's* lineage arose during the third generation (c. 1815) of Hasidism. Gershom Scholem observes:

> The original mystical conception of the bottomless depths of the *Torah* was soon transferred to the personality of the saint, and in consequence it quickly appeared that various groups of Hasidim were developing different characteristics in accordance with the particular type of saint to whom they looked for guidance.[98]

The *tzaddik's* lineage often could be followed in much the same way as that of the Sufi *sheikh* – and there are Hasidic *tzaddiks* operating even today in North America, the Holy Land, Europe and Australia who trace the origins of their power back to the earliest generations of Hasidic masters, representing a Jewish *silsilah* (chain of teaching masters). In the United States the largest include the Lubavitch (founded by Rabbi Schneur Zalman of Lyady, d. 1813) and Bobov (traced to Rabbi Myer Noson Halberstam, d. 1855, in southern Poland), which are centered in the New York area.

A Hasidic tale told of Rabbi Mordecai of Lekhovitz (d. 1811) illustrates the Hasidic chain of succession, which in this case may be traced all the way back to Moses, mirroring the Sufi practice of embedding the origination point of their *silsilah* in the Prophet Muhammad:

The *tzaddik* cannot say any words of his teachings unless he first links his soul to the soul of his dead teacher to that of his teacher's teacher. Only then is link joined to link, and the teachings flow from Moses to Joshua, from Joshua to the elders, and so on to the *tzaddik's* own teacher, and from his teacher to him.[99]

### Jewish *Tariqah*

The organization of novices around each individual *tzaddik* closely resembles the Sufi *tariqah* (order), as well. The Jewish leader gathers his Hasids around him, often counseling and talking to them throughout the day, leading their prayers and working with them into the night. It is a very personal relationship – much more so than the typical interaction between a rabbi and a member of the congregation. Festival days find dozens of acolytes around the leader's table, and the Hasidim are treated to fervent prayers, quiet counseling and teaching tales and legends from the library of the Hasidic master. All Hasidic community and spiritual life revolves around the *tzaddik*.

For the Islamic mystics, a similar relationship had evolved.

The first enduring residential institutions for Sufis emerged in Iran, Syria and Egypt during the 11th century and later. These lodges ... could assume a variety of forms, ranging from a large structure for several hundred residents to a simple dwelling connected to the private home of a master.[100]

The veneration of the master became symbolic of the reverence felt for God Himself. We need only look at these two comments, one each by a Sufi and Hasidic follower, to get a sense of how similar were these aspects of the two paths. This first is a statement by the Sufi *Sheikh* Abu Baker al-Shibli (d. 946):

When I stood in front of him – or any of my teachers – I would start trembling like a leaf in the wind; my voice would change and my limbs would start knocking together.[101]

Compare Shibli's statement with this, from the Maggid (preacher) of Mezhrich, the Baal Shem Tov's principle disciple:

Once – it was on a holiday – the Baal Shem was praying in front of the desk with great fervor and in a very loud voice. It was too much for me, and I had to go into a small room and pray there alone. Before the festival service, the Baal Shem came into the small room and put on his robe. Now, as he was putting on his robe, it wrinkled at the shoulders and I put my hand on it to smooth out the folds. But hardly had I touched it, when I began to tremble. I held fast to the table, but the table began to tremble, too.[102]

Although there are clear differences between the two stories, the central idea that the leader's closeness to God inspires such intense emotion that it produces trembling in the follower was shared by the two spiritual paths.

## Hasidism: A Jewish-Sufi Hybrid?

It is too far a stretch to assert that Hasidism is little more than re-worked Islamic mysticism, packaged in ancient Jewish lore and practiced by Jews from the 18th century through today. However, the influence of Sufism on the development of much post-10th-century Jewish thought cannot be denied, and Islamic inspirations run deeply through Hasidic practice, as well.

It must also be acknowledged that the Sufi impulses which operated on Jewish thinkers hardly passed with the change of eras: Sufism, which first attracted Jewish thinkers as early as 1400 years ago, still plays a strong role in defining Judaic worship and synagogue liturgy.

## Endnotes

1. Scholem, Gershom. *Major Trends in Jewish Mysticism*. (New York: Schocken Books, 1971), p. 288.

2. Scholem, Gershom. *Encyclopaedia Judaica 1st Edition, CD ROM* (Cecil Roth and Geoffrey Wigoder, eds.). (New York: MacMillan and Company, 1997).

3. "Five factors contributed to the overwhelming success of the messianic awakening:

(1)    The messianic call came from the Holy Land, from the center that stood for pure spirituality at its most intense. A message from there would be received in Persia, Kurdistan, or Yemen with a respect that it could scarcely command had it arrived from Poland or Italy. The tremendous prestige of the new Kabbalah that emanated from Safed also played a part.

(2)    The renewal of prophecy with the conspicuous figure of Nathan, the brilliant scholar and severe ascetic turned prophet, helped to obscure the more dubious facets of Shabbetai Zevi's personality which, indeed, played little or no role in the consciousness of the mass of the believers.

(3)    The efficacy of traditional and popular apocalyptic beliefs, whose elements were not relinquished but reinterpreted, played its part. The old eschatological visions were retained but many new elements were absorbed. The conception of the future was, throughout 1666, thoroughly conservative. At the same time, however, the propaganda was also addressed to a widespread group of Kabbalists, to whom it presented a system of ambiguous symbols. Nathan's symbolism satisfied his readers by its traditional terminology, and the apparent continuity enabled the new elements to exist, undetected, under cover of the older Kabbalism.

(4)    The prophet's call to repentance played a decisive role, appealing to the noblest longings in every Jewish heart. Who, even among the movement's opponents, could condemn the one demand that the prophet and the Messiah made in public?

(5) There was, as yet, no differentiation between the various elements taking part in the movement. Conservative minds, responding to their sense of unbroken continuity, saw in it the promise of fulfillment of traditional expectations. At the same time the message of redemption appealed to the utopianists who longed for a new age and would shed no tears for the passing of the old order. The national character of the movement obscured these contrasts in the emotional makeup of its participants." Ibid. Scholem.

4. The Doenmeh sect in Turkey, remnants of the followers of Shabbetai Zevi, remained a separate entity within that society deep into the 20th century, finally disbanding for good sometime after 1960. In fact, the first administration that came to power after the Turkish Revolution (1909) included several ministers of Doenmeh origin. The Jews of Salonika even asserted that Kemal Ataturk himself, founder of the modern Turkish state, was of Doenmeh stock.

5. Scholem, Gershom. *Encyclopaedia Judaica* (Cecil Roth and Geoffrey Wigoder, eds.).

6. Maimonides, Obadyah. *Treatise of the Pool* (Paul Fenton, trans.). (London: Octagon Press, 1981), p. 64.

7. Ibid. p. 64.

8. Elqayam, Avraham. "Shabbetai Zevi's Holy Zohar." *http://www.kheper.net/topics/Kabbalah/Zevi_and_Sufism.html*, p. 2.

9. Ibid. p. 2.

10. Fenton, Paul. "Jewish Attitudes Towards Islam: Israel Heeds Ishmael." (*Jerusalem Quarterly 29*, 1983: 93-102), p. 100.

11. Scholem, Gershom. *Major Trends in Jewish Mysticism*, p. 303.

12. Scholem, Gershom. *Encyclopaedia Judaica* (Cecil Roth and Geoffrey Wigoder, eds.).

13. Scholem, Gershom. *Major Trends in Jewish Mysticism*, p. 303.

14. Buber, Martin. *Hasidism*. (New York: Philosophical Library, 1948), p. 137.

15. Ibid. p. 2.

16. Ibid. pp. 137-138.

17. Idel, Moshe. *Hasidism: Between Ecstasy and Magic*. (Albany, NY: SUNY Press, 1995), p. 82.

18. Bension, Ariel. *The Zohar in Moslem and Christian Spain*. (New York: Hermon Press, 1974), pp. 68-69.

19. Information in this paragraph from Scholem, Gershom. *Encyclopaedia Judaica* (Cecil Roth and Geoffrey Wigoder, eds.).

20. Buber, Martin. *The Origin and Meaning of Hasidism*. (New York: Horizon Press, 1960), p. 119.

21. Lings, Martin. "The Nature and Origin of Sufism." *Islamic Spirituality: Foundations* (S. H. Nasr editor). (New York: Crossroad, 1987: 223-238), p. 230.

22. Quoted in Chittick, William. *Sufism: A Short Introduction*. (Oxford: Oneworld Publishers, 2000), p. 66.

23. Burckhardt, Titus. *Introduction to Sufi Doctrine*. (Bloomington, IN: World Wisdom, Inc., 2008), pp. 63-67.

24. Michon, Jean-Louis. "The Spiritual Practices of Sufism." *Islamic Spirituality: Foundations* (S. H. Nasr, ed.). (New York: Crossroad,1987: 265-293), p. 266.

25. Scholem, Gershom. *Encyclopaedia Judaica* (Cecil Roth and Geoffrey Wigoder, eds.).

26. Elior, Rachel. *The Mystical Origins of Hasidism.* (Oxford and Portland, OR: The Littman Library of Jewish Civilization, 2008), p. 148.

27. Schuon, Frithjof, "The Quintessential Esotericism of Islam." *Sufism: Love and Wisdom* (Jean-Louis Michon and Roger Gaetani, eds.). (Bloomington, IN: World Wisdom, Inc., 2006: 251-275), p. 256.

28. Vajda, George. "The Mystical Doctrine of Rabbi Obadyah, Grandson of Moses Maimonides." (*Journal of Jewish Studies 6,* 1955: 213-225), p. 221.

29. Ibid. pp. 221-222.

30. Ibid. p. 220.

31. Michon, Jean-Louis. "Sacred Music and Dance in Islam." *Sufism: Love and Wisdom* (Jean-Louis Michon and Roger Gaetani, eds.). (Bloomington, IN: World Wisdom, Inc., 2006: 153-178), p. xxv.

32. Idel, Moshe. *Hasidism: Between Ecstasy and Magic*, p. 59.

33. Elior, Rachel. *The Mystical Origins of Hasidism*, pp. 126-127.

34. Scholem, Gershom. *Major Trends in Jewish Mysticism*, p. 334.

35. Idel, Moshe. *Hasidism: Between Ecstasy and Magic*, p. 132.

36. Buber, Martin. *The Legend of the Baal Shem Tov.* (Princeton, NJ: Princeton University Press, 1995), pp. 20-21.

37. Quoted in Peters, F. E. (ed.). *Judaism, Christianity & Islam III.* (Princeton, NJ: Princeton University Press, 1990), p. 241.

38. Idel, Moshe. *Hasidism: Between Ecstasy and Magic*, p. 204.

39. Quoted in Jacobs, Louis. "Hasidic Prayer." *Essential Papers on Hasidism: Origins to Present* (Gershon David Hundert, ed.). (New York and London: New York University Press, 1991: 330-362), p. 332.

40. Ibid. p. 332.

41. Quoted in Idel, Moshe. *Studies in Ecstatic Kabbalah.* (Albany, NY: SUNY Press, 1988), p. 132.

42. Quoted in Ibid. p. 165.

43. Burckhardt, Titus. *Introduction to Sufi Doctrine*, p. 95.

44. Idel, Moshe. *Studies in Ecstatic Kabbalah*, p. 133.

45. Idel, Moshe. *Hasidism: Between Ecstasy and Magic*, p. 13.

46. Elior, Rachel. *The Mystical Origins of Hasidism*, p. 120.

47. Quoted in Schaya, Leo. "On the Name *Allah.*" *Sufism: Love and Wisdom* (Jean-Louis Michon and Roger Gaetani, eds.). (Bloomington, IN: World Wisdom, Inc., 2006: 207-216,) pp. 214-215.

48. Quoted in Jacobs, Louis. *Essential Papers on Hasidism*, (Gershon David Hundert, ed.), p. 351.

49. Quoted in Werblowsky, R. T. Zwi. "Mystical and Magical Contemplation: The Kabbalists in Sixteenth-Century Safed." (*History of Religions I,* 1961: 9-36), p. 22.

50. Jacobs, Louis. *Essential Papers on Hasidism*, (Gershon David Hundert, ed.), p. 351.

51. Werblowsky, R. T. Zwi. *History of Religions I*, pp. 22, 23.

52. Idel, Moshe. *Hasidism: Between Ecstasy and Magic*, p. 18.

53. Ibid. p. 62.

54. Ibid. p. 62.

55. Ibid. pp. 62-63.

56. Quoted in Ibid. p. 63.

57. Lings, Martin. *What is Sufism?* (Cambridge, England: The Islamic Texts Society, 1995), p. 55.

58. Idel, Moshe. *Hasidism: Between Ecstasy and Magic*, p. 157.

59. Ibid. p. 157.

60. Ibid. p. 160.

61. Hallamish, Moshe. *Encyclopaedia Judaica* (Cecil Roth and Geoffrey Wigoder, eds.).

62. Idel, Moshe. "Universalization and Integration: Two Conceptions of Mystical Union in Jewish Mysticism." *Mystical Union in Judaism, Christianity and Islam* (Moshe Idel and Bernard McGinn, eds.). (New York: Continuum Publishing, 1996: 27-58), p. 160.

63. Idel, Moshe. *Hasidism: Between Ecstasy and Magic*, p. 108.

64. Quoted in Ibid. pp. 113-114.

65. Geoffroy, Eric. "Approaching Sufism." *Sufism: Love and Wisdom* (Jean-Louis Michon and Roger Gaetani, eds.). (Bloomington, IN: World Wisdom, Inc., 2006: 49-62), pp. 59-60.

66. Maimonides, Obadyah. *Treatise of the Pool* (Paul Fenton, trans.), p. 91.

67. Arberry, Arthur J. *Sufism: An Account of the Mystics of Islam.* (Mineola, NY: Dover Publications, 2002), p. 78.

68. Sells, Michael. "Meaning and Authority in Sufi Literature around the year 1240 CE: Literary Perspectives." *Jewish Mystical Leaders and Leadership in the 13th Century* (Moshe Idel and M. Ostow, eds.). (New Jersey and Jerusalem: Northvale Press, 1998: 187-198), p. 191.

69. Schatz-Uffenheimer, Rivka. *Hasidism as Mysticism.* (Princeton, NJ: Princeton University Press, 1993), p. 131.

70. Some other examples of *Hasidic tzaddiks'* advocating this ideal are: "The principle is that one should be as if he were not. His body and soul must be totally vacant, to be effaced from this world and from the world to come, in every way and in every place, for the sanctification of His name, may He be blessed ... He has annihilated himself completely and totally as a result of his contemplation of the Creator's greatness." (Menahem Mendel of Vitebsk, quoted in Elior, Rachel. *The Mystical Origins of Hasidism*, p. 113).

"For the purpose of Torah and wisdom in thought, speech and action is to attain the level of nullity, and he should make himself as nothing, and nothingness as its root ..." (Abraham of Kalisk, d. 1810, Quoted in Ibid. p. 111).

71. Ibid. pp. 42, 44.

72. Quoted in Ibid. p. 44.

73. Quoted in Ibid. p. 79.

74. Quoted in Ibid. p. 11.

75. Idel, Moshe. *Hasidism: Between Ecstasy and Magic*, p. 58.

76. Quoted in Ibid. p. 56.

77. Information and quote from Ibid. pp. 56, 57.

78. Ibid. p. 86.

79. Scholem, Gershom. *Major Trends in Jewish Mysticism*, p. 123.

80. Quoted in Elior, Rachel. *The Mystical Origins of Hasidism*, p. 113.

81. Quoted in Idel, Moshe. *Hasidism: Between Mysticism and Magic*, p. 117.

82. Burckhardt, Titus. *Introduction to Sufi Doctrine*, p. 10.

83. Fenton, Paul. "A Mystical Treatise on Perfection, Providence and Prophecy from the Jewish Sufi Circle." *The Jews of Medieval Islam: Community, Society and Identity* (Daniel Frank, ed.). (Leiden: E. J. Brill, 1995: 301-334), p. 316.

84. Idel, Moshe. *The Mystical Experience in Abraham Abulafia*. (Albany, NY: SUNY Press, 1988), p. 131.

85. Fenton, Paul. "Dana's Edition of Abraham Maimuni's 'Kifayat al-Abidin.'" (*Jewish Quarterly Review 82*, 1991: 194-206), p. 205.

86. Idel, Moshe. *Kabbalah: New Perspectives*. (New Haven, CT: Yale University Press, 1988), p. 101.

87. Merkur, Daniel. "Unitive Experience and the State of Trance." *Mystical Union in Judaism, Christianity and Islam* (Moshe Idel and Bernard McGinn, eds.). (New York: Continuum Publishing, 1996: 125-153, 175-183, 230-237, 239-240), p. 178.

88. Quoted in Elior, Rachel. *The Mystical Origins of Hasidism*, p. 118.

89. Idel, Moshe. *Studies in Ecstatic Kabbalah*, p. 113.

90. Quoted in Ibid. p. 124.

91. Ibid. p. 124.

92. Quoted in Ibid. p. 148.

93. Quoted in Elior, Rachel. *The Mystical Origins of Hasidism*, pp. 118-119.

94. Idel, Moshe. *Hasidism: Between Ecstasy and Magic*, p. 279, n. 82.

95. Hourani, Albert. *A History of the Arab Peoples*. (Cambridge, MA: Harvard University Press, 1991), p. 153.

96. Esposito, John L. *Islam, The Straight Path*. (Oxford: Oxford University Press, 1991), p. 105 "The spiritual power of the *sheikh* was passed on or inherited by his successor. While some orders retained the practice of selection or election of the *sheikh's* successors, many opted for a hereditary succession. Leadership of the order often passed to a son or relative of the *sheikh*, keeping control of the order in family hands." Ibid. p. 107.

97. Ernst, Carl. *Shambhala Guide to Sufism*. (Boston and London: Shambhala Publishers, 1997), pp. 127-128.

98. Scholem, Gershom. *Major Trends in Jewish Mysticism*, p. 344.

99. Buber, Martin. *Tales of the Hasidim I, II*. (New York: Schocken Books, 1991), p. 153.

100. Ernst, Carl. *Shambhala Guide to Sufism*, p. 125.

101. Quoted in Fadiman, James and Frager, Robert (eds.). *Essential Sufism.* (New York: HarperCollins, 1997), p. 129.
    102. Quoted in Buber, Martin. *Tales of the Hasidim I, II*, pp. 49-50.

# Epilogue

Islamic inspirations helped to permanently reconfigure the religion of Isaac. As the Jewish scholar, S. D. Goitein (Institute of Advanced Study, Princeton), notes: "Every aspect that we regard as Judaism – the synagogue service and prayer book, law and ritual, theology and ethics, the text of the Bible, the grammar and vocabulary of the Hebrew language – was formulated, consolidated and canonized in the first centuries of Islam."[1]

Today, the Sufi-inspired goals of *hitbodedut*, *devequt* and the Science of the Letters inspire Jewish meditation. Jewish-Sufi *piyyut* (liturgical songs) are sung in synagogues around the world. And the Kabbalah, a medieval Jewish spiritual system that has many echoes of Islamic and Sufi ideas, represents the heart of contemporary Jewish mysticism.

The purpose of this study is not simply to outline the deep connection between Judaism and Islam, but also to begin the vital process of acknowledgement. Although political issues currently separate the two People, their paths are deeply and undeniably intertwined. An academic work such as this may not heal political wounds, but it can offer a vital step toward peace. Jews and Muslims must recognize how much they share at the very core of their spiritual beings.

Lastly, it should be noted that this epilogue could stand as a jump-off point for another entire study on Sufi and Islamic influence on contemporary Jewish meditation and practice. Like the other chapters in this book, this brief epilogue simply hopes to introduce this astounding story, and inspire conversation among and between the religions, and further scholarly investigations of this surprising spiritual fraternity.

## Sufi Influence on Contemporary Jewish Meditation Practice

The influence of Sufism on contemporary Jewish prayer practice is not difficult to discern, stemming from the earlier Islamic inspirations outlined in the body of this book. In a development similar to previous Jewish renewals, today's spiritual leaders often find their inspiration in Sufi-inspired Jewish antecedents, via Jewish-Sufi predecessors who were directly or indirectly influenced by Islamic thinkers. This follows a long-time dynamic of Jewish practitioners sometimes discovering in Sufism, and Sufi-inspired Jewish worship, something special that appeared to them to be missing in exoteric Judaism.

For instance, Rabbi David Cooper (author of *God is a Verb*, *Handbook of Jewish Meditation Practices* and numerous other books), a foremost teacher of contemporary Kabbalah and Jewish meditation techniques, bases his system on the methods of Abraham Abulafia.[2] A recent workshop that he led at the California Institute of Integral Studies was described thusly:

> Seeing through God's eyes is a way to strip aside veils that cloud our view and offers us a way to experience the interconnection of all things. In this workshop, we will use various forms of Kabbalah practices and methods for meditation. We will explore breathing and walking practices that synchronize one's movement through the use of subtle sacred phrases. We will experience an important practice developed by the 13th-century Jewish mystic and "father of ecstatic Kabbalah," Abraham Abulafia, who describes in detail a concentration method for keeping the mind steady and focused for extended periods of time.[3]

It is not hard to see the Sufi inspiration in this short description of Jewish meditation. "Stripping aside veils" defines the quintessence of the Sufi path. The phrase "seeing through God's eyes" echoes the *hadith qudsi* (saying attributed to God): "And when I love him I become the ears through which he hears and the eyes through which he sees and the hands with which he strikes and the feet with which he walks." "Synchronizing breathing and subtle sacred phrases" represents Sufi *dhikr*. And, as we well know, Abulafia's concentration method came from Islamic inspirations, as well.

Like the medieval Jews that inserted these ideas into Judaism, Rabbi Cooper can point to Jewish antecedents in Solomon's *Song of Songs*, the life of King David, Moses' sojourn on the Mountain of God and more recently the Kabbalah and *Hasidism* – but the reason that they are *currently* vital within Judaism has much to do with the Sufis, who helped medieval Jews bridge the gap from the Bible to the Kabbalah, as well as introduced new ideas such as *devequt*.

Another contemporary Jewish meditation practitioner, Rabbi Avram Davis (editor of *Meditation From the Heart of Judaism*), echoes Rabbi Cooper's sentiments, exhibiting even more specific Sufi inspiration. He notes:

> Meditation is designed to bring us to a direct experience of ourselves and of God. "*Ayin*" meditation means "nothingness" and "the void," and it describes the state of complete oneness with God. The active form of *Ayin* is called "*Devequt*" meaning "merging" or "cleaving." Kabbalah (meditation) relies on fierce study, complicated visualizations and recitations.[4]

This sounds not unlike a text taken directly from the 13th-century Sufi-inspired Abraham Abulafia. Much of both of these contemporary practitioners' techniques would have been considered heretical to orthodox practitioners of pre-Islamic Judaism, though they are now accepted as "traditional" Jewish worship.

*Chochmat HaLev* congregation in Berkeley, CA offers prayer services

that "combine both chanting and silence in an alternating sequence to resonate with your soul and connect with the Divine."[5] The *Jewish Community
Center* in Sonoma County, CA, offers programs based in "extended periods of
both chanting and silent meditation, using one as a vehicle to enrich the other.
The experience is enhanced by a Chasidic story/teaching."[6] And on *eHow*, a
website that offers instruction on "just about everything," Jewish meditation
is described in a variety of manners reminiscent of medieval Sufism:

> Chant psalms, prayers and verses from the *Torah* [*dhikr*]. Sound out
> Hebrew letters and/or vowels. Concentrate on their sound, and nothing
> else. Repeat until you are aware of nothing but the sound you're say-
> ing [*Ilm al-Huruf* or Science of the Letters]. Learn a walking-dance-or
> movement based form of Jewish meditation [*sama'*]. Try to achieve
> "*Eyin*," a state of mystical enlightenment that is really like a state of
> nothingness [*fana*]. This technique focuses on silence and breathing
> (*hitbodedut*).[7]

Additionally, the list of classic Jewish-Sufi Kabbalistic texts that are *currently* in print is astounding. *Sha'arei Tzedek* (Gates of Righteousness; c.
1295) by Rabbi Nathan ben Se'adya, a follower of Abraham Abulafia was
published by Providence University Press in 2007; Abraham Abulafia's
*Nair Elohim* (Candle of God) and *Sefer ha-Ot* (The Book of the Sign)
were both published by this same press in 2007, as well. Hayyim Vital's
*Sha'arei Kedusha* (The Gates of Holiness) was reissued in 2007, only this
time with the controversial fourth section intact. The *Sefer Yetzirah* (Book
of Creation, c. 9th century), *Sefer ha-Bahir* (Book of Clarity, c. 1230) and
*Sefer Zohar* (Book of Splendor, c. 1295) have all recently been published,[8]
plus many others.

This contemporary explosion of interest in Jewish esotericism mirrors
past Jewish revivals. Since the time of Hasidism's emergence 250 years
ago, the Jewish mystical impetus has ebbed. But now, with the stimulus
yet again of Sufi-inspired Jewish tracts and practices, Jewish spirituality
is experiencing a rebirth, even becoming known to a wider public through
such American cultural icons as Madonna, Britney Spears and Demi Moore,
all of whom study the Kabbalah![9]

## Ongoing Jewish-Sufi Contacts

Even in our era, direct Jewish-Sufi relations continue, a positive impulse
that often strives to remain hidden, so that the Jewish and Islamic partners
might worship together, free of political and sectarian pressures.

When I appeared at a symposium inspired by my research at George
Washington University (DC), along with Dr. Seyyed Hossein Nasr, University Professor of Islamic Studies and a foremost Sufi scholar, he mentioned in his talk that there were ongoing relations between Kabbalists and

Sufis in the Holy City of Jerusalem. He was unwilling to elaborate upon those interactions, he said, due to the delicate political and social situation in that locale. The message was clear, however: the unbroken chain of Jewish-Sufi interaction continues unabated to this day.

It is a sensitive matter to put into print some of these ongoing contacts; however it is a story that I feel needs to be told. These interactions represent the highest possibility of Jewish-Muslim interactions; and though they are currently operating out of the spotlight of the political and cultural spheres, they have emerged out of centuries of positive interrelationship, and should be acknowledged as central to the Jewish-Muslim historical narrative.

The comments made by Dr. Nasr piqued my interest, and led me to contact a *Rodef Shalom* (peacemaker) living in the Holy land, who replied with this email (I have removed the personal names of the participants, to be respectful of Dr. Nasr's concerns):

> You may be interested to know there are several groups connecting Israeli Jews with Muslim Sufis of the Holy Land. One is a group, *Derech Avraham*, or *Tariqat Ibrahimiya*, a Jewish-Sufi tariqa founded by [a professor] of Bar Ilan U. and a *Sheikh* of the *Qadiri* Sufi center. Also leading this group is a Rabbi of *Midreshet Iyun* in Tel Aviv and a scholar of Sufism who just published a book about the history of Sufism in Hebrew. We had a beautiful Jewish-Sufi retreat in Nazareth recently.
>
> I am also working with a *Sheikh* who runs a Sufi center in the Muslim quarter of the Old City. We have developed a Jewish-Sufi *dhikr*, with passages of the *dhikr* in Hebrew and Arabic, which we lead together at many different Arab-Jewish interfaith gatherings, and when we travel to gatherings in such places as Scotland and Morocco.
>
> The *Sheikh* and I also work with a *Sheikh*, living in London now, but who returns to the Holy Land often. He grew up at the Western Wall in the Moghrabi quarter that was destroyed in 1967; his grandfather had a Sufi *zawiyya* in a room that is now on what is the women's side of the Western Wall plaza.
>
> When we host such gatherings in Israel, and he is in the country and not at the Sorbonne, Professor Paul Fenton gives teachings on the history of Sufi-Jewish influences, especially the movement started by Avraham Ben Maimon (Abraham Maimonides). Are you also aware of the Jewish-Sufi tariqa based in Boulder, Colorado, headed by Reb Zalman Schachter and Pir Zia Khan, called the *Tariqat Inayati-Maimuni*?[10]

Perhaps the most salient in this series of very interesting references, is to *Tariqat Inayati-Maimuni*, which advertises itself as: "an inter-spiritual fellowship of seekers committed to a rigorous path of spiritual development based upon Sufi and Hasidic principles and practices."[11] Here, in 21st-century Colorado, is the completion of the Jewish-Sufi path begun over a thousand years ago in Egypt and Spain! The website continues on to note:

> In the *Maimuniyya*, the Beshtian-Hasidic lineage of the Ba'al Shem Tov (1698-1760) has been joined to the *Inayati*-Sufi lineage of Hazrat Inayat Khan (1882-1927), thus creating a new lineage of *Sufi-Hasidut*. For this reason, we seek to connect to and renew the spirit of the original Egyptian Sufi-*Hasidism* practiced by Rabbi Avraham Maimuni (Abraham Maimonides) of Fustat (1186-1237), our forerunner, who successfully combined these paths as far back as the 13th Century.[12]

The Jewish founder of this line, Rabbi Zalman Schachter-Shalomi (b. 1924), is a Jewish refugee from Nazi Germany who became a *Hasid* in the lineage of Rabbi Schneur Zalman of Lyadi (d. 1813) in 1947. In 1975, he was initiated as a *Sheikh* in the Sufi Order of Hazrat Inayat Khan, leading to his fusion of the Sufi and Hasidic mystical paths.

Although the clearest example of ongoing Jewish-Sufism, it is hardly the only one. A recent note in the Jerusalem Post, Israel's English-language newspaper, advertised for an evening of Jewish-Sufi Storytelling in the Holy City. A Jewish-Sufi woman operating in the Holy Land is introduced in an article entitled: "The Jewish/Palestinian Struggle: One Jewish/Sufi Woman's Journey to Peace." In the piece, the native Israeli describes her attempts to understand the ongoing Israeli-Palestinian conflict in light of her deep and positive experience with both traditions. She achieved a level of deeper understanding by taking part in a peacemaking exercise as part of her contemporary Sufi studies.

Here, Jewish-Sufism is applied directly to the current political situation in the Middle East, channeling earlier conceptions of prophetic legislation, where mystical impulse must be brought to bear on the social reality of the world around us. There is no more powerful manner to honor the long and positive history of these two traditions, than to apply the Jewish-Sufi path in this prophetic manner!

## Sufis in the 21st-Century Synagogue

Adding further resonance to the ongoing Sufi influence on Jewish practice, are a series of medieval Jewish-Sufi works that still inform contemporary Judaic worship. Even a cursory glance at the *Sabbath* (weekly day of rest) and Jewish holiday liturgy uncovers Sufi-inspired *piyyutim* (liturgical songs) and prayers. The penitential poem *Keter Malkuth* (The King's Crown) by the 11th-century Jewish-Sufi Solomon ibn Gabirol has been incorporated into the liturgy of *Yom Kippur* (Day of Atonement), the holiest day on the Jewish calendar. As contemporary scholar Diana Lobel notes in her recent book, *A Sufi-Jewish Dialogue: Philosophy and Mysticism in Bahya ibn Pakuda's "Duties of the Heart."*:

(Ibn Gabirol's) poem draws upon a rich Arabic poetic tradition – one line in particular, "fleeing from You to You," can be traced back to a well attested *hadith* (saying of the Prophet Muhammad): "I fell from You to You," implying that there is no escape from God except in God. Ibn Gabirol tapped into a wellspring of Islamic devotion.[13]

She also notes concurrences between Ibn Gabirol's liturgical work *Keter Malkuth* and the work of Arabic poets Abu Nuwas (d. 810) and Abu Miskawayh (d. 1030).[14] Another of Ibn Gabirol's *piyyut*, *Adon Olam* (Lord of the World), is central to the Jewish *Sabbath*, being chanted during both the Friday night and Saturday morning services.

*Lekha Dodi* (Come my Beloved), written by the Safedian Kabbalist Shlomo Halevi Alkabetz (d. 1580), is sung on Friday nights to welcome the *Sabbath* "bride." Considered one of the most beautiful hymns in the contemporary Jewish service, it not only inserts the sensual imagery of medieval Jewish-Sufis into the synagogue rites, but in the *Sephardic* tradition, it is still chanted to an ancient Moorish melody, imported from the surrounding Islamic milieu from which it originally emerged.

*Yedid Nefesh* (Beloved of the Soul), written by the Safedian Kabbalist Eliezer Azikri (d. 1600), is part of the weekly *Sabbath* liturgy, as well. Sufi-inspired imagery suffuses this piece, including such phrases as "Draw your servant (*avdecho*) to your will" (though some have translated *avdecho* as "slave" instead of "servant," which makes the passage even more Sufic) and "My soul is lovesick for you." Azikri was strongly influenced by Isaac of Acre (13th century), Abraham Abulafia (13th century) and other Sufi-leaning Jewish sources.

The *Metsudah Siddur* (prayer book; published in Brooklyn, 1990) notes that Judah Halevi (d. 1141) mentioned how to correctly chant the *Shemoneh Esrei* (the 18 prayers that constitute the heart of the daily prayer service) in his *Sefer ha-Kuzari*, information that still informs that central Jewish prayer. Halevi's *Sefer ha-Kuzari* was deeply inspired by and interspersed with Sufi ideas and terminology (Chapter 4). These instructions, which are included in the common prayer book to help the 21st-century Jew worship correctly, include taking various steps before beginning to pray and after having finished, keeping the feet together, concentration, silence and other specific directives[15] that might well have stemmed from his contact with Sufis.

According to this same 20th-century prayer book, other liturgy comes from medieval sources that we have already met in this study. Represented are hymns and prayers taken from the *Zohar* (weekday *Shacharis* service; the *Shabbat* service) and Moses Maimonides (weekday *Shacharis* service). There are explanatory notes sprinkled throughout the *Metsudah Siddur* from Abraham ibn Ezra and the *Zohar*.

These poems and songs are woven so tightly into current Jewish practice that their "innovations" – language and ideas that when they were imported, were fresh and, at times, heretical to the conventions of traditional Judaism – have been subsumed into what is today considered normative Judaism. Moses Maimonides, Judah Halevi, Solomon ibn Gabirol, the *Zohar* – all are *now* considered the direct spiritual descendants of earlier Talmudic and Biblical thought, and representative of the lineage of Jewish practice that stem from the earliest Jewish impulses.

## A Wrong that Must be Righted

I am not claiming that Jewish practice, as it exists today, is somehow little more than a Jewish-Islamic amalgam. That would be patently untrue. However, there is the indelible mark of Sufism that runs through contemporary Jewish worship, a bit in the regular prayer services, and much more so in the practice of 21st-century Jewish esotericism. To say anything *but* this is untrue, and represents the pall that the contemporary political situation has cast over this once vibrant relationship.

It is my hope that this study can begin to reintroduce this astounding story into not only the religious narrative between Jews and Muslims, but the political and social worlds, as well. There should no longer be scholarship addressing the history of Jewish mysticism that ignores the strong and positive influence that Sufism has had on Judaism for hundreds of years, inspirations that resonate to this day.

The story of the development of Jewish thinking post 10th century must include references to the origins of the plethora of new ideas. The debt of Jewish spirituality and practice to Islamic mysticism must be acknowledged. To gloss over the strong Islamic influence on medieval Jewish mysticism simply by stating: "We do not have a clear understanding of the roots of the Kabbalah in the generation immediately preceding its appearance,"[16] is unfair to both Judaism and the scholarly ideal.

Even today, many books being written about Jewish mystical history contain not a *single* citation of either Islam or Sufism! *The Mystical Origins of Hasidism* makes no mention of Islam or Sufism. *Essential Papers on Hasidism* brings together 13 of the foremost modern Jewish scholars, including Martin Buber, Louis Jacobs, Gershom Scholem and others, yet there is not a single reference to either Sufism or Islam. In *Safed Spirituality*, part of the "Classics of Western Spirituality" series, there is a complete dearth of citations of either Sufism or Islam. The popular *Essential Kabbalah* makes virtually no mention, either, of the Islamic inspirations on so much of what is being described. *The Early Kabbalah* carries not a single reference to the Islamic mystical path. Book after scholarly book concerning Jewish mysticism treats the subject for hundreds of pages, without ever once mentioning Sufism! Other books have one, two or three spare references, hardly indicating the deep influence of the Muslim spiritual system on the development of Jewish mysticism and worship.

This glaring hole in the study of historical Judaism must be rectified; there should no longer be histories of Jewish spirituality and worship that omit this seminal influence, this explicit relationship that has lasted for more than 1000 years, from the time of the *Sefer Yetzirah* (c. 9th century) through medieval Spain and Egypt, into Safed in the 16th century, the Jewish-Sufi leanings of the false Messiah, Shabbetai Zevi (d. 1676), Hasidism and even into the 20th and 21st centuries, at the *Inayati-Maimuni Tariqat of Sufi-Hasidut*.

We must also make an effort to correct statements such as this one, which was expressed by a foremost contemporary practitioner of Jewish mysticism and doctoral candidate at the Hebrew University in Jerusalem:

> Jewish meditation developed as part of the Jewish religion, and the techniques that it uses to quiet the mind are grounded in Jewish religious concepts: contemplation of God, permutation of Hebrew letters and so on.[17]

This is incorrect.

Many aspects of what is considered today as Jewish esotericism stem from earlier Jewish-Sufi contacts. And while I certainly do not intend to single out specific Kabbalistic instructors or scholars, the fact remains that we would all benefit – Jews, Muslims and anyone concerned with peaceful relations in general – from an honest appraisal of just how threaded together are contemporary Jewish and Sufi history and worship.

## A Fraternity that Runs in Two Directions

In closing, let me add that I firmly believe that a similar book could be written evincing the deep influence of earlier Jewish mysticism – from Talmudic times, and back to the Biblical prophets – on the development of Islamic esotericism. When the first Jewish-Sufis stated that they were simply reclaiming ancient Jewish practices that had become lost to their contemporary Israelites, they were often correct. Many Islamic mystical practices can be traced back to Jewish antecedents, through Jewish converts to Islam, stories of Jewish prophets in the Koran, *Isra'iliyat* (Jewish stories told by Muslim exegetes), early Sufi practitioners such as Hasan al-Basri and other sources.

That important story will hopefully soon be told, as well – and will only further exhibit how deeply interdependent are these two religions at their mystical cores. The goal is not to show which religion had *more* of an influence on the other, or argue the finer points of which might offer a quicker and "better" path to God. The purpose is only to demonstrate how deeply interlaced are the two Abrahamic religions.

While neither religion is simply a hybrid version of the other, it seems possible that no two *other* religions share as much as do Judaism and Islam. Given that fact, the current political calamity in the Middle East and its reverberations around the world are even more tragic and incomprehensible. Perhaps the first stage of peace between these two Biblical cousins can be acknowledgement – acknowledgement of contemporary wrongs committed in the name of God and religion, certainly, but also recognition of the deep connections, respect and even love shared between these two People since the inception of Islam. This book hopes to begin this conversation, and offer a first step toward peace between people who are tied together at their spiritual center.

## Endnotes

1. Quoted in Wasserstrom, Steven. *Between Muslim and Jew: The Problem of Symbiosis Under Early Islam.* (Princeton, NJ: Princeton University Press, 1995), p. 181.

2. Noted by Waxman, Robert. (Author of "Kabbalah Simply Stated,"), *http://en.allexperts.com/q/Kabbalah-3437/books.htm.*

3. *http://www.ciis.edu/publicprograms/fall07/fall07oct.html.*

4. Noted by Waxman, Robert. (Author of "Kabbalah Simply Stated,"), *http://en.allexperts.com/q/Kabbalah-3437/books.htm.*

5. *http://www.chochmat.org/1_shabbat.html.*

6. *http://www.jccsoco.org/meditationprogram.html.*

7. *http://www.ehow.com/how_2031433_practice-jewish-meditation.html.*

8. *http://mysticlink.blogspot.com/2008_02_01_archive.html.*

9. *http://web.israelinsider.com/Articles/Culture/4145.htm.*

10. Personal email message, May 18, 2006.

11. *http://www.sufi-hasidim.org/.*

12. Ibid.

13. Lobel, Diana. *A Sufi-Jewish Dialogue: Philosophy and Mysticism in Bahya ibn Pakuda's "Duties of the Heart."* (Philadelphia: University of Pennsylvania Press, 2006), p. 6.

14. Ibid. p. 7.

15. *The Metsudah Siddur* (Rabbi Avrohom Davis, translator). (Brooklyn, New York: Metsudah Publications, 1990). pp. 115-116.

16. Dan, Joseph (ed.). *The Early Kabbalah.* (Mahweh, NJ: Paulist Press, 1986), p. 4.

17. Michaelson, Jay. *Jewish Daily Forward*, May 4, 2007.

# Timeline

70 C.E.   Destruction of the Second Temple in Jerusalem

c. 150    Rabbi Nehuniah ben ha-Qanah lived, alleged author of
*Sefer ha-Bahir*
Simeon be Yohai lived, alleged author of the *Sefer Zohar*

200-500  Talmudic Age

570      Prophet Muhammad born

600      622 Islam founded
632 Prophet Muhammad dies
634 Abu Bakr, first Caliph of Islam, dies
644 Umar I, second Caliph of Islam, dies

700      711 Muslims cross the Straight of Gibraltar
728 Hasan al-Basri dies
765 Jafar as-Sadiq, sixth Caliph of Shi'a Islam, dies
777 Ibrahim ibn Adham dies

800      801 Rabi'a dies
c. 850 *Sefer Yetzirah* (Book of Creation)
859 Dhu'l Nun al-Misri dies
874 Bayazid Bistami dies

900      c. 900 *Rasa'il Ikhwan as-Safa* (Epistles of the Brethren of
Purity)
910 Junayd al-Baghdadi dies
922 Mansur al-Hallaj dies
931 Muhammad ibn Masarra dies
942 Saadia Gaon dies
961 Caliph 'Abd ar-Rahman III dies
970 Hasdai ibn Shaprut dies

1000    1037 Abd Allah ibn Sina dies
1038 Hai Gaon dies
1056 Samuel ibn Naghrila, the Nagid (prince), dies
1058 Solomon ibn Gabirol dies
1080 Bahya ibn Pakuda dies

1100  1111 Abu Hamid al-Ghazali dies
     1138 Moses ibn Ezra dies
     1141 Judah Halevi dies
     1166 Abdul Qadir dies
     1167 Abraham ibn Ezra dies
     1191 Shihabuddin Yahya al-Suhrawardi dies

1200  1204 Moses Maimonides dies
     1230 *Sefer Bahir* (Book of Clarity)
     1237 Abraham Maimonides dies
     1240 Muhyiddin ibn Arabi dies
     1265 Obadyah Maimonides dies
     1273 Jalalludin Rumi dies
     1291 Abraham Abulafia dies
     1295 *Zohar* (Book of Splendor)
     1295 *Sha'arei Tzedek* (Gates of Holiness)

1300  1305 Moses de Leon dies
     1305 Joseph Gikatilla dies
     1350 Isaac of Acre dies

1400  1415 David II Maimonides dies
     1492 Jews and Muslims evicted from Spain

1500  1520 Judah Albotini dies
     1570 Moshe Cordovero dies
     1572 Isaac Luria dies

1600  1600 Eliezer Azikri dies
     1620 Hayyim Vital dies
     1676 Shabbetai Zevi, the false Messiah, dies

1700  1760 Baal Shem Tov dies
     1772 Dov Baer, Maggid (preacher) of Mezhrich, dies
     1782 Jacob Joseph of Polonnoy dies
     1786 Elimelekh of Lyzhansk dies

1800  1813 Shneur Zalman of Lyady dies

2000  2004 *Tariqat Inayati-Maimuni* (Sufi-*Hasidut* order) founded
     2007 Providence University (Taiwan) reprints Sufi-inspired Kabbalistic works by Abraham Abulafia, Judah Albotini, Moshe Cordovero, Hayyim Vital and others

# Sufi Masters Important to Jewish Mysticism

Early (c. 9th-13th centuries) Judeo-Arabic philosophers were hardly embarrassed about their influences. The medieval Jewish library often contained Sufi tracts in the original Arabic or copied into Hebrew, and made available to the community. As Paul Fenton notes, numerous occasions are documented of Jewish mystics studying directly with Sufis or serving as novices in a Sufi order.[1] A number of specific Sufi influences permeated medieval Jewish thought:

*Ikhwan as-Safa*: The *Ikhwan as-Safa* (Brethren of Purity) was a secretive assembly of Islamic thinkers in 10th-century Baghdad. Their *Rasa'il* (Epistles) was a 52-volume compendium that covered all of the known sciences, including religion and mysticism. There were many passages throughout the Epistles concerning Sufism and its centrality to spiritual attainment.

This book became one of the most important sources for medieval Jews reconsidering their own religion. One aspect that made the Epistles so attractive to Jews was its open-mindedness to and even reliance on Jewish sources. Jews were said to have studied with and joined the secretive *Ikhwan as-Safa*, and the Epistles showed much evidence of Jewish input. For instance, Judaic stories and traditions borrowed from such sources as the *midrash*, the Talmud and the *Haggadah* (Passover holiday text) helped shape ideas propagated by the *Epistles*. Some passages even indicated that the *Torah* was viewed as having as weighty a spiritual import as the Koran.[2]

*Hasan al-Basri*: Hasan al-Basri (d. 728; Babylonia) was a Muslim theologian and scholar born at Medina. Enslaved as a youth, he was later freed and went on to found a *madrassa* (school) in Basra, where he became a renowned teacher. Considered the father of Sufism, it is through Hasan that many of the Sufi orders trace their spiritual descent back to Ali (son-in-law of the Prophet Muhammad), and then to the Prophet himself. Hasan was father of the ascetic school of Islamic mysticism, which slowly was replaced by more socially involved Sufi practice.

*Jafar as-Sadiq*: Jafar as-Sadiq (d. 765; Medina), the Sixth Imam of Shi'a Islam, considered by that group as the direct successor of the Prophet Muhammad, was an astronomer, alchemist, theologian, writer, philosopher, physician and scientist. In addition to being a central religious authority for normative practitioners of Islam, as-Sadiq also was an early *sheikh* on the Naqshbandi Sufi *silsilah*.

As-Sadiq's ideas influenced Jewish thought across a wide range of mystical fields. His concept of the "prophetic legislator" inspired the 12th-century Jewish thinker Moses Maimonides, and subsequently came to define the *Jewish* prophetic ideal. As-Sadiq also helped conceive the *Ilm al-Huruf* (Science of the Letters), theorizing that it was the *letters* of the words in the Koran that had true spiritual import, and not necessarily the meaning of the words they formed. Lastly, as-Sadiq held that sacred texts had duel meanings – an inner and an outer one – stressing the mystical meaning of the Koran, as opposed to its literal meaning. He was one of the first Sufi thinkers to offer a purely mystical reading of the Muslim holy book.[3]

*Ibrahim ibn Adham*: Of princely birth, Ibn Adham (d. 777; Syria) had an awakening while on a hunt, at which point he dropped from his horse and devoted himself to the service of God. He exchanged his princely raiment for one of his father's sheepherder's wool garments, and began the life of a wandering *dervish*.[4]

Although his brand of ascetic practice became less important to later Sufism, he stood as an early master, about whom many stories circulated. He said of poverty that it was a treasure that God kept in heaven, and only bestowed upon those whom He loved. He also said: "Covet nothing in this world or the next, and devote thyself entirely to God."[5] Numerous stories were told about him to demonstrate the spiritual ideal of equanimity – one of which entered the Jewish stream through the writings of Moses Maimonides.

*Rabi'a al-Adawiyya*: Born in Basra, Babylonia, in 721, to a poor but respected family, Rabi'a (d. 801) became the most important female Sufi saint of early Islam. After her parents died, Rabi'a was enslaved, but when her master became aware of her sainted nature, he repented and set her free. She went into the desert and became an ascetic.

She held herself to the high ideal of worshipping God neither from fear of Hell nor for the hope of attaining Paradise, for she viewed emotions such as fear and hope as veils – hindrances to the vision of God Himself. Her name comes up time and again as an influence on important Muslim thinkers such as Bayazid Bistami, Junayd, al-Ghazali, Ibn Arabi and others. Although never quoted by name in later Jewish works, her influence was so strong within Sufism as a proponent of pure Godly love that her ideas were difficult to evade for Judeo-Arabic thinkers.

*Dhu'l Nun al-Misri*: From the Lower Nile and of Nubian descent,[6] Dhu'l Nun al-Misri (d. 859; Cairo) studied under various teachers, traveling extensively in Arabia and Syria. In 829 he was arrested on a charge of heresy and sent to prison in Baghdad, but after examination he was released on the Caliph's orders to return to Cairo, where he died at the age of 63. Legend has it that an inscription appeared on his grave in Cairo's City of the Dead, which read: "This is the beloved of God, who died from his love of God, slain by God," and that whenever it was erased, it would reappear again.[7]

In his writing, he utilized the language of the passionate lover, helping to solidify this characteristic of Sufi poetry and thought.[8]  Later thinkers were assured that if an ascetic devoted entirely to God could use the language of sensuality to define his otherworldly attraction, then it was an acceptable manner of expression for the spiritual path.  His influence ran deep within the practice of Sufism, and found its way into Jewish mysticism.

*Bayazid Bistami*:  Bayazid Bistami (d. 874; Persia) was the first so-called "intoxicated" (*sukr*) Sufi, who uttered a scandalous *shath* (ecstatic utterance): "Glory to me! How great is My Majesty," implying that his personal ego had fused completely with the Divine essence.[9]  His observance of the spiritual path influenced many later Islamic thinkers, helping to turn Sufi practice away from asceticism and toward a more passionate approach.  Little is known of Bayazid's life, though he appeared to personally know the leading mystics of his time.  When Bayazid died, he was over 70 years old.  Before he died, someone asked him his age. He said: "I am four years old. For seventy years I was veiled.  I got rid of my veils only four years ago."[10]

*Junayd al-Baghdadi*:  Junayd al-Baghdadi (d. 910; Baghdad) was born in Persia, but his family settled in Baghdad when he was still a boy.  There, he studied Islamic Law, eventually becoming a chief judge (*qadi*) in Baghdad. He laid the groundwork for sober (*sahw*) mysticism, in contrast to that of God-intoxicated (*sukr*) Sufis.

Junayd was forced to exhibit in a very public manner that intoxicated Sufism was unacceptable to normative Islam.  In the process of the series of trials of Mansur al-Hallaj for heresy, the Caliph al-Muqtadir (reigned 908-932) demanded Junayd's *fatwa* (religious edict) against al-Hallaj, due to Junayd's position as the chief judge of Baghdad.  Although he had been al-Hallaj's teacher, Junayd acquiesced, issuing this statement: "From the outward appearance he is to die and we judge according to the outward appearance, and God knows better."[11]

Junayd helped codify the general doctrine that would emerge at the center of Islamic practice: that of returning from ecstasy (*sukr*) to operate in the world (*sahw*).  Many Sufi *turuq* (spiritual lineages) trace themselves through Junayd back to the earliest Muslim practitioners.[12]

*Mansur al-Hallaj:*  Mansur al-Hallaj (d. 922), al-Junayd's student, played a central role within Sufism, representing the antipodes to Junayd's sober version of Islamic mysticism. Born in 858 in Persia to a cotton-carder (*hallaj* means "cotton-carder" in Arabic), he memorized the Koran as a youth, and often would retreat from worldly pursuits to join other mystics in study. Al-Hallaj later married and made a pilgrimage to Mecca, where he stayed for one year, facing the mosque, in fasting and total silence. After this stay, he traveled extensively, going as far as India and Central Asia and gaining many followers, before settling in Baghdad.

Al-Hallaj provided an ecstatic impetus for the role of mysticism in an already calcifying religion. Although he came along a spare few centuries after the life of the Prophet, al-Hallaj witnessed the overbearing power of Islamic officialdom, which was replacing the possibility of the esoteric readings of the Koran with the rigid structure of religious law. He was declared a heretic by the Muslim authorities and executed for his own ecstatic statement: "I am the Truth," implying that he, like Bistami, had achieved complete God-consciousness.

*Muhammad ibn Masarra*: Muhammad ibn Masarra (d. 931; Cordoba) was the first to bring Sufism to Spain. By the time that he was 30 years old, he had constructed a *zawiyya* (hermitage) for himself on the cliffs outside of Cordoba, and set to educating a few dedicated followers. Like so many Sufis, Ibn Masarra's quiet activities made the local leaders uncomfortable. A respected jurist wrote a book attacking Ibn Masarra's teachings.[13] Growing worried, Ibn Masarra departed on a pilgrimage to Mecca before he could be charged with heresy.

During his time away from his home country, he studied with many of the great Sufi teachers throughout the Islamic world. He returned to Spain with the ascension of Abd ar-Rahman III (in 912) to the Caliphate of Spain. He was a vital early link between Persian and Babylonian Sufism and *al-Andalus*.

*Abd Allah ibn Sina*: Known as the "Leonardo da Vinci of the Muslim World," Abd Allah ibn Sina (d. 1037; Persia) wrote treatises on theology, metaphysics, astronomy, philology, poetry and medicine, including *Al-Qanun fi al-Tibb* (The Cannon of Medicine), a codification of medical knowledge that formed the basis for teaching the medical arts at European universities into the 17th century. Hardly a modest man, he states in his autobiography that there wasn't anything that he hadn't learned by the time he was eighteen.

His first appointment was that of physician to the Emir, who owed his recovery from a dangerous illness to Ibn Sina's ministrations. He then served princes throughout Persia, as both a doctor and teacher. Often falling into disfavor for various reasons, he spent portions of his life in hiding, in jail or on the run. He died at the age of 58, stating: "I prefer a short life with width to a narrow one with length."[14] Much of Ibn Sina's work was translated into Hebrew throughout medieval times.[15]

*Abu Hamid al-Ghazali*: Born at Tus, in Persia, al-Ghazali (d. 1111) had a successful professional career prior to his "conversion" to Sufism. At 33, he was appointed the chief professor at the pre-eminent university in Baghdad, the Nizamiyah College. However, soon thereafter he passed through a spiritual crisis so extreme that it rendered him incapable of lecturing. He abandoned his post in Baghdad and left the region on the pretext of going on a pilgrimage to Mecca. Making arrangements for his family to be taken care of in his absence, he disposed of his considerable wealth and adopted the life of a *faqir*.[16]

Al-Ghazali synthesized Sufi mysticism with orthodox Islam, which led him to be called the "Renovator of Islam." Specific ideas concerning, prophecy, equanimity, images of the seven levels of mystical attainment and other, esoteric, concepts informing the religious path originated in the Islamic thinker's works, and then reappeared in Jewish writings. He was the Muslim thinker most commonly quoted verbatim and mentioned by name within medieval Jewish works.

*Shihabuddin Yahya al-Suhrawardi*: Shihabuddin Yahya al-Suhrawardi (d. 1191; Syria) was born in the town of Suhraward, in Azerbaijan. Already known as a theologian and doctor of Islamic law in his twenties, he entered the Sufi path after meeting Islamic mystics on his travels. He developed one of the most influential Sufi schools, *Ishraqi* or illuminist, which taught that God is pure light, conceived as a cascade of radiance that becomes less intense as God's energy moves through various spiritual levels toward the world of manifested beings.

Having gained notoriety as a great thinker, he was invited by the Governor of Aleppo (Syria) to serve at his court.[17] It was here that he fell into disgrace with the religious authorities in the city, who considered him dangerous to Islam. They asked for his death, and when the governor refused, they petitioned his father, the Sultan of Egypt and Syria, who threatened his son with abdication unless he followed the ruling of the religious leaders. Suhrawardi was imprisoned in 1191, and died at the age of 38.[18] Many of Suhrawardi's books were found in Jewish libraries, translated into Hebrew, including the vast and important collection of David ben Joshua Maimonides (d. 1415) in Aleppo.[19]

*Muhyiddin ibn Arabi*: Muhyiddin ibn Arabi (d. 1240) was born to a wealthy family in Murcia, *Andalusia* who, when he was six, moved to the cosmopolitan city of Seville. A profound mystical understanding came to him in the form of a "spiritual awakening" when he was 15 years old. He spent the rest of his life refining this original, ecstatic event, ultimately studying with more than 90 different Sufi masters and penning more than 850 books, including the *Fusus al-Hikam* (The Seals of Wisdom), an exposition of the inner meaning of the wisdom of the prophets in the Abrahamic line, and the *Futuhat al-Makkiyya* (The Meccan Revelations), a vast encyclopedia of spiritual knowledge.

Firmly rooted in the Koran, his work was universal, teaching that each person has a unique way to the Truth, which unites all paths in Itself.[20] Ibn Arabi taught that "all revelations through prophets and lawgivers were revelations of the same Reality; all men worshipped the same God in different forms."[21] His ideas were deeply influential on the *Zohar* (1295) and the Kabbalah in general.

*Jalalludin Rumi*:  A later ecstatic mystic, Rumi (d. 1273; Turkey) has come to represent the most beautiful aspects of so-called drunken Sufism. Through various English language translations, he currently is the best selling poet in the United States. He also founded the *Mawlawiyya* order of Sufis, known in the West as the *"Whirling Dervishes,"* for the evocative *sama'*, or mystical dance that they perform.

Born in Afghanistan, Rumi became a scholar and a teacher. However, one day a shadowy figure named Shams-i Tabrizi showed up in one of his classes. This foreigner asked a question so compelling that Rumi immediately fell into a mystical state (*hal*). After reviving, he shut himself in a room with his new mentor, with whom he explored Truth. After some time, Shams left him, returned a couple of years later and then disappeared again, possibly murdered by Rumi's son or followers, as Shams had completely monopolized Rumi's attentions. Rumi spent the rest of his life composing heartsick love odes to the One, as well as penning the *Mathnavi* (Spiritual Verses), known to many Sufis as the "Persian Koran."

Although Rumi came along near the end of direct Jewish-Sufi interactions, his work entered the Jewish stream in two specific manners. Sarmad, a 17th-century wandering Jewish-Sufi *dervish*, translated much Persian poetry into Hebrew. Additionally, the false Messiah, Shabbetai Zevi, lived in Anatolia, Turkey after his conversion to Islam, and undoubtedly knew of Rumi's ideas.

These are just a few of the more important Islamic thinkers who influenced Jewish thought. Medieval Jewish libraries held the books and poems of scores of Islamic mystics, and ideas and stories from a wide-ranging group of Muslim thinkers may be found throughout medieval Jewish religious tracts.

Endnotes

1. Maimonides, Obadyah. *Treatise of the Pool* (Paul Fenton, trans.). (London: Octagon Press, 1981), p. 64.

2. Netton, Ian Richard. *Muslim Neoplatonists*. (London: George Allen & Unwin Ltd., 1982), pp. 73, 105.

3. Sells, Michael (ed.). *Early Islamic Mysticism: Sufi, Qu'ran, Mi'raj, Poetic and Theological Writings*. (Mahwah, NJ and New York: Paulist Press, 1996), p. 77.

4. Information from this paragraph from Smith, Margaret. *Studies in Early Mysticism in the Near and Middle East*. (Oxford: Oneworld Publications, 1995), pp. 180-181.

5. Ibid. p. 183.

6. Trimingham, J. Spencer. *The Sufi Orders in Islam*. (New York and Oxford: Oxford University Press, 1998), p. 44.

7. Smith, Margaret. *Studies in Early Mysticism in the Near and Middle East*, p. 192.

8. Information thus far from Arberry, Arthur, J. *Sufism: An Account of the Mystics of Islam*. (Mineola, NY: Dover Publications, 2002), pp. 52-53.

9. Ibid. p. 54.

10. Information in this paragraph from Smith, Margaret. *Studies in Early Mysticism in the Near and Middle East*, pp. 237-239.

11. Information in this paragraph from http://www.onelittleangel.com/wisdom/quotes/al_junayd.asp.

12. Trimingham, J. Spencer. *The Sufi Orders in Islam*, p. 12.

13. *Theosophy Library Online – Great Teacher Series – Ibn Masarra*, www.theosophy.org.

14. http://www.ummah.net/history/scholars/ibn_sina/.

15. Wording and information from *http://www.jewishencyclopedia.com/view.jsp?artid=2168&letter=A*.

16. Arberry, Arthur J. *Sufism: An Account of the Mystics of Islam*, p. 80.

17. Information from Suhrawardi, Shihabuddin Yahya al (Sheikh Tosun Bayrak al-Jerrahi al-Halveti, interpretor). *Hayakal Al-Nur (The Shape of Light)*. (Louisville, KY: Fons Vitae, 1998), p. 27.

18. Information and wording from www.muslimphilosophy.com/hmp/chp19.doc.

19. Maimonides, Obadyah. *Treatise of the Pool* (Paul Fenton, trans.), p. 5.

20. Information from the previous two paragraphs from http://www.ibnarabisociety.org/ibnarabi.html.

21. Hourani, Albert. *A History of the Arab Peoples*. (Cambridge, MA: Harvard University Press, 1991), p. 177.

# Bibliography

Abelson, Joshua. *Jewish Mysticism: An Introduction to the Kabbalah.* Mineola, NY: Dover Publications, 2001.

Ajmal, Mohammad. "Sufi Science of the Soul." *Islamic Spirituality: Foundations* (S. H. Nasr, editor). New York: Crossroad (1987): 294-307.

Ali, Maulana Muhammad. *A Manual of Hadith.* Dublin, OH: Ahmadiyya Anjuman Ishaat Islam Lahore USA, 2001.

Altmann, Alexander (and Stern, S.M.). *Isaac Israeli: A Neoplatonic Philosopher of the Early Tenth Century.* Oxford: Oxford University Press, 1958.

————. *Jewish Medieval and Renaissance Studies.* Cambridge, MA: Harvard University Press, 1967.

————. *Studies in Religious Philosophy and Mysticism.* Ithaca: Cornell University Press, 1969.

Arberry, Arthur J. *History of Sufism.* London: Longmans, Green and Co., 1942.

————. *Sufism: An Account of the Mystics of Islam.* Mineola, NY: Dover Publications, 2002.

Ariel, David S. "The Eastern Dawn of Wisdom: The Problem of the Relation Between Islamic and Jewish Mysticism." *Approaches to Judaism in Medieval Times II* (David R. Blumenthal, editor). Chico, CA: Scholars Press (1985): 149-167.

Assis, Yom Tov. "The Judeo-Arabic Tradition in Christian Spain." *The Jews of Medieval Islam: Community, Society and Identity* (Daniel Frank, editor). Leiden: E. J. Brill (1995): 111-126.

Attar, Farid ad-Din (C. S. Nott, translator). *The Conference of the Birds.* Boulder, Colorado: Shambhala Publications, 1971.

Baker, Rob and Henry, Gray (editors). *Merton & Sufism: The Untold Story.* Louisville, KY: Fons Vitae, 1999.

Baralt, Luce Lopez. *Islam in Spanish Literature From the Middle Ages to the Present* (Andrew Hurley, translator). Leiden: E. J. Brill, 1992.

Beinart, Heim (editor). *Moreshet Sepharad: The Sephardi Legacy.* Lynbrook, NY: Gefen Books, 1996.

Ben-Amos, Dan and Mintz, Jerome R. (translators and editors) *In Praise of the Baal Shem Tov.* Bloomington, IN and London: Indiana University Press, 1970.

Bendiner, Elmer. *The Rise and Fall of Paradise.* New York: Putnam Books, 1983.

Ben-Sasson, Menachem. "Varieties of Inter-Communal Relations in the Geonic Period." *The Jews of Medieval Islam: Community, Society and Identity* (Daniel Frank, editor). Leiden: E. J. Brill (1995): 17-32.

Bension, Ariel. *The Zohar in Moslem and Christian Spain*. New York: Hermon Press, 1974.

Blumenthal, David. "Maimonides Intellectualist Mysticism and the Superiority of the Prophecy of Moses." *Approaches to Judaism in Medieval Times* (David Blumenthal, editor). Chico, California: Scholars Press (1984): 27-52.

——. "Maimonides Philosophic Mysticism." *www.js.emory.edu/ blumenthal*.

——. "Maimonides: Prayer, Worship and Mysticism." *www.js.emory. edu/blumenthal*.

——. "Philosophic Mysticism: The Ultimate Goal of Medieval Judaism." *www.js.emory.edu/blumenthal*.

——. *Understanding Jewish Mysticism*. New York: KTAV, 1982.

Brann, Ross. *The Compunctious Poet: Cultural Ambiguity and Hebrew Poetry in Muslim Spain*. Baltimore, MD: Johns Hopkins University Press, 1991.

Bridger, David and Wolk, Samuel (editors). *The New Jewish Encyclopedia*. West Orange, NJ: Behrman House Publishers, 1976.

Buber, Martin. *Hasidism*. New York: Philosophical Library, 1948.

——. *Tales of the Hasidim I, II*. New York: Schocken Books, 1991.

——. *The Legend of the Baal Shem Tov*. Princeton, NJ: Princeton University Press, 1995.

——. *The Origin and Meaning of Hasidism*. New York: Horizon Press, 1960.

Burckhardt, Titus. *Introduction to Sufi Doctrine*. Bloomington, IN: World Wisdom, Inc., 2008.

——. "Sufi Doctrine and Method." *Sufism: Love and Wisdom* (Jean-Louis Michon and Roger Gaetani, editors). Bloomington, IN: World Wisdom, Inc. (2006): 1-20.

Calder, Norman; Mojaddedi, Jawid; Rippin, Andrew (editors). *Classical Islam: A Sourcebook of Religious Literature*. London: Routledge, 2003.

Chittick, William. *Sufism: A Short Introduction*. Oxford: Oneworld Publishers, 2000.

——. "Sufism and Islam." *Sufism: Love and Wisdom* (Jean-Louis Michon and Roger Gaetani, editors). Bloomington, IN: World Wisdom, Inc. (2006): 21-32.

——. *The Sufi Path of Knowledge: Ibn Arabi's Metaphysics of Imagination*. Albany, NY: SUNY Press, 1989.

Chodkiewicz, Michael. *Seal of the Saints: Prophethood and Sainthood in the Doctrine of ibn Arabi*. Cambridge, England: The Islamic Texts Society, 1993.

——. "The Vision of God According to Ibn Arabi." *Sufism: Love and Wisdom* (Jean-Louis Michon and Roger Gaetani, editors). Bloomington, IN: World Wisdom, Inc. (2006): 33-49.

Cohen, Gerson D. "The Soteriology of R. Abraham Maimuni." *Proceedings of the American Academy of Jewish Research 36* (1948): 75-98.

Cohen, Mark R. "Persecution, Response and Collective Memory: The Jews of Islam in the Classical Period." *The Jews of Medieval Islam: Community, Society and Identity* (Daniel Frank, editor). Leiden: E. J. Brill (1995): 145-164.

Colby, Frederick S. "The Subtleties of the Ascension: al-Sulami on the Mi'raj of the Prophet." *Studia Islamica 94* (2002): 167-183.

Cooper, Rabbi David. *The Handbook of Jewish Meditation Practices: A Guide for Enriching the Sabbath and Other Days of Your Life.* Woodstock, VT: Jewish Lights Publishing, 2000.

Dan, Joseph (editor). *The Early Kabbalah.* Mahweh, NJ: Paulist Press, 1986.

Danner, Victor. "The Early Development of Sufism." *Islamic Spirituality: Foundations* (S. H. Nasr, editor). New York: Crossroad (1987): 239-264.

De Leon, Moses, *The Zohar* (Gershom Scholem, translator). New York: Schocken Books, 1995.

Dinur, Benzion. "The Origins of Hasidism and Its social and Messianic Foundations." *Essential Papers on Hasidism: Origins to Present* (Gershon David Hundert, editor). New York and London: New York University Press (1991): 86-208.

Dubnow, Simon. "The Beginnings: The Baal Shem Tov (Besht) and the Center in Podolia." *Essential Papers on Hasidism: Origins to Present* (Gershon David Hundert, editor). New York and London: New York University Press (1991): 25-57.

———. "The Maggid of Miedzyrzecz, His Associates, and the Center in Volhynia (1760-1772)." *Essential Papers on Hasidism: Origins to Present* (Gershon David Hundert, editor). New York and London: New York University Press (1991): 58-85.

Dupre, Louis. "Unio Mystica: The State and the Experience." *Mystical Union in Judaism, Christianity and Islam* (Moshe Idel and Bernard McGinn, editors). New York: Continuum Publishing (1996): 3-23.

Duran, Khalid. *Children of Abraham.* Jersey City, NJ: KTAV Publishers, 2001.

Efros, Israel. "Saadia's General Ethical Theory and its Relation to Sufism." *The Jewish Quarterly Review 57*, The Seventy-Fifth Anniversary Volume of the Jewish Quarterly Review (1967): 166-177.

———. "Some Aspects of Yehudah Halevi's Mysticism." *Proceedings of the American Academy of Jewish Research 11* (1941): 105-163.

————. *Studies in Medieval Jewish Philosophy.* New York and London: Columbia University Press, 1974.

Elior, Rachel. *The Mystical Origins of Hasidism.* Oxford and Portland, OR: The Littman Library of Jewish Civilization, 2008.

Elqayam, Avraham. "Sabbatai Sevi's Holy Zohar." *http://www.kheper. net/topics/Kabbalah/Zevi_and_Sufism.html.*

Ernst, Carl. *The Shambhala Guide to Sufism.* Boston and London: Shambhala Publishers, 1997.

Esposito, John L. *Islam, The Straight Path.* Oxford: Oxford University Press, 1991.

Ettinger, Shmuel. "The Hasidic Movement – Reality and Ideals." *Essential Papers on Hasidism: Origins to Present* (Gershon David Hundert, editor). New York and London: New York University Press (1991): 226-243.

Fadiman, James and Frager, Robert (editors). *Essential Sufism.* New York: HarperCollins, 1997.

Fakhry, Majid. *Ethical Theories in Islam.* Leiden: E. J. Brill, 1991.

Fenton, Paul. "Abraham Maimonides (1186-1237): Founding a Mystical Dynasty." *Jewish Mystical Leaders and Leadership in the 13th Century* (Moshe Idel and M. Ostow, editors). New Jersey and Jerusalem: Northvale Press (1998): 127-154.

————. "A Jewish Sufi on the Influence of Music." *YUVAL IV* (Israel Adler and Bathja Bayer, editors). Jerusalem: The Magnes Press (1982): 123-130.

————. "Judaism and Sufism." *The Cambridge Companion to Medieval Jewish Philosophy* (Daniel Frank and Oliver Leaman, editors). Cambridge, England: Cambridge University Press (2003): 201-217.

————. "A Judeo-Arabic Commentary on the Haftarot by Hanan'el Ben Samuel, Abraham Maimonides' Father-in-Law." *Maimonidean Studies* (Arthur Hyman, editor). New York: Yeshiva University Press (1990): 27-49.

————. "A Mystical Treatise on Perfection, Providence and Prophecy from the Jewish Sufi Circle." *The Jews of Medieval Islam: Community, Society and Identity* (Daniel Frank, editor). Leiden: E. J. Brill (1995): 301-334.

————. "A Mystical Treatise on Prayer and the Spiritual Quest from the Pietist Circle." *Jerusalem Studies in Arabic and Islam 16* (1993): 137-175.

————. "A Pietist Letter from the Genizah." *Hebrew Annual Review 9* (1985): 159-167.

————. "Dana's Edition of Abraham Maimuni's 'Kifayat al-Abidin.'" *Jewish Quarterly Review 82* (1991): 194-206.

————. "Idel's Studies in Ecstatic Kabbalah." *Jewish Quarterly Review*

*82* (1991): 525-527.

———. "Jewish Attitudes Towards Islam: Israel Heeds Ishmael." *Jerusalem Quarterly 29* (1983): 93-102.

———. "Judeo-Arabic Mystical Writings of the XIIIth-XIVth Centuries." *Judeo-Arabic Studies: Proceedings of the Founding Conference of the Study of Judeo Arabic* (Norman Golb, editor). New York and Milton Park, England: Routledge (1997): 87-101.

———. "La 'Hitbodedut' chez les Premiers Qabbalistes en Orient et Chez les Soufis.*" Priere, Mystique et Judaisme* (R. Goetschel, editor). Strasbourg, France: Centre d'Histoire des Religions (1984): 133-158.

———. "Solitary Meditation in Jewish and Islamic Mysticism in Light of a Recent Archeological Discovery." *Medieval Encounters I* (1995): 271-296.

———. "Some Judeo-Arabic Fragments by Rabbi Abraham he-Hasid, the Jewish Sufi." *Journal of Semitic Studies 26* (1981): 47-72.

———. (& Maurice Gloton). "The Book of the Description of the Encompassing Circles." *Muhyiddin Ibn Arabi: A Commemorative Volume* (Hirtenstein & Tiernan, editors). Oxford, England: Muhyiddin Ibn Arabi Society, 1993.

———. "The Literary Legacy of David Ben Joshua, last of the Maimonidean Negidim." *Jewish Quarterly Review 75* (1984): 1-56.

———. "The Literary Legacy of Maimonides' Descendants." *Sobre la Vida y Obra de Maimonides* (Jesus Pelaez del Rosal, editor). Cordoba, Spain: Ediciones el Almendro (1991): 149-156.

Fine, Lawrence. *Safed Spirituality: Rules of Mystical Piety, The Beginning of Wisdom.* Mahwah, NJ: Paulist Press, 1984.

Finkel, Joshua. "An Eleventh Century Source for the History of Jewish Scientists in Mohammedan Land (Ibn Sa'id)." *Jewish Quarterly Review 18* (1927): 45-54.

Frank, Daniel. "Paul B. Fenton: Deux Traites de Mystique Juive." *Journal of Jewish Studies 39* (1988): 273-276.

———. (editor) *The Jews of Medieval Islam: Community, Society and Identity.* New York, NY: E.J. Brill, 1995.

Gabirol, Solomon Ibn. . *The Kingly Crown* (translated by Bernard Lewis). London, England: Valentine, Mitchell, 1961.

———. *Selected Poems of Solomon Ibn Gabirol* (translated by Peter Cole). Princeton, NJ: Princeton University Press, 2001.

Geoffroy, Eric. "Approaching Sufism." *Sufism: Love and Wisdom* (Jean-Louis Michon and Roger Gaetani, editors). Bloomington, IN: World Wisdom, Inc. (2006): 49-62.

Ginsburg, Elliot. "Idel's 'Mystical Experience in Abraham Abulafia.'" *Jewish Quarterly Review 82* (1991): 207-214.

Glick, Thomas F. (and Steven J. Lively, Faith Wallis, editors). *Medieval Science, Technology and Medicine: An Encyclopedia.* New York and London: Routledge, 2005.

———. *Islamic and Christian Spain in the Early Middle Ages.* Princeton, NJ: Princeton University Press, 1979.

Goitein, S.D. "A Jewish Addict to Sufism." *Jewish Quarterly Review 44* (1953): 37-49.

———. "Abraham Maimonides and his Pietist Circle." *Jewish Medieval and Renaissance Studies* (Alexander Altmann, editor). Cambridge, MA: Harvard University Press, (1967): 145-164.

———. *Jews and Arabs.* New York: Schocken Books, 1964.

———. *A Mediterranean Society: The Jewish Communities of the Arab World as Portrayed in the Documents of the Cairo Geniza (An Abridgement in One Volume).* Berkeley, CA: University of California Press, 1967.

———. "A Treatise in Defense of the Pietists by Abraham Maimonides." *Journal of Jewish Studies 16* (1965): 105-114.

Goldhizer, Ignaz. "Ibn Hud, The Mohammedan Mystic, and the Jews of Damascus." *Jewish Quarterly Review 6* (1893): 218-220.

Goodman, Lenn E. "Crosspollinations – Philosophically Fruitful Exchanges between Jewish and Islamic Thought." *Medieval Encounters I* (1995): 323-357.

Gril, Denis. "The Prophetic Model of the Spiritual Master in Islam." *Sufism: Love and Wisdom* (Jean-Louis Michon and Roger Gaetani, editors). Bloomington, IN: World Wisdom, Inc. (2006): 63-88.

Guenon, Rene. "Haqiqa and Shari'a in Islam." *Sufism: Love and Wisdom* (Jean-Louis Michon and Roger Gaetani, editors). Bloomington, IN: World Wisdom, Inc. (2006): 89-100.

Halkin, A.S. "Classical and Arabic Material in Ibn Aknin's 'Hygiene of the Soul." *Proceedings of the American Academy of Jewish Research 14* (1944): 27-147.

———. "The Great Fusion." *Great Ages and Ideas of the Jewish People* (Leo W. Schwarz, editor). New York: Random House (1956): 215-263.

Hames, Harvey J. "A Seal within a Seal: The imprint of Sufism in Abraham Abulafia's Teachings." *Medieval Encounters 12.2* (2006):153-72.

Hourani, Albert. *A History of the Arab Peoples.* Cambridge, MA: Harvard University Press, 1991.

Hughes, Aaron. "Mi'raj and the Language of Legitimation in the Medieval Islamic and Jewish Philosophical Traditions." *Exploring Other Worlds: New Studies on Muhammad's Ascension* (Christiane Grubar and Fredrick S. Colby, editors). Bloomington, IN: Indiana University Press (2009): 122-191.

————. "Two Approaches to the love of God in medieval Jewish Thought: The concept of devequt in the works of Ibn Ezra and Judah Halevi." *Sciences Religeuses/Studies in Religion 28* (1999): 139-152.

Hundert, Gershon David (Editor). *Essential Papers on Hasidism: Origins to Present*. New York and London: New York University Press, 1991.

Hyman, Arthur, editor. *Maimonidean Studies*. New York, NY: Yeshiva University Press, 1990.

Idel, Moshe. *Hasidism: Between Ecstasy and Magic*. Albany, NY: SUNY Press, 1995.

————. "Hitbodedut as Concentration in Ecstatic Kabbalah." *Jewish Spirituality From the Bible through the Middle Ages* (Arthur Green, editor). New York: Crossroad (1986): 405-438.

————. "Allegory and Divine Names in Ecstatic Kabbalah." *Interpretation and Allegory: Antiquity to the Modern Period* (Patricia Gauch & Jon Whitman, editors). Leiden: E. J. Brill, (2003): 317-348.

————. (& M. Ostrow). *Jewish Mystical Leaders and Leadership in the 13thCentury*. Northvale, NJ: Jason Aronson Publishers, 1998.

————. *Kabbalah: New Perspectives*. New Haven, CT: Yale University Press, 1988.

————. *Messianic Mystics*. New Haven, CT: Yale University Press, 1998.

————. "Universalization and Integration: Two Conceptions of Mystical Union in Jewish Mysticism." *Mystical Union in Judaism, Christianity and Islam* (Moshe Idel and Bernard McGinn, editors). New York: Continuum Publishing, (1996): 27-58.

————. *Studies in Ecstatic Kabbalah*. Albany, NY: SUNY Press, 1988.

————. *The Mystical Experience in Abraham Abulafia*. Albany, NY: SUNY Press, 1988.

Ivry, Alfred R. "Isma'ili Theology and Maimonides' Philosophy." *The Jews of Medieval Islam: Community, Society and Identity* (Daniel Frank, editor). Leiden: E. J. Brill (1995): 271-300.

Jacobs, Louis. *Hasidic Prayer*. Washington DC: Littman Library of Jewish Civilization, 1993.

————. "Hasidic Prayer." *Essential Papers on Hasidism: Origins to Present* (Gershon David Hundert, editor). New York and London: New York University Press (1991): 330-362.

————. *The Jewish Religion: A Companion*. Oxford, New York: Oxford University Press, 1995.

Kaplan, Aryeh. *Meditation and Kabbalah*. York Beach, ME: Red Wheel/ Reiser, 1982.

Kiener, Ronald. "Ibn Arabi and the Qabbalah: A Study of Thirteenth

Century Iberian Mysticism." *Studies in Mystical Literature, Vol. 2, N. 2* (1982): 26-50.

Kister, M. J. "Haddithu 'an Bani Isra'ila wa-la Haraja: A Study of an Early Tradition." *Israel Oriental Studies II* (1972): 215-237.

Kraemer, Joel. *Maimonides: The Life and World of One of Civilization's Greatest Minds*. New York, NY: Doubleday Religion, 2008.

Lasker, Daniel. "Saadia Gaon on Christianity and Islam." *The Jews of Medieval Islam: Community, Society and Identity* (Daniel Frank, editor). Leiden: E. J. Brill (1995): 165-178.

Lazaroff, Allan, "Bahya's Asceticism against its Rabbinic and Islamic Background." *Journal of Jewish Studies 21* (1970): 11-38.

Lings, Martin. *A Sufi Saint in the Twentieth Century*. Cambridge, England: Islamic Texts Society, 1993.

———. "Sufi Answers to Questions on Ultimate Reality." *Sufism: Love and Wisdom* (Jean-Louis Michon and Roger Gaetani, editors). Bloomington, IN: World Wisdom, Inc. (2006): 101-116.

———. *The Book of Certainty*. Cambridge, England: The Islamic Texts Society, 1996.

———. "The Nature and Origin of Sufism." *Islamic Spirituality: Foundations* (S. H. Nasr editor). New York: Crossroad (1987): 223-238.

———. *What is Sufism?* Cambridge, England: The Islamic Texts Society, 1995.

Lobel, Diana. *A Sufi-Jewish Dialogue: Philosophy and Mysticism in Bahya ibn Pakuda's "Duties of the Heart."* Philadelphia: University of Pennsylvania Press, 2006.

———. *Between Mysticism and Philosophy: Sufi Language of Religious Experience in Judah Halevi's Kuzari*. Albany, NY: SUNY Press, 2000.

———. *On the Lookout: A Sufi Riddle in Sulami, Qushayri and Bahya*, Manuscript, 2002.

———. *Sufism and Philosophy in Muslim Spain and the Medieval Mediterranean World*, Manuscript, 2001.

Loewe, Raphael. *Ibn Gabirol*. New York: Grove Weidenfeld, 1989.

Macnab, Angus. "Sufism in Muslim Spain." *Sufism: Love and Wisdom* (Jean-Louis Michon and Roger Gaetani, editors). Bloomington, IN: World Wisdom, Inc. (2006): 117-130.

Mahler, Raphael. "Hasidism and the Jewish Enlightenment." *Essential Papers on Hasidism: Origins to Present* (Gershon David Hundert, editor). New York and London: New York University Press (1991): 401-498.

Maimon, Solomon. "On a Secret Society, and Therefore a Long Chapter." *Essential Papers on Hasidism: Origins to Present* (Gershon David

Hundert, editor). New York and London: New York University Press (1991): 11-24.

Maimonides, Abraham (Samuel Rosenblatt, translator). *The High Ways to Perfection of Abraham Maimonides*. New York: AMS Press, 1966.

Maimonides, Moses (M. Friedlander, translator). *The Guide for the Perplexed*. New York: Dover, 1956.

Maimonides, Obadyah (translation and introduction by Paul Fenton). *Treatise of the Pool*. London: Octagon Press, 1981.

Mann, Jacob. *The Jews in Egypt and in Palestine Under the Fatimid Caliphs II*. Oxford: Oxford University Press, 1922.

Marcus, Jacob. *The Jew in the Medieval World*. New York: Harper Torchbook, 1965.

Massignon, Louis. *Testimonies and Reflections: Essays of Louis Massignon*. South Bend, IN: University of Notre Dame Press, 1989.

Matt, Daniel. *The Essential Kabbalah*. Edison, NJ: Castle Books, 1997.

McGaha, Michael. "Naming the Nameless, Numbering the Infinite." *YCGL 45/46* (1997/1998): 37-53.

———. "The Sefer ha-Bahir and Andalusian Sufism." *Medieval Encounters III* (1997): 20-57.

———. *The Jewish Mystics of Medieval Spain*, unpublished manuscript, 2001.

Merkur, Daniel. "Unitive Experience and the State of Trance." *Mystical Union in Judaism, Christianity and Islam* (Moshe Idel and Bernard McGinn, editors). New York: Continuum Publishing (1996): 125-153, 175-183, 230-237, and 239-240.

Michaelson, Jay. "No Crystals Needed: Even a Stuffy Suit Can Benefit From Meditation." *Jewish Daily Forward*, May 4, 2007 (at *www.forward.com/articles/10634*).

Michon, Jean-Louis. "Sacred Music and Dance in Islam." *Sufism: Love and Wisdom* (Jean-Louis Michon and Roger Gaetani, editors). Bloomington, IN: World Wisdom, Inc. (2006): 153-178.

———. "The Spiritual Practices of Sufism." *Islamic Spirituality: Foundations* (S. H. Nasr, editor). New York: Crossroad (1987): 265-293.

Miller, Elliot. "Sufis: The Mystical Muslims." *Forward* (Spring-Summer 1986).

Moreno, M. Encarnacion Varela. "Cordoba School of Hebrew Grammarians." *The Jews in Cordoba (X-XII Centuries)* (Jesus Peleaz de Rosal, editor). Cordoba, Spain: Ediciones El Almendro (1985): 105-122.

Myer, Isaac. *Qabbalah*. New York: Samuel Weiser, 1970.

Nakamura, Kojiro, "Makki and Ghazali on Mystical Practices." *Orient XX* (1984): 83-91.

Nasr, Seyyed Hossein. *Man and Nature: The Spiritual Crisis in Modern Man*. Chicago: ABC International Group, 1997.

———. *Sufi Essays*. Chicago: ABC International Group, 1999.

———. "The Spiritual Needs of Western Man and the Message of Islam." *Sufism: Love and Wisdom* (Jean-Louis Michon and Roger Gaetani, editors). Bloomington, IN: World Wisdom, Inc. (2006): 179-206.

Netton, Ian Richard. *Muslim Neoplatonists*. London: George Allen & Unwin Ltd., 1982.

Nicholson, Reynold. *Studies in Islamic Mysticism*. Cambridge, England: Cambridge University Press, 1967.

Pakuda, Bahya Ibn (Daniel Feldman, translator). *Duties of the Heart*. Northvale, NJ: J. Aronson Publisher, 1996.

Palacios, Miguel Asin. *The Mystical Philosophy of Ibn Masarra and His Followers*. Leiden: E. J. Brill, 1978.

Pasachoff, Naomi. *Great Jewish Thinkers: Their Lives and Work*. West Orange, NJ: Behrman House Publishing Company, 1992.

Patterson, David (editor). *Greatest Jewish Stories*. Middle Village, NY: Jonathon David Publishers, 2001.

Peleaz de Rosal, Jesus (editor). *The Jews in Cordoba (X-XII Centuries)*. Cordoba, Spain: Ediciones El Almendro, 1985.

———. *Sobre la Vida y Obra de Maimonides*. Cordoba, Spain: Ediciones El Almendro, 1991.

Peters, F. E. (editor). *Judaism, Christianity & Islam III*. Princeton, NJ: Princeton University Press, 1990.

Pines, Shlomo. "On the Term 'Ruhaniyyut' and its Sources and on Judah Halevi's Doctrine." *Tarbiz 57* (1988): 511-540.

———. "Shi'ite Terms and Conceptions in Judah Halevi's Kuzari." *Jerusalem Studies in Arabic and Islam 2* (1980): 165-247.

———. "The Limitations of Human Knowledge According to Al-Farabi, Ibn Bajja and Maimonides." *Studies in Medieval Jewish History and Literature*, (Isadore Twersky, editor). Cambridge, MA and London: Harvard University Press (1979): 82-109.

Poznanski, Samuel. "New Material on the History of Hebrew and Hebrew-Arabic Philology During the X-XII Centuries." *Jewish Quarterly Review 16* (1926): 237-266.

Rapaport-Albert, Ada. "God and the Zaddik as the Two Focal Points of Hasidic Worship." *Essential Papers on Hasidism: Origins to Present* (Gershon David Hundert, editor). New York and London: New York University Press (1991): 299-329.

Rosman, Murray Jay. "Meidzyboz and Rabbi Israel Baal Shem Tov." *Essential Papers on Hasidism: Origins to Present* (Gershon David Hundert, editor). New York and London: New York University Press (1991): 209-225.

Roth, Cecil and Wigoder, Geoffrey (editors). *Encyclopaedia Judaica 1st Edition, CD ROM.* New York: MacMillan and Company, 1997.

Roth, Norman. *Jews, Visigoths and Muslims in Medieval Spain.* New York: E.J. Brill, 1994.

Rothenberg, Jerome and Lenowitz, Harris (editors). *Exiled in the Word.* Port Townsend, WA: Copper Canyon Press, 1989.

Rumi, Jalalludin. *Signs of the Unseen* (W. M. Thackston, Jr. translator). Boston: Shambhala Publications, 1994.

———. *Teachings of Rumi* (E. H. Winfield, translator). London: Octagon Press, 1979.

———. *The Essential Rumi* (Coleman Barks, translator). San Francisco: HarperSanFrancisco, 1995.

Schatz-Uffenheimer, Rivka. *Hasidism as Mysticism.* Princeton, NJ: Princeton University Press, 1993.

Schaya, Leo. "On the Name *Allah.*" *Sufism: Love and Wisdom* (Jean-Louis Michon and Roger Gaetani, editors). Bloomington, IN: World Wisdom, Inc. (2006): 207-216.

———. *The Universal Meaning of the Kabbalah* (Nancy Pearson, translator). Louisville, KY: Fons Vitae, 2004.

Schochet, Rabbi J. Immanuel. *The Great Maggid.* Brooklyn, NY: Kehot Publication Society, 1990.

Scholem, Gershom. "A Note on a Kabbalistical Treatise on Contemplation." *Melanges Offert a Henry Corbin* (S. H. Nasr, editor). Tehran: Institute of Islamic Studies, McGill University (1977): 665-670.

———. "*Devekut*, or Communion with God." *Essential Papers on Hasidism: Origins to Present* (Gershon David Hundert, editor). New York and London: New York University Press (1991): 275-298.

———. *Major Trends in Jewish Mysticism.* New York: Schocken Books, 1971.

———. *On the Kabbalah and its Symbolism.* New York: Schocken Books, 1996.

———. *Origins of the Kabbalah.* Philadelphia: The Jewish Publication Society, 1987.

———. "The Lurianic Myth." *Understanding Jewish Mysticism* (David Blumenthal editor). Jersey City, NJ: KTAV Publishers (1982): 161-168.

Schechter, Solomon. *Studies in Judaism.* Philadelphia: The Jewish Publication Society, 1908.

Schuon, Frithjof. *Sufism: Veil and Quintessence.* Bloomington, IN: World Wisdom, 2006.

———. "The Quintessential Esotericism of Islam." *Sufism: Love and Wisdom* (Jean-Louis Michon and Roger Gaetani, editors).

Bloomington, IN: World Wisdom, Inc. (2006): 251-275.

Schwarz, Leo W. (editor), *Great Ages and Ideas of the Jewish Peoples.* New York: Random House, 1956.

Seeskin, Kenneth (editor). *The Cambridge Companion to Maimonides.* Cambridge, England: Cambridge University Press, 2005.

Sells, Michael. "Bewildered Tongue: The Semantics of Mystical Union in Islam." *Mystical Union in Judaism, Christianity and Islam* (Moshe Idel and Bernard McGinn, editors). New York: Continuum Press (1996): 87-124.

————. (editor) *Early Islamic Mysticism: Sufi, Qu'ran, Mi'raj, Poetic and Theological Writings.* Mahwah, NJ and New York: Paulist Press, 1996.

————. "Meaning and Authority in Sufi Literature around the year 1240 CE: Literary Perspectives." *Jewish Mystical Leaders and Leadership in the 13ᵗʰ Century* (Moshe Idel and M. Ostow, editors). New Jersey and Jerusalem: Northvale Press (1998): 187-198.

Shaddad, Baha al-Din ibn (D. S. Richards translator). *The Rare and Excellent History of Saladin.* Hampshire, England: Ashgate Publishers, 2002.

Sharot, Stephen. "Hasidism in Modern Society." *Essential Papers on Hasidism: Origins to Present* (Gershon David Hundert, editor). New York and London: New York University Press (1991): 511-532.

Sirat, Colette. *A History of Jewish Philosophy in the Middle Ages.* Cambridge, England and New York: Cambridge University Press, 1990.

Smith, Margaret. *Studies in Early Mysticism in the Near and Middle East.* Oxford: Oneworld Publications, 1995.

Steinschneider, M. "An Introduction to the Arabic Literature of the Jews I." *The Jewish Quarterly Review 11* (1899): 585-625.

Stern, S.M. "Isaac Israeli's Book of Substances." *Journal of Jewish Studies 6* (1955): 135-142.

————. "Some Unpublished Poems by Al-Harizi." *Jewish Quarterly Review 50* (1960): 269-275.

Stillman, Norman. "The Jew in the Medieval Islamic City." *The Jews of Medieval Islam: Community, Society and Identity* (Daniel Frank, editor). Leiden: E. J. Brill (1995): 3-16.

————. "The Judeo-Islamic Historical Encounter: Visions and Revisions." *Israel and Ishmael: Studies in Muslim-Jewish Relations* (Tudor Parfitt, Editor). New York: St. Martin's Press (2000): 1-12.

Stoddart, William. "Aspects of Islamic Esotericism." *Sufism: Love and Wisdom* (Jean-Louis Michon and Roger Gaetani, editors). Bloomington, IN: World Wisdom, Inc. (2006): 237-250.

————. *Sufism*. Northamptonshire, England: The Aquarian Press, 1984.

Suhrawardi, Shihabuddin Yahya al (Sheikh Tosun Bayrak al-Jerrahi al-Halveti, interpreter). *Hayakal Al-Nur (The Shape of Light)*. Louisville, KY: Fons Vitae, 1998.

Tobi, Yosef. "Saadia Gaon, Poet-*Paytan*: The Connecting Link between the Ancient *Piyyut* and Hebrew Arabicised Poetry in Spain." *Israel and Ishmael: Studies in Muslim-Jewish Relations* (Tudor Parfitt, Editor). New York: St. Martin's Press (2000): 59-77.

Trimingham, J. Spencer. *The Sufi Orders in Islam*. New York and Oxford: Oxford University Press, 1998.

Twersky, Isadore, *Studies in Medieval Jewish History and Literature*. Cambridge, MA: Harvard University Press, 1979.

Vajda, George "An Analysis of the *Ma'amar Yiqqawu ha Mayim* by Samuel b. Judah Ibn Tibbon." *Journal of Jewish Studies 10* (1959): 137-149.

————. "The Mystical Doctrine of Rabbi Obadyah, Grandson of Moses Maimonides." *Journal of Jewish Studies 6* (1955): 213-225.

Vaughan-Lee, Llewellyn. *Travelling the Path of Love: Sayings of Sufi Masters*. Inverness, CA: The Golden Sufi Center, 1995.

Ventura, David Romano. "On the Life and Work of Maimonides." *The Jews in Cordoba (X-XII Centuries)* (Jesus Peleaz de Rosal, editor). Cordoba, Spain: Ediciones El Almendro (1985): 139-153.

Verman, Mark. *The Books of Contemplation*. Albany, NY: SUNY Press, 1992.

Wasserstein, David J. "Jewish Elites in al-Andalus." *The Jews of Medieval Islam: Community, Society and Identity* (Daniel Frank, editor). Leiden: E. J. Brill (1995): 101-110.

Wasserstrom, Steven. *Between Muslim and Jew: The Problem of Symbiosis Under Early Islam*. Princeton, NJ: Princeton University Press, 1995.

————. "Sefer Yesira and Early Islam: A Reappraisal." *Journal of Jewish Thought and Philosophy III* (1993): 1-30.

Weiss, J. G. "The Kavvanoth of Prayer in Early Hasidism." *Journal of Jewish Studies 9* (1958): 163-192.

Werblowsky, R. T. Zwi. "Mystical and Magical Contemplation: The Kabbalists in Sixteenth-Century Safed." *History of Religions I* (1961): 9-36.

Wertheim, Aaron. "Traditions and Customs in Hasidism." *Essential Papers on Hasidism: Origins to Present* (Gershon David Hundert, editor). New York and London: New York University Press (1991): 363-400.

Whitman, Jon (editor). *Interpretation and Allegory: Antiquity to the Modern Period*. Leiden: E. J. Brill, 2003.

Wijnhoven, Jochanan. "The Mysticism of Solomon ibn Gabirol." *The Journal of Religion 45* (1965): 137-152.

Williams, John Alden (editor). *Islam*. New York: George Braziller, 1962.

Zafrani, Haim. "The Routes of al-Andalus." *http://unesdoc.unesco.org/images/0011/001144/114426Eo.pdf*.

Zolitor, Jeff. "The Jews of Sepharad." *http://www.csjo.org/pages/essays/essaysephard.htm*.

## Holy Books

*The Holy Scriptures*. Philadelphia: The Jewish Publication Society, 1948.

*The Koran* (N. J. Dawood, translator). New York and Middlesex, England: Penguin Books, 1981.

*The Metsudah Siddur* (Rabbi Avrohom Davis, translator). Brooklyn, New York: Metsudah Publications, 1990.

## Web Sources

*allaboutphilosophy.org* (A rational investigation of the truth)

*allexperts.com* (question and answer service utilizing volunteer experts)

*awakenedheartproject.org* (Promoting Jewish contemplative techniques)

*beliefnet.com* (Bible resources)

*britannica.com* (Encyclopedia Britannica)

*chochmat.org* (Jewish congregation)

*ciis.edu* (California Institute of Integral Studies)

*ehow.com* (How-to website)

*eretzyisroel.org* (Jewish perspective on the history of Palestine and Israel)

*forward.com* (Jewish Forward Newspaper)

*ghazali.org* (Everything al-Ghazali)

*haaretz.com* (Israeli newspaper Ha'aretz)

*ibnarabisociety.org* (Muhyiddin ibn Arabi Society)

*isabellafreedman.org* (Jewish retreat center)

*israelinsider.com* (Israel's Daily Newsmagazine)

*jccsoco.org* (Jewish Community Center of Sonoma County)

*jewishencyclopedia.com* (Jewish Encyclopedia)

*jewishgen.org* (Jewish Genealogy)

*jewishvirtuallibrary.org* (Information about all facets of Jewish life)

*learnedoutloud.com* (Educational audio materials)

*meditationspot.com* (Information about meditation)

*mesa.wns.ccit.arizona.edu* (Middle East Studies Association) *mikeshane.org* (Love poems by Rumi)

*muslim-canada.org* (Canadian Society of Muslims)

*muslimphilosophy.com* (Islamic philosophy)

*mysticlink.blogspot.com* (Moshe Yehuda Bernstein's blog concerning Jewish mysticism)

*mysticsaint.blogspot.com* (Sufi and mystical blog)

*olamqatan.com* (Website for Israeli bookstore Olam Qatan)

*onelittleangel.com* (World's religion, spirituality and philosophy)

*ou.org* (Orthodox Union)

*pizmonim.org* (Sephardic Heritage Foundation)

*plato.stanford.edu* (Stanford Encyclopedia of Philosophy)

*submission.org* (Source for Islamic information)

*sufi-hasidism.org* (The Inayati-Maimuni Tariqat of Sufi-Hasidim)

*sufiuniversity.org* (University of Spiritual Healing and Sufism)

*talkreason.org* (Arguments against creationism, intelligent design, and religious apologetics)

*theosophy.org* (Great teachers of humanity)

*trincoll.edu* (Trinity College, Hartford, CT)

*unesco.org* (United Nations Educational, Scientific and Cultural Organization)

*unmah.net* (Information on Islam)

*unu.edu* (United Nations University)

*wordpress.com* (Islamic sciences)

*yachadnetwork.net* (Messianic Jewish movement)

# Acknowledgments

A study of this breadth could never have been completed without assistance from many sources. For their help, I am deeply grateful.

Most importantly is the work that my publisher, Virginia Gray Henry Blakemore put into this book. As she informed me on numerous occasions, the kind of personal attention and editing help that she provided in the preparation of this book was unprecedented. Without her patience and ministrations, this study would certainly never have made it into print.

I am also deeply indebted to Abdallah Schleifer, of the American University in Cairo, who read various versions of the manuscript and made important comments, noting lacunae in the scholarship, as well as indicating what specific themes needed further treatment. Without his help and support, this book almost certainly would not have been published.

I also was very heartened by the help I received from my colleagues in the academic community, who forwarded me manuscripts and ideas when I solicited them. Professor Michael McGaha (Pomona College, CA) was kind enough to share with me his entire unpublished manuscript, *The Jewish Mystics of Medieval Spain*, which provided much important information. Professor Diana Lobel (Boston University) forwarded me copies of two conference talks (which were later included in her books), as did Professor Aaron Hughes (SUNY Buffalo). Rabbi and scholar Michael Paley (Scholar-in-Residence at the United Jewish Appeal, New York) provided support and aid.

Joseph Montville, my mentor in interfaith work, offered constant encouragement, as well as support in a variety of manners, and for this I am eternally grateful. My father, Victor Block, spent many hours gleaning meticulously through the book as my copy editor. And I want to thank the editor of the *Fons Vitae* "Spiritual Affinities Series," Elena Lloyd-Sidle, who offered a series of detailed suggestions, which helped complete the manuscript for the public forum.